DAYS

MUSIC
AND ROMANCE
FOR YOUTH

A COURSE OF STUDY

IN

MUSIC APPRECIATION

FOR USE IN

JUNIOR HIGH SCHOOLS

ALSO IN PLATOON AND CONSOLIDATED
SCHOOLS, ACADEMIES, JUNIOR CLUBS

By

HAZEL GERTRUDE KINSCELLA

RCA Victor Company, Inc.
Educational Department

Camden, New Jersey

780.1

K62m

14751

Table of Contents

Chapter Outline

(For list of musical illustrations see close of each chapter)

PART ONE

PART TWO

PART THREE

Foreword

My Dear Young Music Friends:

The beautiful Spring air is filled with the songs of birds; warm sunshine and the romance of the bursting buds burgeoning on every shrub and tree, give promise of glorious flowering in days to come. In these developing days when your youthful feet are standing reluctant—"Where the brook and river meet"—your thoughts must turn to music, since youth is in music, and the rhythmic flow of melody is in all youth.

The world about you is full of music; but is your own æolian harp attuned to vibrate to the gentle winds of beauty, love, and sweetness that are flowing your way, if only you can catch their message?

Whether we will or no, music is now "In the Air," in every social function, in every part of our daily life. Never before has it mattered so much whether one appreciated or understood music, but now life is so full of it that not to have acquaintance with the world's best music literature is to argue one's self illiterate indeed, uncultured and uneducated.

"Know then thyself," was good advice from Pope; but in these miraculous times of reproduction, of "talkies," and of radio, "Know thy music" has become a necessity for the more abundant life, that now is.

One must recognize the great masterpieces that come over the air, or are heard in a concert; but it is not enough to merely bow to the "Andante Cantabile." Why is it "Andante," why "Cantabile," also is it really both, as its title indicates? To say the name of the "Funeral March" of Chopin means little, if one does not know the great throbbing heartbreak for his beloved Poland that he expressed therein.

Just to name the "Morning Song" of "Peer Gynt" is so pitifully little to know of the life-story of the errant boy and the love triumphant in the final "Lullaby." The opening bars of the "Danse Macabre" mean little if one does not know the poem upon which it is built. The "Overtures" to "Oberon" or the "Midsummer Night's Dream" slip into one ear and out of the other, leaving no residuum, if one knows not his Shakespeare, his fairy lore, and his Greek mythology.

From whence come the Tarantelle, the Rondo, the Dumka, the Valkyries, the Spirituals, Sinbad, and a thousand other interesting facts *about* the music? Also, what are pattern, theme, largo, caprice, serenade, tone-poem, trio, mood, melodic line, rhythmic type, etc., etc., that lie *in* the music itself?

All the lovely pictures in tone that the composers have made for us, become "Things of beauty" and "A joy forever," if only we have the magic key to unlock the treasures hidden away in the tunes, rhythms, forms, and stories which they have used so skilfully, but for which we must hunt diligently if we would make them our very own.

Miss Kinscella, whom many of you know through her Music Appreciation Readers, has woven for you a romantic tale of the beginnings of the music we hear. She has drawn upon her lore of many lands and her fine musicianship in pointing out the salient facts within the music itself, which you must know if you would truly appreciate music.

Miss Kinscella has very wisely refrained from frightening and overwhelming you with the sonata pattern and the analyses of the great symphonies. Those may well be left to the Senior High School, where, building on your splendid foundation of "folk-song" and "folk-dance," "suite," and "overture," they will come easily and beautifully.

To greet the folk of all lands, to mark the theme and pattern of the simple forms, to meet the great composers in their gentler moods, to breathe the romance and essence of really beautiful lighter music leading on to the higher forms to be met in later years, is a feast—colorful, gay, charming, and wholly lovable, for the adolescent youth of the Junior High epoch.

To those "Juniors" in music, though possibly older in years, this book will furnish a rich, understandable, practical introduction to more advanced studies.

Go, then, dear book, "On Wings of Song," carrying thy message of joy and romance to all the thousands of youth, whose fresh young minds and hearts are open to every messenger of Beauty, when his garments are hung with the very bells of heaven, his voice ringing out with the anthems of the ages, and his heralding trumpets skirling forth pæans of praise to Music and to Youth.

FRANCES ELLIOTT CLARK.

Preface

"MUSIC AND ROMANCE FOR YOUTH" has been prepared for the purpose of providing a course in music appreciation keyed to Junior High School requirements, a course so organized as to make a lasting impression upon the listening attitude of the pupils.

It has been the aim, in preparing these lessons, to relate music and its appreciation to life itself, and to set it to work as a training in wholesome use of leisure hours.

The first problems to solve in learning to appreciate and understand music are to establish definite listening habits, and then to learn to hear the dominant musical ideas of the work as a whole.

As one's interest in any subject depends largely upon what he knows of it, the student should also acquaint himself, so far as he is able, with all the fundamental facts and principles which are in any way related to the music to which he is listening. Such informational backgrounds help the pupil to gain a fuller benefit from his listening, and, in the end, lay a solid foundation for permanent listening interest, and for the enjoyable observation and recognition of the many charming and otherwise elusive details of the music heard.

This Course offers an abundant and a widely diversified selection of music for study throughout one and a half years, or three semesters in three different years; or, far better, where circumstances permit the carrying of music as a constant throughout the entire six semesters of the Junior High School, there is an abundance of material, so that each semester's part may be divided and continued for an entire year.

The musical selections suggested with each chapter are chosen from among the most beautiful and nationally characteristic of the world's folk-music, and from the art works of the greatest composers, both classic and modern. Musical taste and judgment are cultivated both through familiarity with music that has won recognition by its enduring worth, and also by being brought into contact with compositions which seek to depict and interpret the life of today.

The book is divided into three parts—each either for one semester of a school year, or it may fill an entire year. Each part is, in turn, divided into sixteen separate chapters, most of which may be studied for more than one recitation period, according to the available time, the needs, and the desires of the class. One lesson, each semester, is planned as a review of the preceding chapters, the form and content of this day's program—which is to be entirely planned and conducted by the class itself—being a practical project in artistic program building. A second special project lesson for each semester may, it is suggested, be in the form of advance preparation for outside hearing, such as attendance at a formal concert given by orchestra or by individual artists, or in listening to some special radio program.

The Victor Records chosen for each chapter are especially adapted to illustrate the chapter topic. As one record will often illustrate points in other lessons to follow, many of the records may be used and heard several times during the progress of the Course. The number of selections to be played during each lesson period is left to the discretion of the teacher.

Detailed suggestions for intensive study and listening are made a part of each chapter outline.

HAZEL GERTRUDE KINSCELLA.

BEAUTIFUL MELODIES, DEVELOPING A LISTENING ATTITUDE

The Importance of Melody. One of the three chief elements of music is Melody. The ability to create a good melody is one of the greatest assets of the skilled composer, especially one who uses the other two elements—Rhythm and Harmony—to enhance the beauty of his melodies.

One of the best ways to learn to appreciate beautiful melodies is to listen to them.

What Melody Is. Melody is a succession of tones, so arranged that they translate feeling into sound.

Why Some Melodies are Beautiful. Some melodies are liked because they are always associated with noble or endearing sentiments, or with some pleasant event. Among such melodies are home songs, national airs, and some national folk-songs.

But the greatest reason for the continued existence and popularity of any melody is *its beauty*. It is beauty which causes the enjoyment of music. There are many ways in which this beauty is produced.

Simplicity. One of the supreme charms of a really great melody is often its simplicity. The simplicity of true art is a quite different thing from the commonplace tune of a popular song. In the first place, both may be easily remembered, but the art melody has in it qualities which cause its popularity to last for years, when the other is soon forgotten.

Examples of this may be found in the exquisite folk-songs of many Old World countries, some of which have been sung for centuries because of their continued appeal to the affections and emotions. Such songs were spontaneously created by a people's feeling. Types of this kind of melody are found in such folk-songs as "Drink to Me Only" (English); "All Through the Night" (Welsh); or "Santa Lucia" (Italian); and in such art music as "Träumerei," by Robert Schumann; "Cradle Song," by Brahms, or "Songs My Mother Taught Me," by Dvořák.

It is, for example, the dignity and simplicity which Dvořák wrote into the *Largo* movement in his "New World Symphony" which gives it its constant emotional appeal. So tender and so haunting is the melody that when the "Largo" was first played by a great orchestra in New York City,* many people who sat in the great audience were moved to tears.

It is this same apparent simplicity which makes a good melody singable. Of all the famous composers of opera, none have been able to write more singable airs, or melodies, than Verdi. It is told of him that on one occasion, when his latest opera, "Rigoletto," was about to be given its first performance, he withheld the principal aria for the tenor ("La Donna è Mobile") from this singer until a few hours before the curtain was to rise. The beautiful aria was so simple and tuneful that if he had not, and the members of the opera company had heard it in even one rehearsal, they would not have been able to keep from humming or singing it on the streets afterwards, and the novelty of the opera would have been gone before even the first performance had been given.

Rhythm. Some melodies are beautiful and retain their popularity indefinitely because their composers have combined a strongly marked rhythm with the tune itself, as a better means of expression.

Slow melodies often seem, at first, to be more expressive than fast ones. Restlessness, or too constant an activity, seldom creates a "favorite" melody. To test this, compare the melody of the Dvořák "Largo" with a Hopi Indian tribal air.

However, some lively melodies have such a contagious "skip and go"—as "Dixie"—that everyone likes to hear or sing them. Most folk-songs and all folk-dances are strongly rhythmic, and some of the greatest pieces of art, or composed music, contain such a strong rhythm that they make the melody one to instinctively wish to keep time with, or hum, or whistle. Examples of this are the famous "Soldiers' Chorus" from "Faust"; the "Toreador Song" from "Carmen"; or "Pomp and Circumstance," by Elgar.

It is the less noticeable but more subtly arranged rhythm that gives the celebrated "Andante" from the Fifth Symphony, by Beethoven its distinctive melody, and places it among the five or six most beautiful melodies in the world.

Harmony. Some melodies are liked because the mind always associates them with rich harmonies. Such is the case with most of the Negro Spirituals, or such a composed piece as the Chopin "Funeral March."

Form. A meandering melody is seldom a "favorite" melody. Even without thinking, the usual choice for "favorites" are those melodies which are written with balance and orderliness. A certain amount of repetition is enjoyed in a melody, and enough contrast to

---

*December 15, 1893.

give it its delightfully distinctive character. Think how the first part of, for example, "Swanee River" is followed by a contrasting theme. But the same first theme is repeated in the chorus to give a sense of balance and completion. This is heard in the "Volga Boat Song," in which the main characteristic phrase—a typically Russian drop from the fourth to the first tone of the minor scale—is repeated nine times in the course of the thirty-two measures which make up the old folk-song.

A good melody must have originality and variety, but not so much as to destroy its unity. It is the balanced combination of repetition, contrast, variety, and unity that constitutes form, without which no melody can be considered beautiful.

Mood. The greatest of all tests of beauty in a melody is in its mood, or in its ability to arouse a definite emotion in the listener, without the aid of a spoken word.

A thoughtful hearing, careful study, and free discussion of those melodic compositions already suggested in this chapter, will bring out the especial thing in each of these particular melodies—in the way of melodic line, length of phrase, sweep of melody or character of construction—which creates in it its own special appeal.

"Drink to Me Only With Thine Eyes" is one of the oldest of English folk-songs. The words by Ben Jonson—sometimes said to be a literal translation of some Greek verses of great age—are set to a gentle, refined, and flowing melody, so old that its origin is lost in mystery. Some people have credited this tune to Mozart because of its lyric beauty, but this claim has never been proved. The melody of "Drink to Me Only" is beautiful, in part, because of its simplicity of form.

Galloway

ITALIAN BOAT SCENE. THE QUAY AT CAMOGLE

The first theme, or phrase, is peculiarly complete within itself, coming to a close on the "home tone" of the key, giving the singer or listener a distinct sense of satisfaction. The second phrase is an exact repetition of the first. Phrase three, higher in pitch, and of a more questioning mood, is answered by the return of the first supremely satisfying air. The form may be diagramed as *a a b a.*

"All Through the Night," a poetic Welsh lullaby, and a very old folk-air, is another proof that mother-love has been common to all races and peoples from prehistoric times. It is an example of the finer type of Welsh folk-melody and is another instance of an air in which the first theme ends upon the "home tone." It, too, has a new theme for its third phrase, this being added for the sake of contrast and balance. The form is *a a b a.*

"Santa Lucia," by Denza, is one of the favorite Neapolitan airs of Italy, a composed boat-song or *barcarolle* so well-beloved and so constantly sung by every fisherman who puts out into the bay from the city of Naples, as well as by every man, woman, or child on land in all parts of Italy, that it is often thought and spoken of as an Italian folk-song. It has been sung wherever there has been an itinerant musician, a fisherman, or a gondolier, and is a real *barcarolle* though folk-song in style. Its name refers to the patron saint of the old Italian city of Naples. The music ably reflects the rowing, rocking sentiment of the words. The chief characteristic of this melody is its carefree and buoyant quality. Notice the way in which the last half of the first theme imitates the first half, only starting on a lower tone.

ROBERT SCHUMANN

"Träumerei," by Robert Schumann, one of the "favorite" melodies of the world, is beautiful because of its simplicity. It is one of a collection of small pieces for piano (now transcribed for almost every instrument of the orchestra, and the entire orchestra itself) known as the "Scenes from Childhood" which, when played in concert by Clara Wieck—later Schumann's wife—attracted the attention of the critics and the general public to Schumann's ability as a composer, which his larger and more pretentious works had, up to that time, failed to secure.

The "Träumerei" is constructed entirely upon one theme, simple, but extraordinarily tender. The first part here given is built upon the very familiar arpeggio or triad, steps 1, 3, 5 and 8 of the major scale of *F.*

(The *E,* inserted by Schumann to give variety and motion to the theme, is printed here with a small note, so as to make clear the steps of the arpeggio.)

A diagram of the structure or form of "Träumerei" and its use of *a,* as we may call the one full theme, is as follows:

a four-measure theme, Key of *F* Major.

a (with differing cadence) *F* Major.

Both these parts are repeated.

a with modulation to Key of *B*-flat Major.

a transposed into key of *B*-flat (slightly altered) and modulation back to *F* Major.

a *F* Major.

a altered into the form of a simple *Coda.*

"Cradle Song" (or "Lullaby"), by Johannes Brahms, is one of the celebrated melodies which this composer evolved, with great art, from traditional German folk-airs. Contrasting this tender air with the exquisite Welsh lullaby, "All Through the Night," the same mother-love is found, but expressed in a slightly different manner in a different land. This song was arranged especially for two of Brahms's little friends, and he wrote, on the side of his manuscript, "For Arthur and Bertha Faber, for their every-happy use. July, 1868."

The "Cradle Song" opens with a two-measure introduction which, with its short "pattern" of double notes, twice repeated, establishes both rhythm and atmosphere of the lullaby. The gentle motion is at once taken up by the voice while the piano (or orchestra) continues in the same type of double-third accompanying figure as that which was a part of the introduction. Each verse of the song is sung to the same air. Each is made up of eight phrases (four "big parts") the second of which imitates the first, while the third and fourth are very similar. This song has been transcribed for many solo instruments.

"Songs My Mother Taught Me," an art song by Antonin Dvořák, is one of a series of "Gypsy Songs," in which the composer tells of the sorrows of a wandering race. This simple and touching melody has such an appeal that, once heard, it is not easily forgotten. It is one of the most beautiful melodies in the world.

"Largo," from Dvořák's "New World Symphony," has for its main theme a romantic and lovely melody. This symphony owes its unusual title to the fact that in it Dvořák, the Bohemian composer, utilized folk-melodies which he had heard and admired during his short residence in the New World. The particular folk-air used by Dvořák here was claimed by some to be an old Negro melody, but Dvořák himself is said to have told Miss Alice Fletcher (noted collector of Indian tribal melodies) that it is an Osage Indian tribal air which he heard sung while in Iowa. William Arms Fisher, a co-teacher of Dvořák in a New York school, sat in the box with the composer at the first presentation of the symphony by Anton Seidel. He says Dvořák remarked to him on that occasion, that the music of the "Largo" as well as the other parts was wholly and entirely original.

The first theme of the Dvořák "Largo" is written in the five-toned pentatonic scale—frequent among Indian tribal airs—and thus immediately achieves a mood and atmosphere quite its own (the second phrase uses a six-tone scale). This rarely beautiful melody from the movement of the "New World" was labeled "Adagio" by Dvořák when he composed the Symphony, but this was changed to "Largo" after the composer heard the first rehearsal of the work by the New York Philharmonic under the direction of Anton Seidel, who played the movement much slower than *Adagio*.

The element of pitch also enters into the appeal. The movement begins with a low, somber, chordal passage, played by horns, trumpet and trombone. This establishes the atmosphere. Then comes the tender melody, played by English horn, over an accompaniment of muted strings.

The last notes of the theme are repeated softly by the clarinets. Then follows a repetition of the poetic chord passage with which the movement opened. It is now in the top register, in the woodwind.

The melody is further developed by being given to two horns as a duet.

The second theme is played by flute and oboe. It, too, is characterized by great simplicity.

This material is developed in the same subtle manner, and after a return to the first theme the movement comes to a close in a lingering, hesitating leave-taking of the air.

Beautiful Melodies

"La Donna è Mobile," a popular aria for tenor, from the opera "Rigoletto," by Verdi, is so spontaneous and tuneful that upon the occasion of its first performance it so stirred the audience present that they burst into wild applause before even the first verse was ended. After the close of the opera the fascinating air could be heard throughout the entire city, being whistled or sung by the home-going opera-lovers.

SCHIPA AS THE DUKE IN "RIGOLETTO"

The *aria,* sung by the Duke in the first part of Act Three in the opera "Rigoletto" —and again in the last act when he thus informs his would-be murderers that he is still alive—is introduced by a remarkable seven-measure prelude which ushers in the main theme of the popular operatic tune, then suspends the interest and arouses an unsettled feeling of expectancy, by a hold over a full measure's rest which replaces the expected eighth measure.

This fine air is here played in unison and at a lively tempo by flutes, piccolo, oboe, bassoon, violin and 'cello, while the rest of the orchestra plays a sturdy, *one,* two, three rhythm.

After one measure of rhythmic chords the aria begins, the Duke's first phrase being an exact repetition of the introduction. There is then added an infectious second phrase in which the composer makes a characteristic use, as he did in the first theme, of transposition of simple two-measure *motifs*—such as this *motif*—which is repeated in higher pitch:

The grace and buoyancy of this simple melody, famous because it is so easily remembered, inspires many great artists to add brilliant *cadenzas* of their own to the aria as they sing it. These, when heard, should be recognized as displays of individual vocal virtuosity, and not as the creation of the composer.

As the second theme is ended the flutes and oboes take up the melody of the delicate interlude, supported by the entire orchestra, the voice echoing itself on the last strain.

con forza

After the orchestral interlude a repetition of the same is heard, after which the entire orchestra takes up the air in first one instrument and then another. The aria is notable for its dramatic grace, its tunefulness, its lyric quality, its appealing warmth and its simplicity.

"Dixie," by Daniel Emmett, one of the old-time minstrels, owes its existence to a chance remark of one of the men in the company (playing in New York—1859) who, tired of the cold of a long Northern winter, made the remark that he "wished he was in Dixie." This gave Emmett his title and the song soon followed. The form of this spirited song is unique. Each phrase of the verse is completed by a refrain, "Look Away, Look Away, Look Away, Dixie Land," the air of this refrain being a series of progressions down the arpeggio. In addition the verse as a whole has a refrain made up of four distinct parts, the first and second of which are similar; the third and fourth make use of *sequence* in the three pairs of upward-moving notes.

The "Soldiers' Chorus," from the opera "Faust," by Gounod, is considered one of the really great choruses of the world. This spirited melody is sung in the great square before the cathedral during the first Scene of Act IV, when Valentine (Marguerite's brother) returns home from the wars at the head of his regiment. The Chorus was not at first intended as a part of Faust, but was written by Gounod for an earlier work which he planned but never completed. When the opera "Faust" came to rehearsal, Gounod very appropriately added this Chorus to the score, where it remains an ever-popular contribution to the opera's music. It is also effective as a concert number.

The "Soldiers' Chorus" is as vigorous and effective a stage march as is to be found in all the world of opera. The short introduction of nine measures introduces a main theme of the chorus, one measure of rhythmic chords and eight measures of rhythmic melody. The melody is of strictly military character, the opening part of the main theme being set upon the notes of a bugle call. All the materials of which the gorgeous melody is made are simple, short scale passages, effective modulations, and many repetitions of phrases. The first phrase, for instance, is repeated six times during the song. Taken at a brisk tempo, the song is march rhythm first, melody second, both blended into a harmonious whole.

"Toreador Song," the great and ever-popular aria for baritone in Act II of Bizet's Spanish opera "Carmen," is a rarely effective and colorful number of similar style, but quite different in mood. The scene in which it is sung is that of a smugglers' Inn, where, during the evening, Carmen has been singing and dancing with her gypsy friends. Suddenly Escamillo, for the moment the popular toreador or bull-fighter, appears, and renews his friendship with the gypsies, who welcome him with gay shouts. Emboldened by his welcome, he begins his famous "Toreador Song," in which, first to the crowd, and later directly to Carmen, he boastfully tells of the dangers and consequent triumphs of the toreador's life. The *aria* is thoroughly Spanish in character, in its melodic figures, its rhythm, and its accompaniment. Many scale passages add sparkling brilliance to the accompaniment as does the rhythm, a typical measure of which is given.

The main and most familiar air of the song is heard again in the refrain participated in by the chorus. Here the main melody is enhanced by an accompaniment in which *staccato* chords are played sharply *with the beats* of the music.

"Pomp and Circumstance" is an example of a piece of music written expressly to celebrate a great event in history, having been composed in 1901 by Sir Edward Elgar, eminent English composer, for the coronation ceremonies of King Edward the Seventh of England, which took place in Westminster Abbey. At the conclusion of the ceremony the bands of the city of London burst into brilliant music, most splendid of all being that written by Elgar, who had composed a whole series of military marches for the day. Finest and most inspiring of all these is the one which is known as "Pomp and Circumstance," and to the middle section of which the Kipling poem, "Land of Hope and Glory," is often sung. This song has become a sort of unofficial anthem of England.

The march is heavily scored for full orchestra. It was Elgar's idea to treat a soldiers' military march in a symphonic manner. After a short introduction, the main theme of the march enters in unison strings, a proud air built upon an individual rhythm.

The first theme of the *Trio,* played more slowly, is the "Land of Hope and Glory" melody in the Coronation Ode. This is introduced by first violin, clarinet and horns, and accompanied by woodwind strings, organ and harp. The second theme of the *Trio* (first violin, flute and 'cello) goes into a higher octave. There is immediately a return to the first march theme, given as before, by the strings in unison. This is followed by a repetition of the broad first melody of the trio, presented this time with full orchestra, *fortissimo.* A brief *Coda,* in which are heard bits of the first theme, running passages, and *glissando* from harps and organ, brings the work to a magnificent close.

Andante con moto, the second movement from the Beethoven "Fifth Symphony," is built upon two lovely themes, each of which is of a quiet, pastoral character. The first, or principal theme, and the one which has won for the *Andante* its imperishable fame, possesses an irresistible grace and a beauty seldom equalled. It is first given out by the 'cellos of the orchestra. The second theme is scarcely less beautiful. The entire movement is conceded to be one of the greatest pieces of musical literature ever written.

The charms of this exquisite music are many, one of the most prominent of these being the individuality created by the melody's refined rhythm. The air moves with dignity, and becomes more interesting through frequent repetition.

1st theme

2nd theme

Following its first announcement, by violas and 'cellos in unison, with a simple *pizzicato* accompaniment from the double basses, it is answered by a touching phrase in flutes and oboes echoed in the violins. The air returns four times during the movement in exactly the same key and form as at its first announcement, no matter what change or developments may have been made in the principal subject. The persistency of the simple phrase makes a profoundly pathetic impression. It appears once in a minor key, and again in an extended form. The end is characterized by violent contrasts.

"Climbing Up the Mountain," an old, but less familiar Negro

Beautiful Melodies

Spiritual, has a melody of tender simplicity, enhanced by rich and colorful harmonies and by a vigorous swinging rhythm.

"Funeral March," from "Sonata, Opus 35," by Chopin, needs no title to designate its mood. It is, in addition, one of the best known and appreciated of the Chopin works, being much more familiar to the general public than the rest of the *Sonata* of which it is a part.

FREDERIC CHOPIN

The "Funeral March" (which is the third movement of the *Sonata*) reflects not so much grief over the death of an individual, as the mourning of a patriot (Chopin) over the loss of its independence by his own native land (Poland).

The mood of the *March* melody is established by its relentless and unchanging rhythm and tempo, and by the insistent alternation of two nearby chords—one in *B*-flat minor, the other in *G*-flat major—under an unchanging melody tone. The first theme—in two-measure phrases—is rhythmic rather than melodic:

This, and a transposed repetition of its two final measures, is followed by a weird one-measure refrain

which in its sinking pitch increases the pitiful dreariness of the atmosphere. This refrain appears later, with embellishments.

There is a constant increase in pitch and volume, but the pace never changes, and the music is awe-inspiring, and presently diminishes to a simple repetition, *piano*, of the second measure theme.

The second theme is an exceedingly sweet air, more impressive in its relentlessness than the gruesome first theme. It is made up of a two-measure theme

Music and Romance for Youth

developed by transposition, after which it returns to the original key of D-flat major.

The first theme with its desolate mood now returns and is repeated to its close.

"The Volga Boat Song" is written in three-part Song Form—A (this is repeated) B A. This is one of the most famous river songs in the world. It is a "working" song of the Russian peasants who laboriously haul the heavily loaded freight barges up the Volga River, keeping time, as they plod along the river's bank, with the words and rhythm of the old melody.

> Yo, heave ho!
> Yo, heave ho!
> 'Gainst the current
> Yo, heave ho!
> Yonder birches on the shore,
> We must pass them, pull, men, more!
> Ai da da ai da,
> Ai da da ai da,
> Pull together
> Onward still we go
> Yo, heave ho!
> Yo, heave ho!
> Pull together.
> Yo, heave ho!

MUSICAL ILLUSTRATIONS

22081	Drink to Me Only (Old English Folk-Air)	Crane
22082	All Through the Night (Welsh Folk-Air)	Crane
20080	Santa Lucia (Neapolitan Boat Song)	Victor Concert Orchestra
19854	Träumerei (Robert Schumann)	Victor String Ensemble
20737	Cradle Song (Johannes Brahms)	Howard
1414	Songs My Mother Taught Me (Antonin Dvořák)	Kreisler
6566, 6567	Largo from "New World Symphony" (Dvořák)	Stokowski and Phila. Orch.
1099	La Donna è Mobile from "Rigoletto" (Verdi)	Schipa
20043	Hopi Indian Tribal Melody	Hopi Indian Chanters
21950	Dixie (Daniel Emmett)	Crane
19783	Soldiers' March from "Faust" (Gounod)	Victor Male Chorus
8124	Toreador Song from "Carmen" (Bizet)	Tibbett
9016	Pomp and Circumstance (Elgar)	Royal Albert Hall Orch.
19783	Land of Hope and Glory (Elgar)	Victor Male Chorus
9030	Andante from Fifth Symphony (Beethoven)	Royal Albert Hall Orch.
20665	Climbing up the Mountain (Negro Spiritual)	Utica Institute Jubilee Singers
35958	Funeral March from Sonata, Opus 35 (Chopin)	Andrews
20309	Volga Boat Song (Russian Folk-Air)	Kibalchich's Symphonic Choir

Beautiful Melodies

Informational Notes

A *spiritual* is a religious folk-song of the American Negro. It is directly inspired by Biblical teaching, and is not "composed."

The Hopi Indians, like the Navajos and the Pueblos, are at home in the great Southwest. Here they reside in small villages, living in cliff-like houses known as pueblos. The Hopi are direct descendants of the people who once lived in the cliff ruins of the Southwest, and they still retain not only many old traditional customs, but re-enact, each year, many of the religious or semi-religious ceremonies of their ancestors. The men are interested in agriculture, and the tribe is noted for the manufacture of beautiful pottery.

Memorizing Melodies

You will wish to learn by heart some of the beautiful melodies that have been written for you by the great composers of the past and present, so that these bits of beauty may be with you always. Know as many beautiful melodies as possible. Whenever you hear a beautiful melody, try to concentrate your attention upon it and in this way help yourself memorize the details of the air. Such melodies will be company and pleasure to you. Try to learn one or two new ones each month.

Suggested Note-Book Work

Make a list in your scrap-book of all the lovely melodies you know and can recognize whenever heard. Include especially any interesting newspaper clippings you may find that relate to these compositions or to the composers who wrote them.

Place in your scrap-book any poem you may find which definitely suggests to you some certain melody or melodic composition.

Questions and Topics for Discussion

1. What are the three essential elements of music?

2. Name and discuss five general characteristics which have their part in making a melody beautiful.

3. If possible, name beautiful melodies which you have heard (either in or outside your classroom) which suggest to you the following moods: Serenity, gloom, somberness, joy, gayety, patriotic fervor, sadness, caprice, tenderness.

4. Compare various melodies which suggest the same poetic thoughts or mood. Tell how you think each composer has achieved his result.

5. What is a *barcarolle*?

6. What is a *theme*? Name an instance in which a composer has constructed a complete composition upon a single theme.

7. What is meant by the pentatonic scale? How does its use alter the appeal of an air from that of one written in the scale with which we are more familiar?

8. What is a *sequence* in music?

9. What is meant by *glissando*? By *pizzicato*?

10. Which of the compositions suggested in this chapter is your favorite? Give some reasons for your choice.

Library Reading. "Land of Hope and Glory," by Rudyard Kipling, and the words of as many songs mentioned in the chapter, as possible. "Songs and Song Writers," by Henry T. Finck, pages 3-12.

PART ONE—CHAPTER TWO

OLD FOLK-MELODIES OF THE OLD WORLD—CONTRASTING MUSICAL TYPES OF MANY LANDS

What a Folk-Melody Is. Folk-songs are signs of the artistic longings of a people. They are never songs that have been written or "composed," but are, as is sometimes said, "the wild flowers of music" which grow into beauty without cultivation, being those songs and dance melodies created by the people themselves, in an unconscious effort to entertain themselves or to express their inner feelings —whether of joy, sadness, longing, patriotism or other emotion. They are handed down, sometimes for centuries, by word of mouth. Learn as much as possible about the peoples of each country themselves, their background, traditions and customs, industries, and ways of enjoying their leisure time, and it will be seen why their songs all differ in type. For, each folk-song or folk-dance reflects, in a very peculiar and fascinating way, the ideals, manners, customs, historical and traditional background of the nation to which it belongs.

The Underlying Fundamentals of Folk-Music. In spite of certain differences found in the folk-music of each nation, it will be easily seen that the three general underlying fundamental characteristics of all folk-music are the same—*rhythm, melody, and mood.*

National Characteristics in Folk-Music. Antonin Dvořák, the best-known composer of old Bohemia, once said: "All races have their distinctive national songs which they at once recognize as their own." A national folk-dance or song is as characteristic a feature of a country as any climatic, geographical or political and historic feature of that land, and may be as easily recognized by a listener who has learned to notice in them types of rhythm, melody, atmosphere, or style.

An example of this may be found in contrasting the folk-airs of the four such closely connected countries as England, Scotland, Wales, and Ireland, now so often grouped together in thought and speech, each formerly an entirely separate identity, and each having folk-airs that had and still retain their national identity; and in contrasting these, in turn, with folk-melodies of Italy and France.

The Folk-Music of England. The beginnings of English folk-music are lost in mystery, but England, at the close of the Middle Ages, had already won the reputation of being the home of song.

Because of the forms of civilization and government which have existed in England for so many centuries, the English people, in their security of home life, created many happy songs. This is evidenced by the many joyous singing games which were sung and danced by grown people as well as by children on the village green on Saturday nights. Of these, "Looby Loo," "Mulberry Bush," and "Oats, Peas, Beans," are good examples.

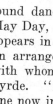

JOHN PEEL

At other times they made merry with the more formal Morris Dances* (brought to them from Spain by invaders in very early days) and in country dances. Of these none were more popular than the old dances † known as "hay dances" or "heys" of the thirteenth century, in which the dancers stepped gayly about in "longways" lines.‡

"Sellenger's Round," one of the ancient round dances, is still danced in its original form in rural England on May Day, around the May-pole and at similar outdoor festivities. It appears in one of the oldest known books of English airs, having been arranged and set down from the original for Queen Elizabeth, with whom it was a favorite, by her music teacher, Dr. William Byrde. "Sellenger's Round" is said to be the oldest country dance tune now in use.

"Green Sleeves" is still another of the popular old-time dances, and is still heard as a popular air on the streets of London. It is a

---

* Morris Dances are sometimes called "bell" dances in rural England, because of the many bells worn on the dancers' costumes.
† These thirteenth-century country dances of England, copied in France, were there called *contre-dances*; in Italy the name became *coranto* and the dance, slightly changed, finally came to be called the *courante*, a popular dance in classic suites.
‡ Some authorities say that "Hey" comes from Hedge, hence "Longways"—like hedge-rows. Such an ancient English dance has been idealized by Percy Grainger in his "Shepherd's Hey."

very old tune mentioned five times in the plays of Shakespeare. There is also a very old song called "Green Sleeves."

English folk-songs have always been noted for their dignity and melodic beauty. Of these "Drink to Me Only With Thine Eyes" * is an example.

"Sumer is icumen in," a quaintly beautiful air, words by Chaucer, is the oldest written *round* or *canon* in the world, and proves the old English claim that the early bards or minstrels used *harmony* at a very early date—some say long before it was used on the continent of Europe. It was written in 1240, and the ancient manuscript may still be seen in the British Museum. The melody is a very simple one, and should be sung, five or six times in succession, in the manner of a *round*.

English Carols. An especially exquisite portion of early English folk-songs were the *carols*. These are folk-songs created to express the emotions brought about by the various seasons of the year, or of the Church calendar—such as New Year's, Spring, or Christmas. Each village had its own carols which were considered the particular property of its inhabitants, who, in turn, respected and admired the carols of other villages. These were sung for almost every occasion, although today the most familiar are those sung at Christmas time.

One of these, "God Rest Ye, Merry Gentlemen," is a fine old song, joyously quaint through being constructed entirely in the ancient pure form of the minor scale (*a b c d e f g a*).

Tabor † and pipe were used to accompany many of the earliest

BURNS' COTTAGE, ALLOWAY, AYR

outdoor dances, while harp accompanied the singing of folk-song. Another early instrument in English life was the roto, which is mentioned by Chaucer, an early English writer. The roto is similar to the ancient lyre.

The Folk-Music of Scotland. Scottish folk-music is outstanding in the matter of nationally characteristic rhythms and types of melody, of the use of certain primitive musical instruments, and of a very old type of scale.

---

* See Chapter One, Part One, *Beautiful Melodies*.
† A tabor was a small drum used as an accompaniment to a melody from a pipe played by the same person.

Characteristic Rhythms. In the characteristic rhythms is noticed the Scotch "catch" or "snap," in which a note of short value is followed by a dotted note of greater value, or the exact opposite. A combination of these two rhythmic forms is very common, as in the old Scotch song, "Comin' Thro' the Rye."

Use of the Five- or Six-Toned Scales. Many of the finest of the old Scotch songs are built on what is called a pentatonic * scale, by which is meant a scale in which only five tones are heard. This scale, with its limited number of tones, was used in many of the old working songs of Scotland.

An old Scotch song, a favorite not only in Scotland but throughout the world, is "Auld Lang Syne," built upon the pentatonic scale, and indebted to Robert Burns for its words. Not only this song, but scores of others, owe their prolonged existence to Robert Burns, who kept so many of the old tunes alive by adding suitable words to them.

The use of the five-toned scale is thought by many scholars to be due to the early form of the bag-pipe, on which only these five tones could be played.

The six-tone scale † is illustrated in the splendid war song "Scots Wha' Hae wi' Wallace Bled." This is one of the greatest patriotic songs in the world, and boldly expresses the defiance of patriotism and daring.

"John Peel," a Scotch hunting song, is an example of the ability of the early Scotch folks to create a stirring song by the use of very few notes. The first theme of the melody of "D'ye ken John Peel" is written on just three notes of the chord, and suggests the sound of the old-time hunting horn.

In the second four-measure phrase of the verse there is a skip up of an octave—also a suggestion of the horn. The chorus is characterized by the same motion and general musical style.

Major and Minor Combinations. In many of the old Scotch reels—the very ancient dances in quick tempo common to all the countries of the British Isles—a use is made of both Major and Minor

---

* See Chapter One, Part One, for discussion of pentatonic scale.
† C, D, E, F sharp, G sharp, A sharp (C).

within a single two-measure phrase, as:

The *reel,* usually danced by two couples at once, is frequently accompanied by the fiddle.

"The Strathspey" or "Highland Fling" is a characteristic dance of Scotland, somewhat slower and more jerky in its rhythm than the *reel.* It possesses real Scotch "snap," and receives its name from the Scotch locality in which it originated.

Welsh Folk-Music * is noted for its great dignity. Its older songs may be divided into two general divisions—that of the quiet pastoral life of the people, and its old-time war songs. The music is essentially harp music, copying the simplicity of the harps of the thirteenth and fourteenth centuries. These old models had only three strings each and were so small that they could be carried on horseback.

HARLECH CASTLE

Many Welsh melodies are inherited from the old-time harpists who gathered, in their wanderings, the loveliest airs and rhythms, and then carried them about through the countryside. So great was the respect in which the harp was held in early days that no slave was allowed to touch or learn to play a harp—he could not then pretend to be a gentleman. The law might seize everything else of a gentleman's wealth, but it might never take his harp—that would be to degrade him.

"Men of Harlech," Wales' most famous war song, takes its name from old Harlech Castle,† which stands upon a lofty rock overlooking the sea on the shore of Meroneth shire. The name is in itself descrip-

---

* One of Wales' sweetest songs is "All Thro' the Night," discussed in Chapter One.
† A Roman fort in the olden days—the original tower of which dates from the sixth century. Other parts of the castle were built in 1468, when King Edward IV ordered an army to Harlech to demand its surrender.

tive of the site, as Ar-lech means "above the rocks." Many interesting stories might be told of the castle and its old towers and turrets.

The song, "Men of Harlech," has a strong martial flavor which well typifies the brave warriors who defended the rock on numerous occasions.

Hark, I hear the foe advancing
Barbed steeds are proudly prancing,
Helmets in the sunlight glancing
Glitter through the trees.

Music of Ireland. The lilting Irish jig is the most strikingly individual dance in Old Europe. No other folk-dance in the world is so gay. Many of Ireland's songs have an equally gay and carefree rhythm, while others are as extremely tender or sad. Special points to notice in a study of Irish folk-music are the scales used in its construction, the construction of the tunes, its emotional character, the highly individual rhythms, and the musical instruments most popularly used.

THE OLD HOLLYBROOK HARP

Many Irish airs are written in the whole-tone scale, others in the ancient Celtic scale, which is pentatonic. (If begun on C this runs $C\ D\ E\ G\ A\ C$. The insertion of F and B would create the scale which is today most familiar.) The number five enters greatly into Irish poetry and music, as, the use of a five-toned scale, five lines in the limericks, and so on. The old "plow tunes" of Ireland, sung or whistled by the plowman as he follows the plow, are of great antiquity, and are built upon this old scale, as:

Antiquity of Irish Airs. The ancient Irish had battle marches, dance tunes and folk-songs in the fifth century. They were among the earliest to use written music, had an army of bards and poets, and a world-famed school of harpers.

Mood in Irish Music. To understand Irish music one must understand the rapid change of spirit among the Irish folk, and the frequent mixture—exhibited in the folk-music—of feelings of deep gloom and extreme levity. Thus in even the liveliest strains of music some melancholy note intrudes.

The romantic character of the music is often enhanced by a characteristic repetition of the closing note of a song * as in "She Moved Through the Fair."

Another feature of Irish music is the great range of its melodies. The rhythms are clearly defined, the *jig* being in six-beat measure and the *reel* in four. A characteristic of the *reel* melodies is their constant reiteration of the first and fifth tones of the scale.

Irish Folk-Instruments. The most popular instruments in old Ireland were the harp and the fiddle, as the violin was usually called. It was the appropriate instrument to accompany the dancing, while the harp was used with singing. The harp emblem was used on the Irish flag. The people of Ireland are among the most musical folk of the world. Real Irish music is as distinctive as that of Spain or Russia.

Galloway

VILLAGE MUSICIANS OF BRITTANY, PLAYING PICCOLO AND BAGPIPE

"The Harp That Once Thro' Tara's Halls" is a favorite Irish air

* Other Irish songs which repeat their closing notes include "Must I Go Bound," "Gartan Mother's Lullaby," "The Weaver's Daughter," "Ballynure Ballad," "The Low-Backed Car," etc.

which commemorates an old custom of the ancient Irish harpers of holding festivals and contests of song at Tara Castle each year. Although the castle has not been used for nearly fourteen hundred years, its outlines still show in the ruins on Tara Hill. The words now sung to the old air are by Thomas Moore.* The form of the song is *a b b a* (modified). Irish music is as greatly indebted to the poet Thomas Moore as Scotch music is to Robert Burns for prolonging the life of the old airs by his creation of new verses to be sung to them.

French Folk-Music. In contrast to the emotional Irish songs are the more formal, and possibly less intense, French folk-airs. These are, however, notable for sweetness, elegance, and formal beauty. The French airs vary in each French province. The general characteristics of the folk-songs of the south of France resemble those of the poetic songs of the early troubadours. Burgundy, in the east-central part, is noted for its charming carols. The characteristic of the songs of Brittany is grave dignity, while songs of Lorraine are often very bright and rhythmic.

Early Military Marching Songs. Some French folk-songs also show the influence of the Crusades which swept across the country for so many years during the Middle Ages. Such a song is the familiar "We Won't Go Home Until Morning"—known in England as "He's a Jolly Good Fellow"—which, as an ancient Crusaders' marching song, bears the title "Malbrouck." There is some doubt as to whether the song originated in France and was taken to Palestine and Arabia by the Crusaders, or whether it came to France with the returning Crusaders.†

Certain it is that it bears a title in which a noble French soldier is named—"Malbrouck to the War Has Gone" (To War Has Gone Duke Malbrouck). It was sung as a cradle song by Marie Antoinette, was sung by Napoleon's troops, and the air was used in 1813 by Beethoven in his "Battle Symphony" as a symbol of the French troops.

Fine   *Da Capo*

---

* Moore's most famous song is "The Last Rose of Summer," set to the old Irish tune of "The Groves of Blarney," the original manuscript of which was sold in New York City, in 1923, for $625.
† The returning Crusaders brought back to France the lute, making it possible, for the first time, to accompany the singing of folk-airs.

The melody is in three-part song form, *A B A*.

More dramatic in its history is the stirring "Marching Through Lorraine." Sung for hundreds of years as an accompaniment for country dancing in the old French province of Lorraine, it became, later on, a marching song for the armies of France.* It is said to have been often sung by the soldiers who followed Joan of Arc's leadership a full five hundred years ago. After the Treaty of Frankfort (in 1871) in which Alsace and part of Lorraine were ceded by France to Germany, the passionately patriotic French people of those districts were forbidden to sing the air. It was, however, kept alive in other parts of France, and during the World War the victorious soldiers of the Allied Army marched into Metz, led by Marshal Foch, singing the "March Lorraine." The march is, singularly, in 6/8, two strong beats to each measure, and is irregular in form.

Folk-Carols of France. Many of the loveliest melodies of France are woven about the festivals of the Church. These old carols, or nowells (also spelled *noël*) take their name from the French word *nouvelles,* meaning "news" or "tidings."

Such carols include the tender Christmas carol, "The First Noël." In form the old folk-carol—also known as Anglo-Norman in its nationality, since it was also sung in England by the Normans during and after their invasion of that land in 1066—uses the quaint old custom of repeating a single theme over and over, and also of ending on some other than the keynote.

"March of the Three Kings," † another French carol, tells of the quaint folk-legend and custom of French boys and girls who watch by the roadsides on Christmas morning for the reappearance of the Three Wise Men. The air proves its great antiquity by its quaint use of the minor in its oft-repeated theme.

---

* Ganne, a French musician, modernized the old air for singing and also for band.
† Used by Bizet in his "L'Arlésienne suite."

Other French folk-songs reflect the occupations of the singers or the tender sentiments of the troubadours.

Songs of Italy. In Italy—another "land of song"—the natural quality of the voices establishes the type of folk-song. Here the folk are endowed with great sensitiveness and a lively imagination. The most familiar Italian folk-dance is the *tarantella*, named from Taranto, where it originated. It is characterized by graceful and rapid motion—usually accompanied by the tambourine, which keeps time to the long-continued and agitated rush of the music.

Galloway

PEASANTS DANCING THE TARAN-
TELLA, ABOVE CAPRI, ITALY

In the Italian folk-song there is a certain graceful refinement and poetic elegance characteristic of the life of the people.

"O Sole Mio" (My Sunshine), by di Capau, is considered as a popular folk-melody, and is sung by all classes of the people. Built over a rhythm which suggests the Spanish *habanera* ♫♫♪ the joyous and graceful downward-moving melody reflects the poetic thought of the Italian folk. It is built upon two separate themes.

"Santa Lucia." One of the loveliest of the Italian popular songs is this Neapolitan boat song, which so ably suggests the depth and sincerity of the feelings of the people. (See Chapter One, Part One.)

Galloway

ITALIAN MUSICIAN PLAYING
PIPES OF BAMBOO

MUSICAL ILLUSTRATIONS

20641	*Shepherd's Hey (English Round Dance—Grainger)*	*Mayfair Band*
20445	*Sellenger's Round (Old English)*	*Mayfair Band*
——*	*Sumer is icumen in (Old English Canon)*	
35788	*God Rest Ye, Merry Gentlemen (English Carol)*	*Trinity Choir*
35878	*Comin' Thro' the Rye (Scotch Air)*	*Victor Mixed Chorus*
35878	*Scots Wha' Hae (Scotch Patriotic Song)*	*Victor Mixed Chorus*
19961	*John Peel (Border Hunting Song)*	*Associated Glee Clubs of America*
21616	*Strathspey (Highland Fling) (Scotch Folk Dance)*	*Victor Band*
20842	*All Through the Night (Welsh Folk Air)*	*Morgan*
——*	*Men of Harlech (Welsh Folk Air)*	

Music and Romance for Youth

INFORMATIONAL NOTES

"Shepherd's Hey," by Percy Grainger, is an art work founded upon thematic material taken from the four differing variants of one tune which were collected by Cecil Sharp in different English communities. Grainger has made use of the outstanding features of each variant by using them in clever *counterpoint*.

In the orchestral version of "Shepherd's Hey" (which is also written for piano solo, for two pianos, for band and for other instrumental combinations) each instrument may be said to impersonate one of the country dancers, and takes its turn of stepping into the line of action. In turn, the stringed instruments (*staccato*), horn and trumpet, woodwind instruments and xylophone, trombones and bass, then oboe are heard—the differing tone qualities of the instruments replacing the variety commonly given by varied themes. The dance moves along in a jolly manner, both tune and the big *pizzicato* accompaniment chords becoming more and more furious as they hurry on to the swirling chromatic runs, many *glissandos,* and chords *ffff* which bring the piece to a hilarious close.

"Sumer is icumen in" is the oldest written music in the world which records both words and music together. It is also the first song to have been written in the language of the people, all previous European music having been in Latin. It is the only music which had a key sign, an invention not used again for nearly four hundred years, and the first song ever written for six voices each of which was to sing a separate part (really a four-part round on a two-part ground or drone bass, imitating the bagpipes). The music itself was first written down in the form of a circle, which was then laid upon a table, so that when the singers gathered about it they found their own parts lying directly before them.

It was at the very old abbey of Reading—a city on the Thames River, about thirty-five miles west of London—that "Sumer is icumen in" was arranged as a canon. In going through the ruins of what was formerly the great Hall, now a roofless, grass-grown enclosure with fragments of stone walls standing and broken towers, there is to be seen, upon one wall, a large plaster plaque with the old canon all written out upon it, illuminated in color, doubtless a replica of the original manuscript and itself very old.

Harlech is a Welsh village many hundreds of years old. The old castle is beside the village on a jutting headland of rock, the entrance way is between two round towers which date back to the Middle Ages. It was the last castle in Wales to hold out for Charles the First. The outside walls and towers of Harlech Castle are still in good condition, built upon the site of an old Roman castle and of succeeding Welsh strongholds. During the War of the Roses, Harlech was defended by an Earl of Pembroke, who made the famous statement that he had held a castle in France "until all the old women in France knew about it," and that he intended to do the same thing in Wales. In spite of his boast he was forced, by hunger, to surrender the garrison. The sea which surges below the castle is a terror to navigators, who avoid its treacherous tides and submerged rocks whenever possible. Parliaments were held in Harlech during the Middle Ages.

The Rye referred to in the song "Comin' Thro' the Rye"— is, like the River Afton, one of the numerous Scotch rivers made famous in folk-song. The Rye is a shallow stream flowing over a stony bed, and it was the custom for the young men of the village to gather on its banks in the evening, to exact a toll from the girls as they crossed over on the stepping-stones.

Tara is the name of a hill in County Meath, Ireland. It was here that the convention of Irish kings, held each three years, was established about 900 B. C. According to the old Irish traditions, the palace of Tara was nine hundred feet square, and contained a hundred and fifty separate apartments. The early kings and queens of Ireland are said to have been crowned there.

The stirring old Scotch song, "Scots Wha' Hae Wi' Wallace Bled" (tune, "Battle of Bannockburn"), was first played—so tradition tells us—in 1344, nine years after the death of the martyred Scottish hero, William Wallace, when Robert Bruce led his daring soldiers to Bannockburn outside the Castle of Stirling. William Wallace (1270-1305) was a popular national hero of Scotland. During the wars between England and Scotland, Wallace was outlawed and driven into the wilds where he surrendered himself to a group of desperate men. Refusing allegiance to the English King, he was accused of being a traitor, condemned to die and executed. His only defense was that he had never sworn fealty to the Crown and was therefore not a

traitorous subject.   Robert Bruce led the Scottish soldiers to victory
at this battle and Bobbie Burns wrote the stirring words four hundred years later.

The province of Lorraine is in the extreme northeastern corner
of France.   Bounded on the east and south by Germany and Switzerland, its most famous village, during the past five hundred years,
has been the quaint village of Domremy, the birthplace and home of
Joan of Arc.

The original kingdom of the great Charlemagne included the
land now known as Lorraine.   When Charlemagne's kingdom was
divided, after his death, this part of the kingdom was given to the
oldest grandson, whose name was Lothair.   Known as the Kingdom
of Lothair, the name became corrupted to Lorraine, and was later
known as the Duchy of Lorraine.   It still retains the very old name,
though now a part of France.   For a long time—hundreds of years
ago, in the time of Joan of Arc, when Lorraine was already thought
of as a portion of France—its inhabitants always thought and spoke
of it as a country in itself, and would talk of ''going into France''
when they left their own province.

Scotch Music.   That music has been a feature of Scotch life for
many centuries is proved by the rare simplicity of the Scottish melodies, and also by the unique sculptured ornaments which have decorated old Melrose Abbey since 1136, in which are seen flutes, violins
and a bagpipe.   A carving of a harp is also to be seen on a nearby
seventh-century church.

Robert Burns, Scottish poet, was born in the village of Alloway,
about two and a half miles from the city of Ayr.   At Alloway a
visitor may visit the Burns cottage, which is kept as a museum, and
will see about it many of the spots immortalized by Burns in his
verse.   The Burns Monument is not far away, near the banks of
the River Doon.   This combines Greek and Roman architecture, its
form being that of a circular open-air temple.   Nine stone columns,
each about sixty feet high, support the dome.   The pedestal of the
monument contains a room in which are shown a number of the
choicest Burns relics.   This exquisite memorial was built by public
subscription.

Dumfries has even more association with Burns than has Ayr.
It was at the village of Ellisland, six miles out from Dumfries, that
he wrote ''Tam o' Shanter.''   In Dumfries is the house on Burns
Street in which the poet spent the last three years of his life.   There
is also a quaint little house known as ''The Hole i' the Wa' '' which
contains a large collection of Burns relics.   Here is also the Globe

Inn, the tavern in which may still be seen a delightful low-ceilinged room, with its original fireplace and the table, about which Burns and his cronies used to sit. Along the nearby banks of the river, Burns, in one of his evening walks, composed the words of the heart-stirring "Scots Wha' Hae Wi' Wallace Bled."

QUESTIONS AND TOPICS FOR DISCUSSION

1. What is a folk-song? How is a folk-melody able to suggest and definitely express national characteristics and sentiments? What are the fundamental elements of the music which help in such expression?

2. Contrast the folk-airs of the four separate countries of the British Isles. How have forms of government and degrees of early civilization affected these folk-songs? What are the typical musical instruments of each country?

3. How did the Crusades influence the music of France?

4. What is a *canon*? A *carol*? What is meant by Scotch "snap"? What is a pentatonic scale? Form a pentatonic scale beginning on *F*-sharp. What is a whole-tone scale? Form a whole-tone scale beginning on *G*.

5. Name at least three evidences which prove the antiquity of Scotch folk-music. How did the use of the early model of the harp influence the form and content of early Welsh folk-song?

6. Name five characteristics of old Irish folk-airs.

7. Tell what you can of, and discuss, the country dances of various countries.

8. What is the most familiar folk-dance of Italy? What effect has the climate of Italy had upon the folk-song of that country? Discuss the typical characteristics of Italian folk-song. In what ways does it differ from the folk-music of nearby France?

PART ONE—CHAPTER THREE

NATIONALITY IN FOLK AND ART MUSIC—BOHEMIA

The National Music Life of Bohemia. Bohemia—now a part of the Republic of Czecho-Slovakia—is a land of music. "Where there is a Czech, there you will hear music," says an old Bohemian proverb.

The Bohemian peasant has a gift for song, and his folk-song is one of the richest of all Europe. In spite of all the other changes which war or other disturbances may have brought to the land during many centuries, the Bohemian has stedfastly retained his own language, his customs and his music.

The country's musical past is rich and full. Though it is not necessary to believe all the romantic legends woven around Bohemian musicality, it is artistically proved that Bohemia was, for a long time, considered the "Music Land of Europe."

Galloway

A SUNDAY AFTERNOON CALL—FOLK COSTUMES IN BOHEMIA

For over six centuries Czech music has been preserved in writing, at first in valuable hand-illuminated manuscripts. Not only were the country people interested in their national folk-songs and dances in early days, but many of the nobles of the land had special music rooms in their castles and maintained private orchestras so that they might, at any time, hear the music of all Europe played, or sung.[*]

Soon it came about that nearly every village in Bohemia had its own band of musicians and its choir. Music was nearly always taught by the village schoolmaster, and many a small country village could boast one or more family string trios or quartets.

While the peasant folk-songs and dances have always retained their own individual characteristics—such as peculiar and unexpected irregularities in the rhythm, or an odd number of measures in a phrase—the national music of Bohemia, like that of all Hungary, Spain, and Southern France, has become embellished and ornamented with brilliant arabesques by contact with the music of the gypsies who have, for centuries, made the land their home.

A Bohemian Dance that Captured the World. Bohemia is not only a land of song, but also a land of dances, and it was from the city of Prague that there came the *Polka,* a Bohemian folk-dance that took the world by storm. The word *polka,* which comes from the Bohemian word *pulka* meaning "half-step," was given to it to describe the peculiar lilting step—always in 2/4 measure with a decided accent on the third beat—with which it is danced.

Smetana, the Father of Bohemian Art-Music. It was upon this solid foundation of the country's music life that Friedrich Smetana, known as the "Father of Bohemian Art-Music," began, during the nineteenth century, to develop what is known as the Bohemian Na-

---

[*] One of these was Count Esterhazy, who, in his palace near Vienna, maintained a private orchestra, of which Haydn was once conductor.

tional School of Music. This does not mean a building, or even an organization, but is a term used to suggest a national movement in which all composers of a country work together along the lines of a great national idea and spirit.

Smetana, better than any other composer of his time, knew his home-land and its people, and the many delightful ways in which it was their custom to spend their leisure time. These he desired to make known to the world, just as they were, without any unnecessary idealization. His principal musical creations were dramatic works.

"The Bartered Bride," a Bohemian opera. This work—a portrait of rural Bohemia—is world famous. In it Smetana has depicted a scene in a typical Bohemian village, so true to life, so natural and so jolly, that a hearer cannot resist its charm.

The story presented is that of an old Bohemian folk-tale, and to tell it Smetana uses much folk-music as thematic material. In one scene at the village inn, a band of strolling players make their appearance and the villagers gather about to watch the street entertainment which they give to advertise their coming evening performance. The "Comedians' March" is one of the particularly effective musical numbers in this scene.

The "Overture" to the opera is an acknowledged masterpiece and is often played by symphony orchestras as an independent concert number. It is built upon several alluring melodies taken from the opera itself, and is so irresistibly gay and jolly that when it was played for the first time on a concert program in the Old World, it was called "Comedy Overture." There are two main features to be observed in listening to this "Overture"; first, the old Bohemian folk-song which comes in a magnificent full chorus of instruments; and second, the spirited

A RURAL SCENE IN BOHEMIA   Galloway

fugue, in which the composer has written a spontaneous dashing about of the strings as though they were taking part in a country jig.

The "Overture" begins at a lively tempo and the chief theme—the old folk-air—is immediately heard from strings and woodwind in unison and in octaves, accompanied by heavy chords from the brass section and the kettle-drums. This theme is the foundation about which the entire "Overture" revolves, and to enjoy the number most completely, one should at once become entirely familiar with it.

As soon as it has been clearly stated, the old tune is developed in a fugal manner, first by the string choir, then the first violins, second violins, violas, 'cellos, second 'cellos and double-bass entering with the air in regular intervals.

This is followed by a loud, joyous episode, full orchestra, after which the music returns to its formal fugal play upon the first theme, the strings now being joined in this by the wind instruments and at last by the full orchestra.

Into this atmosphere of carefree village life comes the second theme, a short and charming melody played first as a solo by the oboe, and then as a contrasting air against a simple tune played by the strings. Once again the first theme is gaily sounded by the wood-winds, by the strings, and in a little *fugue*. The joyous music now gradually sinks to a *pianissimo* before it suddenly bursts forth in the brilliant *Coda* which brings the "Overture" to a close.

The "Comedians' March," from the same opera, is an operatic march written in *rondo* style. It opens with an introduction containing a simple cadence in brilliant chords. This establishes the key, *C*-major. There immediately enters the first theme, a tripping figure in sixteenth notes, very much in the style of a folk-dance.

The form of the "March" may be divided into these several large divisions (note the recurrence of the first theme characteristic of the rondo pattern):

First theme, a tripping figure in sixteenth notes, folk-dance style, *C*-major.

Second theme, very melodic, oboe, then clarinet.

First theme.

Third theme, *A*-minor, trombone; a development section and transitional passages.

Fourth theme, melody in *F*-major.

First theme.

Fifth theme, basses.

First theme.

Coda, reminiscent of several of the thematic passages, *fortissimo* climax.

Throughout the entire march the utmost genial humor and alluring freshness of melodic material prevails.

"Bohemian Dance," Smetana. In this short dance for piano, Smetana has achieved the atmosphere of a rollicking country dance through the constant and clever use of a brief and simple rhythmic figure. This is carried on all the way through the piece, through frequent ascending and descending double-note passages suggestive—because of the speed at which they are taken—of *glissandos,* and even in the slower, quieter middle section.

The rich harmonies used by the composer create an almost orchestral effect.

Following the short, poetic middle section, the music returns, gradually, to its earlier *tempo,* but now, for a short time, continued over an accompaniment figure in the bass,

which, unchanged in pitch or rhythm for several measures, suggests the heavy steps of the peasant dancers.

The "Dance" is extremely brilliant, offers a rare opportunity for technical display on the part of the pianist, but, in its composition, makes no attempt at melodic invention or depth of sentiment.

Another imposing tribute to his native land is Smetana's series of six symphonic poems entitled, "My Fatherland."

Antonin Dvořák, Another Bohemian Composer. Equally patriotic in his use of Bohemian folk-airs and the national *folk-idea,* was Antonin Dvořák, best known to the American musical public through his popular "Humoresque" and his "New World Symphony." Although these two compositions are, in the main, based upon American Negro and Indian airs, they only serve to enhance his reputation as a national composer.

His "Slavonic Dances"—a set of fiery and melodious piano duets based on airs of the Bohemian gypsies—brought him his first fame, and proved his ability as a composer.

The "Slavonic Dance," No. 1, in *G*-minor, is notable for simple conventional harmonies, constant variations of the first theme and its alternation of consecutive phrases between parallel major and minor.

It frequently uses the effect of the *furiant* rhythm (three-beat time measure and duple accents as: $\frac{3}{4}$ ♩ ♩ ♩ | ♩ ♩ ♩ |

The melody of the theme is further varied by instrumental devices, the air being taken or accompanied by first one, then another group of instruments. It ends with a brief *fortissimo* climax immediately preceded by a *pianissimo* melodic phrase in flute, while strings and basses mark the unvarying dance rhythm.

In later works he continued to idealize the folk-airs and folk-rhythms of his native land. One way in which he did this was by using the rhythms of the *Dumka,* an extremely slow and thoughtful folk-dance, as the slow movement in many of his important works for stringed instruments.

The *Furiant,* a wild and noisy Bohemian folk-dance, was often transplanted almost bodily into his art music. The *Furiant,* usually danced toward the close of a wedding or equally important village festival, is unique in its rhythm. The measure is always three-beat (either 3/8 or 3/4), but has *duo* rhythm, $\frac{3}{4}$ ♩♩♩ | ♩♩♩ | ♩♩♩ | ♩♩♩ | etc. the peasant dancers stamping out the vivid rhythm in much the style of a Russian Hopak.

In his beautiful "Quintet" for piano and stringed instruments, Dvořák substituted a brilliant *Furiant* for the traditional *scherzo* so often used in such works.

Josef Suk, a favorite pupil of Dvořák and also his son-in-law, is a modern Bohemian composer who, although he cherishes the national musical characteristics, has a more decided preference for lyrical music than either Smetana or Dvořák. He is a composer of much beautiful chamber music, and a member of the world-famous Czech String Quartet. For many years he lived in an old-style house on a farm just outside Prague, in the same neighborhood in which he was born, with a sign on the gate warning idle visitors not to interrupt his work.

"Polka," the second number of the "Fairy Tale Suite," by Suk (in *B*-major, 2/4 time measure), is for full orchestra. The Suite is a portion of the incidental music written by the composer for a dramatic legend, "Radúz and Mahulena," by Zeyer, a modern Bohemian poet. The "Polka" is based on a little dance with song episode in the first act of the drama. It is real dance music, in which is featured the constant use of double-thirds. Its first part reproduces a folk-dance melody of distinctly Slavic coloring and rhythm. The air is given first to the clarinets.

It is taken up by bassoons, flutes and oboes, and then introduces the *Trio* which is first played by the bassoon. This theme is repeated many times, at last in a diminished form.

Then the first dance is gaily resumed.

"My Homeland," a national song of old Bohemia, corresponds to "America" for the United States, or the "Marseillaise" for France. It is a simple air, having a tendency to return, at the ends of many of its phrases, to the keynote. The melody and the tempo at which it is taken suggest devotion, whether the words are understood or not.

MUSICAL ILLUSTRATIONS

80701	*Overture from "The Bartered Bride" (Smetana)*	*German Opera Orch.*
——*	*Comedians' March from "The Bartered Bride" (Smetana)*	
		German Opera Orchestra
7121	*Bohemian Dance (Smetana)*	*Bachaus*
6649	*Slavonic Dance (No. 1, G-Minor—Dvořák)*	*Chicago Symphony Orchestra*
6649	*Polka from "Fairy Tales" (Josef Suk)*	*Chicago Symphony Orchestra*
79182	*"Where is My Homeland?" (Bohemian National Air)*	
——*	*Dumka and Furiant from Quintet (Opus 81—Dvořák)*	

HISTORICAL NOTES

The land of Bohemia receives its name from *Boemus,* the name of the eldest man of the party of discovery who located in this part of the land and settled it in ancient times.

"Radúz and Mahulena," the play for which the "Fairy Tale" music was originally written, was produced at Prague, April 10, 1898. The *Suite,* made up of numbers from its music, was first played at Heidelberg, June 3, 1901, and its first American performance was by the Chicago Orchestra under Theodore Thomas, November 23, 1901.

Bohemia (Czecho-Slovakia), although still spoken of as Bohemia when discussing events which happened before the reorganization of the old-time provinces, lay in the northwestern portion of the former empire of Austria-Hungary. It was almost entirely surrounded by mountains. Prague was the principal city, and the Moldau the principal river, of the country.

Music and Romance for Youth

Informational Notes

The Bohemian *Polka* owes its invention to a peasant girl named Anna Slezak, who, in 1830, was working at a home in Elbeteinitz. One day she danced for her own amusement this dance of her own invention, and as she danced, sang a suitable tune. Joseph Neruda, who chanced to be in the house as a guest at the time, noted the song and dance and wrote them both down. The next week the dance was played and danced at the students' ball in Prague, from there spreading to all parts of the world.

The "Bartered Bride" was given in 1913 in the open air at Prague.

Questions and Topics for Discussion

1. What is meant by a "national school of music"? How may the life of a people influence their music?

2. How have Bohemian composers used folk-tunes and atmosphere in their art works? What effect has this given to their writings? Discuss three Bohemian folk-dances which have greatly influenced the nation's art or composed music.

3. What is meant by the "folk-idea"? How did Smetana use it in his "The Bartered Bride"?

4. What is the outstanding characteristic of "Bohemian Dance"? How has the composer suggested folk elements in the music? What is the mood of the composition? Is this Pure or Program Music?

5. What is a *fugue*? A *rondo*?

6. Contrast the "Slavonic Dance" of Dvořák with the "Polka" by Suk. How do these differ in type? How are they similar? Give reasons for this.

7. Hear again the "Largo" by Dvořák, studied in Chapter One, and contrast it with the same composer's "Slavonic Dance."

8. Name two special features of Bohemian folk-music that are individual to this country.

9. From what source has both folk and composed music of Bohemia received much of its brilliancy?

10. How may the "New World Symphony," by Dvořák, be said to reflect national characteristics of both Bohemia and America?

11. Contrast the Bohemian folk-airs you have heard with folk-airs from other lands, such as "Drink to Me Only" (English), "Santa Lucia" (Italian), "All Through the Night" (Welsh) or "Volga Boat Song" (Old Russian). All are expressions of national feelings of a people. Give reason why they differ so in type.

Library Reading. "Czecho-Slovakia," by Jessie Mothersole.

Tunes and Patterns

TUNES AND PATTERNS—A LESSON ON FORM

What Musical Form Is. Daniel Gregory Mason has said: "Form is to music what a plot is to a story: it is the order in which things happen."

Form is evolved out of years of experience. The world is, and always has been, full of tunes, but even so long ago as the Dark Ages, when there was no printing, no books to read or to study from, and no rules by which to work, the tunes or folk-songs of the people were unconsciously set together according to patterns. The manner in which such musical patterns are arranged is called *Musical Form.*

To understand Musical Form, it is necessary to recognize the various parts of a piece of music, such as measures and phrases. It is the way in which the separate parts of a composition which are alike, and those parts *which are not alike*, are arranged, that makes up the pattern or form of the individual piece.

The Use of a Knowledge of Musical Form. Just as the knowledge of the simpler rules by which architects or artists work in the creation of a splendid building or a great picture, aids the observer in seeing many otherwise unnoticed details of beauty and artistry, so a knowledge of musical form clears the way for a truer appreciation of beautiful melody or rhythm. The recognition of musical form in a composition may also assist the listener to a more intelligent appreciation and understanding of the composer's intended expression of idea or mood.

There are many kinds of Form. Some of these are very simple, and others are very complicated.

Unary Form. The simplest kind of Form is that which employs just one theme or melodic pattern. An illustration of this—which is called *Unary,* or a Form using one theme—is in the "Wild Horseman," by Robert Schumann. Here the rhythmic and melodic characteristics of this one musical idea—which is built upon a simple broken chord—persist throughout the entire composition.

In the second section of the piece this tune, or theme, is played by the bass, but it is unchanged in either rhythm or melody. In a picture or diagram of this music, giving a letter name to each theme or its reappearance, the letters are *A A,* as the same theme section is repeated twice.

Another small classic by the same composer in which even more extended and more subtle use is made of just one theme, is "Träumerei" (described and discussed in Chapter One, Part One).

Binary Form. Many simple forms are found in old folk-songs and dances in which two or more themes have been used to give contrast and a balanced effect to the music. The first theme in such songs is usually repeated several times, while the second theme offers the contrasting material.

One of the most popular of these simple forms is *Binary Form,* in which two themes are used. These two themes may be arranged in different order, but must be so arranged that there are, in the composition, two definite sections, or musical sentences, each complete within itself, and satisfying; each related to or contrasted with the other in mood; and each of equal length so as to present a true formal balance.

"Barbara Allen"—an old English melody—which is made up of just two themes, each of which is repeated twice, *a a b b,* is, with its two distinct sections, an excellent example of *Binary* or two-part song form. Allowing a capital letter to represent each "sentence," a diagram of the complete form of "Barbara Allen," *A B,* is as follows. Each short phrase is marked by a small letter:

There are slight differences in the *cadence* which closes the repetition of the first and also the second theme, but this does not alter the main characteristics of the themes.

The jolly old Southern tune, "Lil' 'Liza Jane," is also this simple two-part song form.

In "Lightly Row"—a charming old Spanish folk-song—are two main sentences (*A B*), each of which is composed of two smaller divisions, or phrases. The form diagram is *a a b a.*

"Londonderry Air," one of the oldest Irish airs, in earlier days known as "Farewell to Cucullain" (and in modern times transcribed by various composers, including Percy Grainger, whose piano transcription is known as "Irish Tune from County Derry") is in strict two-part form, *A B.*

"All Through the Night" and "O Sole Mio" (as well as hundreds of other folk-songs) are also in the *A B* form.

Perfect examples of two-part song form in small classics are heard in the charming "Minuet," from "Don Juan," by Mozart, and in the "Gavotte" by the same composer. This *Binary* form, in which are heard or felt two distinct divisions, is the most popular of all forms in use in folk-music and in simple

WOLFGANG AMADEUS MOZART

hymns. This form may be recognized also in many of the dance movements of the older suites.

Ternary, or Three-Part Song Form, is that in which are found three distinct "big parts," each of which is usually equal to the others in length, and the third part of which is often a repetition of the first. Each "big part" is generally somewhat contrasted in mood to that which immediately precedes or follows it.

"The Minstrel Boy," one of Ireland's very oldest airs, is known by different names in different sections of the country, but the tune always remains the same. It illustrates the use, in folk-song, of the three-part song form.

"Blue Bells of Scotland" also illustrates this form, in which the third distinct section is a repetition of the first. Such form is diagramed *A B A.*

Popular examples of this form in writings of the Romantic period in music are the "Minute Waltz," by Chopin, and the ever fascinating "Spring Song" of Mendelssohn. The short "Waltz in *A*-flat," by Brahms, also follows this simple pattern.

"Golliwogg's Cake-Walk," by Debussy, is an excellent example of three-part form among modern compositions for piano. Here each "big part" is in a decidedly contrasting mood. Following a brief introduction the gay rhythms of the dance are heard. This first section

(*A*) is immediately followed by a quieter, slower and more thoughtful theme, developed throughout this second section (*B*). A transitional passage, in which *modulations* produce a feeling of expectancy, heralds the return of the first captivating dance, making the complete form *A B A.*

The three-part song form was also, in earlier days, known as *Aria Form,* as a large proportion of operatic arias were composed after this pattern. Such an aria is the familiar and ever-popular "Céleste Aïda," the first *aria* sung by Rhadames, the hero, in the opera "Aïda," by Verdi. In writing out such

CLAUDE DEBUSSY

three-part arias, composers of the early days often used the abbreviation *da Capo Aria* at the close of part two (*B*), instead of rewriting *A,* these words meaning "go back to the head (or beginning) of the *Aria.*"

Tunes and Patterns

Among orchestral works of importance written in three-part song form is the lovely "Largo" from the *New World Symphony,* by Dvořák. (See Chapter One, Part One.)

Development of Three-Part Song Form With Trio. With the improvement and development of the instruments themselves, and also the development of music printing, greater opportunities appeared for the display of instrumental virtuosity. In accord with this there came about a development of still larger instrumental forms, one of the very frequently used of which was the *Ternary* (or Three-Part) Song Form with Trio, which was originally called Minuet Form.

Beethoven's "Minuet in G" is an excellent example of this extended form. In the "Minuet" proper are two gracefully contrasted themes, and just when repetition of the first theme might be expected, for the sake of completeness of feeling, there is, instead, an entirely new section, complete within itself, with two themes. This new section is more lively in character than the quaint old-fashioned minuet, and provides a striking contrast in mood. The three-part form is brought to completion by a *da capo,* indicating the repetition of the entire first section of the "Minuet." Thus the form is diagramed

First Minuet
> 2 themes—*a* and *b* equal one complete section—*A*

Second Minuet
> 2 themes—*a* and *b* equal one complete section—*A*

da capo—repetition of First Minuet—equals *A*

There are, then, two complete minuets within the composition, but, because of the *da capo,* the piece is in three-part form, here also often called simply Minuet with Trio (the word *trio* being used at first because of the then popular custom of playing the second minuet with a trio of instruments).

The Chopin "Funeral March" (with Trio) (see Chapter One, Part One) is another striking example of the use of this simple form in an important art work.

MUSICAL ILLUSTRATIONS

22162	*Wild Horseman (Robert Schumann)*	*Victor Orchestra*
1178	*Träumerei (Robert Schumann)*	*Casals*
4023	*Barbara Allen (Old Border Ballad)*	*Dadman*
——*	*Lil' 'Liza Jane (Southern Melody)*	
20158	*Lightly Row (Spanish Folk-Air)*	*Kinscella*
35781	*Londonderry Air (Old Irish Air)*	*Victor Orchestra*
22082	*All Through the Night (Welsh Air)*	*Crane*
20248	*O Sole Mio (Italian Composed Folk-Air)*	*Neapolitan Trio*
1199	*Minuet from "Don Juan" (Mozart)*	*Landowska*

20440	Gavotte (Mozart)	Reitz
——*	The Minstrel Boy (Irish Air)	
35878	Blue Bells of Scotland (Scotch Folk-Song)	Victor Mixed Chorus
20614	Minute Waltz in D-flat (Chopin)	Schmidt
1242	Spring Song (Mendelssohn)	Chemet
21945	Golliwogg's Cake-Walk (Debussy)	Kinscella
6595	Céleste Aïda from "Aïda" (Verdi)	Martinelli
6566, 6567	Largo from New World Symphony (Dvořák)	
		Stokowski and Philadelphia Symphony Orchestra
20164	Minuet in G (Beethoven)	Victor Orchestra
35800	Funeral March (Chopin)	Pryor's Band

INFORMATIONAL NOTES

The origin of the *Minuet* is lost in antiquity, but its first known existence is as a folk-dance in the province of Poitou, the medieval division of France on the West Coast, between the Loire and the Garonne. In the eighteenth century the *Minuet* became a favorite dance at court, and as such became slower and more stately. Its name comes from "menu," meaning "small," and refers to the small, dainty steps taken by the dancers.

THE MINUET

"Bonny Barbara Allen," as this old romantic ballad is often called, is well known in all the countrysides of England, Scotland, and Iceland. Sung to different tunes in all three of these countries, the words are simply variations of the old border tale, which recounted the woes of this traditional character. Transplanted it is popular and common to all our Southern Mountain States.

"Londonderry Air" takes its name from the Irish city in which it originated, and has been sung for centuries. Cucullain, by whose name the song is also sometimes called, was an early Irish chieftain.

"Spring Song," by Mendelssohn, is one of an inspired collection of "Songs Without Words" by this composer. Many of these were written for Mendelssohn's sister Fanny, in an attempt to describe, musically, events which he had seen taking place. It is said by many that a few of the *Songs* were composed by Fanny. Each one is expressive of a single simple emotion or idea.

QUESTIONS AND TOPICS FOR DISCUSSION

1. What is *form* in music?
2. Name, and discuss the essential difference in the four musical

forms studied in this chapter. Which is the most simple of these forms? Which the most complex?

3. What is meant by the Italian *da Capo Aria*? What is a modulation? How may form be diagramed? By what are the various themes represented? The sections or complete musical sentences?

4. Name a characteristic individual to all gavottes.

5. Select five of the simplest melodies studied in previous chapters, and after listening to them again, describe their formal structure.

6. What is a cadence?

7. How is a knowledge of musical form an aid to greater enjoyment of the music we hear?

PART ONE—CHAPTER FIVE

TYPES OF VOCAL MUSIC—ART-SONGS AND THEIR INTERPRETERS

What Art-Song Is. An art-song is one in which the poet and the composer share honors equally. It is characterized by perfect unity in its expression of the sentiment of both the words and the music.

In the case of many songs of other types, the words may be the most interesting feature, appealing because of their sentiments; or the "tune" or melody, may be so beautiful, so singable or so spontaneous, that it would attract interest if the words were of no value at all.

In an art-song each portion of the sentiment, poetic content, and meaning of the song is reflected in the music, which expresses these sentiments exactly. Such a song is said to be "composed throughout." Occasionally the same melody and accompaniment is used for each verse and the song is then *strophic* in type.

Of all the art-songs in existence none are more convincing than those of Franz Schubert*—the King of Song—the music of many of his songs expressing the message of the words so completely that a title would often be unnecessary, even if the words were omitted.

FRANZ PETER SCHUBERT

"The Erl King" is well over a hundred years old, but it remains the greatest of all classic art-songs.

---

* Familiar art-songs by Schubert are "Hark, Hark the Lark" and "Who Is Sylvia?" "Thou Art Like Unto a Flower," by Schumann, is another example of simple art-song.

The words of this song, by Goethe, are a retelling of a German folk-legend that has been familiar to the world for several centuries. It is a dramatically descriptive song concerning three people—the Erl King (a symbol of Death), the Father, and the Child. The Goethe words which tell the story are reinforced at every point by the Schubert music. The opening Introduction for piano is a direct suggestion of galloping horses. The quality of the musical themes—even the pitch of the music—is expressive and impressive.

Who rideth so late through storm so wild?
It is the father, he holds his child,
And close the boy nestles within his arm,
He holds him tightly, he holds him warm.

"My son, why shrink you in terror, and hide?"
"O father, beside us the Erl King doth ride,
The Erl King so dreaded, with crown and robe."
"My son, 'tis but the mist of a cloud."

"Thou lovely child, come go with me,
Such merry games I'll play with thee,
Many gay blossoms are blooming there,
My mother hath many gold robes to wear."

"My father, my father, did'st thou not hear
What the Erl King whispered so soft in my ear?"
"Be quiet, my child, and do not mind,
'Tis but the dead leaves stirred by the wind."

"Come lovely boy, wilt go with me?
My daughters fair shall wait on thee,
My daughters lead in the revels each night,
There is dancing and singing and laughter bright."

"My father, my father, oh, see'st thou not
The Erl King's daughter in yonder dim spot?"
"My son, my son, I know and I say
'Tis only the olden willows so gray."

"I love thee so, thou must come with me now,
Thou must know to my will thou shalt bow."
"My father, my father, oh, hold me fast, do,
The Erl King will drag me away from you."

The father is troubled, he now rides wild
Holding close in his arms the shuddering child.
He reaches home with doubt and dread,
But in his arms the child is dead.

In this composition Schubert not only tells a story, but he vividly portrays a scene, and throughout the program of the song the hearer seems to see what is happening as well as hearing about it.

The agitated rush and roar of the storm, as well as the beating of the horse's hoofs, are suggested by the wild rhythm and the rapid pace of the fifteen-measure piano Introduction with its incessantly repeated triplets. The voice of each character —the Erl King, the Father and the Child—is given its own distinct personality in the music: the luring, coaxing voice of the Erl King, the terror in

THE ERL KING

the voice of the Child, and the soothing tones of the Father. The incessant galloping of the horse is maintained until almost the last line of the song. The force of the themes is enriched by use of many modulations, as in the case of the Child's questioning appeals and entreaties, each of which rises in pitch above the other, illustrating the growing terror of the boy. A dramatic climax is reached in the sudden hush and pause which immediately precedes the final statement—"But in his arms the child (here there is a brief fearful suspense) is dead!" Two dramatically simple chords which relapse into the minor key conclude the song.

"The Two Grenadiers," by Robert Schumann, is a unique and truly marvelous art-song, which makes an unusual and thrilling use of a national air, the "Marseillaise" of France.

The words of the song refer to the Russian campaign of Napoleon, and represent two soldiers of France as they sadly and wearily return to France after Napoleon's crushing defeat at the hands of the Russians. The soldiers had been, according to the poem, imprisoned in a Russian prison, and now, as they cross the border into their own country, learn for the first time that the Emperor has been defeated and is in captivity. They are so distressed by the news that they desire to die, and request that they may be buried in the old flag.

At this point in the song the speaker takes up the melody of the stirring "Marseillaise" and says:

"So will I lie and listen there,
Like a sentry on guard o'er the forces,
'Til waked by the loud cannon's deafening roar
And the tramp of the loud neighing horses.
O'er my head then will ride my Emperor so brave
While swords are crashing and flashing,
Their ray in the sunlight blending,
Then will I rise, fully armed, from the grave,
The cause of my Emperor defending."

Whereas some art-songs (as "Erl King" or "Lo, Here the Gentle Lark") abound in imitative passages, the stirring "Two Grenadiers" is a marvelous example of *suggestion* in an art-song.

It opens in minor mode, but in martial spirit, with a brief and snappily rhythmic Introduction (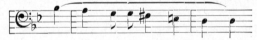) which sets the scene and suggests the marching step of the returning grenadiers. Their saddened feelings are suggested by the downward moving direction of the (altered) minor scale in the second phrase.

A two-measure interlude at the close of the first stanza ushers in the return of the first theme on the second stanza of the poem. Much of the conversation of the two men is carried on in almost recitative style on a melody of very few note changes. Here the piano accompaniment furnishes the suggestion of flurried action of war in a measure in the bass which is repeated seven times in succession as

the soldier completes his directions—"on my bosom place my cross of honor, my musket in my hand, my sword about me buckle." Then follow the broad and stirring strains of the "Marseillaise" (French national air). The song closes with a four-measure *Coda, adagio.*

It is the song-like quality and poetic ideality of Schumann's writings which have so large a share in the beauty of this song.

"Lo, Here the Gentle Lark," by Bishop (poem by Shakespeare), is an art-song for *coloratura* soprano, a type of voice best fitted to sing highly embellished (or "colored") music. It is considered to be one of the principal songs written in England during the past three centuries and is notable as an example of sparkling style. The opening words are set to a joyous melody which rises in pitch as it moves, just as a lark, rising straight toward the sky from its nest in the grass, carries its song upward with it. The beauty of the accompaniment of this delicately charming song is often enhanced by flute obbligato, which reproduces the song of the lark.

SIR HENRY R. BISHOP

It has a piano accompaniment of supreme importance. A rather long and elaborate Introduction in which flute and piano vie with each other in a reproduction of the lark's delicate song, opens the piece, after which, throughout, both voice and flute imitate the lark, first in alternating phrases and at last in a long and brilliant wordless *cadenza* in which both participate. Both flute and voice parts are replete with embellishments—turns, single and double gracenotes, trills and cadenzas of the most brilliant description. This exquisite song is an art-song because of the *character* of the music.

"Songs My Mother Taught Me," Dvořák. This simple work—said to be based upon a theme taken from a gypsy folk-air—is one of the beloved art-songs of the world. The song is *strophic* in type.

Its first individual peculiarity lies in the fact of Dvořák's writing the accompaniment in 6/8 measure and the song melody in 2/4. The song opens with an eight-measure Introduction, this itself a work of art, as it awakens entire sympathy by its simple pathos. It is all built upon a simple one-measure *motif* of three consecutive downward-moving tones, starting on different pitches.

At the close of the Introduction the voice takes up the same air, and it is interesting to contrast the same theme as it is written in the two parts.

6/8 measure

The theme in the Introduction,

2/4 measure

In the vocal score,

The first theme now enters over a quiet accompaniment which

combines a singing melody tone held through each measure (not a theme, but a counter melody) with a soft chordal harmony. Presently the accompaniment begins to develop activity, and works toward its own individual climax, but always in keeping with the tender sentiment of the words.

At the close of the first stanza a four-measure interlude continues the first plaintive theme. The second stanza is sung to the same theme, but in a slightly embellished version, extra notes being introduced into the air, while the accompaniment is embellished with grace-note "patterns." The final phrase is extended, from four, to six measures.

A four-measure piano *Coda* (the first two measures a repetition of the theme, the last two chords *morendo*) concludes the song.

In the second stanza Dvořák has slightly altered the notes (and their rhythm) to fit the different words. Three notes which in the first verse are sung to the word "eye-lids"

are altered to fit the phrase "tears are flowing"—

It is in these and other similar details that the composer displays his artistry. The constant use of the same theme *motif* is highly appropriate, as the mood of the song is unchanged throughout, only its quality becomes more intense.

MUSICAL ILLUSTRATIONS

7177	*The Erl King (Franz Schubert)*	*Schumann-Heink*
6563	*The Two Grenadiers (Robert Schumann)*	*Werrenrath*
6593	*Lo, Here the Gentle Lark (Bishop)*	*Talley*
1319	*Songs My Mother Taught Me (Antonin Dvořák)*	*Ponselle*

Lyric Forms and Types

QUESTIONS AND TOPICS FOR DISCUSSION

1. What is an art-song? What is meant by its being "composed throughout"?

2. Name at least five instances in the "Erl King" in which Schubert has made the piano accompaniment assist in characterizations of living things. How does he use the piano to definitely create and establish the scene in which the little drama takes place?

3. How is musical nationalism introduced by Schumann into his "Two Grenadiers"? Tell, in your own words, the story of "The Two Grenadiers." What is a "grenadier"? Who is the Emperor to whom the words of the song refer?

4. What is a "coloratura" soprano? Name as many present-day singers of this type as you can. Put any clippings that are to be had concerning such artists in your scrap-book. Name also a present-day artist of every voice (soprano, contralto, tenor, baritone, bass) and suggest songs most appropriate to be sung by each. Give reasons for your choice.

5. Why should "Lo, Here the Gentle Lark" be more appropriately sung by soprano than by other voices? What is meant by the term "musical embellishments"? Explain the meaning of *cadenza*, and identify the various embellishments mentioned in this chapter, when heard in the song. Why is the flute selected by the composer as the instrument to furnish the "lark" obbligato, rather than piccolo, violin or other instrument? What is an obbligato?

6. What is a "strophic" type of song?

7. Name and discuss at least four musically artistic devices used by Dvořák in the creation of "Songs My Mother Taught Me." How has he suggested, in the music, the tender appeal of the words? What is, to you, the most dramatic moment in this song, and why? What is the mood of the song?

8. Mention as many ways as you can in which the music of the songs studied during the course of this chapter has strengthened the meaning of the words.

Library Reading. "Famous Composers," by Dole, pages 259-276.

PART ONE—CHAPTER SIX

LYRIC FORMS AND TYPES

Why Lyric Music Is So Called. The name *lyric* was given by the old Greeks to a kind of poetry which was not narrative—did not tell any particular story—and which was chanted or sung to the accompaniment of the *lyre*.* The term has come to be used quite commonly with any music whether it be vocal or instrumental which suggests flowing melody or simple song.

Instrumentally a *lyric* may express many types of emotion, or mood, each slightly different in its rhythm, scope or its personal appeal.

The Serenade. Of the several types of lyric forms, none is more tender in sentiment than the *serenade*, a form which has come to us from the romantic Troubadours of Provence. Their serenades were songs similar to those of their Arabian friends and neighbors, and the song takes its name from the Arabian *sera*, which means "evening." The *serenade* is therefore a romantic evening song.

There are many art-songs written in this lyric form, but none so exquisite as the famous serenade by Franz Schubert.

The Schubert "Serenade," considered to be one of the world's masterpieces among art-songs (see Chapter Five, Part One, for definition of "art-song"), was written by the composer as a birthday present for a friend. It is a real *serenade*, or evening song, an imploring invitation from the singer for someone who is, presumably, in the window above, to join him in the garden below. Here the composer has used the accompaniment most artistically to both "set the scene" and to make it appear more vivid, the frequent chords in the accompaniment definitely suggesting the light stringed instrument in the hands of the serenader. Schubert has here made a unique use of two-measure rests, using them as an artistic device to stress the emotional element in the song. During these pauses the youthful singer listens for a hoped-for reply from the window. The piano interludes also echo both—the melody of the singer and the sentiment of the exquisite verses—

> "Warm entreaties, gently pleading
> Through the night to thee.
> Hear the nightingale so tender,
> Would her strains were thine!
> Ev'ry note, lamenting echoes
> Some fond sigh of mine."

A Romance is another lyric form, not intended by its composer to tell a definite story, but to suggest a fanciful or romantic mood.

The "Romance in F," Opus 50, by Beethoven, is an instrumental song for violin with piano accompaniment (the accompaniment was originally for orchestra), divided into several parts, each of which is simple, tender and gracefully gallant.

---

* The *lyre* was a stringed instrument similar to a harp, and small enough to be held in the hands, which was played by the ancient Greeks.

It opens, without introduction, *adagio,* a quiet, unadorned melody, the notes of the theme lying near to each other rather than skipping about. Both melody and form are of the old classic style. There is a four-measure theme and its answer. After a piano interlude the theme is repeated. There is then heard a development and embellishment of the theme, much altered and extended, but retaining the same winsome mood. A second interlude ushers in the final "verse" or section of the piece which, without deviation from its first expressive style, brings the poetic thought or lyric to a close.

JULES MASSENET

The Meditation. A third type of lyric is the *meditation,* which by its very name suggests thoughtful contemplation of some definite idea. The subject of a musical meditation is seldom definitely expressed by the composer, but is merely suggested to its individual hearer.

"Meditation," by Massenet, is the most famous and familiar of all *meditations.* This thoughtful lyric is played repeatedly during the opera "Thaïs," although it has also won fame as an independent concert piece. It is first heard in the opera in the first scene of Act II, as a symbol of the conversion of Thaïs, who has been wrestling with her thoughts throughout the entire night. It is played again in Act III (Scene 1) as Thaïs disappears into the desert; as a thoughtful "curtain-riser" for the third scene of this act; and finally as Thaïs dies.

The melody—*andante religioso*—is notable for its suave thoughtful character, its flowing style and its irregular phrase formations. The equally important accompaniment (when played at the piano) clearly suggests the soft upward sweep of harp chords. A mystical atmosphere is produced by the use of harmonics at the close of the composition.

A Reverie is an abstract, undirected train of thought, which may be brought about or induced by any incident or happening. Its mood has no connection with time, either day or night.

"Reverie du Soir" (Reverie of Evening), by Camille Saint-Saëns, a portion of that composer's vividly Oriental "Suite Algerienne," is, as its name suggests, a lovely, quiet bit of music in romantic style. It is written in an Oriental manner as to both melody and accompaniment, and is in slow three-beat measure. The musical climax comes in the center of the composition, rather than at its end—as is more customary—but even here it retains its elegant simplicity. Following the climax is heard a tiny descending cadenza which leads into a brief restatement of the theme, this followed in turn by a sequential descent of the music. There is then a return to the melting mood of the music's beginning, exquisite trills played by the wind instruments, and a gradual diminuendo to a quiet and tender *finale.*

CAMILLE SAINT-SAËNS

Barcarolle is the name formerly given to the popular songs sung by the gondoliers of Venice. The word has now come to suggest any music—whether vocal or instrumental—that is written in the style of the gondolier's songs. The rhythm, which can be easily recognized, is always a swaying one, suggesting the rocking motion of the water and the boat.

"Barcarolle," from the fantasy-opera "Tales of Hoffmann," by Offenbach, is one of the very popular pieces of music composed in this form. The charming song is played by the orchestra before the curtain rises on the second act and is then sung as a duet by Guiletta and Niklaus as they land from the gondola. It suggests the beauty of a moonlight night on a canal in Venice. Later in the act the same alluring melody is repeated by the chorus as the gondola and its occupants move away.

The characteristic of the long *entr'acte*—as the music played before the curtain rises is called—is its swaying bass rhythm. As the melody progresses it is accompanied by hárp. The song proper (after the curtain rises) is ushered in by a two-measure introduction.

The most characteristic feature of the entire composition is its ever-swaying rhythm, as the melody, for the first eight measures, is purposely monotonous, moving about over only three tones. As the boat floats away into the distance the music becomes gradually softer and softer, ending at last *ppp* as the chorus and soloists are repeating the syllable *Ah!* on the different tones of the common triad.

The Nocturne is a pensive, thoughtful night-piece written in lyric form. The form was invented and its name given to it by John Field, an Irish pianist and composer who lived during the eighteenth century. Chopin borrowed the name and form from Field and carried the *nocturne* to perfection.

Lyric Forms and Types

"Nocturne in E-Flat," Opus 9, No. 2, by Frederic Chopin, is built upon a simple theme, but one which suggests thoughts of twilight and the stillness of night, through a rich flow of exquisite melody.

The form of the nocturne is as follows:

   a—four-measure theme and answer
   a—theme embellished and spun out by extra notes
   b—second theme and answer
   a—further embellishments and slight alternations
   b—slight rhythmic alternations
   a—rhythmic embellishments, more elaborate.

The *Coda*, which includes inversion of the first part of the first theme, repetitions of various embellishments and a tiny, exquisite

THE GRAND CANAL, MAIN STREET OF VENICE

Galloway

cadenza made up of an extended trill and the *pianissimo* repetition of a dainty pattern of notes, ends quietly with simple chords.

MUSICAL ILLUSTRATIONS

6703	*Serenade (Franz Schubert)*	*Homer*
6606	*Romance in F (Ludwig van Beethoven)*	*Thibaud*
6844	*Meditation from "Thaïs" (Massenet)*	*Kreisler*
9296	*Reverie du Soir (Reverie of Evening) (Saint-Saëns)*	*Continental Sym. Or.*
20011	*Barcarolle from "Tales of Hoffmann" (Offenbach)*	*Victor Concert Orch.*
3043	*Barcarolle from "Tales of Hoffmann" (Offenbach)*	*Bori and Tibbett*
6589	*Nocturne in E-flat (Frederic Chopin)*	*Casals*

INFORMATIONAL NOTES

John Field, inventor of the lyric form known as the *nocturne* (the first of the "Songs Without Words"), was an Irishman born in Dublin in 1782. There, his father and his grandfather were both musicians of standing and his first teachers. Later in his life, Field spent many years in London, where he was a pupil of the noted pianist and teacher, Clementi; and in St. Petersburg, where he was the teacher of Glinka, who afterward came to be known as the "Father of Russian Music." It was in Russia that Field wrote his first nocturnes, and also in Russia that they came to the notice of the younger composer, Frederic Chopin, who perfected the nocturne in form.

The opera "Tales of Hoffmann" is written in three acts, with a *prologue* and an *epilogue*. During the *prologue*, Hoffmann is telling his friends why he has never married. As he begins to tell of his first sweetheart—who turned out to be but a mechanical doll—the curtain descends, to rise again upon a new scene in which the story Hoffmann was about to tell is enacted. Each succeeding act tells of another episode in Hoffmann's life. The first performance of the opera, given after the composer's death, was at the Opéra-Comique in Paris in 1881.

QUESTIONS AND TOPICS FOR DISCUSSION

1. What is a *lyric*? Name six types of lyric music and discuss the essential features of each.

2. From what does the *serenade* take its name? What instrument is most appropriate for use as a serenade accompaniment? What is a lyre? What modern musical instrument most closely resembles it?

3. Contrast the moods of the "Meditation" and the "Reverie." Which is the more definite in its suggestion and appeal? Why?

4. What romantic scene is always suggested by a *barcarolle*? What is an *entr'acte*? Mention another musical term which has much the same meaning.

5. What definite musical characteristics distinguish the *barcarolle* from the *nocturne*?

PART ONE—CHAPTER SEVEN

CHAMBER MUSIC—INSTRUMENTAL COMBINATION— CONTRASTING CLASSIC TYPES

What Chamber Music Is. By the term "Chamber Music" is meant all instrumental music which is appropriate or suitable for performance in a small or private room.

Chamber Music

The Beginnings of Chamber Music. The history of the development of chamber music is a fascinating one. At first the name was used to indicate both vocal and instrumental music.

The earliest songs not religious were often vocal compositions arranged for from three to six voices. These were characterized by grace and lightness. In the sixteenth century there lived, in Venice, a musician named Gabrielle, who wrote *madrigals,* as these songs were called, for instruments, instead of for voices. This was the first real chamber music, and, as the music was played in a room, it was called, in Italy, *musica di camera,* or chamber music.

AN OLD-TIME CHAMBER MUSIC ENSEMBLE

The name was continued in the medieval custom of princes and nobles, of employing the finest musicians obtainable * to furnish them with frequent—sometimes daily—concerts in the private music rooms of their castles.

Although chamber music is now often played in concert halls, and sometimes even out-of-doors, the type of the music remains unchanged.

Chamber music owes a great deal in its development to royal or aristocratic patronage.

Couperin, a Pioneer in Chamber Music. One of the earliest musicians to develop real chamber music was François Couperin, royal organist to Louis XIV, King of France. Each Sunday afternoon during many years of his life, a chamber music concert was given for the king and his court at Versailles, and for these concerts Couperin created many lively concerted works in which he himself played the clavecin—the French type of harpsichord. He was also a favorite with the general public, as he took much care in preparing frequent special concerts for Paris music lovers.

His music is notable for a pure beauty, perfection of form as it

---

* As Haydn was employed by Prince Esterhazy.

was then known, for tender delicacy, exquisite melody, and for much refined ornamentation, the peculiarities and delicacy of his instrument calling for flourishes to help prolong the tones of the melody. A favorite instrumental combination for which Couperin frequently wrote was that of clavecin, violin and 'cello.

"Concertos Royaux" (Royal Concertos), by Couperin. These concertos, in reality suites or collections of small dances, are still played

FRANÇOIS COUPERIN

and still popular, although two centuries old. The word "concerto" had a very different meaning in Couperin's time than it has today. It is now used to suggest a composition written in sonata form and for a solo instrument. In Couperin's day it meant, rather, an exploitation of the various instruments of a carefully arranged ensemble.

"Concerto Royal, No. 2," for piano (clavecin), violin and 'cello. This charming work opens with a "Prélude" (*Moderato, D* Major, 3/4 measure). The eight-measure theme, first stated by the violin, is characteristically embellished by single and double grace notes, and by *mordents*. A distinct counterpoint in the 'cello, which is, during the course of the eight measures, taken up by the bass of the piano score, suggests the type of contrapuntal development that is given the thematic material throughout the entire movement. Delicacy, elegance, grace and symmetry are attributes of this short and attractive "Prélude."

"Allemande Fuguée" (*Molto moderato, D* Major, 4/4 measure). The principal theme, in gay mood, is greatly ornamented, as was the first theme of the "Prélude." Announced by the violin, it is imitated immediately by 'cello and piano. The theme itself, developed in contrary motion, by inversion, and by rhythmic devices, becomes more and more brilliant toward the close of the movement. Gayety and vivacity are characteristics of this dance movement.

"Air tendre" (*Andante,* 3/4 measure). This gentle, expressive movement of the Concerto, which employs an Oriental scale (beginning on *G*) in its construction, is, although richly ornamented throughout by *turns, mordents,* and similar embellishments, of plaintive mood. As is the custom in much primitive music, the air begins on a high pitch and then descends, both in pitch and intensity of emotion, to the end of the phrase. All three instruments share quite equally in the announcement and development of the simple themes.

Chamber Music

"Air Contre Fugué" (*Vivement, D* Minor, 2/4 measure), a short and lively number, has a theme announced by each instrument in turn in strictly fugal manner, with clever note "patterns" and imitations. The theme

is developed in a manner well planned to display all brilliant technical abilities of the players and the possibilities of the early forms and early instruments.

Echos (*Moderato, D* Major, 3/4 measure). The vivid little movement with which the Concerto closes is characterized by several repetitions of the same themes, each time—as is frequent in the variations of a song—in the same form, key and *tempo*, but with altered accompaniment, pitch, embellishments and rhythmic developments. It brings the entire work to a close in an enchantingly dignified and satisfying manner.

Archangelo Corelli, not a pioneer, but a distinguished composer of chamber music, achieved in this line of composition musical results so conspicuously important that his influence was actively felt in the chamber music writings of Bach, Haydn, and Mozart. Corelli's period of chamber music lasted until well past the middle of the eighteenth century. His music is notable for a graceful melody, dignity, fluency of modulation and phrasing, a pure style and elegance of form.

"Pastorale," from the "Christmas Concerto," is one of his most beautiful works. The charm of this music lies in the tender simplicity of its melodies or themes, and in its atmosphere of peace. Written, as it was, for harpsichord and "string band," before the advent of either the modern pianoforte or the orchestra, it holds a place of vital importance in the history of musical development.

The "Concerto" was published in Rome in 1712. The original score was prepared for a Christmas concert and for a solo group made up of two violins and a 'cello, accompanied by a "string band" (violins, viola, 'cello, and bass) and a harpsichord.

In a modern presentation of this music the number of players in the string "band" or orchestra is often increased, and a piano usually takes the place of the harpsichord,* but the general effect of

---

* Some large orchestras find it possible. when presenting this music, to use a replica of the old-time harpsichord.

quaint beauty and tender mood is always retained. The main theme

is repeated many times during the progress of the "Pastorale" and much use is made of muted strings in the accompaniment.

"Gavotte," by Lully. Jean Baptiste Lully, by birth an Italian, and by naturalization a Frenchman, was, for many years, in the service of Louis XIV of France, was a member of that monarch's famous "Band of Twenty-four," and wrote a profusion of court ballets in many of which the king himself danced.

In many of these ballets—music of which has descended to us in the form of instrumental *Suites*—folk-dances of France and other countries were idealized. This quaint "Gavotte" (in common time, beginning on the third beat of the measure, and of moderately quick *tempo*), reflects the atmosphere of the days in which it originated.

"Pastorale," by Scarlatti, best known in its concert arrangement for piano by Carl Tausig, is here transcribed for small orchestra. This short classic was first given to the world as one of a group of harpsichord sonatas, although Scarlatti's use of that word differed greatly from the modern acceptance of the term. It meant, in those early times, merely a sounding piece.

The composition is written in two "big parts," the first of which begins in minor and ends in major, while the second begins in major and ends in minor mode. It has throughout only one theme which is, however, treated in a different manner in each part. The form is *A A*. The melody, a graceful and refined air

is constantly ornamented, in the manner necessary in compositions written originally for harpsichord, in order that melody tones might be prolonged.

The composition closes in a return to the minor key.

Luigi Boccherini and the String Quartet. With the advent of Boccherini, the practice of writing for even smaller groups of players came into fashion. Boccherini is said to have originated the idea and plan of the modern string quartet. Most of the vocal music of his time was in four parts, and this inspired Boccherini to arrange a quartet of stringed instruments.

Chamber Music

In such a quartet, the melody is not carried by any one player, but is distributed among the different instruments, according to the kind of effect desired by the composer. For this reason, no one performer in the quartet is a soloist. Each is equally important and each, as he plays his phrases of the melody, must then possess both the grace and the ability to subordinate his playing and adapt himself to the general effect desired.

In the string quartet each instrument has an individual charm and personality. The first violin is naturally the leader, and, by nature of the instrument itself, plays many of the more brilliant solo parts. The second violin—being the same instrument—plays the same type of music, but usually displays less initiative. The viola, larger in size and possessed of a unique tone quality, assumes the tenor of the quartet, while the 'cello part provides the foundation bass.

Luigi Boccherini

LUIGI BOCCHERINI

Boccherini also wrote much for string Quintet—in which two 'cellos, or one 'cello and one double bass, are employed. His famous "Minuet" was originally a part of a String Quintet, although it is now one of the most popular small numbers in the repertoire of any good quartet organization.

The Boccherini "Minuet" is notable for the charm and grace of its melody and of its *pizzicato* accompaniment. It moves along with a sprightly motion, and with great delicacy, all the strings being muted. The main melody is one of the loveliest ever written to minuet rhythm and is sung by the first violin, while the second violin and viola accompany with simple alternating notes in octaves, and the 'cellos supply the rhythmic figure by *pizzicato* bass.

A new questioning figure heard in second violin, viola, and 'cello, is answered by a graceful downward moving phrase from the first violin.

In the *Trio* there is an interesting play of voices, each half phrase being taken by one group of the quartet instruments and the reply by another. The first upward-moving question is played by viola and 'cello, the downward-moving reply by first and second violins. The second section is characterized by many short phrases and by much use of contrasting touches.

Following the *Trio* a return of the *Minuet* proper brings the cheery composition to a happy ending.

"Allegro," "Gavotte" and "Aria" from "Sonata," No. 7, for piano and flute, by Jean Baptiste Loeillet. The use of flute with piano has always been a very charming combination, and no early music of this duet ensemble type, written in classic form, is more attractive than that written by Jean Baptiste Loeillet, one of the most distinguished Belgian flute players and composers, who lived and wrote during the seventeenth century. His concerts were eagerly attended, not only in his native land, but also in France and England.

As a variation from the strictly formal *sonata,* Loeillet wrote many *suites,* utilizing the forceful rhythms of the old dances, although the name given to the composition may frequently have been "Sonata," as in this case. The lilting "Allegro," the quaintly elegant "Gavotte," and the gentle "Aria," from the characteristically graceful "Sonata" No. 7, all reflect the spirit of the tunes in which the music was written.

A Bach "Trio in G Major," for piano, violin, and flute. One of the charming customs of the Bach household was in the holding of frequent evening concerts played in the family living-room by Bach, his talented wife, his children, and many of the family's friends. The Bachs themselves possessed a number of stringed instruments, as well as several clavichords,* and the number or variety of these was apt to be augmented by instruments which the visitors brought with them.

This "Trio," written during the time when Bach resided at Cöthen, was first set down as for flute, violin, and figured bass. The "Sonata," or "Trio," of which these three movements are a part, is thought to be one of the series of classic chamber music compositions written by Bach for the entertainment of his musical family and that of the many friends who often spent long happy evenings at the Bach home, playing whatever the great master had written during the day.

The *Vivace,* which is the second movement of the Trio, is characterized by a dainty little rhythmic figure, heard first from the flute, then passed to violin, and then to piano.

The entire short movement is in *canon* fashion, written upon this one theme. The contrasting *Adagio* opens with a plaintive air, the small rhythmic pattern of which is carried, with embellishments and much development, throughout the movement, illustrating the splendid use

* A clavichord is a small keyed instrument, a forerunner of the piano.

which may be made, by a great composer, of a very small bit of thematic material.

In the closing movement, *Presto,* the piano takes the lead in stating the subject, which is then treated contrapuntally. It is, in form, a jolly instrumental *canon* which moves along at dashing speed.

"Arioso," by Johann Sebastian Bach. This exquisite example of pure, or absolute music, is notable for its serene dignity and simplicity. In its original version the "Arioso" was a prelude (called Sinfonia) to a church cantata which Bach wrote for performance on the third Sunday after Epiphany. In the transcription for string orchestra new beauties and a variety of delicate effects and shadings are added to a work long known for its earnest expressiveness. In both the original version and in the transcription, the music is suggestive of the four-part chorales which were always sung by the congregation at the close of a sacred cantata in Bach's time and Church.

As time passed on and the piano itself developed, the instrument took an ever increasingly important part in chamber music and from the days of Haydn, Mozart and Beethoven, no combination of instruments has been so popular with artists and amateurs alike, as the piano trio. By this is usually meant a combination

FRANZ JOSEPH HAYDN

of piano, flute and violin; piano, violin and 'cello; or, less common, piano and two violins. Haydn wrote many piano trios which are still considered as models of this type.

"Rondo in C," for piano, violin, and 'cello. Many of Haydn's trios were written for special occasions at the Esterhazy castle, and into these he put much of the brightness and melodic charm so characteristic of many of his larger works. The perfect "Rondo in C," with its ever-recurring theme of tiny rhythmic patterns, and its contrasting themes in scale runs and in related keys, is said to owe much of its sparkling gayety, freshness, and verve, to Haydn's conscious, or unconscious) use of the characteristics and colorings of his well-loved native Croatian folk-airs. The "Rondo" in its daintiness recalls the intimate charm of the old-time harpsichord, and is the brilliant *Finale* from the composer's "Trio in C," for piano, violin, and 'cello. The first theme is given out first by the piano, in the key of *C* Major,

and is immediately repeated by the violin. After an episode built upon *motifs* from this theme (in both major and minor) the entire theme is again repeated, in the bass of the piano and in the 'cello part. A modulatory passage carries the music into the key of *G* in which the second theme is announced. Following this are modulations to various keys, and snatches of the first theme in piano, violin and 'cello parts, in octaves and sixths. Other interesting themes—one made up of scale passages, another of the following small "figure"

with constant recurrence of the first theme—carry the players back to the key of *C*, and to a short, light *Coda*.

The work is notable for delicacy, for elaborate use of one main theme (heard seven times), for open, transparent fluency, and for the classic atmosphere of the old-time *Trio*.

Haydn's position in the world of music is one of first importance. As the father of instrumental music, he not only brought the orchestra to its established form and then divided it into its four separate Choirs (strings, woodwind, brass instruments and percussion), but he also brought the String Quartet * to its present perfection.

"Theme and Variations," from "Emperor," Quartet, Opus 76,

---

* Haydn wrote between forty and fifty string quartets.

No. 3. No more exquisite *theme with variations* * has ever been written than that which Haydn made a part of his "Emperor" String Quartet. The theme † is the air of the "Austrian National Hymn," which Haydn had written in 1797 and presented to the nation on the Emperor's birthday (February 12th), when it was played and sung in all the theatres and public meetings in Vienna. It is because of this use of the National Hymn that the quartet bears the name of "Emperor."

As no set of variations can be truly enjoyed and understood without a certain acquaintance with the theme, its melody is given here.

There are four variations and a *Coda*.

Variation I is in reality a duet, and carries the air in the second violin part, while the first violin plays a *staccato arpeggio* accompaniment. The other two instruments are silent.

Variation II. Here the 'cello sings the lovely theme, while a second counter-melody is played by the second violin. The first violin and the viola furnish an accompaniment.

Variation III. The viola now plays the theme, its tender quality enhanced by the voice quality of the instrument. Here the theme is slightly embellished, and counterpoint is furnished by the violins and 'cello.

Variation IV. The first violin—the only member of the quartet

---

* The theme and variation is a favorite form, frequently used by both classic and modern composers for the display of their skill and technique in writing. A familiar example is "The Harmonious Blacksmith," by Händel.
† Also sung as a hymn, "Glorious Things of Thee Are Spoken."

which has not sung the air—now takes up the melody in a simple repetition with only slight embellishment.

The *Coda* contains but a few measures and these, diminishing to the close, *pianissimo,* contain quiet, hymn-like chords.

"Bagatelles." Beethoven was the first composer to use this title for a series of short compositions, and in them all he reflected the atmosphere of this French word, which means "a trifle." Beethoven wrote four series in all. To the *opus* 119, from which these four pieces are selected, the composer also gave the German title equivalent to *bagatelle,* which is *Kleinigkeiten.*

No. 1, a whimsical composition, opens with a short theme which, in its simple rhythmic pattern, suggests the formalism of an old classic dance.

This is followed by a second theme, *legatissimo,* which, in its lyric beauty and flowing style, is a decided contrast to the opening measures. A delicate transitional passage presently brings about a return to the earlier theme, which now appears in a slightly elaborated version, and which colors the brief *Coda* with which the charming "trifle" ends. The form is *A B A Coda.*

No. 8, which is here played in direct contrast to the more sprightly *bagatelle* which opens the series, is extremely short, *legatissimo,* and characterized by a soaring, flowing melody, which is treated by Beethoven in a style suggestive of an old-time chorale.

No. 3 vividly suggests an old-fashioned German *allemande.* Classic in style, it is written in "question and answer" form easily discerned.

The second main theme is built upon a sturdy succession of chords. The first theme returns immediately, and is presently followed by a *Coda,* in which the second theme achieves much prominence, but which ends with a lightly questioning phrase from the opening theme. The form is *A B A Coda.*

No. 9, built entirely upon a simple ascending broken chord, displays the art of a great composer, who, with this limited material, was able to achieve a particularly pleasing bit of music. The rhythm is that of an old-style valse.

"Canzonetta," from "String Quartet," Opus 12, by Mendelssohn. This "Canzonetta"—or "little song"—composed in 1829, is one of the most charming short movements ever written for the string quartet combination. Dainty, sparkling, in quietly gay humor, it is remarkable for its delicate rhythms and its happy sincerity.

Its first theme, gay, although written in a minor key, is heard first from the first violin.

This, and its equally charming reply, are both repeated, the repetition being followed by an announcement of the lilting second theme, in unison, for all four strings. This, too, is repeated.

The key then changes to the parallel *G* Major and a jolly dance rhythm is heard from first and second violins, while viola and 'cello accompany with long-held tones. The same theme is repeated by viola and 'cello, after which a brief modulatory episode brings the key to the original *G* Minor. A restatement of both first and second themes, and a short and graceful *Coda* conclude this most fascinating little movement.

No composer of the classic or romantic periods in music was more fitted to write for combinations of instruments than Franz Schubert, partly because of the fact that he was so well acquainted with the instruments themselves and with their possibilities of expression.

"Scherzo," from the "Trout" Quintet for piano and strings, by Schubert. The joyous atmosphere of this animated "Scherzo" for piano and strings is essentially that of the open air and out-of-doors. It is interesting to recall that it owes its existence to the inspiration given Schubert by a happy summer's vacation spent in the country near Steyr. Here, during some weeks spent in walking trips with friends, impromptu concerts and frequent work on composition, Schubert set down the separate parts of the Quintet without making a score, and then one evening gave the new work its first performance at the home of some friends, he himself playing the pianoforte part by heart.

In this quintet a double bass was chosen as the fifth instrument in place of the usual second violin. The first theme of the *Scherzo* is played by violin and viola, with a response from the piano. All strings then take up the air. In the second section the piano leads and the strings respond to the phrase question. The work is notable for the skillful blending of themes, and is built in simple, three-part song form with trio.

"Trio in *D* Minor," by Robert Schumann. This chamber music —written for piano, violin, and 'cello, is a beautiful example of romantic and colorful composition. Written by a pianist, the piano is given great prominence throughout the score. There is, however, great artistry in the manner in which all three instruments are used, and the way in which they frequently show the musical interest, with equality of prominence. This work should first be listened to as an exquisite example of pure beauty, of marvelous melodic invention, and of the poetic possibilities of each of the three instruments represented. Each of the four movements possesses an individual charm.

I. *Con energia e passione,* opens with the principal subject— which pervades the entire movement—announced in limpid tones by the violin:

II. *Vivace, ma non troppo.* This short movement, in reality a *scherzo,* has a splendid main theme, and strikes the mood of assertive independence.

The middle section of the movement is in direct contrast, with much flowing beauty of melody.

The form is *A B A* with *Coda.*

III. *Lento, con espressione intima.* The opening bars of this charmingly romantic movement are suggestive of deep mystery. Presently the mood changes to one of vigorous tenderness. The movement is, throughout, a miracle of concentrated beauty.

IV. *Con fuoco.* The animated first theme is here announced abruptly and without introduction by the piano.

This is echoed immediately by the violin, after which the 'cello comes into prominence. Following a delightfully delicate second theme, which is doubled alternately by piano and 'cello, then piano and violin, the work progresses into gorgeous harmonic effects, through frequent but artistic changes of mood and *tempo,* and closes in a swirl of florid runs and chordal passages.

Chamber Music

MUSICAL ILLUSTRATIONS

——*   *Concerto Royal* (*François Couperin*)
21947   *Pastorale from Christmas Concerto No. 8* (*Archangelo Corelli*)
         Kinscella and String Ensemble
——*   *Gavotte* (*Lully*)   *Victor Orchestra*
22448   *Pastorale* (*Scarlatti*)   *Victor Orchestra*
20636   *Minuet from String Quartet* (*Luigi Boccherini*)   *Victor Concert Orch.*
21947   *Allegro, Gavotte and Aria from Sonata, No. 7* (*Loeillet*)
         Kinscella and String Ensemble
21948   *Vivace, Adagio, and Presto from Trio in G* (*Bach*)
         Kinscella and String Ensemble
 9598   *Arioso* (*Bach*)   *Philadelphia Chamber String Simfonietta*
22018   *Rondo in C* (*Haydn*)   *Kinscella and String Ensemble*
 6634   *Theme and Variations from "Emperor" Quartet* (*Haydn*)
         Elman String Quartet
22449   *Bagatelles Nos. 1, 8, 3, and 9* (*Beethoven*)   *Victor Concert Orchestra*
 9245   *Canzonetta from String Quartet, Opus 12* (*Mendelssohn*)
         Budapest String Quartet
21948   *Scherzo from "Trout" Quintet* (*Franz Schubert*)
         Kinscella and String Ensemble
8130-8133   *Trio in D Minor* (*Schumann*)   *Cortot-Thibaud-Casals*

QUESTIONS AND TOPICS FOR DISCUSSION

1. What is meant by the term "chamber music"? Tell what you know of its historical beginnings and compare the writings of the earlier Couperin and Corelli with those of Mendelssohn and Schubert. What was a "string band"? To what present-day organization is it comparable? To what class of people is chamber music indebted for much of its growth and development?

2. Compare the emotional content of the Couperin and the Corelli works heard in the lesson. Contrast the Corelli "Pastorale" with the Boccherini "Minuet." Which is the more poetic? What one word suggests the mood of each? What can you say of the personality or characteristics of each instrument of the string quartet?

3. Contrast the appeal of string quartet and full symphony orchestra. What are the individual characteristics peculiar to each?

4. Discuss the use of folk-rhythm forms (as Gavotte, Minuet, etc.) and melodies in chamber music.

5. What is a *canon*? What is a *canzonetta*?

6. Listen much to single parts in chamber music and try to learn how each composer has achieved his individual result.

7. What is a transcription? After hearing the Bach "Arioso," name at least four essential features of it. What instruments are members of the string orchestra?

PART ONE—CHAPTER EIGHT

MUSIC THAT TELLS A STORY—PROGRAM MUSIC

The Very Old Art of Story-Telling. Ever since the world began, the telling of stories has been one of the happiest ways in which the people of the world have entertained each other. In early days—and even today in some parts of the world, as in Persia, Arabia and other parts of the Orient—the professional story-teller is a very important person, ever welcome. Stories may be told in many ways—as through use of words, by means of pictures, or music. Many of the greatest composers the world has ever known have delighted in writing "Story-telling" music.

Absolute and Program Music. In composed music there have always been two decidedly distinct types of composition. One of these, known as *Absolute,* or *Pure Music,* is written according to beauty or perfection of form, or "pattern," without, in any way, trying to suggest to the hearer any definite object or any special poetic thought. The second type is that which is called *Program,* or *Story-telling Music.*

Program music has, in turn, three general divisions. In the first of these, the composer (who might be called the Narrator, or Story-teller) directly *imitates* certain sounds, whether in the world of nature or in the animal world. Some sounds—such as wind, thunder or singing of birds—may be imitated by musical instruments so cleverly that they can be recognized instantly for what they are. Such music is sometimes called *Imitative Music.*

The second type of program music is not definite in its portrayal of a picture, but seeks to carry the listener to a particular scene, or to describe an event by suggesting, in the music, the emotions surrounding that event, with, perhaps, the addition of associated melodies. Such music is called *Narrative.*

The third—and some people think, most artistic type—is that which merely suggests a story, an idea, or a mood. This suggestion may be either definite or indefinite, but the composer leaves the actual picture to the imagination of the hearer.

The Title a Guide to the Music's Meaning. The composer of Program music usually gives a title to his composition to let the hearer know, at once, what idea or "program" he had in mind when he was writing the story he is about to tell.

"The Victory Ball," by Ernest Schelling. "The Victory Ball," an orchestral fantasy written by an American composer who was also a soldier in the World War, is a magnificent piece of "story-telling" music. After the signing of the Armistice on November 11, 1918, the relief and happiness of the war-troubled world took expression in many parties or gayeties which had been denied it for so long. A ball held in London soon after the Armistice led Alfred Noyes, a prominent young British poet and Oxford graduate, to write some verses in which he expressed the resentment which he imagined the soldiers of all nations, who had suffered and died in the trenches, must be feeling toward the frivolity and the apparently

ARMISTICE CAR—PARIS

thoughtless and forgetful dancers. He called his poem "The Victory Ball."

In the poem the "shadows of dead men watching them" discuss what seems to them the heartlessness of the crowd.

> "Do not reproach, because they know,
> If they're forgotten, it's better so."

But as "the cymbals crash, and the dancers walk," some of the dead soldiers—"shadows" the poet calls them—become very angry. Others try to reason with them.

> "Pish," said a statesman standing near,
> "I'm glad they can busy their thoughts elsewhere,
>   We mustn't reproach 'em. They're young, you see."
> "Ah!" said the dead men, "so were we."

Then the shout goes up—

> "Victory! Victory! on with the dance,"

and

> "Shadows of dead men . . . grin by the wall,
> Watching the fun of the Victory Ball."

The Music of "The Victory Ball." This stirring poem is the story upon which Ernest Schelling has based his symphonic poem and to which he gave the same name. Of it the composer said, at the time it was given its first performance by orchestra:

"I have used two army calls—the 'Call to Arms' and 'Charge'— which ominously usher in the War Vision; and at the very end I have used 'Taps.' The work is a perfectly free fantasy, with, however, a certain amount of thematic development. I had occasion, during the war, to hear the Scotch Pipers, and to observe the extraordinary effect their music had on the troops; and at the end of the

work I have tried to make the whole orchestra a huge bagpipe, perhaps the most pagan and primitive form of music. The piece is scored for full symphonic orchestra, and bears the inscription, 'To the memory of an American soldier.'"

The music follows this "program" very exactly. The introduction of "The Victory Ball" begins very gently and softly, flute, piccolo, harp, and strings participating in the music. Rather abruptly (through the use of full orchestra with harp), the atmosphere of the crowded ballroom is portrayed with its confusion of restless motion.

Presently the music tells that the dancing is about to begin, and there are the noises of an orchestra tuning, first the violins,

ERNEST SCHELLING

then the harps.

Next a sturdy polonaise rhythm is established by the horns and military drum, and by a lone trumpeter who plays a brief two-measure solo, the use of the trumpet suggesting the military atmosphere which is the historical background of this old-time dance. The rhythm changes to that of a fox-trot, following a climax, in a short transitional passage in which are heard descending harmonies in woodwind and celesta. The fox-trot rhythm once established (by strings, harps, and tympani), the violin plays a short and rhythmic eight-measure solo. This is immediately repeated by horns and trumpets, and, after a few measures of rhythm alone, an abrupt change is made to two-four measure. Swirls of sound from the harp carry the dancers into the Spanish atmosphere of the tango. Despite interruptions which are reminiscent of the ballroom dance rhythms, the music is now upbuilded to a tremendous climax, in the midst of which is heard the dramatic call "To Arms" (in solo trumpet) from the ghostly legions who now go marching by.

The trumpet call is repeated by all the trumpets and horns, and the rhythm of the music changes to a quick-step. Over a beating of military drums in strict rhythmic figure, a march, very soft at first, but distinct, brings the troops ever nearer and nearer.

The march is dramatically interrupted by the sound of an approaching aeroplane, suggested by the composer by his use of long *crescendo* chromatic passages in which the organ, with dissonant chords, joins the instruments of the full orchestra; and in which the harps play ascending and descending *glissando* passages, the harp players being instructed by the composer in his score to play "as many notes as possible with flat hands and arms." The terrific climax of sound, *ffff*, now gives way to the eloquent strains of the "Dies Irae" (or Hymn of Death) played in a solemn manner by the instruments of the brass section, the trumpet carrying the melody.

The original version of the "Dies Irae" is written without time signature or measure bars, as are all Gregorian hymns.

Di - es   i - rae, di - es   il - la

The *Coda* begins, *prestissimo,* at the close of a rapid *fortissimo* passage and diminishes until only a roll of the drums and tympani is heard. Then the drums, in turn, slowly die down to a *pianissimo* throbbing, and above this murmur, from an unseen player behind the scenes, there comes, softly and slowly, as though from far away, the "Taps."

As the echoes of the bugle call die away, there come a few measures of a *pianissimo* roll from the tympani, a tap from the drum, sharply *pizzicato* chords from the strings, and silence. The "Victory Ball" is ended.

Music and Romance for Youth

"Omphale's Spinning Wheel," by Saint-Saëns, first a piano solo, was later arranged as a symphonic poem for orchestra by its composer. It is a retelling, in music, of the old Greek myth of Hercules, the "strong man," who, having accidentally killed his friend Iphitus in a quarrel, was punished by being sent as a slave to the court of Omphale, Queen of Lydia. Here Hercules was to serve for three years. During this time he was often ridiculed and tormented by his royal mistress, who not only forced him to wear women's clothes, but also made him try to spin with her serving maids.

The music is built upon three themes, each of which helps to tell the story. In the beginning of the composition, a charming and clever imitation of the spinning wheel is heard, and quick running passages, which are played by the violins in the orchestra, are supposed to suggest the laughter of the Queen's maidens as they watch Hercules in his awkward attempts to use the spinning wheel.

"The Spinning Wheel of Omphale" (written in the free form of a Symphonic Poem) begins *Andante,* the stringed instruments, muted, alternating with flutes in the quiet music, which gradually attains a livelier motion. The "spinning wheel tempo" once established, frequent notes from the horn accent the rhythm while the higher wind instruments add graceful arabesques to the main theme.

A chain of many episodical harmonies (the voices of Omphale's maidens) introduces a lovely song melody, played by wind instruments and occasional strings. The verse is repeated, fuller, the harp adding exquisite harmony in showers of notes, while a drum is tapped lightly and the trumpet plays one single note.

"Hercules air" is now heard, played in the lower strings and the basses of the wind and brass instruments, accompanied by a low roll of the drum and a soft clash of cymbals. As Hercules' rebellious song becomes more intense, trumpets clang, and the drums increase their rolling.

Presently the spinning wheel whirr is renewed (Hercules' strength does not release him from his labor), and again are heard in addition, the light voices of the flutes (the laughter of Omphale's maidens), and the rippling of the harp. The spinning is continued until the close of the day, when, one by one, the workers stop.

The entire composition is graceful, quite short, and very elegant.

MUSICAL ILLUSTRATIONS

1127, 1128	*The Victory Ball (Ernest Schelling)*	*Mengelberg and N. Y. Orch.*
21621	*Dies Irae (Gregorian Chant)*	*Palestrina Choir*
7006	*Omphale's Spinning Wheel (Camille Saint-Saëns)*	
		Philharmonic-Symphony Orchestra of New York

Music That Tells a Story

"The Victory Ball" was begun by Schelling in New York in the spring of 1922, and completed that year in Switzerland, where he has a summer home. Its first performance was by the Philadelphia Orchestra on February 23, 1923.

"Omphale's Spinning Wheel," Symphonic Poem, Opus 31, No. 1, is the first of a series of four compositions written in this form by Saint-Saëns. Composed in 1871 as a piano solo, it was heard in concert frequently during the year. After being arranged for orchestra it was first played in Paris at a Concert Populaire, April 14, 1872, where the "musical myth" was received with great enthusiasm by the Parisian music lovers.

QUESTIONS AND TOPICS FOR DISCUSSION

1. In listening to "The Victory Ball" notice the composer's use of Army Calls, and also of certain combinations of instruments in various sections of the music, to help him tell the story.

2. What nations, whose troops participated in the War, are represented in this music?

3. Could you tell, by simply hearing this music, what War or what period of world history is meant to be suggested by the composer's music? If so, name at least three incidents in the music which prove it.

4. In hearing "Omphale's Spinning Wheel," listen for the various instruments and the part they play in the story-telling, as: the muted strings in the *Andante* (opening section); the flutes with which they alternate; the horn which accents the "humming" and "spinning" of the wheel. What musical instruments produce the music which suggests the spinning wheel?

5. What is *Absolute* music? How does *Program* music differ from it? Name three divisions of *Program* music. To which divisions do "The Victory Ball" and "Omphale's Spinning Wheel" belong?

6. What is meant by the "program" of a composition?

Library Reading. Try to read the complete poem, "The Victory Ball," by Noyes; also the old Grecian myth of Hercules and the Lydian Queen.

OUTSIDE STUDENT PROJECT

Class members should hear and study at least one concert program each semester, in addition to those presented in the classroom. This may be chosen from high-grade entertainments by local organizations or by visiting artists, or it may be selected from the many out-standing programs now being offered by radio, which include some of the world's greatest artists and orchestras.

The program should be approved by the instructor and prepara-tion made in class for hearing it. By then applying the facts and ideas learned in class, as well as the listening habits practiced there, to the concert program, the student will put into application his study in music appreciation. Such concert attendance is excellent training as well as a challenge to the student to get the most from his study.

Correlation should be made between the music heard and other subjects studied. Each class member should write a brief, but definite, discussion of the program, including in it such points as: time and place of concert; names of artists or organizations participating, with interesting facts about them; special character of the music heard; special comment and criticism, both complimentary and adverse, of the concert. Reasons for such criticism should be given in every in-stance.

Part One—Chapter Nine

FORM—RONDINO AND RONDO

(The student should reread at least the first paragraphs of Chapter Four, Part One, "Tunes and Patterns"—before continuing with the study of this chapter.)

An Old Folk Rondeau. In any town or village of Southern

FRENCH FOLK DANCING IN THE MEADOW   Galloway

France, Italy, or Spain, the time of a holiday or festi-val, several hun-dred years ago, would have found the people amusing themselves by play-ing a singing game. Men and women as well as boys and girls of all ages would have been taking part in the same game in which, standing in a circle, with hands joined, they sang and danced an old folk-air.

French Folk Rondo. Since the early days of the Troubadours in

Form — Rondino and Rondo

Provence, taking part in a song in stanzas, with a dancing refrain, has been a popular and well-loved pastime of the French people. Sometimes the words they sang were dramatized or acted out.

The one peculiarity of these old singing games was that the chorus was always sung first, after which a short solo would be sung by anyone in the group of dancers who volunteered. Then the chorus would be sung again; another solo, the chorus and countless new solos alternating until the game was ended.

The chorus was called the *rondeau,* from the French word meaning "to return" or "to come around to the beginning again." The solos were known as *couplets.* (In England the "Round" or "Roundel." *)

"Bridge of Avignon." One of the most popular examples of those early "round dances," or singing games, was the charming old "Bridge of Avignon," which is still frequently danced, as it has

THE BRIDGE OF AVIGNON

been during many centuries, on the quaint old bridge in that French city on the River Rhone.

In this singing game the chorus sings this melody.

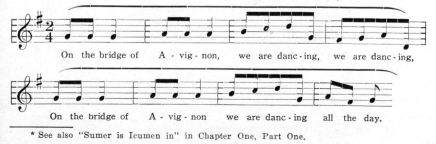

On the bridge of A - vig - non,   we are danc-ing,   we are danc-ing,

On the bridge of A - vig - non   we are danc - ing   all the day.

* See also "Sumer is Icumen in" in Chapter One, Part One.

Immediately a soloist volunteers with this:

The la - dies all do this way: (*Curtsies.*)

Everyone repeats the short phrase and its accompanying action. Then the chorus is repeated, after which new solos, in which all kinds of action are introduced, are alternated with the chorus until the dancers are ready to end the game.

Spanish Folk Rondos. In Spain it is still a custom for friends who have chanced to meet at a tavern to start singing a rondo to the tune of an old folk-song. The guitar is passed from hand to hand, each person to whom it is passed improvising a solo verse, after which the familiar chorus is again repeated. Each succeeding soloist has only the amount of time needed to sing the chorus in which to compose his solo contribution.

The Rondo Form. So the word *rondeau* or *rondo,* as it was afterward spelled, came to mean any piece of music in which the first melody (or theme) was constantly alternated with other melodies.

Composers of music have delighted to imitate the form of the old dancing game in their art-works, and the *rondo* (or *rondino,* which means "a little *rondo*") is one of the most popular of all extended types of musical form. It is often used as the final movement of a sonata or symphony, and also as an independent concert number.

Characteristics of the Rondo. The two essential characteristics of a composed rondo are *variety,* brought about by the use of many themes; and *unity,* created by constant repetition of the first and most important theme.

The first theme is usually a very decided melody, and all succeeding themes are written so as to offer a distinct contrast to it. The first theme, in its several reappearances, may be presented in its exact original manner; or it may be varied (either as to rhythm, melody, pitch, key, or by means of embellishments) in each appearance, but it must always be the last theme heard, as well as the first.

"Gypsy Rondo," from Haydn Trio No. 1. One of the best known of all instrumental rondos, and one in which the main theme is practically unchanged, and so, easily recognized in all its appearances, is the "Gypsy Rondo," the third and last movement of the Haydn Trio for piano, violin and 'cello.

The first main theme—the one which recurs—is given out in *G*

Major by the piano, while the other two instruments add simple chordal accompaniment.

It is immediately repeated an octave higher, and after a short episodical passage, is heard again, this time played by both piano and violin.

The second theme, also in *G* Major, is given out by violin with piano in unison.

The first *Trio* appears, a lively theme in parallel minor key. After this melody has been clearly stated comes the recurrence of the first, main theme; that of the second Trio, also in *G* minor; and that of the main theme, now heard for the last time before the entrance of the *Coda,* which is built upon *motifs* from this theme.

"Gavotte in F"—Beethoven-Bauer. A composition may often be written in rondo form, and still be called by another name. Such a classic rondo is this little-known gavotte by Beethoven (arranged as piano solo, from its original form as a piano duet, by Harold Bauer), the form of which —*A B A C A Coda*—follows the old classic rule that the principal theme shall be heard three separate times during the course of the piece.

"Rondino in E-flat"—Beethoven-Kreisler. A charming graceful rondino is that in which Fritz Kreisler, an eminent modern violin virtuoso and composer, has utilized a short, airy theme composed by Beethoven and com-

FRITZ KREISLER

bined it with themes of his own creation, in a composition for violin with piano accompaniment.

The eight measure Beethoven theme, with which the "Rondino" opens,

is heard six times during the composition, and alternates with two principal themes by Kreisler. The Beethoven theme (with a short *Coda*) brings the dainty number to a close.

The "Rondino" is notable for simple grace, melodic charm and a lilting rhythm.

"Rondo"—Mozart-Kreisler. Another classic rondo, transcribed for violin by Kreisler, is that by Mozart. Written in the type of a per-petual-motion, it displays throughout the characteristic transparent simplicity of the Mozart style, a delicate sparkling *staccato,* and much opportunity for brilliant performance on the part of the violin soloist.

The first theme is made up of tiny note-patterns and scale runs. Solo and accompaniment begin simultaneously. After an extended presentation of this melody, the second theme enters in more flowing style. At its close a short violin *cadenza* precedes the re-entry of the main theme, after this second presentation of which, is heard theme three, in simple triplet figures. Following these figures a sec-ond *cadenza,* more brilliant than the first, featuring trills and intri-cate "figures," announces the first theme again, sounding as it did at first, then repeated and varied by a difficult double-note passage.

The entire composition closes with a third elaborate and strik-ingly ornamental *cadenza.*

"Ronde des Lutins" (Round of the Goblins), Opus 25, by Bazzini, is a fantastic *scherzo* in rondo form. In *presto* tempo, and in the key of *E* minor, the dashing work is a magnificent bit of program music. The main theme appears in both minor and major modes.

"Rondo," Opus 32, No. 2, by Henri Vieuxtemps, illustrates once more the great popularity of this simple form, with composers whose music is written especially for concert performance.

The Vieuxtemps number is one whose captivating charm, bril-liance, and extraordinary effectiveness place it at once in the concert repertoire of every great violinist. With an eight-measure intro-duction by the accompaniment, the work begins, *piano,* and increases immediately to *fortissimo.* The violin enters with sweeping scale passages which reach a *sforzando* climax, after which the various single notes of the theme are ornamented in turn by grace notes— singly, in pairs, in groups, and by frequent trills. The *staccato* ac-companiment is characterized by a fine simplicity.

Form — Rondino and Rondo

Other violinistic features of the various appearances of the main theme and those with which it alternates are much display of octave skips, use of the *G* string, harmonics, arpeggiated chords, tremolo in octaves, extended octave passages, double third passages, and the brilliant running passages in the gorgeous *cadenza* with which the rondo comes to a close.

"Rondo"—Schubert-Friedberg—for violin solo with piano accompaniment, is a sparkling composition which gives great prominence to continued melody of a dazzlingly brilliant kind. The main theme is that of a Schubert song, and starts out in the major, in a brightly cheerful and sprightly manner.

The main theme, which continues in the style of a "perpetual motion," glides smoothly into the second theme, which is similar in style, though not in melodic content.

The first theme returns again, as before, but this time with its beauty enhanced by brilliant arabesques from the piano.

Other secondary themes appear and disappear. The main theme is heard in the minor, then is contrasted with a plaintive flowing melody. Now the music returns to the earlier mood, but not the earlier theme, immediately. It returns after a superbly brilliant transitional passage, and a long extended trill. The theme is now varied by the most brilliant embellishments and concluded in a clever little *Coda* in which the first song theme is repeated first by violin and then by piano.

This is more truly a rondo for violin and piano, each instrument sharing the responsibility jointly, than a solo with piano accompaniment.

MUSICAL ILLUSTRATIONS

19723	*Bridge of Avignon (Old French Folk-Song and Singing Game) Victor Orch.*	
3046	*Rondo all'ongarese (Gypsy Rondo) from Trio No. 1 (Haydn)*	
		Thibaud-Cortot-Casals
6592	*Gavotte in F (Beethoven-Bauer)*	*Bauer*
1386	*Rondino in E-flat (Beethoven-Kreisler)*	*Kreisler*
——*	*Rondo (Mozart-Kreisler)*	*Chemet*
*6159	*Ronde des Lutins (Round of the Goblins), Opus 25 (Bazzini)*	*Heifetz*
H6447	*Rondino, Opus 32, No. 2 (Henri Vieuxtemps)*	*Hansen*
6691	*Rondo (Schubert-Friedberg)*	*Heifetz*

Informational Notes

Avignon, a historical city situated on the banks of the River Rhone, in Southern France, has been a part of France since 1791. Its history is long and varied. Famous for its many beautiful churches, it has long been known as the "City of Bells." Its fame also rests upon the quaint ruins of a stone bridge which once spanned the river, and which, an old tradition tells us, was built by the power of song, nearly a thousand years ago. Only four of the original twenty-two arches remain. It was in Avignon that Francesco Petrarch, the distinguished Italian poet and scholar, received much of his early education.

Avignon was, for nearly seventy years, the home of the Holy See. Here still stands the famous Papal Palace, the largest building of the Middle Ages now standing in Europe. Avignon was formerly outside of France, which country ended with the opposite bank of the River Rhone. The Queen of Naples, to whom it belonged, sold both town and province to the Popes, who continued in its ownership for about four hundred and fifty years, until the French Revolution. At Nimes, nearby, is the most perfect example of ancient Roman architecture to be seen in Southern France.

The "Gypsy Rondo," in perfect form, with its ever-recurring theme in *G* Major and its two contrasting themes in parallel minor, is said to owe much of its sparkling gayety, freshness and verve to Haydn's use of the characteristics and colorings of his well-loved native Croatian folk-airs.

Questions and Topics for Discussion

1. From what simple beginnings has the rondo form descended? Name and discuss two national games or customs of considerable antiquity which were its antecedents. From what does the form take its name?

2. What are two essentials of composed-rondo form? What is a *rondino*?

3. Contrast the moods of the "Gypsy Rondo," by Haydn, and the Beethoven-Kreisler "Rondino." How does each composition display national characteristics? Contrast the Beethoven-Bauer "Gavotte" (really a rondo) and the "Ronde des Lutins," by Bazzini. Which is the more formal? Which is more programatic?

4. Make a diagram of the form of each Rondo heard during the study of this chapter.

5. Name several ways in which Vieuxtemps has made use of artistic skill in varying the several appearances of the first theme in his "Rondino," and at the same time afforded the violin soloist an opportunity for display of virtuosity.

6. How has the Schubert song melody been combined with other melodies so that a rondo is constructed? How does the use of a different instrument, with the same melody, "color" the music in a different manner?

Library Reading. Pages 3-13 in Book III, Kinscella "Readers in Music Appreciation."

Ballet

BALLET—TELLING A STORY IN MUSIC AND DANCE

Ancestors of the Modern Ballet. In the earliest days, men who had no other way of writing told stories or wrote them down by means of pictures. Some of these picture-stories were mere scratches made on the walls of caves or on bits of wood or bone. But after a while, men learned to make such things as dishes and vases from the clay upon which they walked. Then, to make their vases prettier, they decorated them by carving upon them pictures which told stories of the scenes they saw, and of the happenings which took place before their eyes.

In many of the greatest of the world's museums there are valuable old vases and bits of pottery that have been dug out of the earth in old and far-off lands by great scientists. On some of these vases are carved or modelled pictures which tell a very clear story.

The pictures on one such vase in the Metropolitan Museum represent several dancers. One is a girl dancer who is posed so as to suggest the Sun. Other figures on the vase represent other dancers who pose about the Sun in worshipful attitudes. This picture tells as plainly as though words had been written, of one of the earliest dances, known as the Sun Dance, which was a part of the Sun Worship among nearly all pagan tribes and peoples. There are still, in some parts of North and South America, Indians who, at their annual festivals, have picturesque ritualistic ceremonies during which they dance out to meet the Sun.

Other ancestors of the modern ballet were the stirring pageants in which people loved to take part in medieval days; the mystery plays which were sometimes given on church steps or in open squares of European cities in the early times; and the idealized folk-dances which were often introduced into scenes in early operas.

What the Ballet Really Is. Although it is interesting to know where *ballet* * originated, it is still more interesting to know about the modern ballet. It is a story-telling combination of music, dancing and pantomime, all these being aided—as in an opera—by appropriate scenery and costuming. The modern ballet need not be a dependent part of an opera or ceremony, but is complete in itself.

Much of the music of the most famous ballets has also been arranged so that it may be played independently in concert, where it will have a wider hearing. In listening to it thus, the appreciation and understanding of the hearer will be greatly increased if he is

---

* Ballet comes from the Italian *Ballare* meaning "to dance."

first familiar with the ballet plot, or "program." It will therefore be both interesting and helpful to study the plots of some of the more famous ballets.

"The Nutcracker Ballet," by Tschaikowsky. In 1891, Tschaikowsky, the popular Russian composer, received an invitation to write both an opera and a ballet for performance at the St. Petersburg * Opera House. Without much loss of time he chose, for the subject of his ballet, a charming fairy tale by Hoffmann, which tells of a wonderful dream in which "Marie," on Christmas Eve, dreamed that she saw—after the mysterious fashion of things in fairy-land—all her dolls, the Nutcracker and the other toys, come to life. She thought she saw them having a battle with the Mouse King who, with his troops, came to eat up all the goodies on the Christmas tree. The Nutcracker, thus released from the "spell" that had bound him, becomes a Prince, who conducts her to a revel in fairy-land.

Much of the music is of rarely delicate beauty, with a charm and novelty of orchestration which make it, in the opinion of many

APOLLO AND THE MUSES

critics, Tschaikowsky's greatest work. The incidents of the fascinating fairy tale are related, in the suite (or collection of pieces from the ballet), in eight short numbers. Piquant effects are secured by use of the *celesta* in the "Dance of the Sugar Plum Fairy"; of a trio of flutes in the "Dance of the Mirlitons" (automatic toys); and of characteristic rhythms in the "Dance Arabe," the "Trepak" and the "Danse Chinoise." The other three numbers are built upon a similarly dainty plan.

"Overture Miniature," from the "Nutcracker Suite," is, as its

* Now Leningrad.

name suggests, an overture (or prelude) small in compass. It is, however, a classic overture perfect in form, having (as does any sonata movement) two subjects or themes which appear first in related keys, a development section, and a restatement of both themes—called *recapitulation*. The first theme is a dainty melody played by the flute. The second theme is as easily recognized, a smoothly flowing melody played first by the violins, to an accompaniment of soft chords *plucked* rather than *played* by the remainder of the string choir, and by fleeting scale passages. A short development of these two themes, the brief recapitulation, and a tiny *Coda*, ending in swift chords *pizzicato* and a soft clang of the celesta, complete the miniature overture.

"Dance Arabe." This short number owes much of its truly Oriental character to the use by Tschaikowsky of muted strings, omission of all brass instruments, the inclusion of a bass which never stops its droning from beginning to end, its constant use of tambourine, and the Oriental type of melody with its irregular number of notes.

"Dance of the Sugar Plum Fairy." This tiny dance is notable for its delicacy, and for its use in both solo and *cadenza*—of the celesta. There is a dainty orchestral accompaniment.

"Trépak" (Dance Russe), like many Russian dances, when danced in a folk way, to an accompaniment of folk-airs, is featured by much hand-clapping and foot-stamping, and increases, toward the end, in the greatest possible rapidity.

It opens in a very gay manner on a loud chord, full orchestra. The first theme (first violins) sets up a lively atmosphere, which is

enhanced by unusual accents, which fall upon the second beat in many measures of the melody, this syncopated accent being reinforced by sharp, loud chords from the rest of the orchestra.

The main melody receives an answer from the flutes, after which it and its answer are repeated by the same instruments. Many of the orchestral instruments—as flute, clarinet, violins and oboes—now sweep with a noisy rush into the melodic theme, or rhythm copied from it. This section is also repeated.

The next division of the piece is made up largely of rhythmic patterns developing from the previous themes. *Staccato* octave skips in the flute furnish the accompaniment. A real *round* is very nearly created by the rhythmic figures, one group of instruments rushing in with the pattern before another group has finished with it. For some measures kettledrum and the tambourine alternate with each other in keeping up a monotonous rhythmic beating.

The first theme returns and is repeated with tremendous force as the dance increases in intensity and velocity, almost the entire orchestra joining in a rhythmic figure (| ♫ ♫ | ♫ ♫ |) *fff,* while the horns keep up a semblance of the melody, in altered form.

"Marche" (Danse Characteristique). The orchestra which plays this lively and dainty "toy" march contains no 'cellos or double-bass. It is made up of the violins of the orchestra divided into a quartet; the violas divided into two parts; plus the wind instruments, horns and triangle. The little composition opens with a miniature *fanfare* by the clarinets and brass. The first theme is mostly in trumpet and horn, reinforced by clarinets. A reply comes from the strings after a call from the woodwind. A variation of the first theme is heard, presently, in the lower brass instruments, answered by *pizzicato* strings and woodwind.

In the middle section or *Trio* of the "Marche" a series of rapid-running passages (woodwind and strings) is heard followed by a slower strain (bassoons and horns), after which there is an immediate return to the main march theme.

"Danse Chinoise," the dance of another of Marie's Christmas dolls, is only thirty-two measures long, but it is filled with fantasy, and with a captivating and fascinating grace. Simple in construction, it opens after four measures of rhythmic chords with a *glissando*

SPRING RAIN—V. STUCK

across the octave. The accompaniment has an unchanging pattern (played by the bassoons and by the double-basses *pizzicato*). The melody is played by the flutes and piccolos, with many embellishments. The sound of little bells alternates with the string *pizzicato*. The use of bassoons on the low notes and of the flutes on the highest notes suggests the humorous steps of the dancing doll. An Oriental din is produced by rapid arpeggios in the clarinets, and the composition ends with an abrupt bang!

"Danse des Mirlitons" (or toy pipes) is an exquisitely airy composition, the main features of which are the swiftly moving trio for flutes, the frequent use of the piccolo, the *pizzicato* strings, and of colorful *chromatic* passages.

"Waltz of the Flowers," the last composition of the ballet "Suite," is the most glowing of the pieces. It opens with a tiny Introduction (woodwind) and a swirling harp cadenza. Horns give out the main waltz theme after four measures of simple rhythmic *one*-two-three, *one*-two-three chords. Clarinets give the answer. In the second section the strings carry the main theme and the wind instruments the answer, the music, meanwhile, being decorated and beautified with arabesques of melodic phrases.

The third section of the charming and poetic waltz presents still another melody (woodwind) with an accompaniment of singing, *legato* strings and harp. The Waltz is notable for exquisite melody, luxurious chords, and much brilliant display of harp music.

The "Coppélia" ballet, by Delibes (one that was often danced by the world-famous Pavlowa), is a refreshingly jolly story of life in a little Austrian village.

Many years ago, so the old tale runs, there lived in this village an old doll-maker named Coppelius.* So lifelike were the dolls which he made that it occurred to Coppelius, one day, to play a joke upon his neighbors. So, when the doll upon which he had been working was completed, he dressed it carefully and set it in his window, placed a book in its hand, so that it might appear to be reading, and pushed back the curtain.

Many villagers who passed wondered about the beautiful young girl who was visiting at Coppelius' home. Toward evening Franz, a young lad of the village, came by, and, seeing the pretty stranger in the window, stopped and bowed to her, and did not go on until he had become very sure that she would neither notice nor speak to him.

That evening Franz and Swanilda—his sweetheart, who had observed his conversation with the strange girl—quarreled over the affair. Several days later at the great celebration which was held in the village because of a bell which the Lord of the Manor had presented to the town, Franz tried to win Swanilda's forgiveness, but she was still angry.

Coppelius, who had noticed the quarrel, and had decided that his joke had gone far enough, managed to drop his house-key at Swanilda's feet, as though by accident, as he passed her on his way into the village. She, seeing the key lying there, picked it up and, calling to some of her friends to come with her, rushed away to the home of the doll-maker, determined to learn the secret of the silent

---

* This Old World tale has also been made into a stage comedy, and was used as the theme of Act I in Offenbach's opera, "The Tales of Hoffmann."

girl. Soon they learned of the joke that had been played on them, found that Coppélia was only a mechanical doll, and the day ended happily for everyone.

"Dance of the Automatons." This typical bit of ballet music, with its splendid vitality and its ceaseless activity, is built largely upon a single theme. It opens with a rhythmic pattern (strings) over a droning accompaniment, and moves directly into the ballet. The main theme, written in high register and played by flutes, sug-

gests the jerky motion of the automatic dolls, as does the mechanical accompaniment of plucked strings.

"Waltz." The Coppélia Waltz is one of the most popular Valse melodies of the world. It is introduced by four measures of *one*-two-rest, *one*-two-rest rhythmic figure, immediately followed by the soaring melody of the first theme.

This melody is repeated in its entirety, immediately after which alluring *motifs* from it are repeated again and again. A new theme, with slurring, sliding motion, now enters.

This is also repeated (with its *staccato* answering phrase). A transitional passage, built largely upon chromatic patterns, leads to a return of the first Valse theme and a presentation of the alluring melody of the third theme.

Ballet

The entire Valse is notable for wealth and originality of charming melody, and for graceful refinement.

"Sylvia Ballet," by Delibes, is a ballet in three acts and five tableaux, on a classic story, the scene of which is laid in mythical times.

"March and Procession of Bacchus," which occurs at the opening of Act III, is one of its most colorful and attractive numbers. The scene in which this bit of the Sylvia ballet is laid, is a rural site near the shore of the sea, the green spot before the Temple of Diana being shaded by a huge oak. Here a festival of the peasants is in progress. The scene shows a procession in which are seen—and heard—the country people, the buffoons, the trumpet players, and a group of bacchant warriors who dance about armed with javelins.

Before the curtain rises upon the ballet scene, the far away sound of the orchestra (kettle-drums and a murmur of strings) is heard. At the fourth measure of the Introduction the curtain slowly rises, disclosing the festival, where soldiers with switches in hand are chasing aside the peasants and their families to make a passage for the procession. In the music, chromatic passages, abrupt single notes, and a loud trumpet call usher in the procession.

The processional march, in brisk *tempo,* is characterized by a simple but constant rhythmic figure in the bass, and by an airy rhythmic melody—the first theme.

It accompanies the movement of a group of armed men. Trumpet calls in the distance frequently break in upon the melody.

Presently a new theme is heard, announcing the entrance of white-clad flower girls.

The clowns next enter to the accompaniment of a typically humorous air.

Following this come the Muses of the Dance, to a graceful accompaniment of arpeggiated chords from flute, clarinet, harp and *pizzicato* strings. The remainder of the composition is either a repetition of, or reminiscent of, earlier incidents in the music already played, the brilliant *Coda*—in which is again heard the stirring trumpet call —rising to a tremendous climax, full orchestra.

"Valse Lente," another alluring and popular valse from the ballet, is characterized by the wide skips in its thematic pattern. The first (and most important) theme enters in violin and wind instruments with harp accompaniment, and is immediately repeated without change. A second statement of the theme (by horn) is repeated; another, in transposed form (by clarinet), is also repeated; after which the theme returns to its original key. The second theme features arpeggiated figures.

"Pizzicato" (in Act III), most familiar of all the numbers from the Delibes ballets, is the dance of a young slave who wishes to thus attract the attention of the young Aminta. The piece owes its name to the manner in which a large part of it is played—the strings *pizzicato*. It has all the airy grace of the Valse. It opens *Andante* with an Introduction of three long-held chords (woodwind) over arpeggiated chords from the strings. The first and most widely known of its themes is played *pizzicato* by all the strings. The flute is the solo instrument of the second part, or Trio, in which a lyric melody is featured. The form of the "Pizzicato," in large eight-measure parts, is as follows:

Andante Introduction—(three long-held chords)
    a—first theme
    a—first theme (varied in cadence)
    b—second theme
    a—return to first theme

Ballet

Trio—first theme—flute melody repetition of theme—flute and clarinet

Da Capo to first theme (*a*) main section—here four measures and a running-passage Coda. Two final chords are not played *pizzicato,* but with the bow.

"Dance of the Hours" is a classic ballet which was written as a part of his opera "La Gioconda" (The Ballad Singer), (after a tale by Victor Hugo), by Ponchielli, an Italian composer of the nineteenth century.

The scene of the opera is laid in Venice in the seventeenth century. In the third act of the opera, a masked ball is taking place in the Duke's Palace, where Alvise is receiving his friends. For the entertainment of his guests he arranges the ballet, in which the dancers, costumed as the Hours of Dawn, Day, Evening and Night, and aided by cleverly arranged lighting effects, portray the eternal struggle between darkness and light. There are twenty-four dancers. Six are garbed in black decorated with silver stars, im-

Courtesy of Roxy Theatre
A GROUP FROM "DANCE OF THE HOURS"

personating the Hours of the Night; six in pink represent those of Dawn; six, dressed in golden hues, are the Hours of Midday; and six, costumed in mauve, personify the Hours of Twilight.

Although first written as a part of an opera, the "Dance of the Hours" Ballet—as it is always called—has been danced for many years, as an independent ballet. In the same way the ballet music has been played as an independent concert number. In the opera, of which this dance is a recognized part, the ballet is immediately preceded by a brilliant *recitative* sung by Alvise, and by delicate *pianissimo* patterns of running notes. The ballet itself is filled with the symbolism of tone-shading. As the dancers, who impersonate the "Hours of Daybreak," make their quiet entrance, the theme—built upon the three notes of the common triad or chord in the key of *E* Major—is played *pianissimo* with a delicate tremolo of the muted strings as accompaniment. The entrance of the "Hours of Day" is preceded by a *fortissimo* Introduction (in the opera this is sung by a chorus of voices). This ballet music is extremely light and graceful, and moves directly into that which ushers in the "Hours of the Evening." Here the music drops into a lower key (*C*-sharp minor). Contrasting with the considerable use of *staccato* in the first three divisions of the ballet (Hours of Daybreak, Dawn and Midday), the music which accompanies the dance of the "Hours of Night" (in *E* Minor) is an expressive, flowing *legato* melody.

"Faust Ballet Music," by Gounod. This melodic ballet music is a portion of the equally melodic opera "Faust," which is based upon Goethe's dramatic poem of the same name. In this, a tale is told of Faust, an old German philosopher and scholar, who sold his soul to the devil for the return of youth, and the acquisition of supernatural power. The "germ" of the whole story is to be found in German folklore and old "magic" tales of the sixteenth century.

The ballet music was less elaborate in its earlier versions, but was revised at a time when Gounod was making preparation for performances of the opera at the Grand Opera in Paris. During the seven numbers of the ballet several famous women of history and mythology are brought to mind.* The music is now also played frequently, as an orchestral Suite.

1. "Dance of the Nubians" † (*Allegretto movement de Valse*) opens, *fortissimo,* with a fanfare of brass and cymbals. Following the climax of the introduction, the graceful lyric air which constitutes the first theme is heard.

The second theme is more seductive in type, and soars from treble and bass in a "question and answer" manner, after which an immediate return to the first theme, and a short *coda,* bring the piece to a happy ending. The form, which is identical with that of nearly all of the seven dances, is *Introduction, A B A coda.*

2. "Cleopatra and the Golden Cup" (*adagio*) is a contrasting number, being more languorous than the preceding "Valse." Following a chordal *Introduction,* the first theme—built upon a rhythmic pattern—enters.

etc.

---

* Nubian Slaves usually dance the waltz. The *Adagio* introduces Cleopatra. Aspasia steps to the *Allegretto* and Lais to the *Moderato maestoso.* Helen of Troy appears for the *Moderato con moto,* and Phryne dances the *Allegro vivo.*
† Black slaves from Nubia, a former country which lay between Egypt and Abyssinia.

The second theme, a light *staccato* melody, is followed by a repetition of the first melody, and a *coda* in which are heard reminiscences of both.

3. "Dance Antique" (*allegretto*) is in a minor key, and makes use of much syncopation. The lilting air of the first theme

produces an Oriental atmosphere, an effect which is enhanced by the steady and persistent use of the tambourine in the accompaniment. The second theme is in the relative major.

4. "Dance of Cleopatra and Her Slaves" (*moderato maestoso*) is based upon a graceful skipping figure:

The second theme is in similar style.

5. "Dance of the Trojan Maidens"(*moderato con moto*) gives much prominence to the harp. The main theme, one of great elegance, suggests the flowing lines of an ascending scale,

illustrating the very simple means often used by a great composer in the expression of a beautiful idea.

6. " Mirror Dance" (*allegretto*), one of the most familiar airs of the entire ballet, is built upon a rhythmic design which clearly suggests dancing steps.

The second theme, very delicate in effect, features the flutes in single and double note passages.

7. "Dance of Phryne" (*Allegro vivo*), which closes the Suite, is a brilliant and dramatic climax to the entire series. The colorful first theme makes much use of chromatic contrivance.

p expressivo

The conclusion, through its sonority, velocity, and furious climaxes, makes an insistent appeal to the emotions, and culminates in a *coda* reminiscent of earlier themes.

MUSIC ILLUSTRATIONS

6615, 6616, 6617   *Nutcracker Suite (Tschaikowsky)*   *Phila. Sym. Orch.*

6586   *Dance of the Automatons and Valse from ''Coppélia'' (Delibes)*
                                                    Hertz and San Francisco Orch.

35879   *March and Procession of Bacchus from ''Sylvia'' (Delibes)*
                                                          Victor Sym. Orch.

1166   *Valse Lente from ''Sylvia'' (Delibes)*   *Hertz and San Francisco Or.*

1166   *Pizzicato from ''Sylvia'' (Delibes)*   *Hertz and San Francisco Or.*

35833   *Dance of the Hours from ''La Gioconda'' (Ponchielli)*
                                                          Victor Sym. Orch.

9646   *Dance of the Nubians*
       Cleopatra and the Golden Cup   *from ''Faust Ballet'' (Gounod)*
       Dance Antique   *Royal Op. Orch. Covent Garden*
       Dance of Cleopatra and Her Slaves

9647   *Dance of the Trojan Maidens*
       Mirror Dance   *from ''Faust Ballet'' (Gounod)*
       Dance of Phryne   *Royal Op. Orch. Covent Garden*

INFORMATIONAL NOTE

When, in April of 1891, Tschaikowsky set sail for his only trip to the United States—where he helped to dedicate Carnegie Hall in New York City—the first scene of the ''Nutcracker'' ballet was already finished. He returned to Russia in May, and before the summer was over all of the music was written. Urged to do so by his friends, Tschaikowsky conducted a series of pieces selected from the ballet music, in a concert, on March 19, 1892, and so gave them an advance hearing, although the ballet was not given until later. Very appropriately the ballet was given its first performance at the Opera House at the Christmas season (December 18th) before an audience which included the former Czar and all his Court.

SUGGESTED PROBLEM

Include in your scrap-book such newspaper or magazine accounts as you are able to secure of the annual Sun Ceremonies or Festivals of the Bolivian Indians in South America, and of the Pueblo Indians in southwestern United States. Compare these and their very primitive musical accompaniments with the modern composed ballet. File in your scrap-book, also, any accounts of modern ballet that you may find.

Ballet

1. What are the principal elements in a modern ballet which help to tell its story?

2. Tell what you know of the ancestry of ballet. Where, in the New World, are ancient ritualistic dances still a part of worship?

3. How has the early history of the ballet been preserved?

4. After you have heard the music from the four ballets discussed in this chapter, compare the "story-telling" power of the old classic and the more modern works. Which, in your opinion, most completely and convincingly suggests the plot, or story?

5. Compare and contrast the three waltzes given in this chapter. Does each suggest a different type of action, or similar? Explain.

6. Discuss the manner in which Tschaikowsky has used certain instruments of the orchestra in each of the numbers of the "Nutcracker" to suggest different nationality. Name the instruments most appropriate for use with a musical expression of various nationalities.

7. What is a Trepak? How is it danced?

8. Describe appearance and tone of the celesta. Define *glissando, pizzicato, chromatic, legato,* and *staccato.*

9. What is an automaton? How does the music by Delibes definitely suggest the jerky motion of one or more automatons? Name at least two ways.

10. Contrast the three themes of the Coppélia waltz. Which is your favorite, and why? Give a clear statement of the reasons for your choice.

11. Contrast also the three themes given from the "March and Procession." How does each theme ably characterize the persons it is supposed to suggest?

12. What is meant by the "symbolism of tone shading"? How is this employed by Ponchielli in the "Dance of the Hours"?

13. Notice and discuss the various devices—such as tremolo of strings, wide skips in the accompaniment (as in the Clowns' Dance) *glissando,* change of key on the repetition of a theme, and muted strings—used by composers to suggest definite mood.

Library Reading. "Indian Dancers in Bolivia"—pages 100-106 in Book VI, Kinscella, "Readers in Music Appreciation." "The Diverting Art of Ballet," and "The Story of the Dance" in "The Mentor," December, 1926. "Interpretations," by Anna Pavlowa, "Ladies' Home Journal," September, 1924.

A MODERN SUITE—"L'ARLÉSIENNE," BY BIZET

What a Modern Suite Is. A Suite, in music, is a collection of short pieces—usually pieces which are, in one way or another, related to each other.

In early days the Suite—which was then known as *Classic Suite*—was a set of short dance forms of various origins. For example, a composer might write several little dances, imitating in them the styles and forms of a German *Allemande*; a French *Minuet* or *Gavotte*; and a Spanish *Sarabande*. The different dances would be placed in an order best calculated to offer most contrast. These would all be written in the same key, and their composer would introduce them to the audience by means of a *Prelude*. He might also close his Suite by writing a lively little *Jig* (or *Gigue*).

The *Modern Suite* differs from the old Classic Suite in that its greatest desire is to exploit its content—its story-telling possibilities or its poetic mood—rather than its form.

The Modern Suite was at first an experiment with the old form, and was a collection of short pieces, written to be performed in connection with ballet, or as incidental music with stage dramas.

Presently it became quite customary for composers to write modern or story-telling suites for independent concert performance, many of them finding that the short numbers convey the descriptive "program" of the music to the hearers more easily than the longer symphonic poem or symphony.

Of the type known as "incidental" music, which has been arranged in a form suitable for concert performance, is the "L'Arlésienne Suite," one of the most irresistibly charming suites ever written.

The Suite "L'Arlésienne." It was in the year 1872 that Daudet, the renowned French dramatist, requested Bizet, the equally eminent French composer, to write what is known as "incidental" music for his forthcoming play, "The Woman of Arles," or, as the French title gives it, "L'Arlésienne."

Bizet's music consisted of twenty-seven short numbers, each of which was written for the purpose of enhancing the meaning or charm of some individual incident or situation in the three-act drama.

The Daudet play, with the Bizet music, was given its first presentation at the Vaudeville Theatre in Paris, from which, in spite of careful staging, it was necessary, because of lack of public support, to withdraw it, after only fifteen performances.

A Modern Suite

It seemed, at first, that the failure of the drama to attract public attention meant, also, the failure of the Bizet music. But within a few months, Pasdeloup, an orchestral conductor who had been charmed by the beauty of the music, selected four of the most outstanding of the twenty-seven numbers, and played them at a Paris concert.

This combination was soon played by other orchestral conductors, and presently it came, without any effort on the part of the composer himself, to be known as Bizet's "L'Arlésienne Suite."

GEORGES BIZET

Again some conductors selected other numbers from the "L'Arlésienne" music, for concert performance, and a second suite came into being. But of this only the "Farandole" is given frequent hearings. This, with the "Prelude," "Minuetto," "Adagietto" and the "Carillon," are the familiar and popular choice of music-lovers from among the twenty-seven pieces which Bizet had composed.

The Story of "L'Arlésienne." The play, "The Woman of Arles," cleverly combines within itself two complete stories. One is the story of Frederic, a splendid young man who loves a beautiful young woman of Arles. When he learns that she is unworthy of his love and untrue to him, he tries to forget her, but, in spite of Vivette, who truly loves him, he loses control of his emotion on the great festival day and puts an end to his troubles by throwing himself from an upper window in the house, onto the stones below.

Contrasted with this is the beautiful love story of Old Balthazar, the Provençal Shepherd, and Mère (Mother) Renaud, who, in spite of all difficulties and years of separation, remain true to each other.

An artistic and subtle touch on the part of the playwright is that the first of the heroines—Frederic's unworthy sweetheart—is never seen upon the stage, although her influence strongly colors much of the action of the drama.

The "L'Arlésienne" Music. As the action of the play is supposed to have taken place in or near the old Provençal city of Arles, in the south of France, and at Christmas time, Bizet made effective use of many charming old-time folk-airs of Provence in his score. The most important of these, in that it is heard again and again

and seems to dominate the entire Suite, is the familiar and well-loved
Christmas carol, "The March of the Three Kings."

Each of the picturesque, melodious numbers in the Suite is quite
short—some are very short—but each is so complete a musical picture that it cannot be overlooked. Many critics consider the Arlésienne music Bizet's finest work, although he is universally admired
as the composer of the Spanish opera, "Carmen."

The "Prelude" (or Overture) with which the Suite opens, at once
introduces, as its principal theme, the air of "The March of the Three

A VILLAGE FARANDOLE—FRANCE

Kings." Characteristic features of
the "Prelude" are four interesting
variations of the melody, as follows:

Variation I. The melody is
played by clarinet, with smoothly
flowing harmonies supplied by the
flute, English horn and bassoons.
The key of "The March of the
Three Kings" as it here appears is
C minor.

Variation II. Here the melody is played by all the woodwinds
of the orchestra in unison, at first *pianissimo,* with an accompaniment
by the snaredrum and the stringed instruments. The key is still
C minor, but the mood is a livelier one, with much sharply defined
rhythm.

Variation III. In this variation the melody is arranged for
three voice parts and is in the key of *C* Major, the three contrasting
voice parts being taken by two horns and the 'cello, with accompaniment by bassoons.

Variation IV. Here the old carol is repeated as a military march
played by full orchestra, in its original key of *C* minor.

The "Minuetto" was the seventeenth number in the complete version of the incidental music, and is a folk version of an old-time court
dance. The *Trio,* or middle section, is exquisitely tender. In the
Trio, the melody, in its first presentation, is carried by saxophone
and clarinet, with decorative arabesques added by the violins. In
the repetition the order is somewhat reversed, the melody being taken
by violins and 'cellos, with arabesques from flutes and clarinets.

The "Adagietto," the third number of the Suite, is, as its name
suggests, a rather slow and thoughtful bit of music. It is also very
brief. The effect of great simplicity is given by the arrangement of
the music for muted stringed instruments. This is one of the most
popular numbers of the Suite. All of the string section is muted for

this number with the exception of the double-basses, which are here not heard at all.

The "Carillon," * piquant and spontaneous, takes its name from the little musical figure or pattern, of three notes (*G*-sharp, *E*- and *F*-sharp) that is repeated over and over for more than fifty measures, suggesting the unvarying chime of bells. This music, when a part of the drama, formed the joyous prelude to Scene IV, where, at the Court of Castelot, the Christmas Festival (also the betrothal of Frederic to Vivette) is being celebrated. The courtyard is gay with decorations, while overhead the chimes are ringing. Accompanying the chiming bells is a joyous, soaring melody (the first theme) played by the strings.

The contrasting theme which follows was written by Bizet to suggest the entrance of Mère Renaud and the Shepherd Balthazar, who have been faithful to each other though separated for more than fifty years. During this episode there is heard a lovely duet for flutes, suggestive of the two personalities here prominent in the drama.

Then the bells resume their ringing, and continue it until the end of the piece, and the end of the Suite.

The "Farandole,"† in reality a part of the second "L'Arlésienne" suite, is sometimes played as a part of the first one. This spirited number receives its name from an old folk-dance and custom still prevalent in Provence and in the neighboring French and Italian districts.

In it is again heard the stirring melody of the "Three Kings" march, first in unison, and then as a round, or canon. Presently the music stops entirely for a moment, but the rhythm moves relentlessly on, suggested by a monotonous beating upon a tambourine, or little drum. Then the spirited dance (another Provençal folk-melody, originally a Greek dance) begins, and first alone, then in combination with "The March of the Three Kings," brings the "Farandole" to a brilliant close.

The music of "L'Arlésienne" is now orchestrated for and played by the greatest symphony orchestras of the world. But it is interesting to know that when the music was first played in connection

---

* A Carillon is a set of bells tuned in the scale, so that melodies may be played upon them. In the modern orchestra, a series of small steel bars which, when struck, produce bell-like tones, is used to suggest the Carillon. The word was formerly "quadrillon," meaning a chime of four bells. Old folk-dances included several "carillions." One of these is "Le Carillion de Dunkerque," a rapid dance in 2-4 or 6-8 measure, still danced in France.
† A Farandole is a game resembling the well known "Follow the Leader." In it a long line of players moves through the village, pausing at intervals to imitate the action of the leader. In early days the music was supplied by pipe and tambourine—a small barrel-shaped drum. A feature of the Farandole, which is still practiced in rural communities, is the passing of the procession through all the houses of the village.

with Daudet's drama, Bizet had arranged it for an odd and very small combination of instruments: 7 violins, 1 viola, 5 'cellos, 2 double-basses, 1 saxophone, 2 horns, a kettledrum and piano.

MUSICAL ILLUSTRATIONS
"L'Arlésienne Suites," by Bizet

7124	*Prelude*	*Philadelphia Symphony Orchestra*
7125	*Minuetto*	*Philadelphia Symphony Orchestra*
7125	*Adagietto*	*Philadelphia Symphony Orchestra*
7126	*Carillon*	*Philadelphia Symphony Orchestra*
9113	*Farandole*	*Royal Albert Hall Orchestra*
20227	*Pour mal tems* (*Thibaut of Navarre*)	*Dixon*

Historical Notes

Adam de la Hale, one of the most prominent of all the Troubadours, was born in the city of Arles about 1230. He wrote a dramatic

DANCE OF THE WEAVERS

work, "Robin and Marian," which was, in form, a forerunner of the opéra-comique. Adam de la Hale was a master of the *chanson*, a form of song in which the verse alternates with a refrain. Copies of his manuscripts may be seen in the Paris Library. He died at Naples about 1288. In 1896, a performance of the quaint "Robin and Marian" was given in Arles.

Although the Daudet drama "L'Arlésienne" was withdrawn after about fifteen performances, the Bizet music has kept it alive in the minds of all concert-goers. As a result of this continued interest, an English translation was made in 1897, when the play was produced in New York City, with the famous Anton Seidel conducting the incidental music.

Geographical Note

The department of France which is known as Provence is situated in the southeastern corner of the country. It is bounded on the south by the Mediterranean Sea, and on the east by Italy. Its most important seaport is the city of Marseilles, upon the streets of which may be seen people from every known country in the world.

Musical and Historical Background

Provence, the section of France in which the city of Arles is situated, is often called "The Land of the Troubadours." To travel over the highways of Provence is to walk in the tracks of Cæsar's soldiers, and in the footsteps of the romantic Troubadours, who, in the Middle Ages, journeyed from castle to castle, accompanied by princely retinues.

Great events have happened in Provence. From its ports at least two of the Crusades set sail for Jerusalem. Some of its castles or walled towns have recorded history extending back two thousand years. Legend and tradition carry its renown still further.

Galloway

RUINS OF ROMAN THEATRE NEAR ARLES, FRANCE

In the ninth century, Provence became an independent kingdom, with Arles as its capital. Barbarossa (of the legend of the Red Beard) was crowned in Provence, which was also visited by Richard the Lion-Hearted of England. Some of Cæsar's wars were fought on its fields, and he built ships in the dockyards of Arles, which city was, in those days, directly on the shores of the Mediterranean Sea. Since then, many miles of good ground have been swept down and deposited between Arles and the Mediterranean by the River Rhone. This is now a vast gray-green orchard of olive and almond trees.

Provence was occupied, in turn, by the Phœnicians, Greeks and Romans, and it is to them that Bizet owed several of the quaint melodies he used in "L'Arlésienne," as, for example, the old Greek dance, *Danso dei Chivau-Frus,* the air of which he used in the latter half of his Farandole. Provence was made a part of France in 1481.

Provence is steeped in history and in mediæval song. One reason for this is the fact that thousands of Crusaders returning, during the Middle Ages, from the East, passed through this pleasant land, and in passing, acquainted the Provençal folk with songs and musical instruments of the Orient which they were carrying home with them.

Other quaint and lovely folk-airs were brought to Provence in early days by bands of gypsies from the East who wandered over all the southern part of Europe playing and singing.

The third reason for the intense love of song that prevails in Provence is that the influence of the knightly Troubadours who lived and sang here in the Middle Ages is still felt.

The Spanish word *trobar* (in French, *trouvere*) means "to invent," and it is from this verb that the Provençal troubadours received their name. The first troubadours lived in Provence about the year 1100, and for three hundred years they traveled about singing to all the people. They were always men of the nobility and accepted no pay for their singing. Like the minstrels of more northern lands, they invented, or composed, songs in which they told stories of heroic events, sang of the glories of war, of the beauties of nature and of knightly chivalry. Such songs were often known as improvisations.

One very famous Provençal troubadour was Thibaut de Navarre, born in 1201, and educated at the Court of France. He was a Crusader and at last became King of Navarre.*

A famous troubadour song—or *chanson*—is the "Song of Roland," which was composed about the year 1100 in honor of Roland, the nephew and favorite of the Emperor Charlemagne. This song was popular for centuries and was sung by the soldiers of William the Conqueror.

During the twelfth century, Spain and Provence were united by the marriage of a Provençal princess and the Count of Barcelona. Soon Arabian minstrels who had made their homes in Spain, drifted into Provence, and brought with them further Oriental musical influences.

Early in the thirteenth century, war was made upon the troubadours because of their participation in religious affairs. One battle took place in the ancient walled castle and city of Carcassonne—some miles west of Arles—where the soldiers fought to the accompaniment of music played upon the violins and guitars of the troubadours. In spite of this, the castle was overcome, and about this time the carefree reign of the troubadours in Southern France came to a close.

The troubadours developed musical composition and form in many ways. They were among the first musicians to arrange their songs to be sung in definite parts. They often improvised variations upon popular folk-songs. They used many of the old Greek modes, as was natural in view of their partially Greek ancestry; but gradually they came to prefer and use but two of these. One was the *Ionian*,† our major scale, as, *C-D-E-F-G-A-B-C*. The second was the *Æolian*,

---

* Hear the folk-song "Thibaut of Navarre," 20227.
† These scales were named for old Grecian provinces.

A Modern Suite

the pure or ancient form of the minor scale—*a-b-c-d-e-f-g-a*. They also influenced the growth of sacred and secular opera, and taught their associates to sing romantic songs.

The rhythms and tonalities, and the Eastern atmosphere of the old troubadour songs, are found in the Provençal folk-music of to-day, and it was from this rich heritage that Bizet drew when he wrote the charming music of "L'Arlésienne."

The City of Arles

Arles was originally a city of ancient Gaul. The River Rhone passes by its western wall. Here are many interesting pink marble ruins—those of a Greek Theatre (so called, though the Romans built it); a Roman road of great antiquity; of an open-air amphitheatre whose walls are still complete although gladiators fought in it fully fifteen hundred years ago—now used by Provençal folk on holidays; and a remarkable folk-museum.

This Musée Arlaten was assembled by Frederic Mistral, the Provençal poet, who used his Nobel prize money for the purpose. Here rooms are built, or moved in from the country, complete, to preserve the life and customs of the people in bygone days. There is, among the rooms in the museum, an old-fashioned farm kitchen at Christmas. Another room illustrates life on a Provençal farm. Still another shows an Arlésienne mother.

For centuries, to be an Arlésienne (or woman of Arles) was synonymous with being beautiful, and on the streets of this city are still worn the strikingly beautiful Provençal costume and elaborate head-dress of earlier days.

Questions and Topics for Discussion

1. What is a Suite in music? How do modern and classic suites differ? Name three kinds of modern suite.

2. Discuss the folk-music of Provence. How has it affected Bizet's "L'Arlésienne"?

3. Who were the Troubadours? In what period of time did they live? Of what did they sing? Name three ways in which their music was influenced by the music of the Orient. How have the Troubadours influenced modern composed music? Name at least five ways.

4. For what purpose was the "L'Arlésienne" music written? How is it better known? Tell what you know of the story of "L'Arlésienne." What does this title mean?

5. What Provençal folk-air dominates the "L'Arlésienne" music? Suggest three reasons why Bizet may have chosen this particular folk-song.

6. What is a "farandole"? What is a "carillon"? A varia
tion? A canon?

7. What famous and popular opera was written by Bizet? Tell
what you know of the composer's life.

Library Reading. "Old Provence," by Frederic Mistral; "Romantic France" (The Enchanted Land of Provence), by Elsner.
"Footprints of History in Provence," in "Contemporary Review,"
January, 1924. "Touring in France" (pages 272-273), by Shackel-
ton. "Old Towns of Southern France," in "Mentor," November,
1928.

PART ONE—CHAPTER TWELVE

EARLY SYMPHONIC MUSIC

The Standardization of the Orchestra. The story of early symphonic music is a fascinating one.

When the first opera was performed in 1600, the instrumental
accompaniment was furnished by a grave-cembalo, chitarone, lira
grande, theorbo and three flutes, some of which were doubled. The
development of opera called for perfection of an instrument to support the soprano voice, and brought about perfection of the violin,
this being completed about 1650. The little French fiddles were
previously used, also the viols.

Preceded by many years of history in which the "string band" *
—with occasional addition of such woodwind instruments as the flute
or hautboy (oboe)—was the accustomed type of large instrumental
ensemble, the symphony orchestra, as it is now known, became fixed
in its form by about the middle of the eighteenth century.

The great credit for this standardizing of the physical form and
balance of the orchestra—as well as that of the music written for it—
is largely due to Joseph Haydn, who, in his thirty years of residence
at the castle of Prince Esterhazy, just outside Vienna, experimented
daily in orchestral effects. He was the first to introduce the clarinet
into the orchestra. His imagination was constantly at work on melodies, development of themes, and balance of voices. Haydn considered each instrument's voice a distinct contribution to the eloquence
of the orchestra as a whole. There is, in the Haydn symphonies, an
exquisite balance, finish and style not heard in the words of many
other writers, due to the fact that everything he wrote was performed
as soon as completed.

---

* See also Chapter VII, Part I, for description of Corelli's "Pastorale" (originally for
harpsichord and string band).

Haydn's Division of the Orchestra into Choirs. Noting the magical symmetry and balance of music well written, for the string quartet, Haydn proceeded to divide his small orchestra into four definitely organized sections, each of which now had its own place in the orchestral formation.

Thus in the Haydn symphony orchestra (as in a modern orchestra) were:

1. The String Choir, violin, viola, 'cello, double-bass.
2. The Woodwind Choir, flute, clarinet, oboe, bassoon.
3. The Brass Choir, trumpet, French horn, trombone, tuba.
4. The Percussion Choir—those instruments which must be struck to be sounded, and whose use so greatly affects the "color" or atmosphere of the music, or its imitative effects—drums, cymbals, bells, gongs.

Tschaikowsky, the modern Russian composer, has defined orchestration—composition or arrangement of music to be played by the orchestra—as the "distribution of a work among the different instruments." Haydn was a master of such distribution, as well as of formal beauty in music.

Nationality in the Haydn Music. Haydn's music is saturated with the national characteristics of the folk-music of his native village. He seldom traveled outside the limits of his own native district, and Rohrau, the village in which he was born, was the heart of a settlement of Croatians. The family name, Haydn, had been, in earlier days, Hajden—a familiar Croatian surname. He has used Croatian folk-melodies in his composed works in their exact form, or in slightly altered or developed form. He once said, "It is the melody which is the

PASTORAL—A SLAVIC SHEPHERD

charm of music, and it is that which is most difficult to produce." In still other compositions are found not only original themes, but rhythms and melodies that are characteristically Croatian in style.

"Surprise" Symphony. It is these nationally attractive elements and characteristics which give so great a charm to the Haydn symphonies, of which the most familiar and popular is the "Surprise" Symphony, No. 6. The *Andante* movement is said to be based on a Croatian melody.

Many stories have been related concerning this work, written

by Haydn to be first performed by the orchestra which he conducted
at the Esterhazy castle near Vienna for thirty years. Tradition tells
that the Prince was accustomed to take a nap at the concerts. This
offended Haydn, who therefore proceeded to plan a musical joke on
the Prince. He set to work on the composition of this symphony, in
the *Andante* of which—after a passage calculated to soothe the Prince
to slumber—he inserted a sudden *Bang!* which startled the Prince
so that he awoke with such a start that he fell from his chair.

The first movement opens with a short and slow *Introduction*
(*Adagio*) somber in mood, the jolly first theme being announced immediately afterward by the strings, with a reply from the full orchestra. This theme is then somewhat developed, and the second
theme, a contrasting one of a quaintly bright and playful type, is
given out in a related key.

The second section of the movement is a free fantasy in which
both themes receive much development.

The third section is much like the first. Both themes now return
in the key in which the movement is written. There is a very brief
Coda.

The second movement, Andante, is the movement in which the
''surprise'' chords are heard, these being produced by crashing chords
from full orchestra and the tympani.

The third movement, Minuet, is in three-part song-form with
Trio. It is a real dance * and an unsurpassed example of rollicking
fun expressed in music.

The first theme—built in the tones of the arpeggio—is given out
with energy by the flutes and bassoons.

Just before the Trio of the *Minuet* the music indulges in a series
of playful ''antics,'' thirds in the flute and oboe being answered by a
quaintly humorous phrase from the bassoons and 'cellos.

A repetition of the *Minuet* proper follows the *Trio.*

The *Finale* retains the sparklingly whimsical mood of the earlier
parts of the symphony. It is written in the form of a rondo, the
piquantly charming main theme (given out by first violins and im-

---

* Haydn used not only folk-melodies, but his works are also filled with folk-dances and
rhythms, of which the minuet is one.

mediately echoed by the flutes), being the central figure of the whole

movement. It recurs constantly, being repeated five times (once in the minor) before a conventional climax brings the work to an end. The entire *Finale* is written in the characteristic mood of a jovial Croatian country-dance.

Not all early symphonic music was written in the large form of a complete symphony. However, the *sonata form* (or symphony first movement) was frequently used in less lengthy numbers.

"Euryanthe Overture," by von Weber. This overture, written as a prelude to an opera of the same name, has long outlived the opera in popularity. Though written in classic form, the famous overture contains a spirit of romance.

It opens with a spirited and fiery Introduction, immediately followed by the first theme (all woodwind) accompanied by the full orchestra *fortissimo*. The entrance of the second theme, in the violins, brings a fascinatingly lovely melody which presently develops a *fff* climax. This is followed by a group of softly sustained chords for horns and bassoons, then a long-held pause.

Now follows a short fifteen-measure *Largo* so exquisitely beautiful, and so unique, for its day, that it has become famous. In it Weber used *harmonics* (played by eight muted violins) and *tremolo* of violas which were considered extremely "modern" and audacious when they were written and first heard. The mood of the little episode is one of mystery.

The development section which follows uses and embellishes the first theme in a brilliant fugal manner; the second theme is played *fff* by full orchestra.

CARL MARIA VON WEBER

A restatement of both themes in the key of the overture follows and an extremely brilliant Coda closes the classic Overture.

"Pastoral Symphony." An exquisite example of early orchestral music is this delicately scored interlude which furnishes so appropriate an atmosphere, in the first part of Händel's "Messiah."

The word "pastoral" suggests shepherds and their rustic pipings, and this melody is that of an old Italian folk-air, sung for many years by the *pifferari*—shepherds who come down from the hills at Christmas time each year to sing old carols and play them upon their dudelsacks in the streets of the Italian cities. It was heard by Händel in Rome thirty-two years before he wrote the "Messiah."

The orchestra for which Händel wrote this "Pastoral Symphony" and which he assembled for the first performance of the great oratorio in Dublin, was composed of muted strings, piccolo, flute, oboe, clarinet, bassoon and horns in *C*.

Throughout the whole short quiet work (which is in three-part form, and in the key of *C*) Händel has made much use of double thirds. The rhythm suggests a swaying lullaby, quite appropriate for the Christmas season. The simple melody of the first theme is sung by nearly all the voices of the orchestra in unison, very softly and gently, in slow tempo. The pedal-bass suggests the drone of the primitive bagpipe.

The second theme is announced by the horns and strings, providing a contrast, not in melody or in type, but in the tone quality of the instruments.

The first two themes are again heard in repetition after the short Trio in *G,* which was added by Händel, some time after the completion of the work, for greater variety.

The "Unfinished Symphony," by Franz Schubert, written in acknowledgment of his election to honorary membership in musical societies of both Linz and Grau, was given the first Vienna perform-

BIRTHPLACE OF SCHUBERT

ance in December, 1865. The Symphony dates from the year 1822, in which Schubert refused an appointment as Court Organist so that he might have all his time to devote to his music and to his friends. The Symphony was lost for many years, but was discovered about forty years after the composer's death, in an old cupboard in which it was his custom to store his manuscripts. Only two movements and nine bars of a third were found, and from this fact the work takes its name. The haunting melody for which the composition is most famous is heard in the *Andante con moto,* the second movement of the Symphony, and is said to be one of the purest melodies in existence.

Each of the two movements is exquisitely beautiful, both alluring in melody and rhythms, and in perfection of classic form.

The first movement begins with an air of mystery, the lovely melody of the introduction, played by 'cello and double-basses in octaves, being unaccompanied and followed by a quivering pattern

from the strings. Then comes the real first theme, in the violins.

This figure soon becomes an exquisite accompaniment to a soaring singing melody in the oboe.

The well-known second theme is given out by the 'cellos.

This latter theme is echoed *pianissimo* in the violins, with syncopated chordal accompaniment.

Notable features of this part of the work are the delicacy of the orchestration, and a gorgeous stream of pure melody.

A *motive* from the first phrase is developed in a canonical form, and rises to a dramatic climax. Full orchestra announces the theme in unison following which a return is made to the original bass figure and the fascinating delicacy of the first melody.

A short *Coda* in the desolate atmosphere of the first theme brings the work to a close.

The second movement, *Andante,* is introduced by a quiet melody in the strings.

Presently a duet is developed between the *staccato* bass and the *legatissimo* of the violins.

Many modulations from key to key produce a touching effect. The second theme, a simple charming melody, enters with clarinets.

MUSICAL ILLUSTRATIONS

7058, 7059, 7060 *Surprise Symphony, No. 6 (Joseph Haydn)* *Boston Sym. Orch.*
9398 *Euryanthe Overture (Weber)* *Berlin State Opera Orchestra*
20620 *Pastoral Symphony (Händel)* *Victor Concert Orchestra*
6663, 6664, 6665 *Unfinished Symphony (Schubert)* *Philadelphia Sym. Orch.*

INFORMATIONAL NOTES

The "Surprise Symphony" was composed by Haydn in 1791. Its first performance was in London in March, 1792. The melody which Haydn used as the theme for his variations in the *Andante* (second) movement, was also used by him as the theme in the aria, "With joy the impatient husbandman," in "The Seasons," where it is played by a piccolo.

The opera "Euryanthe," of which the suggested Overture was an important part, was written by Weber upon the request made by the director of a Vienna theatre in 1822. The first performance of the opera—of which Euryanthe is the heroine—was on October 25, 1823, in Vienna. The opera was never a success, because of its distorted story or "libretto," but the Overture is a perennial favorite.

QUESTIONS AND TOPICS FOR DISCUSSION

1. Name several characteristics of early symphonic music. What was the "string band"? How does the modern orchestra differ from that known and used previous to Haydn's day? For what two developments is all orchestral music, since his day, indebted to Haydn? What incidents concerning Haydn's residence and his duties there contributed to his accomplishment of these developments?

2. Name the four main divisions of the orchestra, and the principal, or leading, instrument in each. How do the voice qualities of these Choirs differ?

3. Describe the style of each movement of the Haydn Symphony. How is nationality expressed in Haydn's symphonic music? Which movement of the "Surprise" symphony is most influenced by folk-music? Discuss and compare the moods of the four movements of the "Surprise." Is it melody or rhythm which has created the Symphony's distinctive atmosphere? Give reasons for your answer. What is a minuet? What is the form of the "Minuet" movement?

4. Discuss the appeal of the "Euryanthe Overture."

5. Name and discuss the outstanding feature of the Haydn Sym-

phony. Contrast that music with the "Pastoral Symphony" by Händel. Which work more clearly suggests the old-time atmosphere? By what two simple means has Händel indicated the serenity of the Christmas season?

6. How has Schubert developed the formal orchestral style of Haydn? What are the most important features of this beautifully poetic work—melody, rhythm, harmony, mood or "program"? Give the reasons for your answer. The melodies of this "Unfinished" Symphony should be memorized so you may always have them with you.

7. Which of the four symphonic selections heard and studied in this lesson is your favorite? Give reasons for your preference.

PART ONE—CHAPTER THIRTEEN
NATIONALITY IN MODERN SYMPHONIC MUSIC

Causes Which Influence Nationality in Music. Much symphonic music, as well as the folk-music of the world, bears witness to the influence of historic events and of geographical and political changes. An increased use of folk-airs and of the folk idea, in addition to a strict devotion to formal structure and beauty, has given to much modern symphonic music a colorfulness and nationalistic individuality, and a type of vigor or vitality, not found in earlier orchestral writings. This is particularly true in lands where the people have been forced to endure much suffering and privation. It is for this reason that much of the modern symphonic music possesses an emotional appeal much deeper than that of the more formal classics. The growth of the orchestra and the inclusion in it of instruments hitherto unused have aided in display of nationality.

THE HOME OF EDVARD GRIEG AT TROLDHAUGEN

"Peer Gynt," by Grieg. In no modern symphonic music is such nationality more evident than in the writings of Grieg, especially the familiar, ever-popular music written for the Norwegian drama "Peer Gynt," by Ibsen.

In the drama, Ibsen tells a story of a rough Norwegian lad, who worries his mother and all his older friends by his fantastic talk and wild dreams of adventure. Presently these dreams come true, and Peer Gynt—after numerous startling adventures in Norway—sails away to Africa. There he steals a horse and robe and goes to Arabia, where he is entertained in the grandest possible manner by the Arabian chieftain. Anitra, the chief's daughter, and her maidens, dance for him. After many experiences and narrow escapes from death, Peer returns home to die, his final repentance brought about through the unending faith of two good women: Ase, his mother, and Solvejg, his wife.

Grieg's music exactly reflects the sentiment and incidents of the drama. Four of the very attractive selections from this incidental music have been brought together in a suite for orchestra, in which such national traits as characteristically Norwegian melodies and harmonies, frequent use of consecutive open fifths, and of primitive harmonies—or, in "Anitra's Dance," of Oriental scales and instruments—are heard.

"Morning Mood." This idyll, a portrayal of a mood, as its title suggests, is the prelude or "beginning piece" of the first Peer Gynt suite.* It is built almost entirely upon a single theme. It begins gently, with a delicately wavering broken chord played by flutes, accompanied in part by very simple chords from the rest of the orchestra. The high notes of the theme are repeated for four measures by the flutes and are then taken up by the oboes in a lower octave. The theme alternates once more between flutes and oboes and is then divided between them in a short four-measure duet. Finally all the strings (save double-basses) join in the fluttering air in unison. After a moderate climax, in which the theme now appears in both major and minor keys, it is echoed by the woodwind. The "Mood" comes to a tranquil ending in a *pianissimo* restatement of the first theme, enhanced by many exquisite trills and ornamental figures in the flutes.

"Ase's Death." This brief composition is as compelling in its tragic mood as many a longer funeral march. It is written entirely for muted strings. The simplicity of both the minor theme and its chordal accompaniment, and the relentless slow-march rhythm create a dramatic tone picture.

"Anitra's Dance." The Oriental character of this music is stressed not only by its melody and rhythm, but also by the instruments which the composer has chosen. It is a dance written for stringed instruments and triangle (suggestive of similar instruments

* See complete listing of music from Suite I and II in "Music Appreciation for Children," pages 242-243; also complete analysis in "What We Hear," pages 453-454.

118

of the desert). The strings are at first muted, with conspicuous use of the oboe in imitation of the Arabian flute or "oud."

"The Hall of the Mountain King," arranged by Grieg for full orchestra, is a masterly study in climax building, both in volume of tone and in velocity. Grieg's love and frequent use of the characteristically Norwegian open fifths are displayed in the opening measures. Here the elements of mystery (quick, short steps of the little people —Trolls) are suggested by the rhythmic skippings about of the bassoons in fifths, *pianissimo*. A *pizzicato* melody in muted 'cellos and

INTERIOR OF EDVARD GRIEG'S MUSIC HOUSE

double-basses enters. Various other instruments join in the repetition of this melody until a terrific climax is reached.

"The Marche Slav," by Tschaikowsky, is an outstanding expression of Slavonic patriotism. It was written in 1876, at a time when Slavic patriotism ran high in Russia because of the war between Turkey and Serbia. Many public demonstrations took place in Russia during the year, one of them a benefit concert for the wounded Serbian soldiers. The concert was arranged and managed by Nicholas Rubinstein, who invited Tschaikowsky to write a new orchestral composition to be played on the occasion. The new work, when completed, was called "Marche Slav," and in it Tschaikowsky has made an artistic use of an old Serbian air, and of the National Hymn of the former Empire of Russia. It is said that Tschaikowsky was fond of calling it his "Russo-Serbian March." The Serbian folk-air used is one customarily sung to the words

> "Come, glittering sun,
> You do not shine the same."

This plaintive melody is made the main theme. The composer opens with a few measures of *tremolo* from the strings in the tempo of a funeral march.

The principal melody enters softly in the bassoons and violas, with a counter melody in horns. An answering melody sings, very sweetly, in woodwind and strings. Then follows a development-like conversation between the theme and the counter-theme. The main theme is sounded as a climax by clarinets, horns, trumpets and 'cellos, followed by a unison passage, full orchestra. Following an episode in major key, the Russian hymn is sounded, as a solo by the tuba and unison strings, while calls from trumpets resound. Soon a full verse of the main song

GRIEG'S MUSIC HOUSE OVERLOOKING THE SEA

is heard again, and also a medley of lively military *motifs*. Once more the Russian hymn is sounded, in stately measured tempo, by all the horns and basses. The "Marche" then ends in a dashing and magnificent fanfare.

The "Fire Dance," by De Falla. This is a spectacular scene taken from a complete modern ballet, "El Amor Brujo" (Love, the Magician), written by Manual de Falla, one of the foremost Spanish composers of the day. The colorful music is written for an effective combination of ballet, voices and orchestra.

The story, or plot, is one developed from an old gypsy tale of Andalusia—a southern province in Spain—and tells of a ghost who persists in returning to torment his former sweetheart. The flickering fire, the cavern, the gypsy dancers and the cruel ghost, create a picture seldom surpassed in ballet.

Nationality in Symphonic Music

De Falla is a student of both his native folk-lore and folk-music, and the music of the ballet is typically Spanish. There is a frequent repetition of single phrases as is common in the Spanish folk-dances.

The fascinating gypsy scene and ballet is complete in two scenes, one act. It was first performed in the Spanish city of Madrid in April, 1915, when its vivid melodies and rhythms, and brilliant Andalusian arabesques created a sensation.

"Fire Dance" opens with an extended trill passage from viola and clarinet, and is accompanied by the 'cello *pizzicato,* and detached accompaniment notes in piano, double-basses, horns and tympani. The typically Spanish melody, which appears in the oboe, soon becomes a duet between oboe and clarinet, characterized by many rhythmic irregularities, and a melody of distinctly Andalusian type. It is now taken up by violins and flutes in unison, then by piano and wood-wind and the other strings, and accompanied constantly by a characteristic rhythmic figure, in which the piano and kettledrum keep up a strumming accompaniment of a Spanish guitar type. Piano and harp indulge in arpeggiated chords until the return of a trill section similar to the opening measures.

An interlude is followed by a new and more simple melody in horns and first violin. This second theme moves to the flutes, while the tympani keep up a monotonous beating. This solo theme now moves to first one, then another instrument of the orchestra, making use all the while of typically Spanish embellishments. The violins and flutes give out the third theme. A development of the three themes follows, and, ornamented by many flying scale passages, ends in a *coda* which is made very Oriental in character by its relentless monotony.

CHARLES SANFORD SKILTON

"Two Indian Dances," by Charles Skilton. Truly American—in that it is the idealized music of the American Indian—is the series of "Indian Dances" for grand orchestra, by Skilton. The complete series of "Indian Dances and Suite Primeval" includes six numbers, in their order, Deer Dance, War Dance, Sunrise Song, Gambling Song, Flute Serenade and Moccasin Dance. The melodies and rhythms used are authentically Indian, and were given to Mr. Skilton personally by members of the tribes. In the "Dances" which were first written for String Quartet, and within a year after their first performance as quartet music, arranged by Mr. Skilton for orchestra, the composer has made use of an Indian drum, the rattle, and the tom-tom in a peculiarly effective manner. Instruments common to the orchestra— as xylophone and harp— are used in particularly telling fashion.

"Deer Dance," with which the series opens, is a unique composition. Information concerning its tribal significance, given by Mr. Skilton at the time of the first performance of the music, tells that a "Deer Dance" is a part of the annual memorial service of Rogue

INDIAN BRAVES DOING A WAR DANCE, NEW MEXICO   Galloway

River Indians of Oregon. The opening melody is intoned by the 'cello, the chief singer, then taken up in turn by the whole orchestra. Then there is a commemorative speech by chief (*cadenza,* solo 'cello), after which the melody is repeated. The Dance proper begins with a livelier melody in 2/4, accompanied by drums in 3/4—a combination or cross rhythm frequent in Indian music.

A primitive ensemble is used in the accompaniment while the melody is being intoned by the chief singer, the women and middle-aged men. The interval of the young men's song is characterized by a rising third, while that of the song of the very old men has a similar falling third. The drum beats incessantly. While this goes on the whole company stands in a half-circle, alternately men and women, the dancers passing out and in between them, imitating the hunter pursuing the deer, and exploiting the deeds of those hunters who have now gone to the Happy Hunting Ground.

The music of the Skilton "Deer Dance" opens *Adagio* in 4/4 measure, and in the key of *G* Minor. The quite elaborate Introduction, carrying out exactly the plan of the ritualistic ceremony, begins with a single tone (*basso ostinato*) in the bass and a swinging "pattern" or "figure" played by all the 'cellos. Single notes are added by the other strings, creating the desired effect of monotony.

A short 'cello *cadenza* (the commemorative speech by the chief) is followed by one other short passage in which the earlier monotonous phrase is repeated by harp and *pizzicato* strings. This ushers in the dance, *Andante,* in two-beat measure.

Here is found the most definitely "Indian" feature of the entire work, the steady, relentless, never-stopping beating of the dull-toned Indian drums, beginning and continuing in 3/4 measure, although the melody or theme is constantly in 2/4 measure. The theme, given out by first violins, is then taken by the oboes, from whence it

moves, with a *glissando,* to flute and strings. In another repetition, it is played by these instruments combined with muted trumpets, and harp, and accompanied by the tympani, cymbals and the ever-beating Indian drum.

The music now returns to the first *Adagio* 4/4 measure—the Indian drum is silent. The earlier theme is now given a new treatment.

It is heard twice in its entirety, once in the woodwind and then from the strings and woodwind. Characteristic running passages bring the "Dance" to an abrupt end, the tympani playing alone at the close.

The "War Dance" ceremony is idealized as the second number of the series. This is based upon a Cheyenne melody, and has for instrumentation, in addition to what is planned for the "Deer Dance," a piccolo, rattle, tom-tom and xylophone. The "War Dance" is music of a barbarian type, and moves at a furious speed, all the time being strongly accented, accompanied throughout by the Indian drum. It opens 2/4 with the monotonous Indian drum | ♫♫♫ |. The same effect is emphasized by the 'cellos, viola and second violins, each of which in turn enters on the same rhythmic figure. The rhythm established, the first violins announce the first theme, with the many syncopated accents.

A repetition of the same theme—ushered in with a short rush of notes of a staccato scale—is played an octave higher (oboes, clarinets and all violins). The music grows in intensity. A *glissando* from the bottom to the top of the xylophone ushers in theme once again, still another octave higher. The harp enters *glissando* and adds firm *fortissimo* chords to the general *crescendo,* in which chromatic passages (clarinet and viola) add to the primitive din. Quite suddenly the music diminishes, only to burst forth with renewed energy after the temporary lull, during which, however, the Indian drum beats constantly, and the xylophone is repeatedly used. A rattle and a tom-tom are heard occasionally.

The music comes to a spectacular close, with full orchestra, much use of chromatics, and a constant *glissando* up and down on both harp and xylophone, and *sforzando* chords.

"Sioux Flute Serenade," No. 5, from "Suite Primeval," by Charles Skilton. The melody of this exquisite idealization of a tribal melody and custom was given the composer by George La Mere, a member of the Winnebago Indian tribe of Nebraska.

The melody which Mr. Skilton has here idealized is a traditional one among the Sioux and is played by them on a large wooden flute about twenty-four inches long, and blown from one end (not the side, as is a modern flute).

The piece begins *Adagio,* with the exquisite four-measure theme of the old Sioux Indian love song, played by flute. After the momentary pause which follows the conclusion of the plaintive air, there arises a gentle murmur from the stringed instruments ('cello and bass), of trills from the tympani, and its response from the entire orchestra. The flutes repeat the gentle air an octave higher. There is again a response from the entire orchestra and succeeding flourishes from flutes and piccolos on exquisite *motifs* from the main theme.

All of the woodwinds now take up the melody, *forte*, to accompaniment of harps and the remainder of the orchestra. After a brief but agitated development section, the music rapidly diminishes to a dramatic anti-climax, when again the air of the beseeching love-song is heard, *piano*, this time adorned by many trills. The mood of the music becomes steadily gentler and more subdued.

The tender melody is heard still another time, *pianissimo*, from flute alone; there are rhythmic figures and a long-held high note, piercingly sweet; *pizzicato* chords from the strings; and silence.

MUSICAL ILLUSTRATIONS

35793	*Morning Mood (Edvard Grieg)*	*Victor Symphony Orchestra*
35793	*Ase's Death (Edvard Grieg)*	*Victor Symphony Orchestra*
20245	*Anitra's Dance (Edvard Grieg)*	*Victor Symphony Orchestra*
20245	*In the Hall of the Mountain King (Edvard Grieg)*	
		Victor Symphony Orchestra
6513	*Marche Slav (Tschaikowsky)*	*Stokowski and Philadelphia Orchestra*
6869	*Fire Dance (de Falla)*	*Hollywood Bowl Orchestra*
22174	*Deer Dance (Skilton)*	*Victor Concert Orchestra*
22144	*War Dance (Skilton)*	*Victor Concert Orchestra*
——*	*Sioux Flute Serenade from "Suite Primeval" (Skilton)*	

INFORMATIONAL NOTES

Tribal courtship has been described by Francis la Flesche, son of the last chieftain of the Omaha tribes and now an important member of the Government Ethnology Department at Washington, D. C., as follows: Among many Indian tribes the custom of courtship, in early days, was for the lover to conceal himself, at dawn, in a tree or behind clumps of bushes near the spring to which the maidens came each morning for water. When the maiden of his choice appeared, the lover would then serenade her by playing to her, on his handmade Indian flute, his own original, or a traditional air. If favorable to his suit, the maiden would show her preference; if not, she would pretend not to hear the music at all; and the youth was often obliged to play his plaintive air for many dawns before finally attracting the attention he craved.

The "Indian Dances" were originally written for string quartet, and were given their first performance by the Zoellner String Quartet, to whom they are dedicated, in January, 1916. During the summer of 1916, Mr. Skilton arranged the dances for full symphony orchestra, while spending a short time at the MacDowell Colony at Peterborough, New Hampshire. The first orchestral performance was in October, 1916. The native Indian melodies which are used as thematic materials in the two *Dances* were supplied to Mr. Skilton by the chief of the Rogue River Tribe of Oregon. The manner in which the themes were secured by Mr. Skilton is related by the composer as follows:

"There is near Lawrence, Kansas [where Mr. Skilton makes his home], the Government Indian School, Haskell Institute, the center of Indian education in the United States. One day in 1915 an Indian graduate of this school, Robert R. De Poe, who was their bandmaster, stopped me down town and asked for theory lessons. He came to my study after that, Saturdays mornings, and brought with him a drum which he had made from a chopping bowl and a piece of skin. After lessons he would sing me the melodies of his tribe and others, and proposed that I should write them down. After some six melodies were notated he was called to another post in the Northwest, and I have never again met him.

"The first melody he sang was that of the Deer Dance, in the middle of which occurs a passage in two-four measure accompanied by the drum beating three-four; when I asked him if he knew how difficult a thing he was doing, he shook his head and said, 'We always do it that way.' He was hereditary chief of the Yah Shoo Wee clan of the Rogue River Indians of Oregon, and described this as the annual service for those who have died during the year.

"The opening strain is a lament sung by the chief singer without drum accompaniment; after sufficient repetition of this, the chief makes a speech in praise of the departed, which is briefly suggested by the *cadenza*. The dance begins at the two-four section, some dancers putting on the skins and horns of deer and other animals, while others, in the garb of hunters, pursue them in and out among the spectators, who stand in a semi-circle, men and women alternately, marking time with the left foot. Mr. De Poe further assured me that the young men sang a rising third in the tenor and the old men a falling one in the bass, combining with the melody and three-four drum-beat to make a curious primitive ensemble. The piece is to be conceived as an expression of primitive religion.

"The 'War Dance' is a Cheyenne melody. Mr. Hervey Peairs, then superintendent of Haskell Institute, heard it played by the Minneapolis Symphony Orchestra and told me that it recalled vividly an occasion twenty-five years before, when he had heard it sung by three thousand men of the Cheyenne nation on their last war-path.''

An Indian drum is about the size of a snare-drum, but has no snares, and gives forth a dull tone. (By snares are meant those several cords of catgut which are usually stretched across the lower head of the side- or snare-drum, and which rattle against it with every stroke). As each tribal ceremony has its own individual drum rhythms, it is often possible to tell, from a great distance, exactly what is going on in an Indian camp. In early days, before the advent of cities on the plains, it was the custom for Indians approaching a camp to place an ear to the ground—which is a splendid conductor of sound—and thus learn in advance what was taking place there.

HISTORICAL NOTES

In January, 1874, Ibsen wrote to Grieg telling him of his contemplated drama for performance on the stage, and asking him, ''Will you write the incidental music?'' The first performance of the ''Peer Gynt'' music was at the Christiania (now Oslo) Theatre, February 24, 1876. Both drama and music had a real success. Some of the exquisitely beautiful and expressive music was arranged as the first ''Peer Gynt'' suite and later additional numbers were arranged in a second suite. Later, Grieg was given a life pension by the Norwegian Government.

QUESTIONS AND TOPICS FOR DISCUSSION

1. Name several causes for an increased display of musical nationality in modern symphonic music. How has the development of the orchestra itself helped to bring this about?

2. Name four typically Norwegian musical characteristics heard in the ''Peer Gynt'' music, and point out definite sections of the particular composition in which they are used. How has Grieg created the exquisite effect of mood in the first number of the ''Peer Gynt'' suite? By what means has he suggested the Orient in ''Anitra's Dance''?

3. Name and discuss three distinct divisions of the ''Marche Slav.'' Of what is each division characteristic? How does Slavic national music differ from that of Norway?

4. How does the De Falla ''Fire Dance'' suggest the folk atmosphere of Spain? Name two characteristic features of the ''Fire Dance.'' What instrument gives out the principal theme? What instruments suggest a characteristically Spanish accompaniment? How does this music suggest the Orient?

5. What instruments, in addition to those which are a part of a standard orchestra, has Skilton included in his instrumentation for the "Indian Dances"? Name several musical effects produced which are peculiarly typical of Indian tribal music? What are the two main characteristics of the "War Dance" theme? How has Skilton, in his idealization of this air, contrived to give us an authentic portrayal of the scene and the happenings of an Indian camp during a war dance? What kind of a scale is used toward the end of the composition to suggest the fervid emotion of the dancers and assist to create a climax? What instrument furnishes brilliant embellishments for the dance music? What is the outstanding characteristically Indian feature of the "Deer Dance"?

6. Describe the old Indian custom of courtship. How has the composition, "Sioux Flute Serenade," suggested the continuation of the courtship through several dawns? Why is the flute so prominent in Skilton's orchestration of the music?

Library Reading. "The Indian in Song and Story," by Alice Fletcher; pages 202-211, of "My Long Life in Music," by Leopold Auer.

Part One—Chapter Fourteen

THE "FINGAL'S CAVE OVERTURE"

How "Fingal's Cave Overture" Came to Be Written. Many concert overtures of a descriptive character are written to commemorate some great event in history, or some phenomenon of nature.

FELIX MENDELSSOHN-
BARTHOLDY

The "Fingal's Cave Overture"—sometimes called the "Hebrides Overture," by Felix Mendelssohn, was inspired by a visit which the composer made to this great natural curiosity in 1829, when he was just twenty years old.

What Fingal's Cave Is. Fingal's Cave, on Staffa, one of the Hebrides, or Western Isles of Scotland, is one of the most marvelous of nature's exploits. Staffa is a small island, scarcely a mile in length from north to south, and half that at its greatest breadth from east to west. The island rests like a table upon a wall of strangely formed and colored stone columns, and the Cave which has made it so famous is near its southeastern corner. The formation of the rocks is similar to that of the Giant's Causeway, many miles away.

The "Fingal's Cave Overture"

The Highlanders, in earlier times, called the cavern the Cave of Finlin—some say, after the Celtic giant who, legend tells us, built the Causeway so that he might step over from Ireland to Scotland on dry land. From Finlin, the name gradually changed to Fingal.

Still another name by which the spot was known in early days was the Cave of Music, this name having been given it because of the sonorous and monotonous murmur of the waters as the tide enters and leaves it in calm weather. When the seas are heavy, the huge waves pound through its caverns with such force that they shake the earth and fill the air with thunder.

The Cave is safely entered only when the day is calm and no rough seas are present to dash the small boats, which attempt the entrance, and their passengers, against the rough stone roof and walls; or to wash the more venturesome from the narrow, slippery path which runs along the tops of some broken columns.

Mendelssohn's Visit to Fingal's Cave. Mendelssohn visited the Hebrides in 1829 and was so deeply impressed by its weird grandeur that he wrote to a friend: * "In order to make you realize how extraordinarily the Cave affected me, the following came into my mind there." Then he added this theme from the Overture:

A companion named Klingermann wrote to a friend: "We were put out in boats, and climbed, the hissing sea close beside us, over the pillar stumps to the celebrated Fingal's Cave. A greener roar of water surely never rushed into a stranger cavern—comparable, on account of the many pillars, to the inside of an immense organ, black and resounding, lying there absolutely purposeless in its utter loneliness, the wide gray sea within and without."

In September Mendelssohn wrote from London: "The Hebrides story builds itself up gradually." From

THE ENTRANCE OF FINGAL'S CAVE Galloway

* On August 7, 1829.

that time on, through many months, the composer worked upon the Overture until its completion. The first public performance of "Fingal's Cave" was in London on May 14, 1832.

How the Overture Is Written. "Fingal's Cave" is a concert overture written in strictly classical style and form. Mendelssohn evidently felt that the inspired short theme he mentioned in the first

Galloway
THE SEA FROM WITHIN FINGAL'S CAVE

letter written after his memorable visit was entirely typical of what he had heard and felt in and about the Cave, for he used it as the principal melodic theme or subject of the composition.

As the Overture opens, this theme (first in *B* Minor) is played, in turns, by the bassoons, the violas and the 'cellos, in various keys and with differing degrees of force. Then the first and second violins take it up, the flutes, then the clarinets, until nearly every instrument of the orchestra has sung it.

A quieter second theme (in relative major key of *D*) is introduced by the 'cellos, as a contrast, accompanied by a waving figure from the strings. But, throughout the entire composition there is no forgetting the constant motion of the sea, for, even when the melody of the first theme itself is not heard, its peculiar rhythm ♩ ♪ ♫ ♪ ♪ is repeated in the accompaniment, over and over. Other accompaniment to the main theme is furnished by groups of swirling notes and many chromatic passages. The second theme is much elaborated, until presently the return of the first theme is heard. After a free development section, in which the second theme is much extended, and a recapitulation, the Overture ends quietly, as it began, the simple little "sea" theme being repeated by the clarinets softly, three times within the last five measures of the short *Coda*.

MUSICAL ILLUSTRATIONS

20744   *Skye Boat Song (Old Highland Rowing Measure)*   *Brown*
 9013   *Fingal's Cave Overture (Felix Mendelssohn)*   *Ganz and St. Louis Orch.*

Early Italian Opera

Fingal's Cave is 227 feet long, 42 feet broad, from 50 to 100 feet in height and at ebb tide contains a twenty-five-foot depth of water. The roof of the cave is in the form of an arch.

The Hebrides Islands are famed in old English and Scottish history. "Prince Charlie's Cave" on the rocky coast of one of the Hebrides is one of the numerous caves where the Young Pretender is said to have once lain in hiding.

Skye, one of the Inner Hebrides, is the classic home of the Scotch bagpipes, because of the college of piping established there.

Questions and Topics

1. With what does the music begin and end? Find the short musical theme which describes the music of the waters. Is this a definite or indefinite description, a story, a mood or an impression?

2. Describe the mood which is suggested to you by the main theme of this Overture. Is it somber or gay? Has it dramatic, pictorial or poetic characteristics? Give reasons for your answer.

3. What does the composer's use of his first theme tell you about the ocean and Fingal's Cave?

4. How may the "Fingal's Cave Overture" be said to belong to both types of music—Pure and Program?

5. Name other pieces of instrumental music that you know which describe or suggest water.

Theme Topics. 1. What I have learned from magazines about Mendelssohn. 2. A report on Fingal's Cave, Hebrides Islands. 3 What Mendelssohn's Overture has told me about Fingal's Cave.

Library Reading. "A Journey to the Western Islands of Scotland," by Samuel Johnson; "Fingal's Cave" (sometimes called "Staffa"), by John Keats; and "Sea-Distances," by Alfred Noyes; "Mackrimmon's Lament," by Sir Walter Scott.

Part One—Chapter Fifteen

EARLY ITALIAN OPERA—"IL TROVATORE"

What Early Italian Opera Really Is. There are styles and fashions in opera just as there are in dress, in conveyances, or in public amusements. Just as there is usually something of worth and beauty in each changing style, so there are qualities which charm in each type of operatic music.

An early Italian opera—unlike many of the present-day operas, or the music-dramas of Wagner—had, usually, a very simple, conventional story, or plot. Its music was often an artificial arrangement, or grouping together, of solos, duets, choruses, or other musical ensembles, which were written for the special purpose of displaying the brilliant vocal gifts of the singers, rather than to help tell the story. The orchestral accompaniments were often very superficial also.

Many of these early operas have outlived the years, and every change of taste and fashion, and are as popular now as when they were written and first sung, nearly a century ago.

The main reasons for this lie in the fact that each of the early Italian operas usually contained a wealth of beautiful and expressive melodies; plenty of lively and strongly marked rhythms; and that they were very dramatic. It was the combination of these three essential qualities which brought about the lasting popularity of the old "singing operas" of Italy.

GIUSEPPE VERDI

Some Early Italian Opera Composers. Prominent writers of early Italian opera were Rossini, Donizetti and Verdi, and chief among these was Verdi, whose magnificently tuneful opera, "Il Trovatore," remains a favorite among all his works.

CHARACTERS IN THE OPERA, "IL TROVATORE"

LEONORA, a noble lady of the Court of a Princess of Aragon.

AZUCENA, a wandering gypsy from the province of Biscay.

INEZ, Leonora's attendant.

MANRICO, a young chieftain under the Prince of Biscay, who is of mysterious birth, in reality a brother of the

COUNT DI LUNA, a young noble of the Prince of Aragon.

FERRANDO, Captain of the Guard under Di Luna.

RINZ, a soldier in Manrico's service.

An old Gypsy, Messenger, Jailor, Soldiers, Gypsies, Attendants, etc.

The Scenes in Which the Opera Is Laid. The scenes in which the four acts of "Il Trovatore" are laid are in Biscay and Aragon, two important Spanish provinces.

The Time. The events of the opera are supposed to have taken place during the fifteenth century.

Early Italian Opera

The Story of the Opera. The title of this opera, "Il Trovatore," when translated, means "The Troubadour"; and the opera story relates the romantic adventures of Manrico, the gypsy troubadour, who is found, in the end, to be the long-lost brother of his rival, Count di Luna. The opera is sometimes spoken of as "The Gypsy's Revenge."

Act One is often called "The Duel." It opens in the vestibule of the old palace of Aljaferia, in the Spanish city of Saragossa, in Aragon, where Ferrando, the talkative Captain of the Prince's guard and in the service of Count di Luna, is gossiping with a group of soldiers. He tells of the Count's love for Lady Leonora, and his jealousy of a mysterious troubadour whom she seems to prefer. He relates, then, an old tale of the troubles of the di Luna family—that he and the Count are at all times watching for a certain old gypsy woman, who, about twenty-five years earlier, had committed a great wrong against the di Luna family. This gypsy's mother having been burned as a witch by the order of the Count's father, this gypsy had either burned or kidnapped Garzia di Luna, the Count's younger brother. Many of the Count's followers are sure that she threw the child

OPERA HOUSE AT NAPLES

into the flames. Others think that he is still living, but that he has been brought up as a gypsy rover. All this Ferrando relates to the soldiers, ending his weird tale, as midnight strikes, with an assurance that he would know the woman anywhere. The story ended, the troops march into the palace to take up their night guard-duty.

Meanwhile Leonora has stolen quietly out of the palace to meet Manrico, her Troubadour. When he does not come to the usual meeting place, she returns to the palace, just before Manrico and the ever-suspicious Count di Luna both arrive. The two men, both now suspicious and jealous, engage in a duel there in the old garden.

Act Two, The Gypsy Camp. Manrico had wounded the Count in the duel, but spared his life. In the meantime, Leonora fled from the palace and took refuge in a retreat. Having since been wounded in the border warfare between Aragon and Biscay, Manrico has come to the village—a Biscayan gypsy settlement—to visit Azucena, whom he has always regarded as his mother. During his visit, Azucena, who is now quite old and witless, sings a wild song in which she partly betrays the secret of her mother's cruel death and her own secret revenge. Manrico, who hears the song, begins to suspect his own true name and station. However, he is not certain, and Azucena's savage command, "Avenge me!" is hardly uttered before his attendant, Ruiz, enters and informs him of the Count's plan to abduct Leonora that very night. Manrico departs with Ruiz, arriving just in time to rescue Leonora from di Luna and his followers.

Act Three, often called "The Gypsy's Son." The opening scene finds Manrico and Leonora hidden in a solitary fortress which the

AZUCENA—"IL TROVATORE"

Troubadour holds for his Prince. They are about to be married, but the fortress is being besieged by Count di Luna. Just at this moment an old gypsy woman—evidently a spy—is captured near the camp and recognized by Ferrando. She denies any connection with the deeds of which he accuses her, but boasts that she is the mother of Manrico, the Count's rival. At this the Count orders her burned—at that time the usual punishment given gypsies suspected of treason; Manrico learns of what is taking place in his rival's camp, and in horror summons his soldiers to help him rescue Azucena, calling out as he does so, "I was a son before I was a lover."

In Act Four—"The Torture"—Manrico finds himself not only defeated in his efforts to rescue Azucena, but is himself captured. Both of them are chained in a lonely tower of the Aljaferia palace. Leonora, who escaped, returns to Aljaferia to either rescue Manrico or say good-by to him—possibly both. From outside the tower she hears him singing his pathetic farewell to her, and at once offers herself to the Count, if he will only release Manrico. When the Count agrees, she takes a slow poison, so that she may live only long enough to free Manrico. When Leonora dies, the Count breaks his pledge and has Manrico killed in the courtyard, at which the old gypsy rouses from her stupor just long enough to tell him that he has killed his own brother. Her revenge is indeed complete.

The Music of "Il Trovatore." The pathos of many of the scenes of the opera, and the vividness of the many intensely dramatic situations are made doubly appealing by the rhythmic and melodic beauty of the music. From the stirring bugle call in the orchestral introduction of Act One, to the dramatic Finale of Act Four, the melodies are fresh and expressive. The most popular melodies of this opera are not all sung by the soloists. The magnificent "Anvil Chorus," sung by the gypsies, and the famous "Misérere," sung by an unseen chorus in the prison tower, are examples. So is the pathetic duet, "Home to Our Mountains," which Manrico, her foster son, sings with Azucena, the old gypsy, comforting and soothing her during her last night in the tower.

The "Anvil Chorus" opens with a brilliant orchestral introduction, a unison passage, decorated by countless trills, unique rhythmic figures and beating of triangles. The male chorus enters, accompanied by strings alone, in a theme which is compelling by its very simplicity. There is, in the melody, a constant sequential rising of the melodic figure built upon the arpeggio.

Presently the men take up their hammers and begin to accent their singing by strokes on their anvils, the basses on the strong beats, and the tenors on the weak ones. Here there is a full orchestra accompaniment, and a unison melody, stirring and forceful.

"Stride la vampa," sung by Azucena, follows immediately, to an accompaniment of *pizzicato* strings. The melody is characterized by rhythms of an Oriental type, the use of the Oriental scale (pure minor with an augmented—or raised—fourth), and embellishments of a Moorish type.

The same theme is constantly repeated during the progress of the aria, often sequentially, in different tonalities. The song is in clear three-part song form.

"At My Mercy Lay My Foe." Here Manrico is describing to Azucena a scene of his meeting with the Count di Luna, and of how he spared the Count's life. As the opportunity came to kill his enemy, Manrico was, he tells his foster mother, "in that moment spellbound"—the real cause having been his intuitive though unconscious recognition of relationship. Manrico sings of all this in a simple melodious aria.

"Di quella pira" (Tremble, Ye Tyrants) In this brilliant tenor *aria* in Act III, rhythm plays an important part. Manrico has recognized his foster mother in the captive of the enemy, and prepares to fly to her rescue. The *aria* is in three-beat measure and in the key of *C* Major. It is introduced by one measure of a rhythm which is, thereafter, almost constant in the basses and bassoons which have their part in accompaniment of the voice ( ). This rhythmic figure( ) is a frequently heard feature of the vocal part.

The "Misérere." This is heard toward the beginning of the last act, and immediately following Leonora's aria in which she meditates upon her love for Manrico. Suddenly the death bells are heard tolling, and an unseen male chorus is heard in the solemn death chant. This chant (the "Misérere") is interspersed with Leonora's questionings, and her singing is, in turn, interrupted by Manrico, who, in the tower, sings, *pianissimo*, the well-loved air

The blending of the solo music written for Leonora (who stands below the tower), Manrico and the male chorus, creates one of the greatest of all vocal ensembles.

"Home to Our Mountains." As she rehearses the remembered terrors of her mother's tragic death at the stake, and is comforted by Manrico, Azucena begins, presently, to sing (accompanied softly by *pizzicato* strings in the orchestra),

Home to our moun-tains thou yet shalt take me

to which Manrico replies, in an upward moving melody,

Rest thee, my moth-er, to heav-en wing-ing

Their voices then join in an exquisite duet, accompanied at its close by only the muted strings. The duet ends tenderly, an extremely emotional effect being achieved by the placing of the voices just a third apart.

Early Italian Opera

Historical Notes

In this opera Verdi made use of real Spanish names. The Counts of Luna are a famous old Zaragoza family. Their home—the Casa de Los Gigantes, or House of the Giants—may still be seen, with the huge figures at its door which gave it the quaint name. The coat of arms of the di Luna family is a moon, and this is seen in all the decorations of the palace.

Galloway
THE CASTLE OF ALJAFERIA, SCENE OF THE "MISÉRERE"

"Il Trovatore" was given its first performance in the Apollo Theatre in Rome, on the evening of January 19, 1853. Such an intense interest in the new Verdi opera had been aroused in advance that, although the weather was bitterly cold and, for some days preceding, the River Tiber had been at flood stage and had invaded the whole section of the city in and about the Apollo Theatre, so that water and mud were over all the streets, crowds stood in line from early morning until evening, the day of that first performance, to make sure of securing a seat. No opera ever became so popular as did "Il Trovatore," for it was soon being given all over Europe, sometimes at three opera houses in one city at the same time.

Music and Romance for Youth

Literary Sources

Years before Verdi wrote his colorful music, the main features of the story upon which the libretto of the opera was written were made into a drama, "El Trovador," or "The Troubadour of Aljaferia," by Antonio de la Vega, a Spanish dramatist. This was a tale of a border war in the fifteenth century. "Il Trovatore" is the Italian translation of the title.

Geographical and Historical Setting

The opening and closing scenes of "Il Trovatore" are laid in a quaint and historic castle which still stands, after nearly a thousand years of use, near one of the gateways of the old city of Saragossa (Zaragoza) in northern Spain. This old citadel is called the Aljaferia, and was originally built as a palace by the Moors. Late in the fifteenth century it was assigned by King Ferdinand and Queen Isabella to the Inquisition. Since that time it has been used for military purposes.

Saragossa was, in turn, the residence of the Moorish kings and the headquarters of the Aragonese court; and is now the capital of the province of Aragon. It is a very old city whose written history dates from 25 B.C., when it was made a colony by Augustus. It has been besieged by many heroes of history, including Charlemagne.

The Aljaferia stands just outside the Portillo Gate of the city, just a few yards along the Madrid highway.

Questions and Topics for Discussion

1. Locate the Spanish provinces of Aragon and Biscay on a map. Locate, also, the city of Saragossa.

2. Notice Verdi's very high art in closing this opera in the same setting as that in which it opened. Discuss the setting.

3. Discuss the art of the composer in making the old gypsy the real heroine of the opera, rather than the young and beautiful Leonora. How does he bring this to pass? When is Azucena first called to our attention, and by whom?

4. How does Verdi first suggest the military atmosphere which surrounds much of the opera?

5. What incident in the opera most strongly proves Manrico to be a true hero?

6. Which of the two men, Manrico or Count di Luna, do you most greatly admire? Why?

7. The music of the "Anvil Chorus" suggests a very vivid scene. Describe it in your own words.

8. What feeling does the singing of the "Misérere" and "Home to Our Mountains" arouse in you? For whom have you the greatest sympathy? Give a reason for your answer.

9. Name general characteristics of the early Italian operas.

10. Discuss Verdi's music. What are its greatest characteristics? Name other operas or famous arias by Verdi.

Library Reading. Read the story of Marie Agustin (known as the "Maid of Saragossa"), the historic defender of the city of Saragossa, as told by Byron in "Childe Harold." Pages 255-258, in "Spanish Sunshine," by Elsner. Pages 216-219, in "Spanish Towns and People," by McBride.

PART ONE—CHAPTER SIXTEEN

OUTSIDE STUDENT PROJECT

A program may be made up of musical numbers heard and studied during the semester, the selection and arrangement of which has been made by members of the class. This concert, the planning of which is a practical lesson in artistic program building, may be general in character, vocal or instrumental, seasonal, symphonic, formal, programmatic, or may stress nationality in music.

The numbers of the program may be selected by a committee of class members, under the guidance of the supervisor, or by popular vote of the entire membership. The arrangement of material should secure *unity* and *variety*, with compositions of like type or appeal grouped and with contrasting types used effectively to secure interest. Program notes on these numbers may be written as a correlated exercise in English. These should consist of short annotations or analyses of noteworthy details in the music, or facts about the composer. They should be in the student's own words and the result largely of his own experience, thought and research rather than mere copying of printed matter. Previous to the playing of each number a member of the class whose work has shown real thought and appreciation may be designated to read his program note on that particular composition. Throughout the program concert, habits of silent listening should be observed.

FAMOUS PRELUDES—VOCAL AND INSTRUMENTAL

What a Prelude Is. A Prelude is an introduction to something which is to follow. There are many words that are synonyms for the word prelude, as overture, preambule, or the Latin praeludium. Preludes have been used as "beginnings" for classic suites, for opera, for ballet, and as independent art works. They have been both vocal and instrumental.

The first real preludes came into being at the time of the composition of the first classic suites.

The Bach Preludes. It was between the end of the sixteenth and the first of the eighteenth centuries that the classic suite came into its own. During this time, when collections of dance tunes were often introduced by a prelude, it was often a simple movement in sonata form. A charming example of this is in the Bach "Partita in B-flat" in which the little set of pieces opens with a miniature prelude of the utmost delicacy and grace.

In his "Preludes and Fugues" from the "Well-Tempered Clavichord," the Prelude is often an irregular combination of arpeggios and scale passages, without having or following any definite form. It is, as the composer intended, a "starting piece." A familiar example of this is heard in the first of these Preludes (the one which Gounod used as the accompaniment for his "Ave Maria," some years later), in which the flowing arpeggios appear—

but which leave, in the ear of the listener, the clear suggestion of a simple melody:

Famous Preludes

Since the word overture is so easily interchangeable with the word prelude, it is interesting to note that almost every opera written opens with music intended to "set the scene." Such overtures are usually planned so as to include many of the prominent musical themes of the opera, and thus introduce them to the audience in advance of their appearance in connection with the action of the opera. Frequently it has happened that an opera overture became more popular than the opera itself, and was later played as an independent concert piece.

"The Hänsel and Gretel Overture," by Engelbert Humperdinck, very completely establishes the atmosphere, and sets the scene for the opera which is to follow, for in it are distinctly heard many of the important themes which add so greatly to the charm of this "fairy" opera.

The overture begins, without any introduction, with the melody of the "prayer theme" which is brought into each act of the opera to show that no harm will befall the children. It is here played by the horns.

Presently a second theme enters, the "hokus-pokus" theme (played by trumpet), which is the "magic" used to turn children into gingerbread.

That the antidote may also be at hand, Humperdinck has included the theme of the children who had been turned into a gingerbread fence by the wicked witch, but who have been disenchanted by Hänsel and Gretel.

A reference is made to the exquisite air sung by both the Sandman and the Dew Fairy.

The prelude closes with a slightly altered, but still easily recognized statement (horns) of the old German folk-song which Hänsel and Gretel sing as they go to sleep in the forest.

Overtures have often been written in strict sonata form, but many have been written in a free form, with more care given to the material and poetic content of the music.

"Magic Flute" Overture, by Mozart, is of this latter type. When Mozart was invited by Schikaneder, the author of the opera libretto, "The Magic Flute," to write the music for the opera, he replied: "But I have never written any magic music."

However, he became interested in the fanciful story of the magic pipes and set to work. He had many interruptions and so he was finally installed by Schikaneder in a tiny garden house or pavilion not far from the theatre, where he worked, surrounded by members of the opera cast and a few other friends. The opera was to be presented on September 30th, and on the morning of the 28th the overture was not yet written. But when evening came it was completed, one of the most enchanting bits of fairy music ever written.

The overture is unique in many ways. Contrary to custom, Mozart used in it only one thing which appears in the opera, this being a series of three magic chords, played very loudly by the full orchestra immediately following the very slow introduction. These are, it is suggested, the magical formulæ which open the gates to fairyland. The overture is also unique in that it is written in fugal form, one piece following another into the music as do singers in a round. The first announcement of the fugue's theme is by the clarinets, followed a few bars later by the cornets. These are followed in turn by every instrument, in the brilliant finale.

Throughout the fugue Mozart plays with voices as though they were a part of some happy game. In about the middle of the overture the three magic chords suddenly sound again.

Famous Preludes

The "Magic Flute" overture, which is one of the greatest of its kind, soon began to be played in concert as an independent piece, and won the regard of other composers to such an extent that they tried to copy its style and form.

GARDEN HOUSE IN WHICH MOZART WROTE "THE MAGIC FLUTE"   Galloway

An Overture for Ballet. The "Overture Miniature" with which Tschaikowsky sets the scene of his delightful Christmas ballet, the "Nutcracker," is a prelude in miniature. The dainty voices of flutes and violins carry the greater part of the melody. There is, in the middle section, a flurrying as though in anticipation of the many strange things which are to occur during the progress of the ballet itself.

Preludes As Art Works. The Preludes of Chopin * are a series of short suggestive and imaginative pieces which do not follow any set form. They bear no individual titles, but each is a bit of *Absolute* music. Each has a certain character, some being dramatic, others idyllic, and one or two suggesting an element of tragedy or melancholy. Of this latter type is the "Prelude in D Flat"—very often called the "Raindrop" Prelude.

The Chopin "Prelude," Opus 28, No. 15—not a prelude in a "formal" sense—best known by its acquired title of "Raindrop Pre-

---

* The late Henry T. Finck, a noted music critic, once said: "If all pianoforte music in the world were to be destroyed excepting one collection, my vote would be cast for the Chopin Preludes."

lude,'' is notable for an exquisitely singing melody, and for the persistent sounding of the *A*-flat in its accompaniment. This *A*-flat continues through the entire short composition, at times seeming to be a part of the regular harmony of the music, but becoming ominous, at last, in its relentless repetition. This Prelude may be thought of as being in three parts with a tiny *Coda*.

Tradition tells that Chopin, who was, at the time of its writing, on an island in the Mediterranean Sea, imitated, in its constantly and softly monotonous repeated notes, the falling of the raindrops as he heard them dropping from the eaves outside the house. If this be true, the composition should be classed as program music.

LAWRENCE TIBBETT AS TONIO IN "PAGLIACCI"

Vocal Preludes are written to be sung rather than played by instruments.

''Prologue'' (another synonym for prelude) from ''I Pagliacci,'' by Leoncavallo, is one of the most remarkable as well as most popular preludes ever written. It is a reversion to the type of the ancient prologues of the early Greek tragedies, in which one of the actors always came before the audience, preceding the opening of the play, to explain to them his sentiments.

In this short and realistic opera there is, on the stage, a play within a play, the principal characters being a wandering troupe of Italian players. The most famous aria of the opera is the famous ''Prologue'' in which Tonio, a clown, puts his head through the curtain before it rises and, in song, tells the audience with both humor and pathos, that clowns are ''as other men,'' and that they suffer as do other men.

The orchestra begins a spirited Introduction, the first two-measure statement being answered by a correspondingly brief passage from piccolo and flutes. Statement and answer are repeated in a transposed key, after which a rush of notes ushers in a song-like air. The first introductory phrase is again repeated immediately before the appearance of Tonio, who thrusts his head through the curtain, and, in a *recitative style,* sings:

> "A word allow me!
> Sweet Ladies and Gentlemen,
> I pray you, hear
> Why alone I appear . . .
> I am the Prologue."

He then *speaks* to the audience, while at the same time the solo 'cello plays a tender *obbligato* above a *pianissimo* orchestral accompaniment.   Tonio presently takes up the melody from the 'cello and sings his famous dramatic aria to its end, when, after another short *recitative,** and with a dash of artificial gayety, he turns and calls for the curtain with the words, "Come on! Ring up the curtain!" The curtain then rises upon the first act, disclosing a scene which is a stage-picture of a Sicilian village, where a traveling circus has just set up its tent, and the actors, in a donkey-cart—with Canio beating the drum—are just entering.

Since the advent of this Prologue many modern operas have employed a vocal prelude.

"Siciliana," from "Cavalleria Rusticana," by Mascagni, is another illustration of this, in which, back of the closed curtain (following a few brief measures that are

PIETRO MASCAGNI

played by the orchestra to set the atmosphere), Turiddu—one of the principal characters—sings a tender song disclosing his love for Lola. "Siciliana" differs from the "Pagliacci" Prologue in that it is sung entirely behind the curtain, and thus loses some of its dramatic force. The orchestra opens *pianissimo* and in three short pages of music the Preludio changes its *tempo* and general style, six times. Two measures of arpeggiated chords from the harps signal the beginning of Turiddu's *aria,* in which, in a typically Italian operatic melody, he sings the "key song" of the opera, placed on or near one high tone for many consecutive measures.

The Prelude or Overture As a Formal Concert Number. Very often a composition is written in the style of the prelude or overture, but not to introduce any particular opera.   In this type the

* A recitative is a vocal composition written to be performed in a declamatory style.

composer merely makes use of the form of the prelude to present his ideas in a concert number.

"Carneval Overture," by Dvořák, entitled by the composer and so announced at its first performance in Prague, "Bohemian Carneval," is narrative in style. It suggests three distinct moods— lively humor, pathos and pastoral simplicity—each of which is represented by a highly individual theme, and by a particularly appropriate choice of instruments.

It opens (*A* Major, *C, Allegro*) with full orchestra, the first four-measure theme "setting the scene" for the jolly, boisterous Old World carnival.

The theme is immediately repeated (in the key of *E*) by the first violins over a sprightly accompaniment of all other strings (*pizzicato*) and of trills and embellishments from flutes, oboes, clarinets and bassoons. A second repetition, which brings the first "big part" to a stirring climax, is played full orchestra, *fortissimo,* the theme being heard in unison from nearly all members of string, woodwind, and brass choirs, and being embellished by a brilliant accompaniment from the percussion instruments.

The sharply contrasted second theme, played by solo oboe, suggests, in its moving simplicity, the tender pathos which is so frequently an attribute of the folk character.

This theme is developed briefly, after which the music moves gently into a mood of pastoral charm and serenity. Here (Key of *G* Major, 3/8, *andantino con moto*) are alterations in tonality, time and tempo, and in the personality of the instruments playing the prominent parts. The chief melody of this brief section (theme three of the "Carneval") is first played by solo English horn, then by flute.

It is accompanied by muted strings.

This lyric melody is followed by a return to the spirited melody, rhythm, tempo and mood of the first section, in the original key of *A*. The carnival gayety of the Slavonic merry-makers is brought to a tremendous closing climax by vivid *crescendos* and acceleration of *tempo*.

"Praeludium," by Järnefelt. Of all the music written by this composer none is so happy or so gay as this, written to be played as a concert number by a symphony orchestra.

ARMAS JÄRNEFELT

This short composition is built upon folk-dance tunes of the Finnish peasants. It begins with an odd pattern of notes that is played over and over by the 'cellos, and which, because it continually goes on "keeping time" in the bass, is called *basso ostinato*. This is one way of saying that it is an obstinate bass, which does not change for anything. The little tune is not played with the bow, but is plucked from the strings by the players. It is heard four times before the real melody begins, making everyone who hears it want to take part in the dance. Here is the dance tune.

After this has been played, the jolly melody, with its little scale runs, begins.

After the first two tunes—the *basso ostinato* and this folk-dance melody—a third tune is heard. This new melody is a slow, soft and tender air, played by the French horn in the orchestra.

Then the *basso ostinato* returns, leading the way back into the tripping dance melody. At the end of the "Praeludium" the dancers seem to stop singing, and only the sound of their feet is heard as they keep time to the first little bass tune.

This quaint tune is played over and over, up from the deepest bass to the high treble. Each choir in the orchestra plays it in turn, and as the string choir finishes the dainty playing of it, the composition comes to a sudden end.

Music and Romance for Youth

INFORMATIONAL NOTES

The "Hänsel and Gretel" opera libretto is based entirely upon an old folk-legend of the German Black Forest. The music of the opera was written by Humperdinck, bit by bit, for the amusement of his own children and that of his sister. It was this sister who arranged the words of the folk-tale so that they might be set to music.

"Cavalleria Rusticana" was written as an offering for a competition in which a prize was offered by an Italian publishing house for the three best one-act operas submitted. The winning opera was to be produced in Rome, free of expense. Mascagni saw the notice of the prize offering in a newspaper, and hurriedly wrote his friends for libretto. This came in piecemeal, sometimes a few lines appearing on a postal card which came in his morning mail. The work was completed scene by scene—some say, in eight days—only to be thrown away at its completion by the dissatisfied composer. His wife rescued the manuscript from the fire and sent it to the judges, receiving in return shortly, a telegram of congratulation. The first performance took place about two months later, on May 17, 1890, and roused the audience present to a frenzy of enthusiasm. The composer was called before the curtain twenty times, and was honored in every way by his home town, of which he was made an honorary citizen, and by the King of Italy, who made him Chevalier of Honor of the Crown of Italy.

The scenes of the opera are laid in a Sicilian village. Sicily is the largest and most populous island in the Mediterranean, is a part of Italy, and is separated from it by the Strait of Messina, a channel of water about two miles wide. The opening prelude, "Siciliana," takes its name from the old country dance of the peasants of Sicily, which is set to a smooth, flowing melody of much grace, resembling a *pastorale*.

"I Pagliacci" had its first performance at Teatro dal Verme,

Milan, May 21, 1892. The libretto is founded upon a real happening in an Italian village, an incident which had been tried in his father's court. The opera is in two acts and because of its shortness, is often combined with "Cavalleria Rusticana," by Mascagni, to make a full evening's entertainment. The first American performance of the opera was in New York City on June 15, 1894.

The "Carneval Overture," by Dvořák, is one of three large works written by the composer during his summer holiday, in 1891. It had its first performance in Prague on April 28, 1892, at an elaborate farewell concert given by musicians of that city in honor of Dvořák before his departure to America, where he was to teach in New York City for a term of years. Dvořák conducted the overture himself, as he did again in the autumn of the same year, when the brilliant work had its first American hearing at Carnegie Hall, New York City. The composition is dedicated to Prague University.

The overture, when contrasted with Dvořák's "New World Symphony," furnishes an interesting contrast of moods in the works of a single composer. The symphony contains melodies which have a sad and serious character, melodies which are beautiful but with an undertone of heartache in their beauty. In the Carneval overture, however, the complete colorful picture of a festival of country life is portrayed, with all its extremes of pleasure and gayety.

Questions and Topics for Discussion

1. What is a *prelude*? Name several synonyms for this musical term, and a composer who has written an example of each.

2. What is a *fugue*? How may it sometimes differ from a *canon*?

3. Discuss the appeal of the Mozart "Magic Flute Overture." By what musical means has the composer achieved his "fairy-like" effects? What and where are the "magic chords"? Is this Absolute or Program music?

4. Reread the story of the "Nutcracker" music. How does this exquisite "Overture Miniature" prepare the listener for the musical delights which are to follow?

5. What is the form of the Chopin "Raindrop" Prelude? Is this Absolute or Program music? If Program, is it imitative, descriptive, narrative or impressionistic?

6. Contrast the two vocal preludes suggested in this chapter. Which is the more dramatic? Why? Give at least three reasons. What is a *recitative*? How does it often add reality and dramatic fervor to an aria?

7. Contrast the three principal themes of the *Carneval* Overture. How has Dvořák intensified the mood of each theme by his choice of instrumentation? What is meant by "personality of instruments"?

8. What is meant by *basso ostinato*? How has Järnefelt made use of this type of musical figure to suggest the tireless repetition and charming monotony of a folk-dance? How many times is the figure repeated? Discuss the structure of the "Praeludium." Try to hear each of the three themes mentioned in the chapter.

9. Contrast the Bach "Prelude in C" from the "Well Tempered Clavichord" and the Järnefelt Praeludium. Which is more suggestive of the life of a people? Why? Which is more "atmospheric"? What musical means are employed to make it so?

10. What preludes suggested in this chapter show influence of national folk-music?

11. What is your favorite among the preludes suggested in the chapter? Tell why.

Library Reading. "Hänsel and Gretel," Music Appreciation Reader, Book IV, pages 15-30, Kinscella; "Chopin and Other Musical Essays," by Henry T. Finck.

PART TWO—CHAPTER TWO

MUSIC OF THE ORIENT

The Great Antiquity of Oriental Music. In listening to true music of the Orient the music of today seems left behind, for little has been changed for a thousand years or more. The same odd scales, weird, fantastic melodies, and driving, resistless rhythms as were played in the days before Abraham or before Marco Polo's romantic journey to the Far East, may still be heard.

Much more may be known regarding the songs and dances of the Orient or of its many musical instruments than concerning those who wrote the music.

Early Types of Musical Instruments. In all Oriental countries three types of primitive musical instruments are used—stringed, wind, and percussion instruments. The percussion group is, in turn, divided into two types—instruments with vibrating membranes, as drums; and instruments made of sonorous substances, such as bells, gongs or "stones."

Character of Oriental Scales. The Orientals have as many as fourteen scales or modes, in which the half steps are arranged or changed in order in as many ways, thus producing frequently weird and primitive effects.

These, with the five-toned and the whole-tone scales, offer much variety. In an Oriental scale a common feature is the absence of the seventh or leading tone, of the scale.

Oriental Embellishments. An Oriental characteristic easily recognized is the constant use of embellishments. If an Arab is singing a song, and accompanying it with an instrument, he will usually improvise, at the close of each verse, a series of flourishes (*ritornello*), and will, at the same time, embellish the accompaniment with all the profusion of *pizzicato* grace notes, turns, and mordents of which he is capable.

Chinese Music and Musical Instruments. Chinese music is so old that its beginnings are lost in mystery. Many of the enchanting legends of China (including fanciful tales of magical flutes, and of birds with miraculous songs) contain references to music and musical instruments, and these were told and sung a thousand years ago by the native minstrels who wandered from village to village in China. Long before any other nation had done so, China had invented a system of octaves and scales in which tones and half-tones were used.

The Chinese still classify their instruments according to various sounds of nature, these including Sound of Skin (drums and like instruments of percussion); Sound of Metal (gongs, cymbals, bells and brass horns); Sound of Silk (lutes, guitars, violins and similar stringed instruments); Sound of Wood (xylophone and castanets); and Sound of Bamboo (flute, clarinet and other wind instruments).

The Chinese form of oboe is one of the most popular of instruments in the Far East. It consists of a wooden pipe with a copper bell, and, of course, a double-beating reed. When it is heard in the morning, it is supposed to announce a funeral; in the afternoon, a wedding; but usually it plays all day anyway. It is not fitted with keys, but has seven holes on the upper side for the fingers and one underneath for the thumb. Its tone is, to Western ears, harsh, high and shrill.

JAPANESE GIRL PLAYING THE SAMISEN

Although many Chinese musicians use a scale divided into twelve half-tones (like our Chromatic scale, *C, C*-sharp, *D, D*-sharp, *E, F, F*-sharp, *G, G*-sharp, *A, A*-sharp, *B, C*), the oldest scale used was the pentatonic or five-tone scale.

Japanese Music and Instruments. The musical traditions of Japan, like those of China, are very old, but differ from those of other Oriental countries as much as do the music of Japan and of America. In fact there are many Japanese scales which are not un-pleasant to Western ears, and in balance and design of composition there is a marked similarity to Occidental music. Many, if not all, Japanese instruments are very like those of China.

STREET ENTERTAINERS IN JAPAN USING MOON GUITAR

The Koto is probably the most popular instrument of Japan. It consists of a long, narrow sounding board over which are strung thirteen strings of even length, made of tightly twisted silk soaked in wax. It is tuned by means of movable bridges under each string. When played, the Koto is laid upon the ground, the player squatting near the upper end of it and plucking the strings by means of ivory finger pieces. The tone is gentle and pleasing.

The Samisen, another favorite instrument, is built on the principle of the lute. It has a hollowed out body over which is stretched snake or cat skin. There are three strings which are tuned to correspond with those of the Koto.

In Primitive Java the natives play upon strange tom-toms, bamboo flutes and curious little two-stringed instruments made from gourds with strings stretched across the opening. Some of the folk-melodies of Java are very lovely.

Music of India. In India music has always played an important part in all games, and in the ritualistic ceremonies of worship. In ancient days music was used by the natives of India to assist them in their pleas for rain and for a bountiful harvest, and to this day

JAPANESE TEMPLE GONG

seasonal songs are heard all over India in connection with any kind of agricultural work.

There is the "Ploughman's Song," sung in the fields, the workers being often urged on by special singers who accompany their singing by beating on long, narrow Indian drums or on little metal castanets. The "Wellman's Song," sung to the oxen which tramp back and forth to help the laborer draw up from the crude well the skins of water which he uses for irrigation, and the "Rice Song," are both "working songs," in that all the laborers move together on the accented syllables of the words.

A STREET BAND IN INDIA

There is, in India, an absence of harmony such as that of Western music, much use of unfamiliar scales, and therefore much use of strange Oriental melody. Most Indian folk-music is also embellished with a profusion of grace notes.

Stringed, wind, and percussion instruments have been in use in India since almost prehistoric days. The drummers, who attain to a marvelous facility in playing—with palms of their hands, not with sticks—their long narrow drums, seek for unique rhythmic independence of both hands. Trumpets six and seven feet long are often made from the stems of plants, and flutes are made from bamboo. Wooden tambourines are made of native wood and goatskin, with small jingles or clappers of wood set loosely in the frame.

The Native Musical Instruments of Arabia and Persia. Persian and Arabian music fills in the period between those early ancient musical forms and the medieval days of music, when these near neighbors contributed so greatly to the music-life of Europe through the instruments, songs, scales, and other musical characteristics taken home to Europe by the returning Crusaders.

Present-day Arabian music is almost exactly the same as that of the Middle Ages. First in importance among native Arabian musical instruments is the rhythmic drum, which may be either square or round. The usual orchestra is one in which all the musicians play in unison on drums of various sizes, a sort of rhythmic harmony. In a military band the melody is played in unison, with rhythmic accompaniment for big drum and many side drums.

The most popular instrument is the Oud or Oboe, which is often only a reed having three holes in it. A favorite instrument is a form of violin, in which the box—shaped like a mandolin and having from one to four strings—is held on the knee.

Influence of Primitive Oriental Music Upon Occidental Music.

In no land do the characteristics of folk-music exert so powerful an influence upon the composed music, as in that vast expanse known, in general terms, as the Orient. Because of lack of conventional training among musicians of the Orient in general, much of the present-day so-called Oriental music is written by composers of other nations, especially those of Old Russia, a nation close to the Orient in both location and musical atmosphere.

THE SARUNGI, A HINDU VIOL

"Danse Orientale"— Alexander Glazounow. No Russian composer has written music more typical of the Orient than Glazounow, who, in this brief orchestral number suggests a fantastic Arabian dance. The composition opens with a four-measure rhythmic introduction from the drums, and in the melody is heard, at once, an echo of Oriental phrasing and scale, and a primitive downward motion of the theme. The drums are constantly sounded as in a native orchestra, and alternation between three-, then four-beat rhythms produces a singularly irregular and fantastic effect.

The second theme equals the first in Oriental color and makes subtle use of Oriental minor and the whole tone scales. The music is at first faint and distant, and then fiercely barbaric in effect.

"Melodie Arabe," by Glazounow, transcribed for violin by Paul Kochowski. This short, but vividly suggestive, number opens (*Vivo*) with a cadenza-like violin introduction in which primitive bagpipe effects are accomplished through double-stopping and *pizzicato*. The sonorous melody which follows (*andantino*) is in minor mode, within the narrow range of a fifth, and is Oriental in all its characteristics. It is accompanied by simple harp-like chords. Following a two-measure piano interlude, the violin takes up a more passionate air, in which emotional appeal is made through the composer's continuous use of chromatics. A return to the lively strains of the introductory passage serves as a *coda*.

"Orientale," by César Cui, number nine from the "Kaleidoscope" (a set of twenty-four pieces for violin), is a distinctly original composition with strong Eastern flavor. Muted violin and monotonous Oriental rhythm give the melody a mysterious charm, while the piano accompaniment adds odd intervals which subtly suggest the tinkling of camel bells in the desert.

"Song of India," by Rimsky-Korsakow. This popular *aria*, better known as an instrumental concert number than as an *aria* in an opera, is, nevertheless, an important song in the mythological opera "Sadko," in which the God of the Sea heaps riches upon Sadko, the hero, in return for his gift of music. Sadko, who becomes a wealthy merchant, invites his merchant visitors from foreign countries to tell him of their homelands, in song. "The Song of India" is the *aria* sung by the Indian merchant visitor. In use of intervals from the whole-tone scale, subtle harmonies, poetic mood, and Oriental atmosphere, the song is unequaled.

"Tambourin Chinois," by Fritz Kreisler, is an attractively characteristic, Oriental composition. Its first theme makes frequent use of monotonous rhythms, of the whole-tone scale, of abrupt modulations in both single and double notes, of sequential progression, high delicate harmonics, and dazzlingly brilliant velocity.

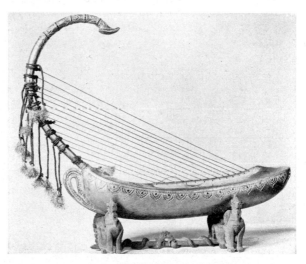

A SONNG THIRTEEN-STRINGED HARP OF BURMA

The second and middle section of the composition is Viennese, rather than Oriental, in style.

The first theme is repeated exactly as first given out. The form of the composition is *A B A*.

"The Nightingale" (Le Rossignol), by Igor Strawinsky, is a vivid opera-ballet in which the charming Chinese legend * of the Emperor and the Nightingale is retold in appropriate music. The legend tells of a Nightingale, which, after being invited to the Palace to sing for the Emperor, is lured into a cage. It finally escapes and returns to the Fisherman, to whom it talks of its adventures in the Palace.

Meanwhile the Emperor falls ill, and a mechanical bird is brought to sing for him, but without any helpful influence upon the Emperor's health.

---

* This legend has also been retold by Hans Christian Andersen.

Presently the real Nightingale learns of the Emperor's trouble, and reaches the window ledge of his room just in time to drive Death away. Then it sings, and its sweet song revives the failing monarch so that when his courtiers come, next morning, to mourn his death, he greets them with a happy "Good Morning!"

In his orchestral music for the ballet, Strawinsky has made use of every device and characteristic of Oriental—and especially Chinese —primitive music that good taste will permit. Strikingly effective numbers are the "Chinese March," the "Nightingale's Song" (always sung by an unseen soprano from the orchestra pit when the work is given as an opera), and the humorous "Funeral March."

"Chinese March" is written almost entirely in the five-toned scale, and is both fanciful and grotesque in its *fortissimo* pomposity at the moment at which the Emperor arrives upon the scene. A *staccato* ascending and descending passage, carried by two bassoons and ornamented by weird harmonics from the solo violin, introduces the Nightingale.

"Song of the Nightingale." This gentle bird is impersonated by the silvery-toned flute. A delicate *cadenza* (the Nightingale's song) is first heard, and then an enchanting melody from flute, clarinet, and solo violin, while harp, piano, and celeste furnish an atmospheric background.

The music changes to a tiny *presto* fanfare from the trumpets, announcing the envoy with the mechanical bird. After a dramatic pause in the music, the bird begins to *whirr* and sing (piccolo, flute, and oboe).

Next, the "Song of the Fisherman" (to whom the real bird returns) and the short musical dialogue between Death and the Nightingale are heard.

"Funeral March" is a masterpiece of Oriental humor. *Glissando* passages from muted trombone, harps, and strings usher in the dutifully mournful but entirely mistaken courtiers. A sudden chord, *sforzando,* and a dashing upward-moving *glissando* from the harp break into the mournful march melody as the Emperor says "Good Morning!"

The work closes with a reminiscence of the Fisherman's Song.

"Bacchanale," from "Samson and Delila," by Saint-Saëns, is a brilliantly composed and orchestrated Oriental dance which occurs during the second scene of the last act of this Biblical opera. The music is the accompaniment to the barbaric dance of Delila and her attendants.

The magnificent music is gorgeous in its Oriental flavor. As the dance progresses, the music becomes more aggressively primitive. Soft, but unceasing, beating of drums, use of whole-tone scale, themes of Oriental type played by oboe and English horn, and glittering rhythms sounded by the tambourine and castanets, contribute to the spectacular effect.

MUSICAL ILLUSTRATIONS

50170	*Samisen and Flute Duet (Japanese)*	
42480	*Chinese Orchestra (Bells, Gongs, Flutes)*	
P5865	*Flute Solo (Hindoo)*	
73466	*Oud Solo (Arabian)*	
50279	*Dojoji (Japanese) (Vocal solo with piano, two samisens and tomtoms)*	
50314	*Yasugibushi (Japanese) (Vocal solo with two samisens, flute, koto and tomtom)*	
1335	*Danse Orientale (Alexander Glazounow)*	*Stokowski and Phila. Sym. Or.*
1354	*Orientale (César Cui)*	*Elman*
45531	*Song of India (Rimsky-Korsakow)*	*Ganz and St. Louis Sym. Orch.*
6844	*Tambourin Chinois (Fritz Kreisler)*	*Kreisler*

*   { *March Chinese*
        Song of the Nightingale   } *from "The Nightingale" (Strawinsky)*
        Funeral March

6823   *Bacchanale from "Samson and Delila" (Saint-Saëns)*
                  Stokowski and Philadelphia Symphony Orchestra

(Hear also "Danse Arabe" and "Danse Chinois" from the "Nutcracker Suite," by Tschaikowsky; "Arabian Dance" from Second "Peer Gynt" Suite, by Grieg; and "Scheherazade," by Rimsky-Korsakow; mentioned in other chapters.)

INFORMATIONAL NOTES

The Koto is the national musical instrument of Japan. While the instrument of today has been much improved by the development of many years, the form of the Koto has always been the same, and is said to represent the dragon, symbolical, to the Japanese, of all that is noble. The length of the instrument is a little more than six feet.

There are heard, in Chinese temples, choirs of instruments which include brass cymbals, wooden blocks for pounding, a small brass bell with a jade hammer, and some parchment-covered drums. In some temples there may be seen and heard old-time lyres and silken-stringed lutes.

The Arabian oud was an instrument introduced into Europe by the Crusaders, and there developed into the lute, the ancestor of the modern guitar and mandolin. Various forms of this instrument were carried by armies into all parts of Europe. The popularity of the lute declined with the advent of the violin, and passed altogether with the introduction of the pianoforte.

A primitive form of the harp is used in Arabia frequently, but in an exaggerated size. It has, sometimes, as many as seventy-five strings, but is of light weight because of having been made of dried skin stretched over a harmonic box. The instrument is laid across the knees of the player, who uses either quills or his fingers in playing the strings.

"The Nightingale," by Strawinsky, which had its first performance in London, June 25, 1914, was at first a symphonic poem. Arranged by the composer as a ballet (the work was really started in 1909), it had its first performance in this form in 1921. The music moves along in continuous episodes. This is but one of the many effective dramatic musical works which have had their source in the literature of the Orient. Another, "Turandot," by Puccini, which had its beginnings in the Arabian Nights tales, was not produced until after the death of the composer.

QUESTIONS AND TOPICS FOR DISCUSSION

1. Name and discuss three characteristic scales commonly heard in Oriental music. Suggest a composition which is based upon each. How does the use of a certain scale affect the atmosphere of a composition?

2. Compare the musical instruments used by natives of the Orient with the tribal instruments of the American Indian. How do the scales used by the two races compare?

3. Which is more colorful in atmosphere—the native music of Arabs and Persians, or that of China and Japan? Give reasons for your decision.

4. What primitive instruments of the Orient are now used regularly in a modern symphony orchestra?

5. What musical devices has the composer used to produce the Oriental atmosphere so vividly suggested in "Melodie Araba"?

6. How has Strawinsky made use of appropriate instruments to help tell the fanciful story of the Emperor and the Nightingale? Contrast the "Danse Chinois" of the "Nutcracker Suite" and the "Tambourin Chinois," by Kreisler. What similar musical devices have both composers used to suggest this Oriental land? What European country most closely resembles the music of the Orient in its composed music? Give reasons for this. How may the native rhythms, melodic characteristics, and musical instruments of the Orient be said to have exerted a powerful influence upon our modern symphonic music? Give instances.

NATIONALITY IN FOLK AND ART MUSIC—SPAIN

Origins of Spanish Folk-Music. A story of music in Spain and a story of Spain itself are much the same thing, for the history of this interesting country and that of its music are one. Each invader who marched into Spain during the centuries brought his own land's music with him, and, whether he himself stayed for a long time or not, left a trace of his music's characteristic style behind him.

So, in the music of Spain—or in the scales and modes it employs—are found traces of the Iberians, of the Celts, a reminder of the coming of the Greeks and the Phœnicians, the invasion of the barbarians, the descent of the Visigoths, the conquest of the Romans, and later of the Arabs, who came over into Spain from their native land by way of Morocco in Africa.

In no country of the Old World is music more a part of the daily life of the people than in Spain, and of all the outside influences which have come to it, none is more distinctly heard and felt today than that of the Moors—a word used to indicate the Arabians.

The Moorish Influence on Spanish Music. More than twelve hundred years ago the Moors added Spain to their long line of conquests, and immediately, upon their coming, the whole country took on a new and better life. This was true in regard to literature, science, engineering skill, road making, general life of the people, and all the fine arts.

Moorish influence in architecture is still to be seen in Spain, and is most noticeable in the rare and intricate arabesques (a word which suggests exquisite embellishments and decorations "like those of the Arabs") which adorn such old Moorish palaces as the Alhambra at Granada. The same influence in music expresses itself through the use of Oriental scales (*as A, B, C, D-sharp, E, F, G-sharp, A*); picturesque Oriental rhythms; and endless arabesques.

It is the music most Moorish in type which is generally spoken of in discussing Spanish music. This really "Spanish" type is that which comes from the province of Andalusia, the portion of Spain first settled by the invading Moors.

The Four Main Divisions of Spanish Music. The folk-music of Spain easily divides into four distinct groups, although it is sometimes said that there is a different music for each Spanish province. This is because each province still retains its own certain customs, costumes, and dances.

In the south (including Andalusia), the folk-songs and dances are influenced not only by the Moors, but by the gypsy musicians of past days. The guitar is a popular instrument, and the most popular dances are the *fandango* and the *malagueña*.

In the Basque country to the north, is found the music of Biscay and Navarre, very irregular in rhythm and melody. The *jota** is the characteristic dance of these provinces and of Aragon and Valencia as well. It is usually in three-beat measure and is sung, as well as danced, in the old twelfth-century style, at all merry-makings, weddings, and festival days.

Still another division of the Spanish folk-music is that heard in the provinces of Castile and Galicia. This is very bright and gay, and has strongly marked rhythms in its dances, the *bolero* and the *seguidilla*.

The fourth type is that heard in Catalonia, where the influence of the French Troubadours is plainly felt. A folk-dance found nowhere else in the world, save in Catalonia, is the *sardaña*, a polite and extremely refined step, danced to almost savage, barbaric music which is usually played upon a primitive kind of wind instrument.

There are, besides, quaint working songs, common to all Spain, as, for example, the weird "Date-Pickers' Song" sung by the men who work at the top of the date-palms in certain sections and lighten their labors by the rather monotonous singing.

A dance common to all Spain (also danced in the revivals of folk-dance in England) is the *Morisco*, a Moorish dance. In early days this was done as a burlesque. Some of the dancers would be costumed as Buffoons, riding "stick-horses" (suggesting knightly tournaments), while others, equipped with swords, and with bells jingling merrily from their arms and legs, would move about in step to the music.

Still another dance, native of Madrid, is the *pasodoble,* a kind of quick-step, still often played when the toreadors enter the arena for a bull-fight and sometimes continued throughout the fight itself.

The Art-Music of Spain. The art or composed music of Spain is a direct outgrowth of that country's folk-music. Many Spanish musicians have been wise enough to appreciate the worth of their own folk-melodies and to use them, or their characteristics, in their compositions.

Among the most eminent Spanish composers whose works reflect these national characteristics is Pablo Sarasate.

"Zapateado," Opus 23, No. 6, by Sarasate, displays the possibili-

---

* A Moor whose name was Aben Jot is given the credit of being the originator of this dance. The *jota* is something like a waltz, with more picturesque freedom of movement, and with much more fire.

ties of brilliant violin technic as well as presenting a jolly "Shoe-maker's Dance."

The introduction is shared by the piano—which here sounds like a gypsy cembalom *—and the violin, which plays both in octaves and harmonics. The rapid three-beat dance theme (in major key), twice heard, is notable for much syncopation and use of simple rhythmic embellishments. A second theme is presented and repeated, in slightly varied version, with harmonics. Transition is made to the Trio, in which should be noticed contrasting use made of major and minor modes; and by the violinist of double-note passages, plucked chords, *pizzicato*, delicate shadings of tone, and harmonics. A return to the theme, mood, and style of the opening passages precedes the brief *pizzicato Coda*.

PABLO SARASATE

A modern Spanish composer whose writings reflect the influence of the folk-music of his land is Manual de Falla.

The "Jota" for voice and orchestra, by de Falla, is the fourth of a series of "Seven Popular Spanish Songs." It combines song and dance as does the traditional *jota,* and is notable as an art work which incorporates within it many of the characteristic features of the old Spanish folk-dance of the same name.

The de Falla "Jota" begins with plucked violin—a suggestion of a Spanish guitar. The rhythm is distinctly Spanish. The rather long dance prelude in three-beat measure presents a typically Spanish melody which is repeated with simple variations, as two or three different individuals will often vary the air or rhythm of a folk-song in singing or playing it. The voice part which now enters with a slower, more flowing melody, contains the peculiarly uneven rhythms of the dance.

Presently the first theme (orchestra) and the second (voice) are combined, then followed by an orchestral interlude (built on the first theme), a repetition of the song, a short interlude, and a vocal *Coda* in which the flute echoes the voice.

"Tango" in *D,* by Albeniz. The music of this Spanish composer makes free use of old national rhythms and of the atmosphere of Spanish folk-song. For this reason it makes an insistent appeal to the senses. This short and graceful composition is built upon the Habanera rhythm (2/4 | ♩. ♫ | ♩. ♫ |) and is much ornamented, through use of

---

* A cembalom is a series of wires strung above a sounding board, their tone being produced by the performer striking them with padded hammers. The cembalom is a popular instrument in Hungary.

single and double grace-notes, and mordents. The very effective melody is at once suave, simple, and elegant.

The composition closes, as it began, with a series of rhythmic chords.

"Sierra Morena" (Serenata Andaluza), by Monasterio, is, as its name suggests, written in the prevailing style and rhythm of a typical Andalusian folk-air. Written for violin solo, it displays the use of the mellow and sonorous *G* string in the main melody, and such embellishments as mordents, trills, and turns. Brilliant double-note passages (double stopping) in the central melody preface the return to the first theme and its pulsating rhythm. The piece ends in a swift but emotional manner, on the *G* string.

The "Theme and Variations," by Sor, is written for guitar, the popular household instrument of Spain. The composition is not only a clever set of variations written in formal style, but also displays to good advantage the possibilities of the guitar in the hands of a Spanish master.

"Spanish Dance," No. 2 (Andalouse), by Enrique Granados. This idealization of a quaint melody from the south of Spain (as the subtitle of the composition indicates) is notable for the insistent pedal-point, or *basso ostinato*, of the accompaniment. Written originally as a piano solo, new and delightful national characteristics are added by the orchestral transcription. The melody is introduced by a weird rhythmic introduction in which constant use is made of *pizzicato* and *basso ostinato*. Throughout, the air alternates between minor and parallel major tonalities. A short poetic section in the middle of the piece is given a spiritual quality by being played slowly and in a hymn-like manner, by the strings, solo voices being taken in turn by violin and oboe.

Galloway

SPANISH FOLK DANCERS—
GRANADA

This section is followed by an immediate return to the first melody, heard in minor, major, then minor modes. The composition ends with a brief *codetta* in the major key.

"Spanish Dance," No. 3 (Rondalla Aragonesa), opens in a lively manner, with a theme very simple and monotonous in character. It develops rapidly to a climax, after which there enters, immediately, an exquisite, plaintive air. This haunting melody reflects the picturesque characteristics of the music of the Orient. Phrase endings are here emphasized by sparkling passages from the castanets. The air develops, presently—although with no change of *tempo*—to a passionate utterance. A roll of drums precedes the entrance of the earlier theme. This is taken up by various groups of instruments, and rises in pitch, and increases in dynamic intensity and velocity. A *codetta,* dominated by extreme velocity, swirling *glissando,* and crashing chords, brings this unusual composition to a close.

THE PAINTING "DUCHESS OF ALBA," INSPIRATION OF "GOYESCAS"

"Goyescas," a truly Spanish opera from the pen of Enrique Granados, is based upon two suites of piano solos, written by the same composer, in which he sketched, in music, the life of early nineteenth-century Madrid. The piano solos were inspired by famous Spanish paintings of Francesco Goya. The opera, which was developed from the suites, is a colorful work rich in Spanish atmosphere. The Moorish influence is noticeable in all the music.

The "Intermezzo" from the opera is written in the style of a polished *minuetto,* suggesting more the elegant airs and dances of nearby Provence or Southern France than the Oriental or Asiatic influences which are strong in so much Spanish music. Features of the music are the constant syncopation of the melody and the slightly Oriental influence in the intervals upon which the melody is built. The opening measures of the "Intermezzo" are played *pianissimo* by multiple quartets made up of strings of the orchestra. The first theme, after its first statement, is repeated with new harmonies and with the bassoon in a running accompaniment. Alluring and characteristic Spanish atmosphere is suggested by use of castanets. The Intermezzo, at its close, leads directly into the famous scene of the lantern-lighted ball.

Much of the most striking of the so-called "Spanish" art music has been composed by musicians of other lands than Spain. French composers who successfully copied the Spanish style are Bizet, who wrote the Spanish opera, "Carmen"; and Chabrier; while Rimsky-Korsakow, a Russian, has written the most superb "Spanish Caprice" ever composed.

"Caprice Espagnole," by Rimsky-Korsakow, is one of the most

remarkable pieces of music ever written for orchestra. The composer is said to have written to a friend, "The opinion of both critics and the public that the 'Capriccio' is a magnificently orchestrated piece is wrong. The 'Capriccio' is a brilliant piece for orchestra." Both statements are true. Within the limits of this composition Rimsky-Korsakow provides a solo for each instrument or choir.

ARABESQUES IN SPANISH (MOORISH) ARCHITECTURE

The "Caprice" is divided into five separate and distinct sections. The first of these is the *Alborado*.

I. "Alborado." This Spanish word has several differing meanings or translations, all of which refer to morning music. Often translated as "serenade," in this instance it has rather the meaning of music played at daybreak in honor of a military officer, as is customary in many old Spanish or Moorish barracks.

The music opens with a flourish, full orchestra and *fortissimo,* the theme being in the style of a military piece, though in the prevailing rhythm of a Spanish dance. The secondary theme is presented by the instruments of the woodwind section. Each theme is repeated twice by the clarinet, accompanied by *pizzicato* strings, after which a delicate *cadenza* (much *staccato* and embellishment) for solo violin brings the selection to a *pianissimo* ending.

The form of the *Alborado* is very simple. It may be described as being written in four large parts.

II. "Variations" is exactly what its name suggests, a series of distinguished variations which Rimsky-Korsakow wrote upon an old Spanish folk-air, in three-beat measure.

A quartet of horns gives out the short theme within two measures of the beginning of the piece, these brief two measures being a rhythmic Introduction. At once the air is accompanied by a swaying pattern from the strings, which, within eight measures, begin the first variation. The second variation is in the form of a duet between the English horn and French horn. Variation Three gives the melody to full orchestra. Variation Four gives prominence to the woodwind, two horns and two 'cellos, with a clever accompaniment by chromatic passages in the violins. Variation Five is another brilliant setting of the air for full orchestra. A *cadenza* in chromatics played by solo flute closes the movement.

III. "Alborado." This movement is practically a repetition of the first, but creates a very different impression, as in it Rimsky-Korsakow has used a quite different instrumentation. It is also transposed a half-step higher than the first "Alborado" for the purpose of securing added brilliancy.

The subject or theme is announced at the very beginning, as in the first movement, but is now played by piccolo, oboe, and clarinet of the woodwind choir. Here the clarinets and the violins exchange parts—the solo previously taken by the clarinet is now played by solo violin. The *cadenza* previously played by violin is now taken by solo clarinet.

Notice should be made of the typically Spanish manner in which Rimsky-Korsakow treats the short violin solo, much use of *pizzicato* suggesting the popular guitar of Spain.

IV. This "Scene and Gypsy Song" is really a series of brilliant and characteristic *cadenzas*. The momentary silence between the "Alborado" and the "Scene" is broken by a loud roll of side drums and a fanfare of horns and trumpets, in the nature of a *cadenza*. The drum roll diminishes to an extreme *pianissimo*. This is followed, like an echo, by a second *cadenza* from solo violin—the chief theme—

derived from a Spanish gypsy folk-air. The soft accompanying roll of military drums continues.

The third *cadenza* is extremely brilliant and presents the air much embellished by flute, the accompaniment, as before, being from the drums. *Cadenza* four displays the brilliant possibilities of the clarinet, which is accompanied in its version of the melody by a roll of cymbals, the oboe, for a moment, pronouncing the theme. The fifth and last of the *cadenzas* is for solo harp with triangle. The song or theme proper begins after a decorative *glissando* from the harp. A vigorous phrase from the violins, chords from trombone and tuba, and strokes of the cymbal add to the brilliancy. Presently the *cadenza* theme enters, full orchestra, with a secondary theme added by a solo 'cello. The characteristics of a Spanish accompaniment are maintained throughout, and strongly suggest the rhythm of the Spanish *fandango*.

V. "Fandango or Finale." This brings the work to a close. Further use of brilliant *staccato*, *pizzicato*, and chromatic passages, with the use of gorgeously rhythmic patterns, provides the accompaniment for the simple but stirring melody.

This is presented by trombones and tuba. A related theme follows in woodwind, and both themes are repeated by other instruments. A variation in dance form provides a solo for violin and allows display of violin harmonics. The main theme given by clarinet with "fandango accompaniment" of castanets, triangle, and cymbals brings the dance to a still more furious brilliance, when a sudden change is made to the quieter 2/4 measure and mood of the opening "Alborado." Here it is livelier than in the first or third movements, and in a short and rapid *Coda* brings the complete work to a dashing close.

"España," by Chabrier, is a free fantasy in Spanish style by a French composer. It is built upon two original tunes in the rhythms and tempo of the *jota* and the *malagueña*. It opens in 3/8 measure with a real Spanish *malagueña*, an old folk-dance which received its name from the Moorish city of Malaga. This dance resembles the *fandango,* but is infinitely more poetic. So beloved is it, that in Spain, where it is heard in many villages, a person at one end of a street may start it very softly, and before many minutes have passed, the entire length of the street will be alive to the melody. Everyone will be singing it. It is always in a minor key, is in two-part song-form, and takes its name from both the province and city of Malaga.

Chabrier spent much time in Spain studying the music and dancing of its people, and "España," or "España Rapsodie," as it is also called, is a tone picture of this romantic country.

The opening measures contain no melody, only the sharply beaten rhythm of the castanets, which, first in the middle, then at the first of a measure, set the tempo for the principal melody which presently appears in the strings and muted trumpets. Soon it is repeated by cornets, bassoons, and oboes, and then by full orchestra. The rhythm is now maintained by harp, strings, and trumpet.

A jolly tune is introduced by bassoons in the tranditional rhythm of the Spanish *Jota* which is, in rhythm and melody, daintier than the *Malagueña.* There is scarcely any use of castanets. After an episode of song at the climax of which the fascinating melody is played by the violins, while the wind instruments and harp strike the rhythmic figure sharply, a short murmuring transitional passage (harps, strings, and trombones) leads into a noisy phrase which announces the return of the *Malagueña.*

Notable in "España" are the two highly contrasting dances, the characteristic folk-style of both melody and rhythm, and the use of instruments (as strings, castanets and so on) in popular use in Spain.

"Habanera," from the opera "Carmen," by Bizet, was written in the midst of an opera rehearsal to please the leading lady of the original "Carmen" cast. It appears as the fifth number of the first act, where it lends authentic atmosphere to the scene. It is sung to José by Carmen and a chorus made up of girls and workingmen in the cigarette factory.

The *aria* is introduced by a four-measure rhythmic phrase on the figure | ♪♫ ♫ | ♪♫ ♫ | (a typical Habanera rhythm). The theme (a free adaptation of a Spanish gypsy folk-air) consists of a simple descending melody of four measures, which is repeated by Carmen in its entirety, four times. The melody is immediately taken up by the chorus while Carmen sings an alluring obbligato of short phrases above it, following which she resumes her solo which now includes a secondary theme. The entire section is repeated, and the *aria* closes with a *Coda* in which *motifs* from both themes are heard. The *aria* in the opera is danced, as well as sung, as are many of the Spanish gypsy tunes.

MUSICAL ILLUSTRATIONS

6695	*Zapateado (Shoemaker's Dance) (Sarasate)*	*Heifetz*
1153	*Jota (Manual de Falla)*	*Schipa*
1445	*Tango in D (Albeniz)*	*Bachaus*
6841	*Sierra Morena (Serenata Andaluza) (Monasterio)*	*Menuhin*
6766	*Theme and Variations (Sor)*	*Segovia*
35977	*Spanish Dance No. 2 (Andalouse) (Granados)*	*Goosens-Sym. Orch.*
35978	*Spanish Dance No. 3 (Rondalla Aragonesa) (Granados)*	
		Goosens-Sym. Orch.
6635	*Intermezzo from "Goyescas" (Enrique Granados)*	*Casals*
6603	*Caprice Espagnole (Rimsky-Korsakow)*	
		Hertz and San Francisco Symphony Orchestra
1337	*España Rapsodie (Chabrier)*	*Gabrilowitsch and Detroit Symphony Orch.*
8091	*Habanera from "Carmen" (Bizet)*	
		Jeritza and Metropolitan Opera Chorus

INFORMATIONAL NOTES

The guitar and many other similar musical instruments were brought to Spain from the East by the Moors. It is a descendant of the lute, an Arabian instrument of medieval days. Early guitars were often played with a bow, as is the violin. At the close of the eighteenth and the beginning of the nineteenth centuries, the guitar became one of Spain's most fashionable instruments. This vogue was furthered throughout the continent of Europe and in England by Ferdinand Sor—the composer of the "Theme and Variations" discussed in this chapter—who, soon after the Peninsular Wars of 1808 (in which Napoleon endeavored to secure control of all Southern Europe) dazzled the concert-going public of the various countries by his virtuosity on the instrument.

The Spanish castanet has a fascinating history. Since the earliest days of prehistoric times it has been the custom for onlookers at a folk- or festival-dance to assist the dance along by the rhythmic clapping of hands. It is thought that such rhythmic expression preceded even a melodic accompaniment of song. Presently it came about that pairs of "clappers" were made of shells, later of wood. The word castanet comes from castaña, the Spanish for chestnut, the wood from which Spanish castanets are usually made.

The "Goyescas" was the first Spanish opera to be given in the United States in the Spanish language. It contains three episodes such as might have occurred during the height of the career of the famous Spanish painter Goya, who lived in Madrid about the beginning of the past century. The portrait of the Duchess of Alba—the supposed heroine of the opera—by Goya, hangs in the Hispanic Museum in New York City.

The three scenes used in the first presentation at the Metropolitan were painted after a study was made of the original paintings by Goya, in Madrid, by an artist sent there by the management of the opera house. The opening scene shows a group of laughing men and girls tossing a *pelele* (a straw man) up in a blanket. This is a favorite amusement at Spanish peasant festivals. The story of the opera concerns a popular toreador, Paquiro; a Spanish maiden, Pepa; Rosario, a lady of rank; and Fernando, a Captain of the Royal Guards.

The rhythms of the music are true to Spanish life and easily suggest the surging movement of the light-hearted throng. The melodies, throughout the opera, are short, and the choral and orchestral parts make a blending of the gay folk-tunes and dances of the folk.

The first performance in the world was given in the Metropolitan Opera House, New York City, in 1916.

Malaga, the Spanish sea-port from which the picturesque *malagueña* derives its name, is one of the oldest of the Mediterranean ports. Established by the Phœnicians, it was called Malaga from their word *malac,* meaning "to salt." Here they set up a great trade. It was ruled, in turn, by the Romans; by the Arabs, who captured it in

711; and by Ferdinand and Isabella. It is noted for its mild winter climate.

Bolero. The rhythm of the dance—this being usually given out by the castanets of the dancers themselves—is as follows:

QUESTIONS AND TOPICS FOR DISCUSSION

1. Name and discuss four general divisions of Spanish folk-music. Why is the music in the different parts of this comparatively small country so varied in type? Which division is most distinctly "Spanish" in type, and why?

2. Name three general ways in which Moorish influence is most evident in Spanish folk-music. How may this be compared to Spanish architecture of the Moorish period?

3. What is an arabesque in music, and from what does it take its name?

4. Name and discuss at least five characteristic Spanish dances.

5. How does the art music of Spain reflect the unusual characteristics of the nation's folk-music?

6. Compare the folk-music of Spain with folk-songs or dances of other countries. Discuss the national traits of each. Which do you prefer, and why?

7. What musical instrument is most commonly in daily use in Spain? What can you tell of its ancestry?

8. Locate the various provinces of Spain on a map, if possible, before you hear the music of each province.

9. What unique use has Rimsky-Korsakow made of orchestral instruments in the "Caprice Espagnole"? Discuss and contrast the five different sections of the composition. What is the interpretation which Rimsky-Korsakow has made of the term *Alborado*? Contrast the instrumentation of the two presentations of the *Alborado*. Which choice of solo instruments seems to you most interesting and appropriate for this music? Why? What variation of rhythm, tempo, instrumentation, melodic alteration, or style has Rimsky-Korsakow employed in each of the variations? How does transposition to a higher or lower key sometimes affect the mood of a theme or composition? How does the composer use the violin to suggest a stringed instrument popular in Spain? What is a fanfare? What instruments most commonly participate in one? What distinct type of embellishment is used by Rimsky-Korsakow in the "Scene" for the purpose of displaying instrumental possibilities? What is a *glissando*? What is the

rhythm of the *fandango*? To what section of Spain is it native?
What instrumental Choirs are most appropriate for use as accompaniment to the *fandango*?

10. What is a fantasy? Tell what you know of the *Malagueña*,
its origin, type, and rhythm. Contrast its rhythm with that of the
jota. From what early custom of dance accompaniment has the castanet come? Which of these two dances is most often accompanied by
song?

11. Give the rhythm of the *habanera*. Name two essential features
of a *habanera*. Of a *Bolero*?

12. Contrast the Granados "Intermezzo" with other Spanish
music previously studied in this chapter. How does it differ? How
is it similar? By what folk-music would it seem to have been influenced? What is a multiple quartet?

13. Compare the "Jota" by de Falla with the *Jota* which constitutes the second section of the Chabrier "España." Which more
nearly suggests the traditional folk-dance? Why?

14. Name and discuss several distinct ways in which display of
virtuoso violin technic is combined with presentation of melodically
and rhythmically characteristic Spanish airs in the "Zapateado" and
the "Serenata Andaluza."

Library Reading. "Spanish Sunshine," by Elsner, pages 17-18;
"Spanish Towns and People," by McBride, pages 189-195; "My
Musical Life," by Rimsky-Korsakow.

PART TWO—CHAPTER FOUR
A LESSON ON FORM—THE THEME WITH VARIATIONS

What a Variation Is. With the invention of printing, and the
evolution and development of musical instruments, composers began
to wish to write longer and more brilliant pieces of music. One of
the ways in which they accomplished this was to write sets of variations upon simple folk-songs, or upon airs which they themselves created.
Thus composers were able to secure great variety, and as the use of
the new form continued, it became one of the most brilliant types of
display pieces for both composer and performer. Variations have
been written for full orchestra, band, and for every solo instrument.

In a theme with variations, the theme must be a whole tune,
rather than a small portion of it. This may be repeated as often as
the composer desires, but each time in a different manner. The early
classic variations were written to spin out the length, without much
reference to development or alternation of the theme. Some ways in

Form—Theme with Variations

which variations are frequently constructed are to vary the theme by changing its mood (frequent alternation between major and minor); inversion or alteration of the theme; changes in the rhythm; changes in key; change in the placement of parts (as, the shifting of the solo from one voice to another); change of tempo; and dynamic shadings, from *pianissimo* to *fortissimo*. A study of

ESTERHAZY PALACE, WHERE HAYDN WROTE THE "SURPRISE SYMPHONY"

series of variations written for different instruments will display the manner in which composers have used these devices.

One of the most perfect examples of classic variations is that which Haydn wrote as the "Andante," or slow movement, of his famous "Surprise" Symphony in *G* minor.

The theme of the "Andante" (in the key of *C* major) is a simple folk-tune.

This first section of eight measures is immediately repeated, and at the end of the repetition is heard the famous *Bang!* Another eight measures follow and these are repeated with changes in the instrumentation.

Variation I. The first of the variations (still in *C* major) follows immediately. The air sounds, at first, almost exactly as it did before, but by the end of the second measure a gracefully flowing melody has been added by the violins. The adding of this new melody to the theme is the most interesting feature of the first variation.

Music and Romance for Youth

Variation II is in the parallel key of C minor, extremely loud and bold in style, where, before, it was rather dainty and modest in character.

This variation ends, very softly, in the major, after which a downward-moving passage of scales and little figures leads into the next section.

Variation III. Here the original melody is presented in quickly repeated notes, oboes and violins carrying the air, which is again in C major.

After the conclusion of the first eight measures the melody is taken up by the strings as in Variation I, and a new and beautiful secondary or counter melody is added by the oboes and flutes.

Variation IV opens, with no preamble at all, in a very gay and boisterous mood. The original melody is again presented, but it is, this time, so covered with ornamental note-figures played by the violins, with vivid accompanying chords in the bass, that it is almost unrecognizable. The theme is further varied by the strikingly abrupt changes in volume—ranging from *forte* to *piano*—which lead to the brilliant climax. This is at once followed by one other presentation of the original theme. It is now played in tender mood, with a soft accompaniment of chords, and moves along through many new and interesting harmonies.

The tiny *Coda* or ending is a dainty, gentle repetition of the opening measures of the first theme.

Themes and Variations are also written for the voice, but in comparatively limited number.

"Theme Varie" (Ah, vous dirais-je *)—Mozart-Adam—is one of the most brilliant works of this type. The air or theme of this

* "Ah, if I should tell you."

Form—Theme with Variations

bravura aria for soprano and flute is the old French folk-air known as the "A B C" song.

The melody is said to have been first sung about 1776, at the time of the American Revolution.

Some time afterward, Mozart wrote a set of twelve showy variations upon it. Then it was, presently, included in an *opéra buffa* written by Adolphe Charles Adam and entitled "Le Toreador." The greater part of the opera has long since been forgotten, but this brilliant series of variations (reconstructed from a vocal trio * which stood as number five in the opera) has remained for years one of the most splendid concert numbers for soprano.

It opens with a two-measure Introduction and a simple statement of the old theme, *allegro*.

In the first variation (*Andante*) the melody is unchanged, but interesting embellishments are added to the vocal part.

In the second variation (*Allegro*) the voice part returns to its earlier simplicity while the accompanying piano supplies the variation features through its use of arpeggiated chords.

The third and last variation displays to the utmost the flexibility, agility, and skillful technique of the singer. Toward its close, rapid trills and vocal arpeggios are added, resulting soon in a dazzlingly brilliant *cadenza* in which the flute and voice share.

The "Carnival of Venice" (Arban-Benedict) offers a coloratura soprano opportunity for a brilliant display of vocal technique. Part One opens with an orchestral introduction, after which the slow and melodious theme (one upon which Paganini once wrote and played a set of brilliant variations) is announced by the voice. The theme is then taken up by the orchestra, while the voice adds delicate embellishments. Part One closes with a vocal *cadenza* in the old-time Italian manner.

Part Two, notable as an illustration of vocal variations, is based upon a familiar theme in bright folk-song style. The theme is announced by the orchestra, and is then varied in the following ways:

Variation I. The voice presents the theme over a *pizzicato* rhythmic accompaniment.

Variation II. In this variation the voice and flute alternate in chromatic embellishments of the greatest purity and brilliancy.

---

* The principal melody is sung by Caroline, the heroine.

Variation III. The theme is now presented at a faster *tempo,* and with much *portando* from the voice.

Variation IV. This variation is unique in that in it the voice echoes itself, beginning each phrase in a low register and echoing it an octave higher. At frequent intervals the flute contributes a second echo. The variation closes with a series of bird-like upward-moving vocal *cadenzas,* each of which is echoed delicately by the flute; and by rushing chromatic *glissandos.*

"Turkish March," from the "Ruins of Athens," by Beethoven-Rubinstein, is an effective piano solo written in variation form and displaying a subtle control over dynamics (volumes of sound) rather than the usual types of variation. The unusual melody of this short number is that of a Russian folk-song which Beethoven is said to have heard, one day, in Vienna, and jotted down in his ever-present pocket notebook.

Some time afterward he wrote a set of "Six Variations in *D*" (Opus 76), using the simple folk-tune as his theme. Two years later he again used it in the incidental music which he wrote for a dramatic piece by a man named Kotzebue, for the opening of a new theatre at Pesth, and called "Ruin of Athens," after which the special number was transcribed for piano solo by Anton Rubinstein, the renowned Russian concert-pianist.

ANTON RUBINSTEIN

The piano piece makes use, from beginning to end, of double-thirds, whether it be with or without additional octave. The first four-measure theme and its reply begin *pianissimo,* as though the marching soldiers were very far away.

After a four-measure modulatory passage, the first variation of the air is heard *mezzo-piano,* with a deeper bass and fuller chords than when it was first sounded.

The following variation shows a development in octaves, *forte*—the procession is coming nearer and nearer.

The third presentation of the self-same air is played *fortissimo,* as though the procession were marching directly past the listener. This is the climax of the short composition, after which the theme is repeated three other times, each time with less elaborate bass and less volume. The *Coda* is no more than a *ppp* repetition of a fragment of the theme—scarcely more than its rhythm. The entire piece has made use of grace notes in embellishment of the first chords in each statement of the theme, and the whole composition is an exquisite study in tone-shading.

The Tartini-Kreisler "Variations" for violin upon an air by Archangelo Corelli (*Allegro non troppo*), is a composition which provides opportunity for a short but brilliant exhibition of the possibilities of the violin. The theme statement is made in simple manner,

Variation I is characterized by *staccato* arpeggio figures in the violin part with a singing *legato* melody in the piano. *Variation III* presents the melody in brilliant chords. A short *Coda* brings the number to a close.

"Theme Varie,"* by Ferdinand Sor, a modern Spanish composer, is an unusual Theme With Variations in that it is written for and played by guitar, unaccompanied. It is not surprising that this dashing display of virtuoso technique should come from Spain.

The theme (2/4 time measure) is a slightly decorated air—in form *a a b a*. The charm of this theme is enhanced by six variations, each of which is more brilliant than the one which precedes it, the sixth one being made up of arpeggiated chords. The entire series is, curiously, followed by a tiny, apparently unrelated minuet, in three-beat measure, which closes with a series of brilliant chords and guitar harmonics. Few compositions written for guitar so deftly exhibit the possibilities of the instrument in the hands of a gifted player.

No study of variations would be complete without a reference to the unique set for harpsichord written and published in 1720 by George Frederic Händel.

"The Harmonious Blacksmith" (theme and variations for harpsichord). This charming composition is one—the fifth—of a set of Lessons which Händel wrote for the use of his royal pupil, Princess Anne of England, daughter of the Prince of Wales.

The theme of the "Harmonious Blacksmith" is the air of a very old church hymn, and is developed by Händel in a very *rhythmic* manner, each variation displaying more brilliancy and velocity than the preceding one.

Variation I, with the melody played by the right hand, places an extra note between each original note of the theme and plays the theme twice as fast.

---

* See Part II, Chapter 3, Page 5.

Variation II inverts the music and gives the air to the left hand.

Variation III repeats the theme but in triplets, the melody in the right hand.

Variation IV inverts the music of the preceding variation, giving the air to the left hand.

Variation V is made up almost entirely of scale passages, the melody appearing in a very vague way.

(In hearing a recording of this composition, the student will find it interesting to compare the tone of the harpsichord to that of its modern descendant, the piano.)

"Seven Variations on a Theme from the Magic Flute"—Mozart-Beethoven. Beethoven wrote three sets of concert variations for 'cello and piano, but of these only this one is now heard. It is one of the early works of Beethoven and has no *opus* number. The variations are written upon an air (from Act III of the Mozart opera), which has so unmistakably a folk-flavor that it has been said to be "not an *aria*, but a song."

Both instruments share equally in the presentation of the theme, the piano prominent at first, and then giving way, on each alternating phrase, to the 'cello.

Variation I. The theme is here varied by being played *staccato* throughout, and in a question and answer manner. The 'cello leads in prominence.

Variation II. In this variation the principal notes of the theme are embellished with swift scale passages.

Variation III. The 'cello leads at first in the statement of the theme, which is presently taken up by the piano, in a slightly ornamented version, and accompanied by brief two-measure phrases from the 'cello.

Variation IV. Here the piano states the theme slowly (*adagio*) as a lyric air, with delicate arabesques, and is then repeated in a more sonorous and classic manner by the 'cello.

Variation V is characterized by brilliant episodical passages from both instruments, arpeggio figures ascending and descending serving as embellishments for the 'cello, and a dazzling climax at its close.

Variation VI. Here a return is made to the quieter mood of the original statement of the theme, which is now simply stated by the piano and repeated by the 'cello. This variation closes in the manner of a *recitative*.

Variation VII is characterized by a series of short *staccato* two-note phrases from each instrument, a dramatic development Section, and an abrupt *sforzando* ending.

Form — Theme with Variations

MUSICAL ILLUSTRATIONS

7059 *Theme and Variations for Symphony Orchestra: Andante from
  "Surprise Symphony" (Haydn)*   *Boston Symphony Orchestra*

H6364 *Voice: Ah, vous dirai-je maman (Mozart-Adam)*   *Hempel*

6614 *Carnival of Venice (Arban-Benedict)*   *Dal Monte*

1196 *Piano: Turkish March from "Ruin of Athens" (Beethoven-Rubinstein)*
                     Rachmaninoff

H710 *Violin: Variations (Corelli-Tartini-Kreisler)*   *Kreisler*

6766 *Guitar: Theme Varié (Sor)*   *Segovia*

1193 *Harpsichord: Harmonious Blacksmith (Händel)*   *Landowska*

3048 *Violin and Piano: Seven Variations on a Theme from "Magic Flute"
  (Mozart-Beethoven)*   *Casals-Cortot*

INFORMATIONAL NOTES

"Carnival of Venice" is an old folk-melody of Venice which the violinist Paganini used during the eighteenth century. Inspired by Paganini's use of the melody, Arban made it into a composition for piano and later Sir Julius Benedict, the English composer, made arrangements for voice and orchestra.

There are many stories told regarding the composition of "The Harmonious Blacksmith." One story is that Händel was inspired to write the *Air* by watching and listening to the singing of a blacksmith one day while on a walk, when he was forced to take refuge from the rain in a blacksmith shop. The name of this "harmonious blacksmith" is said to have been William Powell, of Edgware, a village in England. In the cemetery at Edgware, where William Powell is buried, there is carved upon his "marker" this legend—"Here lies the original of the 'Harmonious Blacksmith,'" also a hammer and anvil, a floral design, and a bar of the music. Others say that the publisher of many of Händel's compositions, including the suite or series from which the "Air and Variations" was taken, was formerly a blacksmith named Lintern, who later went into the music business. Some say that, as a joke, he named the composition by his own nickname, "The Harmonious Blacksmith."

QUESTIONS FOR TOPICS AND DISCUSSION

1. What is a *variation*? Why were they first used?

2. Name and discuss eight ways in which a theme may be varied. In what particular way has each composer whose *theme with variations* is studied in this chapter, most greatly varied his theme?

3. Listen very carefully to the theme (several times when possible) before studying its variations. This will help you to hear and recognize it in its varied form.

4. What is a *preambule*? A *transcription*? What are the *dynamics* of a sound? What is meant by *mezzo-piano*?

5. Name three unusual features concerning the Sor "Theme and Variations."

6. What is meant by *Portando*? Contrast this series of vocal variations in "Carnival of Venice" with the "Harmonious Blacksmith," and with the variations on the air from "The Magic Flute." By what similar musical devices have these three composers achieved their results?

PART TWO—CHAPTER FIVE

TYPES OF VOCAL MUSIC—OLD FLORID ARIAS AND THEIR INTERPRETERS

What a Florid Aria Is. The word *aria* is taken directly from the Italian, meaning, literally, air, song, or melody. This general title has been given to those melodic vocal solos which form so important and popular a part of oratorio or operatic works.

There are several types of *arias*—those written and sung in dramatic, or more purely lyric manner, and those which have been written for the express purpose of displaying the vocal abilities of the performer. Such decorative airs are known as *florid arias,** and display, not so much sentiment as, according to the individual number in question, wide range of voice, extreme flexibility or agility, and brilliance of vocal technique.

Florid arias are usually remarkably melodic, the underlying form of the song being often very simple, the decorative musical flourishes—such as trills, roulades,† *cadenzas,* and other similar embellishments—furnishing the elaborate brilliancy. This was especially true in the days of the composition of early Italian opera, when the singers were the masters of the composers, whose songs were merely a foundation upon which to place all the ornamental embroideries it was possible for them to sing.

An exquisite example of a florid aria for *coloratura* soprano—by which is meant a soprano voice especially fitted by nature for singing this spectacular music—is the "Shadow Song," from the opera "Dinorah," by Meyerbeer. This is an *aria* which has delighted and dazzled an admiring public for scores of years.

The "Shadow Song," from "Dinorah" (Soprano). The opera "Dinorah" is founded upon an old tale of Brittany, in France, and the scene is laid near the Breton village of Ploërmel. There are three principal characters—Dinorah, a peasant girl (sung by soprano);

---

* See also "La Donna è Mobile" in "Rigoletto," Chapter One, Part One, and "Stride la vampa" from "Il Trovatore," Chapter Fifteen, Part One.

† A *roulade* is a melodic passage composed of short tones arranged in groups, and sung on one long syllable.

Hoël, a goatherd (baritone); and Corentino, a bagpiper of the mountains (tenor).

In the opera, Dinorah's cottage is destroyed by a storm, and so that he may be able to rebuild it, Hoël goes searching for hidden treasure in a haunted region of the mountains. Dinorah, so deserted, loses her reason, and wanders with her goat through the mountains hunting Hoël.

One moonlit night, while in a birch wood, she notices her shadow and thinks it to be a companion ready to play with her, and to it she sings her famous and appealing waltz song, "Fleet shadow that pursues my steps."

The predominating characteristic of the *aria* is grace. It opens with a short prelude in simple *one*—two—three valse rhythm. The *aria* begins very lightly on the fourth measure of the prelude.

GALLI-CURCI AS DINORAH IN "DINORAH"

O ten-der shad-ow that hov-ers near me Thou shalt not fear me, no, no, no

On she goes, singing to her shadow—"Capricious fairy, so dim and airy, Thou shalt not stray, no, no, no." "Do not fade away," she begs it, and alternately follows and dances with it as the orchestra plays the short interludes between parts of her song.

Presently she directs a colorful, light, rapid, and *cadenza-like* phrase (sung on *ah*) to the shadow, ending, "Reply!" Then she echoes, herself, as though singing for the shadow, with extreme delicacy and exquisite brilliancy.

Now she applauds herself (her "shadow" song) with, "Well sung." Over and over she sings long, brilliant passages, and then repeats them, like an echo, *pianissimo*. These are followed by numerous short phrases and their delicate echoes, by trills, and by a return to the first theme.

Dinorah kneels to talk with her shadow. A cloud passes, the shadow disappears, and, in a sad voice, she sings, "Cruel thus to leave me." But a ray of light returns the shadow to her, and with airy joy she sings, "Ah . . . welcome!" The first theme finally appears again, followed by the dance which Dinorah and the orchestra both accompany with most exquisite and daintily brilliant *cadenza-like* passages in valse rhythm.

The "Jewel Song," from "Faust" (Soprano). Few florid arias have achieved the popularity of the "Jewel Song" in Gounod's opera.

GOETHE'S STUDY WHERE FAUST WAS WRITTEN

It is sung by Marguerite, the simple village maiden, as she finds the casket of jewels which has been laid upon her doorstep by Faust. At the same time there lies near a simple nosegay of flowers brought her by Siebel. This is unnoticed, as Marguerite opens the box, examines the jewels, and adorns herself with them, singing, all the while, of her delight and amazement at the rare gift.

The "Jewel Song" is as sparkling as the ornaments of which she sings, and is considered one of the most brilliant *arias* ever written for the soprano voice. The *aria* opens, after a brief, lightly *staccato* introduction, with a prolonged trill and a gay running passage to a brilliant high tone.

> "Ah—what joy past compare,
> Such bright jewels to wear."

and later—

> "No . . . no . . . this is not I!
> —Some king's daughter I do spy!"

The accompaniment seconds the *leggiero* phrases of the soprano's melody by light interludes, and with echoes of some of the vocal passages. The *aria* requires a voice of great range and flexibility.

Florid Arias from the "Barber of Seville." This brilliant Italian opera by Rossini is remarkable for its abundance of sparkling melody. In this one opera there are florid *arias* for all voices. It is an opera with a simple plot and a happy ending. In it Rossini took care not to descend to farce, but in even his highest comedy now and then adds a touch of sentiment.

The story of the opera tells of Count Almaviva, who loves Rosina, the ward of crusty old Dr. Bartolo, who wishes to marry her himself. Almaviva persuades the village busybody, Figaro, to arrange a meeting for him. Presently Almaviva gains entrance to the house in the disguise of a soldier, but is arrested by the guardian. He then pretends to be Rosina's music teacher, and the real teacher appears, but not before a plan for an elopement has been made. The lovers finally outwit the old Doctor and marry just as he arrives with officers to arrest the Count.

The first scene opens in the square of the old Spanish city of Seville, at the left of which is seen the house of Dr. Bartolo, its windows barred and their blinds closed.

The Count's servant enters, lantern in hand, leading a group of musicians who are to assist his master in his evening serenade of Rosina. The musicians tune their instruments, the Count appears and begins his *aria,* a smoothly flowing instrumental introduction presenting the melody of his song. The clarinets announce the tune, which is immediately repeated by the flutes and oboes, with brilliant, rapidly repeated notes and grace notes as embellishments.

RUFFO AS FIGARO
IN "THE BARBER
OF SEVILLE"

"Dawn With Her Rosy Mantle," the Count's *aria* (tenor), is sung to the accompaniment of stringed instruments and guitars.

Dawn with her ro - sy man - - - tle

The brilliant flourish of the ending of this two-measure theme is a symbol of embellishments which are to follow. Each succeeding phrase surpasses the others in increased difficulty and brilliancy.

In this *aria* the same theme is repeated four times in succession, with additions on each repetition, of rhythmic as well as melodic embellishments.

The second theme (*Allegro*) begins after a two-measure interlude of truly Spanish rhythms. Notice that the presentation of the second theme is shared almost equally by the orchestra and the voice. The woodwind instruments, horns, *pizzicato* strings, and guitars play this theme,

to which the voice immediately responds with this theme.

The whole phrase is then repeated with more elaborate chromatic passages. The third repetition displays an accompaniment which is still more rhythmically embellished. The voice part also develops in exceedingly rhythmic patterns. The *aria* is built upon melodic lines easy to remember, and is so filled with elegance and spontaneity that its effect is prodigious.

"A Little Voice I Hear" (soprano) is sung within the house by Rosina, who has heard the graceful serenade, and now enters the room. This popular *aria* opens with a remarkable introduction, full orchestra, with responses from the strings and woodwind instruments, which is very florid, almost every note of the melody being embellished by a group of grace notes. From this very simple beginning

the air steadily advances in brilliancy, this development being aided by such florid devices as scale passages, "patterns" of notes, grace notes and rhythmic groups.

"A Little Voice I Hear" is considered by many to be the finest *coloratura aria* in the world. The beginning of its second part is a brilliant example of the use of vocal elaboration in a melody. Some prima donnas, in singing it, add personal *cadenzas* to it.

"Largo al factotum della citta" (room for the city's factotum) (baritone) is a third notable *aria* from the "Barber of Seville." While not strictly florid in style, it is famous in its vocal requirement of extremely rapid diction and vocal agility. The famous "patter" *aria* is sung by the light-hearted Figaro to accompany his gay entrance on the scene. Figaro thinks very well of himself, and his own good spirits are reflected in the music. The first theme

is repeated several times and in different keys. The pace gradually quickens, many grace-note groups (as ♫♪) being heard in the accompaniment. In the last part of the *aria* he tells how he is constantly "in such request," and uses his own name, Figaro, as a theme upon which he creates his very individual *cadenza*. The *cadenza* is notable for its limited note range; its speed; and its carefully calculated monotony of both words and music. Its unaccompanied reiteration of the name Figaro, increasing to *ffff*, is followed by sudden modulations. The song is a masterpiece of comedy.

Types of Vocal Music

"Brindisi" (It is better to laugh than to sigh), from the opera "Lucretia Borgia," by Donizetti, is a musical and florid *aria* sung by a contralto who takes the rôle of the male character, Maffeo Orsini. The *aria* is sung during the course of a banquet at which Lucretia Borgia—for whom the opera is named—has served poisoned wine. The contrast between the careless, light-hearted words of the *aria* and its dashingly gay valse melody, and the tragedy which immediately follows, is striking.

The melody, in valse rhythm though written in 6/8 measure, is given out first by the instrumental introduction.

The phrase which follows is brilliantly embellished with vocal ornaments. After the statement of the second theme the first is repeated. The chorus now repeats the same theme and adds harmonic, rhythmic responses at other points. Many artists add individual arabesques and *cadenzas* to the melody, thus increasing the splendor of the *aria,* which is also notable for the extremely wide range.

"Air of the Drum Major" (bass), from the opera "Le Caid," by Thomas. This two-act comic opera was written by a composer who had an inborn instinct for scenic effects and orchestral coloring, and who was a master of stagecraft. The scene of the opera is laid in an Algerian village. Throughout the opera is much beating of drums, much parading of soldiers, and much military atmosphere. Michel, the pompous young drum-major of the 20th Regiment, hopes to become the son-in-law of the *Caid,* or chief, the most important man of the village. So he takes every opportunity to display his brilliant uniform and to tell of his own great importance. During the "Air," which occurs in Scene X, Act I, he boasts that

> "A sign of his cane,
> Like a watchword
> Puts in motion
> A whole regiment."

This *aria* opens with a dramatic *recitative* in which the singer sets forth some of the glories attached to his duties and public position. Then follows a brief Introduction and the opening of the *Andante* section of the brilliant *aria,* the theme being created (in 9/8 measure) from the tones of a military bugle call:

The air moves along with a smooth ease, quite flowing in style, and ornamented slightly with single grace notes or grace-note groups. At the close of this section there is a florid *cadenza* which suggests the type often sung by a *coloratura* soprano.

In the *Allegro Moderato,* which immediately follows in 2/4 march rhythm, the boastful drum-major sings again, in an agreeably aggressive manner, of the light-hearted gayety of his calling and of its many spectacular triumphs,

Our Drum Ma - jor   gay   al-ways wins the day, Priz-es   fall   be - fore   him

to a simulated light beating of military drums. Several brief interludes suggest the call of trumpets. A second florid passage for the voice leads to a repetition of the first theme.

The third large section of the *aria* is announced by a military interlude and a tuneful melody very martial in atmosphere.

Here the melody, which moves with a fine rhythmic swing, is embellished by frequent trills, arabesques, and ornamental passages which require and display the utmost flexibility of voice and vocal agility, and breath control. The *aria* is closed by a series of short *cadenzas* of brilliant, dashing style.

MUSICAL ILLUSTRATIONS

Soprano:

1174 *Ombra leggiero (Shadow Song) from "Dinorah" (Meyerbeer)*
                                                                 Galli-Curci

7179 *Jewel Song from "Faust" (Gounod)*   *Rethberg*

7110 *Una voce poco fa (A Little Voice I Hear) from "Barber of Seville" (Rossini)*
                                                                 Galli-Curci

Contralto:

1367 *Brindisi (It is better to laugh than to sigh) from "Lucretia Borgia" (Donizetti)*   *Onegin*

Tenor:

1180 *Ecco ridente in cielo (Dawn With Her Rosy Mantle) from "Barber of Seville" (Rossini)*   *Schipa*

Baritone:

7152 *Largo al factotum from "Barber of Seville" (Rossini)*   *Granforte*

Bass:

6710 *Air du Tambour Major from "Le Caid" (Thomas)*   *Pinza*

Types of Vocal Music

The first production of "Dinorah" was on April 4, 1859. The opera is composed in three acts.

"The Barber of Seville," a two-act opera, had its first production in Rome in 1816. The character of Figaro is patterned after that of a real man who once lived in Seville in the little Plaza of St. Tomás just outside the celebrated Alcazar, where his home and place of business are still shown. Rossini is said to have written the whole opera in thirteen days. His librettist, Sterbini, stayed in the same house with Rossini all this time, writing words to tunes as the composer hummed them to him. During the thirteen days neither librettist nor composer took much time for rest, and, at the conclusion of their work, the opera was presented within a month. Rossini was paid about four hundred dollars for the opera and for presiding at the piano and conducting the first three performances. On the first night there were many mishaps and many hisses from the audience. On the second night everything went smoothly, and the work was so great a success that Rossini was serenaded at his home at the close of the evening. The scene is laid in historic old Seville.

The opening *aria* of the Count ("Dawn With Her Mantle") was substituted by Rossini at the second performance of the opera for a Spanish folk-song which he had, at first, included. The *aria* had been used before in two previous works by Rossini, one as opera, the other a cantata.

The "Largo al factotum"—Figaro's comedy *aria*—is written in the key of *C*, but is often sung in the key of *B*-flat for added effect.

"Lucretia Borgia" has for its title *rôle* an impersonation of the real Lucretia Borgia of patrician family and notorious fame in Italy in the fifteenth century. The opera is written in a prologue and two acts, with words after a Victor Hugo novel. The first performance was in New York in 1876. It was featured again in 1882, and later in 1902, when it was sung at the Metropolitan with Caruso in the cast.

"Jewel Song," from "Faust." The grand opera, "Faust," based upon the tragedy by Goethe, was first produced at Paris, March 19, 1859, with indifferent success. After repeated performances, none of which aroused any enthusiasm, it was given at London, England, its success being instantaneous and overwhelming. Ten years elapsed before Paris suddenly awoke to the fact that it was a masterpiece and since that time it has remained the most popular of all French operas heard in the French capital.

The third act of "Faust," the garden scene, is full of fascinating detail, and breathes the very spirit of poetry and music, combined in a picture of love which has hardly been excelled in tenderness and beauty on the operatic stage. Of the many lovely songs in this scene none are more beautiful than Marguerite's brilliant waltz song when she discovers the casket of jewels, left by Faust and Mephisto, to tempt her heart.

QUESTIONS AND TOPICS FOR DISCUSSION

1. What is a *"florid" aria?* Why is it not especially fitted to convey many types of emotion. What is the origin of the word *Aria?*

2. Discuss the "Shadow Song." How has the composer made of this a real art song? How has he introduced fantasy into it? What is the emotional appeal of the *aria?*

3. Contrast the "Shadow Song" with "Jewel Song" and "A Little Voice I Hear." Name some of the musical devices used to produce the spectacularly brilliant effects displayed in these *arias.*

4. Why is "Largo al factotum" called a "pattern" song? What are the characteristic features of this *aria?* What is its mood?

5. What are the predominating characteristics in each of the individual *arias* suggested in this chapter? Which is the most dramatic? Which is the most appealing? Why? Which contains the most humor? What musical means has each composer used to create an opportunity for the display of great vocal virtuosity?

PART TWO—CHAPTER SIX

MORE STORY-TELLING MUSIC

(Before listening to and studying the music of the five pieces of Program music suggested for this Lesson, the student should carefully review the first five paragraphs in "Music That Tells a Story —Program Music," Chapter Eight, Part I.)

"Sorcerer and Apprentice," by Dukas. In this clever *scherzo,** written in free form, the French composer Dukas describes in picturesque music the efforts of a sorcerer's apprentice to accomplish some of his master's magic, and his troubles when they succeed too well.

The Sorcerer, upon leaving home for the day, leaves orders with his helper (or apprentice, as he is called) to do certain household duties before his return. These include the bringing in of pails of water from a nearby brook. The Apprentice, enjoying his unusual holiday until nearly time for his master's return, resolves to have

---

* A *scherzo* is a composition in humorous, playful mood.

magic perform his duties quickly, as he had seen his master do. He speaks to the broom a formula which he has overheard the Sorcerer use, and orders it to carry in the water for him. This the broom at once proceeds to do.

Presently all the pots and pans are full, but, in an unfortunate moment, the boy forgets the magic word which will turn his servant into a broom again. He tries cutting the broomstick in two, but now he has two servants instead of one, both of whom hurry from brook to house and house to brook, bringing in water and emptying it on the kitchen floor. Just then the Sorcerer arrives, and says the necessary magic word, while the Apprentice runs away, hoping thus to escape his proper punishment.

This composition is an example of "symbolism" in music. There is a symbol—either in the music itself or the instrument which plays it—for each important incident in the story.

The effect of mystery—so necessary for the performance of magic—is created by the long and vague introduction and by the first theme. Here harmonics on violas and 'cellos are combined with peculiar chord effects played on flutes and piccolos.

The second, and, in this composition, more important, theme is introduced by the wind instruments, beginning with the clarinet. Both themes are repeated by muted trumpet, then flute, then harp, thus suggesting the "three magic words" which set the broom to work. The second theme now takes up the burden of the tale, and the bassoons (the clowns of the orchestra, impersonating the magic broom), accompanied by pizzicato strings, begin the story of its thumping from house to river and back again, carrying the water.

Presently there are two parts for the bassoons—the broomstick has been sawed in two and there are now two brooms at work.

The Sorcerer's return is announced by a loud blast from the trumpets, trills from the wind instruments, and tremolo from the strings. The mysterious first theme re-enters, and, with a downward rush of notes, the broom runs back to its corner.

"Danse Macabre," by Saint-Saëns. The "Danse Macabre," or Dance of Death, was a favorite topic for exploitation in art and literature during the Middle Ages. In fragments of a celebrated fresco painted over five hundred years ago, and still to be seen in a cathedral at Basle, are some quaint and familiar figures which inspired Goethe to tell their story in verse. Goethe's poem, part of which is given, in turn inspired Camille Saint-Saëns, French composer, to give the story a musical setting.

> "The Warden looks down at the mid hour of night
> On the tombs that lie scattered below;
> The moon fills the place with her silvery light,
> And the churchyard like day seems to glow.
> When see! First one grave, then another, opes wide,
> And women and men stepping forth are descried
> In garments snow white and trailing.
> . . . And a rattle and clatter soon rises high
> As of one beating time to the dance."

Another fantastic poem was written by Henri Cazalis upon the same grotesque subject, and these lines from it were copied by Saint-Saëns upon the score of his "Dance Macabre":

> "Zig and Zig and Zig, Death plays in cadence,
> Beating time with his heel upon a tombstone;
> Death plays a dance tune, Zig and Zig and Zig, on his fiddle.
> The winter wind blows, the night is dark;
> Groans come from under the lindens;
> White skeletons flit across the gloom,
> Running and skipping in their capacious shrouds.
> Zig and Zig and Zig, capers every one;
> You hear the dancers' bones rattle.
> .   .   .   .
> But whist! Of a sudden they quit their dance;
> They rush off helter-skelter, the cock has crowed."

The "program" of the music is very simple, and follows the traditional tale very closely. First the hour of midnight is indicated, in the orchestra, by the harp. Then Death tunes his fiddle, and to give this incident the necessarily weird and ghastly atmosphere, Saint-Saëns has him tune it to a minor rather than a perfect fifth, as *a* and *e-flat*.

Here follows the "clatter of bones" realistically and gruesomely suggested by the xylophone. As morning comes and the first faint light of dawn appears, the cock crows (played by an oboe), the signal for all the ghosts to scuttle into their graves.

The music is based on two themes, the weirdly gay first one in dance measure; and the second one, in a more serious strain, which is a symbol of night and the lonely graveyard.

The stress has been laid by Saint-Saëns upon the choice of the appropriate instruments for use in each incident of this musical story, rather than upon widely varied thematic material.

Features in the music and its instrumentation, which should be noticed, include the use of violin harmonics, and of weird chords in the Introduction to suggest the tuning of his fiddle by Death; the narrow range (within a third) of the first theme or melody (played by flute); the rhythmic significance of the simple waltz accompaniment; the use of xylophone and cymbals in the accompaniment to suggest the "clatter of bones"; an elaborate use of chromatic runs—often employed by composers to suggest emotion or atmosphere; the choice of the oboe to play the "cock call" at dawn; and the use of tremolo and of a swift upward-moving figure in the strings to suggest the hurried departure of the ghostly dancers. The composition ends with two chords, *pianissimo*.

"Valse Triste," by Sibelius, is another story-telling composition built upon a similar legend. The themes, exquisitely melodic, carry out the mood of the title which the composer has given to his music. Of simple design, the piece has a general appeal and is equally as popular for its somewhat classic beauty as for its programmatic character.

JAN SIBELIUS

The story or "program" given to the music by its composer is of a sick mother whose bedside is being attended by a devoted son. Weary with watching, the boy falls asleep, and during his sleep sees a strange vision in which his mother rises from her bed and begins to dance to the dreamy waltz melody and rhythm which floats into the room. As she beckons, ghostly dancers appear. Just as the gayety has reached its climax there is a knock at the door, the mother utters a low cry and sinks down exhausted; the guests vanish into the air; Death enters.

"Valse Triste" is scored for flute, clarinet, two horns, kettle-drum in *D*, and strings. It begins on muted strings, with 'cello and double-bass playing, while the viola and second violin are being plucked. The melody (first violins) begins on the ninth measure of the valse, followed by a counter melody in the bass, and soft but insistent *one*-two-three, *one*-two-three accompaniment from the strings.

The second theme, the haunting waltz melody which has had so great a share in the winning of a lasting popularity for "Valse Triste" is announced by the flute and is presently heard, first in clarinet, then in first violin and viola.

At the close of the "Valse" is an eight-measure *Coda* in *lento* tempo, the final four measures of which, in simple chords, are played by a quartet created by dividing the members of the violin division in the orchestra.

"Norwegian Bridal Procession," by Edvard Grieg. This composition is a musical portrait of home customs in Norway, where—

NORWEGIAN BRIDAL
PROCESSION

more than in almost any other European country—there are still retained many of the picturesque customs and costumes for wedding festivities. In many districts of the country the wedding party and the guests are all obliged to go to the church service by boat, and, when this is the case, those who are in the first, or "lead" boat, often start many appropriate songs, which are then taken up by singers in the other boats. When the trip can be made by land, it is even more effective.

In some provinces all of the wedding party and the guests go on foot, the little procession being led by the village musicians—mostly fiddlers.

In hearing the "Norwegian Bridal Procession" imagine being seated on the grass by the side of the country road. Suddenly in the distance is heard a soft strain of music, so far away that possibly little but the chief melody can be distinguished. This is repeated and the procession, or people playing and singing in it, is coming nearer, so it is heard more plainly. Gradually the procession comes into sight and the music grows in power and intensity until presently the players are going directly past the watcher, with their musical instruments playing full force. The music then becomes fainter and fainter as the wedding party moves away, until finally all sound dies away in the distance.

"Carnival of the Animals," by Saint-Saëns. This extraordinary Suite of descriptive pieces for symphony orchestra was written by Saint-Saëns in the spirit of humorous satire, and truly carnival gaiety.

In it the composer included snatches of several familiar melodies and clever parodies of others which were calculated to furnish both amusement and astonishment to the audience which assembled to hear its first performance.

After a few very well-received hearings, Saint-Saëns forbade its further performance, with the exception of the exquisite "Swan," a solo for 'cello which appeared as number twelve in the

NORWEGIAN BRIDAL PARTY AT CHURCH

Suite. By a clause in his will, the composer revoked this edict, and the "Carnival" again appeared on concert programs.

A noticeable feature of the work is the individual treatment given in it to appropriate instruments for solo passages, and the prominence given the piano.

1. "Introduction and March of the Lion" opens with a *pianissimo* tremolo from the piano, followed by a theme which gradually increases in volume and pomposity. After a mock fanfare, a ludicrous Oriental tune—which suggests nothing so much as an Eastern Fakir—ushers in the ascending and descending chromatic runs in the bass which depict the angry roar of the approaching Lion.

2. "Hens and Cocks," a very brief composition (reminiscent of the quaint descriptive pieces of Rameau), is a clever imitation of these domestic fowl. Lively grace notes and little canonical passages from the strings and clarinet help in the production of this effect.

A timid "cock-crow" from the piano and an abrupt chord bring the humorous bit of fantasy to an end.

3. "Hemiones" (from a Greek word descriptive of wild horses capable of unusual speed) is played by two pianists only, and was intended as a joke on those artists who have only speed and no poetic interpretations. Continuous rapid running passages, played *forte* throughout, produce the desired effect.

4. "Tortoises." A tremolo, played softly by the strings, furnishes a background for the introduction of a charming melody from Offen-

bach's "Orpheus in Hades." Unique contrasts between the melody and its accompaniment, and the playing of the melody—usually taken at a sprightly *tempo*—at the pace of a tortoise, are the outstanding features of the short work.

5. "Elephants," in three-beat rhythm, features a light, graceful melody in the lower strings, contrasted with a ludicrous accompaniment. In this work Saint-Saëns included a snatch of Mendelssohn's "Scherzo" from "Midsummer Night's Dream."

6. "Kangaroo" features a hopping phrase, which easily suggests the peculiar gait of these unusual animals.

7. "Aquarium" is a charming number in which a quiet flowing melody from flute and strings, punctuated by scintillating passages from the celesta (which in modern performances replaces the Harmonica for which Saint-Saëns originally wrote), is given a rippling arpeggio accompaniment. Swirls of rapid-note passages suggest the gleam of the fishes' scales.

8. In "Personages With Long Ears," Saint-Saëns displayed a crude humor, and in a duet between the first and second violins, imitates the braying of these "personages."

9. "Cuckoo in the Woods" is a dainty bit of music suggesting, by means of sonorous chords from a piano, the calm of deep woods. A clarinet voices the familiar song of the cuckoo.

10. "Birds" needs no title. It is joyous, descriptive music, in which a fluttering tremolo, and rapid scales and arpeggios from the flutes, suggest the swift flight and soft chirping of the feathered folk.

11. "Fossils." In this amusing piece, Saint-Saëns took the opportunity to ridicule certain too well-known (as he asserted) melodies both of his own and others' writings. The composition opens with *pizzicato* chords. A xylophone then features the popular melody of Saint-Saëns' "Danse Macabre"; airs from four French folk-songs—"J'ai du bon tabae," "Ah! vous dirai-je Maman," "Au clair de la lune," and "Partant pour la Syrie"—are heard; a clarinet burlesques Rossini's best-known *aria* from "Barber of Seville"; and the announcement of "fossils" ends with a repetition of the "Danse Macabre."

12. "The Swan." This ever-popular composition for 'cello solo is lovely both for its exquisite melody and for the undulating rhythm of its arpeggiated accompaniment.

13. "Pianists" is an amusing parody on familiar five-finger exercises transposed as in a Czerny technical study.

14. "Finale" is reminiscent of the Introduction and of themes from others of the Carnival "sketches." It closes with a brilliant climax in miniature.

More Story-Telling Music

INFORMATIONAL NOTES

"The Sorcerer's Apprentice" story has been told in literature many times—once in verse by Goethe, the great German poet. Certain of his verses suggest the exact episodes so clearly portrayed by Dukas in his scherzo.

The origin of the *waltz* is lost in mystery. Some say that it is a descendant of the old Ländler, or German country dance. The name comes from the German *wälzen,* meaning "to revolve." This dance came from the Enns valley in lower Austria. Probably the oldest waltz in existence is the jolly "Ach du Lieber Augustin," which was surely sung and danced by strolling musicians three hundred years ago, possibly longer. It was first written down in 1670.

Sibelius's "Valse Triste" was written as incidental music to a drama called "Kuolema" (Death), by Arvid Järnefelt, the composer's brother-in-law.

QUESTIONS AND TOPICS FOR DISCUSSION

1. What is meant by *Absolute* and *Program* music? Name two main divisions of *Program* music and discuss.

2. What is a *scherzo*?

3. Who is an apprentice? What famous opera is based upon this plan of learning?

4. After listening to the music of "Danse Macabre" discuss the manner in which the composer has achieved the gruesome realistic result heard. Contrast this weird music with that of "Valse Triste." Which is the more realistic? Which is more suggestive of the words of the related poem?

5. Discuss the use of appropriate instruments in the "Sorcerer and the Apprentice" and in "Danse Macabre." What are the qualities or individual characteristics of each instrument which have caused it to be chosen for its particular use?

6. Which of these four numbers is the most poetic? Why?

7. Contrast the two themes of "Danse Macabre." Name at least five devices much used by composers for the purpose of producing certain definite effects, which are employed by Saint-Saëns in "Danse Macabre." Discuss the musical and poetical appeal of this music.

8. Characterize various instruments of the orchestra. Which ones, used singly, would you employ to suggest humor, pathos, delicacy, clumsiness, or mystery? Give reasons for your answer.

9. What is meant by "symbolism" in music?

PART TWO—CHAPTER SEVEN

MUSIC OF THE AMERICAN INDIAN—TRIBAL AND IDEALIZED*

Great Antiquity and Variety of Indian Songs. "Long before the white man chanced upon these shores, there sounded in forest, desert, and prairie, the song of the American Indian, the music of a race that once peopled the entire continent, representing different types of culture and various grades of development," said Natalie Curtis, a distinguished student of Indian lore.

The music of the Indian has always been a part of his life, as

OLD SUN DANCE RITUAL IN SOUTH AMERICA

through it he communicates with the unseen world; worships, plays games, works, hunts, and fights. The romantic quality and wide variety in his music are therefore unequalled. There is special music for all his ceremonies, such as prayer songs for rain, or bountiful crops; thanksgiving songs in case of victory; songs of love; and songs of war.

Characteristics of Indian Songs. The tribal music of the Indian —which corresponds to the folk-music of other peoples—is fascinating and unique, and has gathered within itself much of the poetry, romance and history of the race. Some of the many reasons for its great appeal are its lyric charm and its unusual rhythms.

Many Indian songs begin high in pitch and end low. The climax

---

* See also Skilton "Dances," Chapter Thirteen, **Part One.**

of the song comes first, then the tune trails off to the bottom of the scale. Indian songs are also short and simple; often built upon a five-tone scale (corresponding with the usual possibilities of the Indian's hand-made flute); and often syncopated and irregular in meter. They are sung in unison, rather than in harmony.

Indian Singers. Among the primitive peoples much importance is given to the possessor of a good voice, and although tribal and cosmopolitan standards of criticism may differ, the Indians are always extremely cautious in their choice of a "first voice"—the Indian singer whose duty it is to lead the tribal singing and to pass on the hereditary songs from one generation to another.

Favorite Musical Instruments of the Indian. Drums and rattles are the only instrumental accompaniment used by the Indians when singing. The type of the drum may vary

Galloway
INDIAN DRUMMER OF AMAZON VALLEY, SOUTH AMERICA

from the low, flat "tom-tom" with its dull monotonous tone, to the larger drum. The rattle is often made from a gourd, although primitive rattles have often been made by Indians of the Southwest by tying together dried turtle-shells onto a leathern thong and rattling them against each other.

INDIAN FLUTES

The flute is the closest link between primitive and art music. In the making and use of the flute, the Indian of both South and North America has always been a skilled artisan.

In South America many of the Peruvian Indians still use a kind of primitive syrinx, made in the form of the Pipes-o'-Pan, by tying together hollowed out reeds of different lengths.

The flageolet or flute of the Indian is often quite perfect in workmanship and the material is of the finest selection, quite often of cedar. It produces tones of beautiful quality, made by blowing into the end of the instrument. The scales vary, but most Indian flutes have but five or six tones. The pentatonic, or five-tone scale, is therefore commonly used. Flutes are used by Indians to imitate the songs of different birds—such as the cry of the night owl—as well as to play melodies.

Use of Tribal Airs in Art-Music. Many skilled composers and students of folk-lore—including Charles Sanford Skilton, Edward MacDowell, Thurlow Lieurance, Charles Wakefield Cadman, Carlos Troyer and Victor Herbert—have found in Indian tribal music, with its diversity of moods, its unique coloring and flavor of out-of-doors, and its genuine melodic loveliness, a thematic background for the composition of some of their most famous works.

The idealizing and harmonizing of Indian airs, and the incorporating them into art music, seem to be increasing and the opportunity for such musical activity is made possible by the research of interested musicians. Among those who have visited the Indians in their own homes and recorded many of their fast-disappearing ceremonies and songs, is Thurlow Lieurance, who has, in his travels, visited more than thirty tribes.

One melody, which Mr. Lieurance recorded in Taos, was the "Pueblo Lullaby," a quaint air which he heard crooned from the house-top of the pueblo one clear cool night after the camp-fires had been lighted. This tribal melody was later idealized by Mr. Lieurance, who used the air as thematic material in his song "Wi-um," an Indian word meaning "sleep." (The Pueblo flute upon which this is played in this recording is made of cotton-wood, and has six tones.)

"Winnebago Love Song" is an individual type of love song after which many flutists of the Winnebago tribe of the present day model their melodies. Its plaintive and questioning phrases make it a classic among tribal airs.

"Love With Tears" (Cheyenne Love Song). In direct contrast to the Winnebago love song is the Cheyenne melody, "Love With Tears." It is more primitive and commanding, suggesting, the Indians say, the note of a wild bird. The composition and property of one Indian flutist, for the Indians respect ownership of a melody as though it were copyrighted, it is an individual confession of love.

"Omaha Ceremonial Song" is played as a ritualistic tribal air upon a hand-made cedar flute about two feet long. The tone of the old-time Indian flute of the Omahas resembles the crooning of a turtle dove. The lower tones are made to have a vibrato by the adjustment, by the player, of the tuning plug on the mouthpiece of the flute.

"Her Blanket" (also known as "The Weaver"), by Thurlow Lieurance, is a song in which, to the tune of an idealized Indian tribal air, the singer tells of the weaving of her life story, by means of pictures and symbols, into a blanket. A Crow Indian melody, in its original form, furnishes the instrumental introduction.

It then furnishes the first and main theme of the short song, which is notable for its pathos and for its simplicity.

Ceremonial Music of the Hopi Indians, quite well known to tourists who frequently visit the annual fiestas, includes the elegant, expressive Eagle Dance, and the more turbulent Snake Dance.

"The Eagle Dance." Each Indian tribe has its totem (an individual symbol) and should this totem be an eagle, then the individual tribal dance of those Indians would be a picturesque "Eagle Dance," the inflections of the music rising and falling with the rising and falling of the eagle's wings, as represented by the arms of the dancer. The soaring of the eagle as he flies from rock to crag is illustrated by wonderfully impressive *pianissimos* rising to astonishing *fortes.*

"The Snake Dance." This Hopi ceremonial dance, which is used to accompany the rhythmic movements of the dancers in this weird and highly dramatic conclusion to their annual nine-day fiesta, is wild and extremely monotonous.

Traditional Songs of the Zuñi Indians. A pioneer Californian who devoted his life to the collection and preservation of Indian tribal music was Carlos Troyer, whose harmonization of Zuñi songs has brought these quaint melodies to the notice of the concert-going public.

PUEBLO OF ZUNI, NEW MEXICO

"Lover's Wooing" (or "Blanket Song"), by Troyer, is a recording of a picturesque Zuñi custom, in which the brave, dressed in his most gorgeous attire, visits the home of the maiden of his choice and there sings and dances to attract her attention. According to the words of his song, if she favors his suit, they will thereafter "beneath one blanket walk." She may, however, pretend not to hear him, and the brave may have to repeat his song on many evenings before winning the desired acceptance of his plea.

The song opens with a long and slowly moving introduction, mostly rhythmic. The melodic first theme displays a characteristically peculiar feature of much Indian music, beginning on a high pitch and moving downward toward the end of the phrase. The second theme makes much use of skips in thirds. The song is in three-part song form with *Coda* (*A*—repeated—*B A Coda*).

"Sunrise Call," by Troyer. This is a marvelous musical picture of a morning ceremonial, which has been celebrated daily for centuries among the cliff-dwelling Zuñis.

Just before the break of dawn, vibrating chime-plates are struck together by the Sun-Priest, and their *whirr,* sounding through the pueblo, awakens the sleeping Indians, who soon come to the roofs of the houses. The Sun-Priest then makes his morning prayer to the "Mighty Sun-God," and at its close sends the "sunrise call" out to the more distant mesa.

This song opens with an introduction which simulates the sounding chime-plates. The opening words—"Rise, Arise!"—are pronounced in declamatory manner on an interval of a third, and an echo comes back (as though from the stone walls) very slowly. The melody of the main theme, as in that of the "Blanket Song," descends from a higher to a lower pitch. Both "sunrise call" and the song melody are repeated while an imitation of Indian drums is sounding in the bass. The song closes on the more distant call and its *pianissimo* echo.

"Dagger Dance" from "Natoma," the opera by Victor Herbert. The romantic story upon which the American opera is constructed had its setting in the olden days in southern California when the Spanish ruled there.

During a fiesta scene in Act II, on the plaza before the old mission church in Santa Barbara, when the coming of age of Barbara (an important character in the opera) is being celebrated, Castro, a half-breed Indian, who is in an ugly mood, strikes his dagger into the ground and demands that someone shall dance with him the ancient dagger dance of the Californian Indians.

Castro's challenge is not met until Natoma—the Indian maiden about whom the romance of the entire opera centers—steps down from her seat of honor on the grandstand, draws a dagger from her belt, and strikes it into the ground beside Castro's. He then refuses to dance, but is forced to do so by Natoma. The wild and barbarous dance follows, during which Natoma plucks one of the daggers up and stabs Alvarado, Barbara's cousin, who is about to kidnap her. The dance comes to an abrupt end.

The orchestral music of the "Dagger Dance" was constructed by Victor Herbert upon an old Indian theme in minor mode.

The orchestral version opens with a *fortissimo* four-measure introduction of barbaric mood. This is followed by two measures in which only the dull throbbing rhythm of the Indian drums is heard in sinister, monotonous beating, ♩♩♩♩ ♩♩♩♩ before the entrance of the Indian melody. Throughout the dance, which comes to a close with a dramatic clash, the same theme is repeated over and over.

CHARLES WAKEFIELD CADMAN

"Land of the Sky-Blue Water," by Charles Wakefield Cadman. This charming song, one of a cycle entitled "American Indian Songs," was based, by the composer, upon a tribal melody of the Omaha Indians.

The melody of the Omaha love song upon which the Cadman song is built is very simple.

This is made the opening theme of the song, following an alluring introduction copied from a flageolet love call of the Omahas. The song also closes with a repetition of the flute call, and throughout, Cadman has maintained such attractive characteristic features of the tribal air as the syncopated rhythm and the falling intervals of a third. Both verses of the song are set to the same theme, and are united by a characteristic four-measure interlude.

"Onaway! Awake, Beloved!" from "Hiawatha's Wedding," by Coleridge-Taylor. A spectacular piece of concert music, influenced and colored in both atmosphere and musical characteristics by the legend and song of the American Indian, is the magnificent secular cantata "Hiawatha's Wedding." In it the Afro-English composer has utilized the rich thematic material and suggestion of myth and poetic imagery of the Indian.

The text to this rapturous *aria* is from Henry Wadsworth Long-fellow's "Hiawatha," from Part XI, with the sub-title, "Hiawatha's Wedding Feast." Here is a gracious description of the Indian wedding celebration; of the sumptuous feasting; of the tales of Iagoo, the story-teller; and of the dancing of Pau-Puk-Keewis.

The accompaniment opens with an exquisite chordal introduction, *pianissimo*, which sets the mood for the song. The main theme (in G-flat Major) is in impassioned declamatory style, and is a complete musical statement within itself. It is repeated immediately. The second section of the *aria* is filled with questioning. A feature of the return of the music to the first melody is that, with the exception of the addition or alteration of a few notes to meet the needs of the word-phrases—the entire melody is raised a half-step in pitch (to the key of *G* Major), thus enhancing the dramatic effect.

MUSICAL ILLUSTRATIONS

20043 {*Hopi Snake Dance* / *Hopi Eagle Dance*} (*Hopi Tribal Airs*) Hopi Indian Chanters

78280 *Fantasy on Old Inca Airs* (*South American Indian Melodies*)
Spanish Orchestra International

21972 {*Winnebago Love Song* (*Winnebago Tribal Song*) / *Love With Tears* (*Cheyenne Air*) / *Pueblo Lullaby* (*Pueblo Melody*) / *Omaha Ceremonial* (*Omaha Indian Song*)} (*Lieurance*)

22316 *Her Blanket* (*Lieurance*) Princess Watahwaso
——* *Four Penobscot Tribal Songs* Princess Watahwaso

20983 {*Lover's Wooing* (*Blanket Song*) / *Sunrise Call*} *Zuñi Melodies* (*Troyer*) Caupolican

——* *Dagger Dance* (*Victor Herbert*) Victor Herbert's Orchestra
1140 *From the Land of the Sky-Blue Water* (*Charles Wakefield Cadman*) Lewis
——* *Onaway! Awake, Beloved* (*Coleridge-Taylor*)

INFORMATIONAL NOTES

The Pueblo settlement at Taos, New Mexico, about ninety miles north of Sante Fe, was one of those visited by Thurlow Lieurance in gathering his Indian melodies. The Pueblo village here is like two great apartment houses. No one knows when the two huge pyramidal piles of dwellings of mud, built story upon story, were made; they have certainly been a part of the desert for centuries. The little Pueblo River, crossed here and there by bridges built of hewn logs, runs between these houses. Near them are the corrals where the wheat is threshed by driving goats or burros over it, around and around; the adobe ovens where the women bake; and all other features of the community's life, with its many ceremonies, each of which has its interpretation in song.

One of the quaint customs of the Pueblos is that of building *kivas* or underground rooms which are entered by a ladder reaching down into the ground. These *kivas* are sacred spots and are constantly guarded, and in them secret councils are held and treasured warsongs are taught in secret to those who are to sing them. The Indian uses music as a ritual to illustrate a fixed purpose in life. Words are seldom used except in the love-songs and in prayers and petitions to the Deity. Other songs are sung to syllables, as *hay-uh*, and *high-uh*.

The Zuñi Pueblo—about ninety miles from Gallup—is one of the largest of the pueblos. The houses rise like a pyramid to the height of five stories, occupying a plain on the southern bank of the Zuñi River. Zuñi is the heritor of the storied seven cities of Cibola, whose presence there in 1540, when the Spaniards came, has formed one of the romantic chapters of the history of the Spanish-American Southwest. The present pueblo (Spanish word for town) stands on the site of one of the earliest of the cities of Cibola. The town is older than the Spanish Conquest. The older houses are extremely compact, and rise tier after tier. The center of the older part of the town is laid out in a large irregular plaza, in the center of which are the ruins of an old Spanish adobe church. Ladders protruding from the roofs are the only means of entrance to the older pueblos.

The Hopi Indians, living on the high mesa in the Painted Desert (so called by the first Spanish explorers because of its multi-colored sands), celebrate many traditional and picturesque festivals. A part of one of the most famous of these is the Snake Dance, during which tribal songs of great antiquity are sung—a ceremony with each song. During the singing, the dancing is done by Hopis arrayed in ceremonial costumes which suggest mythical characters of the old rituals, such as the War God, and the Katzinas—the intermediary gods who took the prayers from the Indians to their gods. The whole ceremony is a dramatization of a ritual which had its origin in a myth, and is a cry for rain and harvest to keep the tribe from starvation.

"Natoma" is one of two grand operas written by Victor Herbert, and the historical events suggested in it took place about 1820. The actual site of the old Presidio * in Santa Barbara, California, is now,

---

* The Presidio was a fortified place or Spanish garrison. San Francisco was once a Spanish Presidio.

of course, greatly changed. The church is no longer there, and these blocks are now occupied by chief business properties of the city.

The composition of "From the Land of the Sky-Blue Water" has been described by Mr. Cadman as follows:

"The themes I used in 'Land of the Sky-Blue Water' are of Omaha origin. I obtained them from Alice Fletcher's book 'Indian Story and Song.' Nelle Richmond Eberhart (who, by the way, spent her girlhood in Nebraska and taught school in the 'sand hills') first collaborated with me back in 1905. She was always interested in Indian folk-lore and in turn interested me. We felt that the thematic material in Miss Fletcher's 'Monograph' (Peabody Museum Papers) and in the 'Indian Story and Song' was good background upon which to build such songs as we afterwards 'built.' Mrs. Eberhart in her texts tried to reflect the spirit of the Indian, and so together we read all we could get on the subject in 1907 and 1908. My success with my Indian cycle led to my personal acquaintance with both Miss Fletcher and Francis La Flesche, and my visit to Walthill, Nebraska (on the Omaha Reservation), and my recording of over two hundred Indian songs and flute pieces."

"The Land of the Sky-Blue Water" was actually composed in Pittsburgh, Pa. Mr. Cadman had gone, one cold winter day, to practice the program for the following Sunday at the church where he was organist. The zero weather rendered the auditorium too cold, so he was forced to practice on a piano in an adjoining chapel. In these more comfortable quarters and with the winter sun shining through the stained glass windows, he completed his practice, then all at once thought of the poem "Land of the Sky-Blue Water," which had been left until the last for composition. He had formulated the other three songs of the cycle, but seemed to have difficulties in finding just the right lilt for this song, though he had planned using two Omaha themes as a basis.

Suddenly and inspirationally the whole composition formed itself and within half an hour the song was written, just as it is today. Mme. Lillian Nordica sang it for the first time at the Cleveland Hippodrome in 1909.

QUESTIONS AND TOPICS FOR DISCUSSION

1. What primitive music is used as a theme in the "Natoma" "Dagger Dance"? Tell of the historical setting of this opera. At about what date does the opera open? Read in your history of the actual historical happenings of that time and place.

2. How has use of the characteristics of both tribal and art music

brought about a blending of interest in the Coleridge-Taylor choral work?

3. How vital a part of tribal life of the Indian is music? Discuss.

4. Name and discuss at least eight musical features common to Indian song.

5. What are the favorite musical instruments of the Indian? Describe an instrument used by Indians of South America. To what historic instrument is this related?

6. How do symbolism and ceremony influence the tribal music of the Indian?

7. Contrast the moods of the two Hopi songs and those of the Zuñi Indians. Give reasons for the vast differences in the moods of these songs.

8. Is rhythm, or melody, the more important feature of the "Dagger Dance"? Of the Zuñi "Sunrise Song"? Of the "Land of the Sky-Blue Water"?

9. Compare the music of the American Indian with folk-music of other lands. In what points is it similar? In what, dissimilar?

10. To what extent does imagery influence the music of the Indian? Is the music of the Indian chiefly hereditary, or improvisational? How does this compare with the music of the American Negro?

PART TWO—CHAPTER EIGHT

FANTASY IN COMPOSED MUSIC

The Power of the Imagination. A noted English scholar once said, "It is far greater to suggest, than to merely state," by which he himself suggested the importance of allowing the *imagination* of the reader (in case it be written words), or the hearer (in case it be music), to supply the many charming details which are often the most fascinating elements of a story.

"Music begins where speech ends," is an old saying, and many fantastic or fanciful stories have been most artistically and eloquently related by great composers by means of music. Especially is this true in the case of instrumental music, with which no words are sung, as instruments have a great power, both of imitation and of emotional expression.

"The Oberon Overture" (Weber). There is nothing in all fairy music more delicately made, fancifully planned, or more descriptive of the "horns of elf-land faintly blowing" than the magical overture to the opera "Oberon." The scene which the music of the overture brings to the imagination of the hearer, might be a bosky dell at the foot of a tiny glen, at the bottom of which a little stream, over-shadowed by leafy trees, sings on its way to join the river. The music of the entire opera is concerned with Oberon (the king of fairy-land), fairy folk, and their wonderful adventures. The overture sums these adventures all up within itself in such a delightful fashion (because in it are used the three or four most powerful and important of all the lovely "fairy" tunes, or *themes,* in the opera) that it is most often played as an independent concert number, although first written for operatic performance. Thus it gives its hearers a feeling that they have had at least a glimpse into the magic land of the elves.

The whole duty of an introduction is to prepare the audience for what is to follow, and the real introduction of this fairy overture is the group of three notes which form the "magic spell."

The whole dramatic story of "Oberon" is founded on the very old romance of "Huon of Bordeaux," who has been sent by Charle-magne to visit the Caliph of Bagdad. The elf-king—Oberon—has given Huon a magic horn to help him in his adventures. By blow-ing the horn, Huon will be able, at any time, to summon Oberon and the helpful fairies.

Almost immediately after the voice of the horn has been heard in the opening of the Overture, comes the music symbolical of the fairy folk as they trip along—a rush of little notes.

After a pause and a sharp chord, the lively rush of gay music begins—the adventure is on.

Later in the overture comes the tender love melody, the "tune"

by which many people always remember the "Oberon" overture or opera.

These are the principal musical themes of the opera, and the remainder of the Overture is taken up with their development. By many critics, "Oberon" is considered one of the most characteristic bits of joyous fairy "fantasy" ever written into music.

The use of fanciful subjects as background for their musical writings is nowhere more prevalent than among the Russian composers, and a possible explanation for this—if any be needed—is in the rich profusion of fairy tales and folk-tales in Russia.

A Russian composer who delighted to use such tales as subject material in composition was Rimsky-Korsakow.

"Flight of the Bumble Bee," from "The Fairy Tale of Tsar Sultan." The charming bit of fantasy which formed the basis for this artistic work by Rimsky-Korsakow, was an old Russian fairy tale, from which he developed the plot and music for the opera, "The Fairy Tale of Tsar Sultan." This opera deals with a legend (put into verse in 1831 by Pushkin, the great Russian writer), in which a fairy princess is cast under a magic spell, and, so transformed into a beautiful swan. During the third act of the opera, a huge Bumble Bee —the disguised Prince from a far-off land who has come to rescue the Princess and release her from her enchantment—having flown over the sea to an enchanted island, makes its appearance and buzzes about that swan as she floats upon the quiet water.

The music which Rimsky-Korsakow has written to suggest and describe the coming of the Bumble Bee is so cleverly composed, with whirls and swirls of buzzing sound, that no title is necessary. It is scored for flutes, oboes, English horn, bassoons, horns, trumpets, trombones, and strings.

"Scheherazade." * In this marvelous suite Rimsky-Korsakow related anew many of the sparkling tales from the ever-popular "Arabian Nights." One of the most picturesque compositions ever written for orchestra is this truly Oriental masterpiece written by a

---

* For thought analysis see "Music Appreciation for Children." pages 178 and 179.

composer whose own career was almost as romantic as his marvelous music.

Nicholas Rimsky-Korsakow as a naval officer had an opportunity to become thoroughly familiar with the mysteries and dangers of the sea, and with the gorgeous splendor of the Orient, before translating into sound the fascinating tales from the "Arabian Nights."

The art of music soon lured the young sailor from his naval career. The colorful and dramatic "Scheherazade" was written in 1888, and in it Rimsky-Korsakow narrates in music some of the fantastic things told the Sultan Schahriar during the thousand and one nights by his clever story-telling Queen. The composer made it very clear to those who first heard the "Scheherazade" music that he did not pretend to follow a definite "program" in any of the numbers, or movements, of the Suite, but in each one he endeavored to suggest the imaginative atmosphere of the tale in question.

"The Sea and Sindbad's Ship." In the music of the first movement of the Suite, he presents first a musical theme, or brief melody (sometimes called a *motif*) to represent each principal character in the story. Here is the *motif* which, whenever heard, is meant to suggest the Sultan.

(With unison octaves)

"Scheherazade's" characteristic theme, or *motif*, is quite different, an enchantingly dainty melody, played by a solo violin.

Presently the music begins to tell of the sea. There is a suggestion of the waving, rolling waters of the sea in the restless music, and at last, above it, floats a serene, typically Oriental melody—the symbol of Sindbad's boat as it floats upon the water.

Fantasy in Composed Music

This movement, or individual section, of the Suite comes to a quiet close.

II. "The Tale of the Kalender Prince."* In the Introduction (Lento, *B* Minor 4/4 measure) "Scheherazade's" theme is heard, almost immediately, first in solo violin with harp accompaniment, and then, somewhat altered, in a new *cadenza* in double-stopping. This is a clever suggestion that the Queen has begun another of her famous stories.

Then (*Andantino,* 3/8 measure) the voice of the bassoon (the Kalender Prince) is heard.

The rather clumsy theme suggests the burlesque of the masquerading dervishes, and this effect is furthered by a double-bass accompaniment so written as to imitate the droning bass of primitive musical instruments.

Presently the *tempo* hastens, the time changes to 2/4, and the scene becomes more lively. Fanfares from trumpet and trombone are heard, and a brilliantly aggressive mood is established. A long development section, in which the voice of the Kalender is often heard, follows, and at the close of his story, the sweet theme of "Scheherazade" is once more sounded, by clarinet and bassoon, in turn.

III. "The Young Prince and the Young Princess" is a truly romantic idyl at once suggestive of a glamorous scene in an Oriental garden. The two lyric themes are similar in all essentials, and suggest folk-songs in their simplicity. A peculiarity of this movement of the suite is that, between the melody phrases of song-like quality, there are constantly heard swirls of rapidly ascending and descending scale passages, played by clarinets, flutes, and violins.

The Prince is heard immediately in a seductive and suave melody (*Andantino quasi allegretto, G* Major, 6/8 measure) played by all first and second violins in unison.

* Kalenders were, in Persia (and in Turkey), a sect of wandering dervishes. Three Kalenders figure in the Arabian Nights Tale, disguised as Princes.

This is at once repeated on the *G* string, with sensuous effect.

The Princess theme enters presently (*piu mosso*, 6/8 measure) in clarinet, accompanied by varied effects from snare-drums, tambourines, cymbals, and triangle.

Songs of both Prince and Princess have now and then been interrupted by suggestions of the "Scheherazade" theme, which is now, at the close of the movement, heard in its entirety, played by violin.

IV. "Festival at Bagdad," in which is heard a musical description of a riotous, clamorous Oriental fair, opens with the foreboding theme of the Sultan, and the cadenza-like response from "Scheherazade," who still lives and spins out her tale for the entertainment of her cruel husband.

The Festival (*Allegro molto e frenetico, E* Minor, 6/8 measure— later *Vivo in tempo*) features in its first theme the shrill and noisy instruments most frequently heard in Bagdad.

This is played by piccolos, flutes, clarinets, oboes, bassoons, and all strings, with a noisy and barbaric accompaniment from triangles, tambourines, and drums.

While the fun is at its wildest there is suddenly heard a transition to the mysterious and ominous theme of the Sea, from "The Sea and Sindbad's Ship," the first movement of the Suite. This is now played in unisons and octaves, and in its complex development depicts the surge, and the rise and fall of the stormy waters. The elaborate development comes to a dramatic climax—the ship has been wrecked upon a rock. Out of the ensuing silence there is heard for the last time the sweet voice of Scheherazade (violin) as she comes to the triumphant close of her story-telling.

"The Sleeping Beauty"—Ballet Suite, by Tschaikowsky, another Russian composer who was successful in creating musical imagery so skillfully written that all who listened could understand its meaning,* is one of the world's masterpieces.

This old French fairy tale, on the story of the Sleeping Beauty, tells of a princess of whom it was foretold, the day she was christened,

---

* See also the "Nutcracker" music, Chapter Ten, Part One.

that she would die on the day she pierced her hand with a spindle of a spinning wheel. A fairy who overheard the wicked curse lessened its power by saying that the Princess should not die, but that she would fall into a sleep that would last a hundred years. The King immediately banished all spinning wheels from the kingdom, but one day, when she was about sixteen years old, the Princess found one in a turret of the castle, pricked her hand while trying to use it, and fell into a magic slumber. Her good fairy now cast a spell of sleep over all the castle inmates, and caused a thick forest of thorn bushes and briars to grow up about the castle grounds, so thick that no one should be able to penetrate it except the chosen Prince who should come to waken her. Finally he came, and, the enchantment ended, a feast

PETER ILYTSCH TSCHAIKOWSKY

was spread in the great dining hall. After the feast came the marriage of the Prince and the Princess, and music and dancing for all the guests.

Tschaikowsky was very fond of this story and wrote to a friend while working on the music: "The subject is so poetical, so grateful for musical setting, that I have worked at it with all that enthusiasm and good will upon which the value of a composition so much depends."

After the ballet had been produced, Tschaikowsky assembled the more attractive of the pieces from it into a suite. Last and most brilliant and attractive of these is the exquisite "Valse."

"Valse," from the "Sleeping Beauty," by Tschaikowsky. This is one of the most sumptuously gorgeous pieces of dance music in the world. It opens abruptly (key of *B*-flat) without any introduction, the first note of the composition being the beginning of a soaring, luxurious theme played by all the woodwind and stringed instruments.

This is immediately developed in a brilliant manner. The four measures are repeated at once one full step higher, beginning now on *C*; are then repeated in part, from *D* (two measures); from *E*-*flat* (two measures); in its entirety from *E*; the added brilliancy of this soaring development being followed by twelve measures *ff* of trills (the entire woodwind choir) over musical "figures" in the strings and rhythmic chords from the brass instruments. Eight measures of descending arpeggiated chords bring the waltz from the first climax

SCHEHERAZADE AND THE KING

to a series of four measures (full orchestra) of *one*-two-three, *one*-two-three rhythm, which establish the *swing* of the waltz.

On the fifth measure of this the valse theme proper begins.

The exquisitely singing waltz melody is carried through much development in the way of transposition, keeping, at all times, its lilting, swaying character. Presently it is heard on the warm-toned *G* string of all first and second violins, a soft-toned bell adding charm to the rhythmic beating of the accompaniment.

Then comes a second and contrasting waltz theme, at the close of which is a slight extension of the last phrase in a bright cadenza-like manner, leading back, in a graceful way, to the first fascinating waltz theme. This carries the listener on to an engaging *Trio,* with its charming bell effects.

Again there is a return to the first waltz melody, now heard in brass and strings; on the *G* string; from all violins (with a skipping octave accompaniment in woodwind and *pizzicato* viola and 'cello). A conventional but brilliant climax and a short *Coda* bring to a close one of the most gracious melodies in all the world.

"The Fire Bird," by Strawinsky. It was during the summer of 1909 that the late Diaghilev, the noted ballet director, invited Strawinsky to write a new ballet for him, and urged him to base it upon the famous old Russian legend of the Fire Bird. The Russian composer became so enamored of the idea that the music score was ready for delivery the following May, and in June, 1910, the ballet was given its first public performance at the Opera at Paris.

In studying the legend upon which the ballet is written it is of interest to note that it had also interested other Russian composers. Balakirev once went so far as to plan and sketch an opera on the subject. Rimsky-Korsakow wrote an opera—"Katschei, the Immortal"— upon it, and included it in his opera "Mlada." Following the performance of the ballet, Strawinsky arranged much of the music from it into an orchestral Suite, and it is in this form that it is best known.

The old Russian legend tells of an ancient castle about which there lies a beautiful enchanted garden. Ivan Jsarevitch, the hero of many tales, comes to the castle while hunting at night, and there beholds a wonderful bird with flaming golden plumage. While the bird is in the act of plucking golden fruit * from a marvelous silver tree, Ivan captures her, but releases her in answer to her ardent entreaties. In gratitude, the Fire Bird presents him with one of her feathers and tells him of its magic power.

As this incident closes, thirteen enchanted princesses come from the castle and play with the golden apples, and dance. They warn Ivan to approach no closer and tell him of the horrible monster, Kastschei, who lives in the castle and decorates it by turning captured

---

* An old Croatian legend also tells of the golden apples of youth and beauty. Wagner made use, in "Rheingold" of a similar Teutonic myth, in which Freia, "Goddess of Eternal Youth," cared for the golden apples.

travelers into stone images. Although warned of his possible fate, Ivan enters the castle. Protected by the magic feather given him by the Fire Bird, Ivan compels the monster and his followers to dance until they are exhausted, and then, from one of them, learns the secret of Kastschei's horrible power. This is found to be in a magic egg kept by the sorcerer in a basket. Ivan at once breaks the egg. Immediately, the monster and his retinue die, the castle vanishes, the petrified travelers are restored to life, and Ivan at last weds the most beautiful of the thirteen princesses.

The music of the "Fire Bird" Suite follows the action of the legend in a programmatic way.

I. "Introduction and the Fire Birds Dance in the Enchanted Garden." The introduction with which the Suite opens has no tempo markings, but that of the ballet immediately following is *molto moderato*. The theme of the ballet is an air from an old Russian folk-song. The mood is one of mystery.

II. "Dance of the Princesses" opens in a high register with an air of alluring and dainty beauty. The *tempo* is slower than that of the "Fire Bird's Dance."

III. "Infernal Dance of King Kastschei" (*allegro feroce*) is a gruesome dance, filled with weird dissonances and employing the whole-tone scale frequently.

IV. "Berceuse." This is the lullaby which is supposed to rock the most beautiful Princess to sleep. It opens *andante* with a shrilly sweet melody of Oriental style.

The Strawinsky "Fire Bird" music—especially when contrasted with the extremely virile "Petrouchka" music by the same composer —is a wonderful illustration of the combination of the "program" idea with music of an elusive, atmospheric impressionism.

MUSICAL ILLUSTRATIONS

6738- } *Scheherazade Suite (Rimsky-Korsakow)*
6742 }   *Stokowski and Philadelphia Symphony Orchestra*
6579   *Flight of the Bumble Bee (Rimsky-Korsakow)*
        Stock and Chicago Symphony Orchestra
6872   *Valse from "The Sleeping Beauty" (Tschaikowsky)*
        Hollywood Bowl Orchestra
9122   *Overture from "Oberon" (Weber)*   *Coates and Symphony Orchestra*
6773-6775   *The Fire Bird (Strawinsky)*   *Stokowski and Phila. Sym. Orch.*

INFORMATIONAL NOTES

The fairy opera "Oberon" was, contrary to usual custom, written originally in the English language. The work was ordered from

Weber for Covent Garden, London, and the great composer is said to have taken more than a hundred lessons in English so that he might be able to understand the libretto.

"The Fairy Tale of Tsar Sultan." The first performance of this opera was before the Private Opera Company of Moscow in 1900. Contrary to usual custom, the orchestral Suite had its performance in advance of the opera's first hearing. The Scherzo, "The Flight of the Bumble Bee," is heard during the first scene of Act III.

QUESTIONS AND TOPICS FOR DISCUSSION

1. How may suggestion, in music, be sometimes more powerful and more artistic than actual imitation?

2. What is meant by "fantasy"?

3. Why have Russian composers so frequently built important compositions upon stories taken from folk- or fairy-lore?

4. What is a *motif*, as used in suggesting definite personality?

5. Where is Bagdad? What instrument most frequently plays the Scheherazade theme? Why is this an appropriate choice? What tells us that Scheherazade is still living? Contrast the fantastic tale of Prince Kalender (and its musical themes) with the lyric themes and the story of the Prince and Princess. Name as many characters as you can who might be seen at a Bagdad Festival.

6. Study the various themes shown in the chapter, and discuss the manner in which each suggests the definite idea the composer had in mind when he wrote it.

Library Reading. Rimsky-Korsakow's "My Musical Life."

OUTSIDE STUDENT PROJECT

Class members should hear and study an outside program in addition to those presented in class. See Chapter Eight, Part One, for detailed instructions to be followed in hearing this program.

PART TWO—CHAPTER NINE

THE CLASSIC SUITE

(Before taking up the study of the Classic Suite, it will be well to read paragraphs one and two of Chapter Eleven, Part One, for a description of the origin of the Classic Suite and its usual form, also Chapter Twelve, Part One, Early Symphonic Music.)

There were in all lands, in the earliest days of the fifteenth century, just two kinds of music—the music of the church and the music of the folk. There was, at this time, a wealth of primitive dances among all the folk of the then known world, these serving as an expression of communal feeling.

When sufficient development of instruments had taken place to make it possible to have the dance tunes played as well as sung, these old dances were put together in sets, or suites.

(The word *suite* is from the French, and means "a succession or series of pieces.")

As all pieces which became a part of a *classic suite* were supposed to be written in one key, the contrast and balance, which are the foundation of all suites, were necessarily furnished by the character of the music itself.

In very early days when the term *suite* was first used, it was associated with both vocal and instrumental music. Gradually, however, the instrumental suite gained in charm and in public favor and the vocal suite was almost forgotten. This was partly due to the intimate charm of many of the early musical instruments as the harpsichord, the pipes, and the early stringed instruments with sweet and delicate tone-quality, well fitted to play the quaint old dance tunes, combinations of which made up the *classic suites,* usually consisting of four or six numbers, alternating between fast and slow.

To fully appreciate and understand a classic suite, it is of interest to know the origin, nationality, and character of the various small dance-forms upon which the classic writers drew in composing their works.

Air is a word which, in the sixteenth and seventeenth centuries, represented any cheerful strain of music. About the beginning of the seventeenth century part-songs became very popular, and an air came presently to mean not only vocal music, but also an instrumental melody which was accompanied by subordinate instruments. As such it took its place in the suite.

Allemande, an important form in many classic suites, is of German origin, in 4/4 measure, and is still a favorite dance of the peasants of Swabia and Switzerland. The *Allemande* of the suite is usually of earnest character, in moderately quick *tempo.* It always follows the *prelude,* and is followed by a quick dance.

Badinerie (from the old Provençal word meaning "a sprightly jest") was a gay and lively movement often included in a suite for the sake of contrast.

The *Bourrée,* a native of Auvergne, in France, is cheery in mood, and more fluent than the *gavotte.* In 2/4 or 4/4 measure, its characteristic rhythm is that two short notes usually follow a long one. It always begins upon the last or unaccented beat of the measure.

The Classic Suite

The name *Courante* comes from the French verb *courir* (or Italian *correre*) meaning "to run." The *Courante* is therefore a sparkling, lively, quickly moving dance, and is often written with *doubles* (variations).

Galliard is an interesting dance in triple time and of French origin. It was originally for two dancers and of spirited, though not extremely rapid, tempo. It is considered by many historians to be the forerunner of the *Minuet*.

The *Gavotte,* a French peasant dance in 4/4 measure, receives its name from the Gap-men who, in early days, were inhabitants of Gap in the Haute-Alps. A *gavotte* always begins upon the last half of the measure. *Musette,* an imitation of an old bagpipe tune, with a *basso ostinato* imitating the quaint drone of the bagpipe, is often connected with the gavotte, the accepted form of the simple "gavotte and musette" being in three-part song form.

The *Gigue,* or *Giga* (6/8 measure), the lively dance-form with which so many suites end, is a native of Southern Italy. Bach made much use of this form, often composing for it in contrapuntal style.

The *March,* sometimes found in these classic combinations of formal miniatures, is also of German origin, and very old. The regular form is usually in two distinct parts—the *march* proper, with *trio*.

The *Minuet,* always in three-beat measure, originated in the French province of Poitou. It was taken to the French Court, where it opened every ball, and later migrated with royalty to the English Court, and from there to colonies in America. The minuet is notable for grace and elegance. In early days the dance was usually accompanied by a violin and a keyed instrument. It was customary for a third instrument, often a flute, to be added when the music reached the part now called the *trio,* and it was thus that the name of this section of the musical form originated.

Pavan (or *pavanne*) is a slow and solemn dance in four-beat measure and of Italian origin. It derives its name from the Latin *pavo* (peacock), owing to a resemblance to a peacock's tail which was brought about by the sumptuous robes and costumes worn by the court dancers as they swept in and out of the stately and elaborate figures of the dance. In early masquerades, weddings, or religious ceremonies, a pavan was frequently played as processional music. The earliest pavans were both sung and danced and were usually accompanied by the lute.

Polonaise, a stately processional dance of Polish origin, is looked upon by many as a survival of the dignified and formal pavan. As a dance the polonaise consists of a procession in which both old and young participate, usually moving several times about the room or hall in solemn order. The tempo is that of a march, and the measure is usually three-four.

Rondeau is a name often given to a simple old-time French circle dance.

The *Sarabande,* in stately triple measure, was made an important part of the suite by Bach, who gave great prominence to this slowly moving dance from Spain—where it is danced to the rhythmic accompaniment of castanets. The *Sarabande* is said to have been invented by a Spanish dancer named Zarabanda, about the middle of the sixteenth century.

Siciliana (or *Sicilienne*) is a slow dance rhythm popular from very early times in Sicily. There it was always sung as it was danced, was often in rondo form, usually in six-eight measure, and in the tempo of a pastorale. An instrumental Siciliana is often written with a drone or "obstinate" bass, in imitation of the simple sounds and melody of a shepherd's pipe.

"Suite, No. 2," by Johann Sebastian Bach. During the years in which Bach was chapelmaster and director of chamber music to Prince Leopold of Cöthen, he wrote four classic suites for orchestra, each of which was composed for a different combination of instruments, and each of which gave a decided prominence to some solo instrument.

This, the second of this series of suites, is written for strings and flute,* with a figured bass (called *continuo* by the composer) to be elaborated by the player of the harpsichord. The instrument given especial prominence here is the flute, a favorite solo instrument with Bach. The *Suite* is made up of seven movements.

I. The *Overture* (*B* Minor, 4/4 measure) with which the *Suite* opens, is written in a quaint old-time style, with a slow movement first, which leads directly into a spirited four-voiced fugue. The fugue is built upon a subject announced by flute and first violins, and is, during its development, embellished by many unusual rhythmic variations, trills, and grace notes. At the end of the fugue, a short slow movement (now in 3/4 measure) concludes the *Overture*.

II. *Rondeau* † (*B* Minor, 2/2 measure). This movement was Bach's first use of the rondo form, and in it the principal theme

is heard three times.

* The original score calls for one flute, two violins, viola and bass.
† See Chapter Nine Part One. on Rondo.

III. *Sarabande* (*D* Major, 3/4 measure). This dance begins on the third beat of the measure, with flute and first violin, which announce a quaintly charming melody.

IV. *Bourrée* (*B* Minor, 4/4 measure). Here are two bourrées, both in the same key and each in two-part form. A peculiarity of the Bourrée is that it always begins upon the last beat of the measure and ends upon the third.

Bourrée No. 1, the melody of which is given out in *B* Minor, by

flute and first violin, and then repeated immediately in the relative key of *D* Major, makes much use of *basso ostinato*.

Bourrée No. 2 is very similar in style and in thematic material.

V. *Polonaise** (*B* Minor, 3/4 measure). This unusual suite movement is here written in three-part song form. The first theme, in

which solo violin and flute play sparklingly brilliant parts, is followed by a double or variation.† There is a *da capo* back to the first theme.

VI. *Minuet* (*B* minor, 3/4 measure). This sprightly air never departs from its traditionally courtly manner and style (but when played as a concert number it is always faster than could be danced) and is developed in a charming though simple manner.

VII. *Badinerie* (*B* minor, 2/4 measure). This short last move-

---

* See Chapter Eight, Part One, for note on Polonaise.
† See Chapter Four, Part Two, on Theme and Variation.

ment of the *Suite* (which takes its name from the French verb *badiner* —badinage meaning "to jest" or "to play with") is in jolly mood and lively tempo. The main theme—

a passage of "figures" constructed upon a descending arpeggio, gives great prominence to the agile flute.

The entire *Suite* is characterized by distinction, elegance, grace, and perfection of form.

The "Ballet Suite" (so called) by Gluck. This was not originally a suite, but is a collection or set of ballets which were chosen from

CHRISTOPH WILLIBALD
GLUCK

Gluck popular operas and arranged in suite form for performance by symphony orchestra, by Felix Mottl, about the end of the nineteenth century. The score of this *Suite* was published in 1900. Many of these Gluck operas still retain a popularity, but the ballet music contains many of the composer's most famous melodies. In some single movements of the *Suite,* themes from more than one opera are included and developed.*

The nine distinct sections of the "Ballet Suite," the order in which they are heard, the operas from which they have been selected, and the musical characteristic of each dance form, are as follows (the year in which each opera was first published is also given).

The "Introduction," from "Don Juan" † (1761), has a theme built in the form of a rhythmic triplet figure in *staccato* notes, announced by the string choir, horns, and bassoons.

With no break other than a momentary pause, the music moves on directly into "Air Gai," from "Iphigénie en Aulide" (1774), which is, as its name suggests, a jolly, piquant melody set forth by

* See also Chapter Ten, Part One, on "Ballet."
† Not to be confused with the "Don Juan" by Mozart.

woodwind and strings. This simple "gay air" is presently transferred

to the delicate-voiced flute which, though retaining all the simplicity of the theme, develops it to a real climax, over an accompaniment of *staccato* horns and *pizzicato* violins and viola.

"Lento" (from the same opera), scored for strings only, provides, in its clear expressiveness, a contrast to the previous sprightly melody. The theme (first violin) is remarkable for its crisp phrasing and typical imitation of airs even older than those of Gluck's time.

Following the graceful "Lento" is a repetition of the "Air Gai," which sounds much as it did at first, with the exception of an added brilliancy and a more general climax. This completes the first large movement of the "Ballet Suite."

The second large movement of this classic suite opens with the "Dance of the Blessed Spirits," a gracious air from Gluck's best known opera, "Orpheus and Euridice" (1762). This is arranged for strings, two horns, two flutes and English horns, thus creating a distinctive atmosphere very suggestive of that of the very first orchestras. Flutes and first violins carry the main theme.

This is elaborately developed during the progress of the short dance.

At the conclusion of this elegant bit of real chamber music, the violins alone take up the well-loved melody of the old familiar air.

"Musette," from "Armide" (1777). This one quaint melody is probably better known to music lovers than any other air from Gluck. The "Musette" is written in three-part song form with its first theme

(after its announcement by the violins) repeated in turn by flute, and a full orchestra composed of strings, woodwind, horns, and trumpets.

After the announcement of a brief second theme, and a *da capo*, a *Codetta* is heard which closes with two *pianissimo* repetitions of the last phrase of the familiar, picturesque, solo theme.

"Air Gai." This buoyant movement returns for the third time, here repeated with variation in both the rhythm and melody. This is followed by the tender "Sicilienne" (*Andantino*), from "Armide," and a fourth, and concluding repetition of "Air Gai." With many double-thirds, and elegantly dainty grace-notes, and with swinging motion, the theme is announced.

A lovely second melody is played by flute and horn, softly.

The *finale* ("Air Gai") adds the vivacious note which is so frequently heard in the closing section of a conventional concert number.

All of this Gluck music suggests action of a definite type, as is necessary in ballet music. In addition, it presents themes of real beauty and rare artistry, of so winsome a type that they have, for more than a century and a half, withstood the tests of time and changing fashion.

MUSICAL ILLUSTRATIONS

6914-
6915 } *Suite, No. 2 (Johann Sebastian Bach)*   *Chicago Symphony Orchestra*

Overture }
Rondeau } *Sarabande*
Bourrée
Polonaise
Minuet
Badinerie

9278 *Ballet Suite (Christoph Willibald Gluck)*
                              Blech and Berlin State Opera Orchestra
Introduction from "Don Juan"
Air Gai from "Iphigénie en Aulide"
Lento from "Iphigénie en Aulide"
Air Gai (Repeated)

Music of the Northlands

Dance of the Blessed Spirits from "Orpheus and Euridice"
Musette from "Armide"
Air Gai
Sicilienne from "Armide"
Air Gai

QUESTIONS AND TOPICS FOR DISCUSSION

1. What is meant by "classic suite"? How does it differ from a modern suite?

2. Name and discuss the essential characteristics of eight or more dance-forms frequently used by composers of early suites. Contrast the various types, and the moods commonly created by their performance.

3. How has the development of the modern orchestra contributed to the development of the modern suite? What was the type of orchestra usually available for the performance of the early classic suite?

4. How has Bach, in this "Suite," written entirely in one key, managed to suggest diversity of mood and appeal? What musical devices has he used to achieve his effective contrasts?

5. By what one means has Mottl—the arranger of the Gluck "Ballet Suite"—achieved a unity throughout the entire composition?

6. What section of either classic suite discussed in this chapter is your favorite? Why?

PART TWO—CHAPTER TEN

MUSIC OF THE NORTHLANDS * (NORWAY, SWEDEN, AND FINLAND)

The Folk-Lore of the Northlands. One of the oldest civilizations of the Old World is that of the Scandinavian countries. These northern lands preserved, through many centuries, legends and historic folk-lore of the greatest value to all the world, by means of the *sagas,* and the *runes,* which were sung and chanted by their *skalds* —the bards of the northlands.

Folk-Instruments. Here in these old northern lands the folk-musicians still play the quaint folk-instruments which their fathers and grandfathers played in earlier days. In Sweden the romantic lute of the Troubadours of the Middle Ages is still heard —the only land in the world except in the Near East where it is

---

* See Chapter Thirteen, Part One, and Chapters One and Six, Part Two.

still to be found. In Norway the lur—a crude, long horn made of fir wood (like an Alpine horn)—is used by mountaineers and by the girls who watch the flocks and herds near the lonely *saeters*.* Here may be heard, also, the old Hardanger fiddle with eight strings— the four extra strings being added to produce sympathetic vibrations, not to be played upon. The native musical instrument of Finland is the kantele, an instrument having five strings made of copper wire. The kantele looks very much like a zither or a harp. It has been played in Finland for so many hundreds of years that its origin has been lost in legend. One may be seen in almost any home in Finland.

The Folk-Music of Finland. Some of the least known but most fascinating folk-music is in Finland, often called the "land of a thousand lakes" because of the large number of small bodies of water that lie within it. Because its northern part lies within the Arctic Circle, it shares with Norway the title of "The Land of the Midnight Sun." For about six weeks in summer-time there is no night. During this time the sun is seen for the whole twenty-four hours of the day. The

NATIONAL COSTUME OF
EASTERN FINLAND

nights are called "white nights" as no stars are seen. People may read at midnight without any artificial light, for the sky is always bright. When at last the first pale star is seen in the sky, the Finnish people know that autumn is not very far away.

During these long summers there are many parties and festivals of every kind. In many homes the neighborhood spinners and weavers gather, keeping time with their work by singing old Finnish folk-songs.

There is also a "rune" or ballad-singing choir in almost every village, and it is in these choirs that many of the boys and girls of Finland learn to know the folk-songs of their land. The odd name of the choirs is taken from the very strange way in which the old-time bards or minstrels of this country wrote down their songs. They would burn the music onto bits of bark with heated points of metal, indicating the melody by the letters of the alphabet. Such songs were called *runes,* the word *rune* meaning an "air" or "ballad." The name rune was also given to the ancient Finnish folk-song, in which long hero tales were recited, in sing-song manner, to the accompaniment of the kantele, whose five tones were

---

* A Saeter is a mountain top dairy used in Norway during the Summer.

equivalent to the *la-ti-do-re-mi* of the modern scale. Presently a step was taken from indefinite sing-song to a more definite form, in which the rather monotonous melodies were often arranged in five-beat measure—an irregular rhythm frequently found in folk-airs of northern peoples. The name *rune* adhered to these ballad-like songs.

Each summer the choirs of Finland hold several national festivals of singing. These are held in different cities each year, so that all the people may hear the singing, and often as many as a thousand singers take part in one festival.

Finland has many splendid composers, and of these, two who are best known are Jan Sibelius and Armas Järnefelt.

"Sorrow is the source of singing," says an old Finnish proverb. Among the Finnish-speaking people of the land, the sad note is the most prominent in their folk-songs. Loneliness and sorrow are common themes or topics of the songs, many of which are written in a curious 5/4 measure.

This national sadness will be more easily understood if mention is made of the history of Finland, of the war of 1808-1809 between Sweden and Russia, during which Finland passed from the control of Sweden to that of Russia. This war was of Napoleon's making— a plan of his to distract Russia's attention from Turkey. In the fighting the Finns resisted Russia, and even though they were defeated, the Russians had to recognize the unbending Finnish nationality.

The Tone-Poem "Finlandia." Like Chopin, Sibelius suffered in thinking of the woes of his native land, and in 1894 he wrote the tone-poem "Finlandia" as his personal protest against the Russian rule of Finland. The composition is written to express the feeling and impressions of an exile upon his return to his home in Finland after a long absence, and had so exciting an effect upon the Finnish people when it was first heard, that its further performance in Finland was forbidden.

It is said by some that the opening theme, or melody, of "Finlandia" is a Finnish folk-song, but Sibelius himself says that it is not, but rather an original theme written in the rough and rugged style of a folk-song melody.

One mood continues throughout this entire tone-poem, becoming gradually more and more intense. From first to last the sinister roll of the drums, now *piano* and now *fortissimo,* plays a prominent part in the creation of this mood. The composition opens with a dramatic *Introduction*—ominous chords from heavy-toned horns, trumpets, trombones, tubas and basses, *fortissimo,* and an agitated theme, suggesting revolt.

The first theme in the brasses—hymn-like in character—with a reply from the strings and woodwinds, enters, followed by a long succession of rhythmic chords from the brass instruments and a roll of drums. Military effects, *fortissimo*, full orchestra and *allegro*, with ever-constant roll of drums, and unrest in the figures played by strings, produce a climatic effect, after which the hymn-like melody is again heard. The second theme is heard first in strings (a response in woodwinds), and is repeated, in turn, by strings, 'cello, and violin.

A series of thematic developments, full orchestra, and played *fortissimo* and with tremendous force, brings this intensely nationalistic composition to a stirring close, amid steadily increasing excitement and a spirit of wild defiance.

Several changes in meter and in specific rates of *tempo* contribute to the forceful expression of the composer's sentiments.

"Berceuse," by Järnefelt. This tender melody by another Finnish composer is in quite a different mood. It was originally written for violin and piano, but transcribed for orchestra. It is written in the minor mode and is played *andante*. It opens *ppp* with a four-measure Introduction of the simplest possible kind. The rather sad and plaintive melody is presented by the violins three times, each section of the piece, as are the verses of a song, being united with the next by a short interlude. The first repetition is played in unison by heavier strings and woodwind; the second, one octave higher, in a slightly altered form, and with a broader accompaniment. A brief and simple *coda* which ends in *pizzicato ppp* closes the short number.

Folk-Music of Norway. To a certain extent the lands of Norway and Finland have the same characteristics. Both have rugged landscapes, and Norway, to a lesser degree, shares with Finland the loneliness of the long and extremely cold winters.

But Norway's history is a happier one than Finland's, and this contentment is reflected in the nation's music.

Norway, although one of the new nations of the world—through its separation from Sweden in 1905—has one of the oldest histories in the world. The ancient *sagas*—historical ballads and epic poems sung by the *skalds,* or minstrels of the North—relate not only the heroic deeds of the primitive Norsemen, but have also recorded the strongest traits of the race—honesty, proud reserve, self-respect, simplicity of expression, and faithfulness to authority whether this be an authority of law or one of affection.

All of these national characteristics have had their effect upon and been made a part of the greatest in Scandinavian literature, art, and music.

Edvard Grieg, Norwegian composer. Of the really "national" music of the land, none is more fascinating than Grieg's, whose best known compositions are such short and lyrical pieces as "To Spring," "Norwegian Bridal Procession," "Norwegian Dances," and the "Peer Gynt" suite. He has also written music of a heroic type.

"Triumphal March"—"Sigurd Jorsalfar," by Grieg, is a com-position which depicts a romantic and patriotic scene in early Norwegian history, an extremely brilliant march. The gorgeous music which we know as "Sigurd Jorsalfar"— sometimes called "The March of the Vassals"—is a portion of the incidental music written by Grieg to be played during the progress of a drama written by his friend Bjornson. Later

NORWEGIAN FOLK DANCE

Grieg selected three of the pieces from the incidental music and wrote them out as piano solos. These are, "Introduction," "Intermezzo" and "Triumphal March."

The story of "Sigurd Jorsalfar" is one of the old hero tales of Norway. Sigurd, known as "Sigurd, the Crusader," was a younger brother of two kings who ruled Norway jointly in the Middle Ages. Quaint old runic inscriptions found carved upon ruined walls in certain parts of Norway tell many historic facts concerning the Jorsalfars. One of these tells of "the blessed earl" who led a Crusade to Palestine in 1152.

It is at the time (in the play) of Sigurd's return from the Cru-sade that the "Triumphal March" is played. It is majestic music and suggests the enthusiastic welcome that is being given the returned prince by those who owe him allegiance. The music is rich in melody and in harmony, and Grieg made a careful choice of instruments to get those which would best express the patriotic emotion of the crowd.

The "March" opens with a fanfare of trumpets and rolling drums, which might suggest the returning Crusaders, the standards of battle and adventure fluttering in the breeze, the tramp of horses' hoofs, flashing of swords, and clashing of shields. After a moment's pause, the music continues with a quiet but stately melody given out in march time.

This is immediately repeated *fortissimo,* and with abruptly clipped phrase endings. Presently the brass instruments are heard in a lovely bass melody which gradually increases and broadens out to a splendid climax. Then the first theme, or melody, returns again, *fortissimo,* after which a transition is made to the *Trio* by means of the snare drums. As these continue to mark the time, an exquisite lyric melody very characteristic of the happier folk-songs of the people, is heard. With, or after it, are heard a series of interesting modulations to other keys and developments of this melody, after which, once more, is heard the welcoming fanfare of the trumpets and drums, and the stately march of "Sigurd Jorsalfar."

SWEDISH GIRLS FROM DALECARLIA

Folk-Music of Sweden. Sweden, lying directly next to Norway, is subject to similar influence of climate, scenery, and tradition. Sweden is rich in folk-dance music.

"Vermeland." Of all the Swedish folk-music, none is more charming than "Vermeland," an old folk-song of a little province which lies near the border between Norway and Sweden. The melody of the old song is quiet in mood, plaintive, and of a strongly nationalistic nature.

The form is simple; *a* (in minor), eight measures long; *a* (repeated); *b* (in relative major, four measures).

"Swedish Wedding March," by August Johann Södermann, a representative composer of modern Sweden, draws a picture in music of Swedish peasant life. In it he has employed a Swedish folk-melody, and has further suggested characteristic features of a rural "band" by cleverly writing a monotonous drone bass for the melody's accompaniment. The "March" is very simple in its construction.

The first section (in *F* Major) of sixteen measures is made up of two repetitions of the entire first theme.

The second large section—in the minor—characterized by many heavy chords in the bass, is followed by a return (*Da Capo*) to the first section. This is immediately followed by the *Trio,* in which is heard a subject similar to the first theme, and an extended fanfare, reminiscent in its rhythmic patterns (♩♫♪ ♩ ♩ ♪) to that earlier theme.

Four measures, not melodic, but rhythmic, preface the final return to the first march theme.

MUSICAL ILLUSTRATIONS

9015	*Finlandia (Jan Sibelius)*	*Royal Albert Hall Orchestra*
20374	*Berceuse (Armas Järnefelt)*	*Victor Concert Orchestra*
35763	*Sigurd Jorsalfar—Triumphal March (Edvard Grieg)*	
		Victor Symphony Orchestra
19923	*O Vermeland (Swedish Folk Song)*	*Victor String Ensemble*
20805	*Swedish Wedding March (August Johann Södermann)*	
		Victor Concert Orchestra
20151	*Norwegian Mountain March (Folk Dance)*	*Victor Military Band*
77555	*The Kivle Maidens Dance (Norwegian Springar)*	*Hardanger Fiddle*
35885	*Herd Girl's Sunday (Ole Bull)*	*Munson*
20450	*Klappdans (Swedish Folk)*	*Victor Band*
20432	*Carrousel (Swedish Folk)*	*Victor Orchestra*
——*	*Pretty Sister-in-Law (Finnish Dance)*	

INFORMATIONAL NOTES

A *berceuse* is a cradle song. This form has long been used by the leading composers when wishing to write a short poetic composition. The rhythm used is usually a gently swaying one. This "Berceuse," by the Finnish composer Järnefelt, is a general favorite.

Finland is a beautiful country, with clean, bright cities, fine farms, good schools and century-old castles. One of the things which a visitor to Finland always notices is the love that the country people have for music. There is still much weaving of cotton cloth done, and spinning of flax into linen.

"Sigurd Jorsalfar" was written in a very short time. Grieg wrote to a friend: " 'Sigurd Jorsalfar' is a folk-piece. The play is to be produced at the Christiania Theatre after a short preparation

I am allowed only eight days to write and orchestrate the music." But, though the time was short, the music was completed for the first performance of the play (1872).

"Vermeland" (or "Värmland") is the Swedish province on the Norwegian frontier, north of Lake Vänern. It is a land of iron ore and charcoal, of far-reaching lakes and countless forests, and also of poets, legend, and romance. Its mining industry has traditions dating from the Middle Ages, for, as early as the fifteenth century, forges were built, and several of the large iron works in use there today have been in existence for nearly four hundred years. Selma Lägerhof, noted author and Nobel prize winner, is a native of Vermeland, and in this province was also born the famous engineer John Ericsson, the inventor of the propeller and of the U. S. S. "Monitor" of Civil War fame.

QUESTIONS AND TOPICS FOR DISCUSSION

1. Name several general characteristics of Scandinavian music. How is the folk-music related to the folk-lore of the Northland? Tell what you can of the *sagas* and *runes*. Who were the *skalds*?

2. Name and discuss musical instruments characteristic of Norway, Sweden, and Finland.

3. Give reasons for the loneliness and discontent sometimes displayed in Finnish music.

4. Discuss "Finlandia." How does it employ national characteristics?

5. Compare the folk- and composed-music of Norway and Finland. Give possible reasons for differences you may find.

6. How has Grieg used music to tell an old history tale of his native land? Name other composers who have done this same thing in other lands.

7. What is the difference between lyric and dramatic music? Classify, under these two heads, all the compositions listed in the "musical illustrations" for this chapter.

8. How do climate, geography, occupation, and use of leisure time influence a nation's music?

9. Contrast the "Finlandia," by Sibelius, and the "Berceuse," by Järnefelt. How is each typical of life and musical nationalism of Finland? What instrumental means has Sibelius used to depict the gloom and terror of political conditions in his homeland? Contrast, and discuss, the "Introduction" and the first theme of "Finlandia."

Library Reading. Chapter Nine, on "Painting and Music," in "Finland and the Finns," by Arthur Reade; "The Story of Edvard Grieg," in the "Mentor," February, 1929; "Sweden," in the "Mentor," April, 1929.

PART TWO—CHAPTER ELEVEN

FAMILIAR CLASSICS—BEAUTY OF STYLE AND FORM

Types of Music. There are two kinds of music—*Program* music, which tells or suggests a story; and *Pure* music, which does not try to suggest any special thing to the listener, but only to charm because of *its beauty of melody and of form*. Each part of this kind of composition fits upon another part and is so planned as to fit, just as material is laid in careful order in the building of a structure.

"It is not wise to be always hunting pictures in music," a noted critic is quoted as saying. So, in many familiar (and therefore popular) classics, there is much to admire and enjoy in the way of decidedly melodic themes; the lyrical grace and beautiful form with which they are expressed; the careful contrasts, modulations, voice leadings, and climaxes, so artfully worked out by the

GARDEN HOUSE (PETIT TRIANON) OF MARIE ANTOINETTE

composers as their poetic means of expression; and the loveliest of formal balance and unity.

It should prove of interest to hear and study, in turn, the six selections suggested in this lesson, and then to contrast them and learn how each composer has achieved his individual musical results.

"Amaryllis"—an old French air. This sparklingly dainty dance (gavotte), popular for nearly four centuries, is a real classic.

The air is said to have been composed by a court musician to Henry the Third, of France, about the middle of the sixteenth century, and is known to have been played in 1581 at the royal wedding of Margaret, of Lorraine, and the Duc de Joyeuse. It has been much played in later years in the form of a transcription for piano by Ghys.

The first theme (in major mode) and its reply are notable for a sprightly movement and a delicate *pizzicato* from the strings of the orchestra. The second theme appears in parallel minor. The first theme returns, after which the third theme, in a new and contrasting key, is heard. Each thematic statement is crisply detached from that which precedes or follows it. In the distinct form of the *rondo*, each of the themes takes its turn, like a dancer, of appearing again, and at the close of the piece it is found that the form (if a letter represents each theme) is *a a b a a c c b c a a.*

"Largo," by George Frederic Händel, is an air from "Xerxes," one of this composer's Italian operas. As a part of the opera it was known as "My Plane Tree"—a eulogistic *aria* to a beautiful tree. Much more familiarly known as "Largo," the charming melody is loved for its dignity and simplicity. The composition is written with a fine sense for effect, the voice (or *air*) rising by stages higher and higher. The melody is both fluent and graceful, abounding in sustained phrases.

"Marche Militaire," Opus 51, by Franz Schubert. No one ever had a greater melodic gift than Schubert, many of whose famous

FRENCH WEDDING PARTY LED BY A FOLK MUSICIAN

masterpieces were written either for the voice or for instruments of the orchestra. He has, in the "Marche Militaire," written one of his most charming works, and one which has won for itself a lasting popularity. First written as a simple, though effective, piano duet in the key of *D* major, it has been arranged as a concert solo for piano by the famous Carl Tausig and others; transcribed for band, and for almost every type of instrumental combination.

It opens with a stirring six-measure *Introduction* in the style of a fanfare. Then follows the gay and dashing melody, *pianissimo.*

The second theme, in gay martial mood, is heard very soon.

Each repetition of the first theme—of which there are four—brings the parading troops nearer as the music grows in volume with a steady *crescendo*. This first section of the "Marche" ends in a triumphant climax.

Then follows the *trio* with its two delicately melodic themes—one of the most inspired bits of music Schubert ever wrote. The first theme is a lilting air, in major; the second a more plaintive one in minor mode. A brief fanfare brings about a return of the "Marche" in its original key and the composition ends in glorious climax.

"Adagio" (first movement), from the "Moonlight" Sonata, Opus 27, No. 2, by Ludwig van Beethoven. This Sonata, best known to many music-lovers because of the un-authenticated story of Beethoven playing to the blind girl, is an exception to the general rule in that its first movement is written as a free fantasie rather than in strict sonata form.

This movement may well be thought of as "impressionistic" music, such an effect being produced by the *pianissimo* and gently undulating arpeggiated chords in the triplet rhythm with which it opens. The mood produced might be said to be one of imaginative musing. The melody, in four-measure phrases, is interwoven with the broken-chord accompaniment. It develops a real climax, then recedes downward slowly and diminuendo, sounding

REAR VIEW OF BEETHOVEN'S BIRTH HOUSE, BONN

softly but clearly each note of the *C-sharp* minor chord in turn. *C-sharp* is the last of these sustained tones.

The "Minute" Valse, in *D-flat*, Opus 64, No. 1, by Chopin, is a short illustration of a romantic and expressive use of an old dance form. The waltz, or valse, known for many years as a characteristic dance form, has here been subjected to a poetic idealization. It is one of a series of valses by Chopin written for piano solo, which treat the old rhythm in this idealistic manner, and of which a noted critic once said "these are valses for countesses."

Music and Romance for Youth

The form of the Valse is very simple. It opens with a four-measure *Introduction* which moves directly into the Valse itself. The first theme is a simple "pattern" or "figure" of notes. The second theme is similar in character. The most exquisite contrast is afforded by the lovely singing melody of the Trio section, an air which is immediately repeated with slight alterations in harmony, and with delicate grace-note ornamentations. Following an extended trill, a return is made to an exact repetition of the first theme which is brought to a close by a daintily spun-out, downward-moving scale run and a simple chord. The form is a three-part song; Introduction *a a* || *b b* || *Trio a—a* and arabesques; eight measures interlude; *a a* || *b b*—creating the form *A B A*.

"Moment Musical," in *F* minor, by Franz Schubert, is folk-dance in type, although a "composed" work. Its simplicity, its constant use of *basso ostinato*, and frequent repetition of the same themes, all add to its highly artistic appeal. Opening with a two-measure rhythmic introduction, *staccato* and *piano*, the theme (in key of *F* minor), with its attractive embellishments, is presented and immediately repeated. The second theme, smoother in type, is in the related key of *A-flat* major. This, too, is repeated. The third thematic melody is in the prevailing key of *F* minor, the air moving along over a dominant *basso ostinato* and moving at its close to the major key. A repetition of this theme, a *pianissimo* re-statement of the first theme, and a *Coda*, end the composition. The *Coda* is built upon *motifs* taken from the first theme, and ends as though running down, like a music box. The form of the piece in diagram is *a a b b c c a Coda*.

MUSICAL ILLUSTRATIONS

20169	*Amaryllis (Old French Rondo)*	*Victor Concert Orchestra*
6648	*Largo (Händel)*	*Stock and Chicago Symphony Orchestra*
6639	*Marche Militaire (Franz Schubert)*	*San Francisco Symphony Orchestra*
6591- 6592	} *Adagio from "Moonlight Sonata" (Beethoven)*	*Bauer*
20614	*Minute Valse, Op. 64, No. 1 (Chopin)*	*Schmidt*
1143	*Moment Musical (Schubert)*	*Casals*

INFORMATIONAL NOTE

"Marche Militaire" was written as a compliment to the Austrian Imperial body-guards, a crack regiment of grenadiers or heavy infantry, which was officered by some of the highest nobles of the realm.

QUESTIONS AND TOPICS FOR DISCUSSION

1. Name and define two general types or divisions of music? From the instrumental music you have heard or studied, name and describe five examples of each division.

2. Name at least eight elements of beauty usually found in a composition of classic form.

3. For which of these elements is the "Amaryllis" notable? Contrast the "Amaryllis" and the "Largo."

4. How has Beethoven suggested a definite mood in this *Adagio*?

5. Compare the definite form of "Marche Militaire" with the more vague atmosphere of the "Adagio." Which do you prefer? Give definite reasons for your choice.

PART TWO—CHAPTER TWELVE

ILLUSTRATION OF NATIONAL CHARACTERISTICS THROUGH A STUDY OF MODERN SUITES

(The student should carefully review the first five paragraphs of Chapter Eleven, Part One, on "What a Modern Suite Is," before continuing the study of this lesson.)

Nationality in Modern Suites. In addition to its ability to tell a story or suggest a definite mood, the modern Suite often displays a distinct nationality, by which is meant that, in it, the composer has employed either melodic characteristics, rhythms, atmosphere, or style individual to some country.

NATIVE ORCHESTRA IN TURKESTAN

To do this, the composer need not always belong to the race whose music he suggests or imitates, although he usually delights in exploiting the musical traits of his own land. Both possibilities are found in many compositions.

"Danse Russe," from the "Nutcracker Suite,"* is a splendid example of nationality, in which a composer uses the rhythms and style of his native land. It is sometimes called by the title "Trépak," the name of an old and popular folk-dance among the Russian peasantry. The Trépak is a dance of rapid, sturdy character and is always very strongly accented, the dancers crouching near the floor and balancing as they keep time to the rhythms. It is a short, vividly

---

* See Chapter Ten, Part One, for "Nutcracker" story.

vigorous Russian dance, characterized by a tragic abruptness, and is played by full orchestra.

In the "Second Suite," from "Peer Gynt," * Edvard Grieg, Norway's foremost composer, has displayed the ability to accurately present the national characteristics of two widely separated lands and races—Arabia and Norway. Much less familiar to the general public than the first, it contains several unusually attractive numbers. Of these none is more typically national in character—but of Arabia and the Orient, not Norway—than the second number, "Arabian

AN ORIENTAL DANCE

Dance." This was written by Grieg as a bit of music to enhance that part of Ibsen's drama in which Peer Gynt is a guest in the camp of the Arabian chieftain, whose daughter (with all her maidens) dances for his entertainment.

The "Arabian Dance" is so typically Oriental in melody, rhythm, and style that a title is scarcely necessary. At first it is the rhythm and the rhythmic effects which suggest the Orient, rather than the melody. But presently are heard other instruments, the odd intervals, and the use of the whole-tone and Oriental minor scales which are so typical of the East. The dance progresses. At its end the drums are heard again, alternating with the tambourine. The rhythmic beating grows gradually softer but no slower. Soon there is no sound of the tambourines—only the drums still beating softly as they are

* See Chapter Thirteen, Part One, for "Peer Gynt" story.

gently struck by the *hands* of the players—then silence. It is a picturesque composition, opening with a two-measure introduction in which the tempo of the dance is suggested through the rhythmic figure played by triangle and tambourine. The first theme

is not so Oriental in its melodic type as in its orchestral presentation. It is followed in turn by the second theme, a more typically Arabian air.

The development section of the short dance is notable for the use of many double-thirds and sixths, and the entire composition reaches an agitated and violent climax in a series of consecutive double-thirds. A supremely effective anti-climax, or *Coda,* is created by a diminution to *ppp* and the use, during the last four measures, of only rhythmic percussion instruments.

"Sunshine Song." The second "Peer Gynt Suite" contains an orchestral version of a vocal solo. Toward the end of Act IV of the "Peer Gynt" drama, an unusual and attractive effect is obtained by stage devices. From behind a closed curtain Anitra and her maidens are heard, the somewhat picturesque music being sustained by the orchestra as the curtain rises. The stage being revealed, the audience sees Solvejg—Peer Gynt's wife—sitting in the sunshine, and hears her singing her song of faith that Spring will come again, and that with it Peer Gynt will also return. This is often called the "Sunshine Song." After Solvejg finishes her song the curtain slowly descends, the orchestral accompaniment continuing softly, and gradually changing into the sea music which introduces the fifth act.

The principal melody of the "Sunshine Song"—a Norwegian folk-air—is heard twice in the drama, once in its original form as

A NORWEGIAN SAETER

sung by Solvejg, and as an orchestral introduction to another act. The air is genuinely Norwegian in character, alternately plaintive and happy in mood, and is the orchestral prelude which Grieg uses in the "Second Peer Gynt Suite." It is one of the most effective numbers in the Suite and is written for an unusual combination of instruments —muted strings, flutes, clarinet, horns and harp. It alternates from minor to parallel major and back again.

The song opens with an eight-measure Introduction which is characterized by short phrases very Norwegian in style, and which ends in a dramatic pause. After the pause and two measures of simple rhythm in horn and harp, the first theme of the "Sunshine Song" begins, a simple but plaintive melody.

At the close of the first theme statement the brighter second theme is heard (in parallel major key).* It is this portion of the melody which has won for the song its subtitle, "Sunshine Song."

But the mood changes almost immediately to that of the less hopeful and more plaintive air, which brings the song to completion.

The form, or large divisions, of this simple song might be diagramed as, Introduction, first theme (in *A* minor, and preceded by two-measure of rhythmic figure), second theme (*A* major), first theme in original key, brief *Coda*.

"Solvejg's Cradle Song," which shares equally with this character's "Sunshine Song" in fame and popularity, opens with a short *pianissimo* instrumental introduction which at once establishes the atmosphere of a tender lullaby, and which, in the final two measures immediately preceding the entrance of the voice, contains no melody but only groups of rhythmic chords.

The first part of the song is constructed in odd three-measure phrases, reminiscent of the irregular meters of the historic runes. Here the simple two measure vocal melody (first theme) is imme-

Lento

diately followed by the added measure in the accompaniment which completes the three-measure phrase.

---

* Parallel minor and major have the same keynote, different signatures.

A Study of Modern Suites

This unusual formation is repeated four times in succession, after which is heard the second section of the song, *poco animato,* made up of longer, more sustained phrases. Here the artistic accompaniment plays an important part in the creation of mood and atmosphere by its rhythmic alternation of groups of swaying chords with groups of simple arpeggios.

An instrumental *Codetta,* similar in style and content to the Introduction, closes the "Cradle Song." *

"Marche Militaire Française," by Saint-Saëns.† In the "Suite Algérienne," of which this "Marche Militaire" is a part, Saint-Saëns has recorded his musical observations of northern Africa. A French composer writing in the style of a race not his own, but of one which is governed by his own land, he was familiar with the city of Algiers through frequent visits to it, even being there on a visit at the time of his death. On the title page of the *Suite* he wrote, "Picturesque Impressions of Voyage to Algiers."

The Marche is a brilliant composition reflecting his impressions and sensations upon visiting the old French Fort Blidah, not far from the city of Algiers, and in it the composer has incorporated many of the musical characteristics of the native bands.

The music of the native exhibits many Oriental tendencies, both in melodic features and in the instruments used. The native Algerian has a great liking for much sounding of drum and clashing of cymbal, and these instruments are seen in great numbers in the native bands.

The music opens (string choir) with a lively flourish in distinctly military band style, and in double-quick tempo. On the twelfth measure there is a *glissando* of the

A REGIMENTAL BAND IN ALGERIA

strings, which then carry the theme to its repetition by the woodwind, brass, and kettle-drum. After the presentation of the first themes, the transition to the *Trio* section is made by a fanfare of bugles. Here is heard a simple martial melody, with snappy "after-beats" in the accompaniment, of a blood-stirring style. In one part of the composition there is heard a persistent droning bass, suggestive of the drone of certain primitive instruments—as the bagpipe of Scotland, which finds its counterpart in the native Egyptian bagpipes.

---

* This selection should be heard both in its original form as a song and in its transcription for symphony orchestra.
† See also "Reverie du Soir," in Chapter Six, Part One.

Music and Romance for Youth

With lightning-like swirls of sound the music returns to the first theme, after which, with a high, clear military bugle-call and grand flourish, it comes to a close in a spirited and brilliant *Coda*.

Galloway
ALGERIAN STREET MUSICIANS

The frequent use of brass and percussion instruments (including cymbals) is extremely characteristic of the band music of the native troops.

The Ballet, "Le Cid," * by Massenet, is a brilliant display of Spanish nationality in music written by another French composer. It is from an opera of the same name by Massenet which tells of the adventures of the mythical Spanish hero, Rodrigo Diaz de Bivar—better known as Le Cid (or the Chief)—who lived in Spain in the eleventh century.

The "Castillane," from "Le Cid" (which takes its name from the ancient Spanish province of Castile), is an animated dance in 6/8 measure. It is much like a rondo in form, as the melody and rhythm of the first theme return many times, alternating with various secondary themes. A special feature of the entire composition is the characteristic primitive rhythm 6/8 and syncopation, which underlie the main body of the piece. In the "Castillane" Massenet also makes use of consecutive double thirds. The dance ends with a brief *Coda*.

The "Andalouse" (which takes its name from the southern Spanish province of Andalusia, and is characteristic of the locality) moves slowly and deliberately over a definite rhythmic "pattern" bass resembling the Habanera rhythm 2/4 and which accompanies almost all of the brief work.

Uneven rhythmic groups in the simple melody, as 2/4 are characteristic of the first theme. There are two themes, both in A minor and similar in character, both also showing Moorish influence. The form, in a large way, may be described as *Introduction* (four-measure), *A B A* and *Coda*.

"Love Song," from the "Indian Suite," by Edward MacDowell. This charming "Indian Suite" was one of the first attempts in America to idealize the tribal music of the American Indian.

In making the "Indian Suite," MacDowell was apt to say he did it as a "stunt," because of his wish to use the fine themes, rather

---

* See Chapter Ten, Part One, "Ballet, Telling a Story in Music and Dance."

A Study of Modern Suites

than that he thought that in doing so he was accomplishing something of national importance. MacDowell was very certain as to what seemed to him the absurdity of any so-called National American School of music being developed from the tribal or folk-music of the American Indian or Negro. His feeling was that the great composer in America might use either Indian or Negro airs as thematic material, but that these themes would always remain either Indian or Negro, as these peoples have never touched our daily lives or those of our ancestors.

The thematic material for the Suite is authentically Indian, the individual theme of the "Love Song" having come from the Iowa Indians, and being built upon the five-toned scale. The music begins with a soft beauty which gradually develops and increases in power. The mood is that of a tender *reverie*, the flutes being most prominent in the playing of the very lyric melody.

The song is built upon one chief theme which is announced immediately by the wind instruments. It is highly interesting to compare the Indian tribal air and MacDowell's idealization of it, and to note the very slight changes which the composer made in his use of the melody.

Theme of Iowa Indian "Love Song":

The MacDowell version, played by flute at opening of "Love Song":

The theme is developed by the use of two episodical phrases—one a bit of response from the strings, the other a more vigorous melody first given out in the minor by the woodwind instruments.

The effectiveness of the work is disturbed by no abrupt climaxes, and after establishing a definite atmosphere of tenderness and delivering its brief message, it comes to a quiet close.

MUSICAL ILLUSTRATIONS

9296 *Marche Militaire Française from "Suite Algérienne (Saint-Saëns)*
       Continental Symphony Orchestra
1406 {*Castillane* \ *from "Le Cid" Ballet Suite (Massenet)*
       {*Andalouse* { *Hertz and San Francisco Sym. Orch.*
6615 *Danse Russe from "Nutcracker Suite" (Tschaikowsky)*
       Stokowski and Philadelphia Symphony Orchestra
9327 {*Arabian Dance*   } *from "Second Peer Gynt Suite" (Grieg)*
4014 {*Solvejg's Sunshine Song* } *Goossens and Symphony Orchestra*
       {*Solvejg's Cradle Song* }   *Marsh*
20342 *Love Song from "Indian Suite" (Edward MacDowell)* *Victor Orch.*

Informational Notes

"Solvejg's Sunshine Song" and "Cradle Song" present Peer's faithful wife in two distinct moods, each of which is dominated by her extreme love for her unfaithful mate, but each displaying this love in a different manner. The "Sunshine Song" shows Solvejg patiently and hopefully waiting the day of her husband's return, her love buoying her spirits with the assurance that he must return to her. The "Cradle Song," in contrast, is a manifestation of love, expressed in the reception and forgiveness of the broken and weary Peer, who, when he needs the ministrations of a loving hand, finds them here.

Algeria, on the north Mediterranean coast of Africa, is a dependency of France, and has long been indebted to the French for internal improvement, such as draining of swamp-lands, planting and cultivating thousands of acres of barren land, digging artesian wells in what seemed a desert, planting orchards, and battling with plagues of locusts. The fishermen and merchants of France have traded with natives of Algeria since the days of the Crusades.

The city of Algiers is built about a curving bay and has a famous harbor. The old city is an almost even mixture of ancient and modern buildings and streets. In the older part, or native city, which had always the greatest fascination for Saint-Saëns, the Moorish influence is immediately noticed. It has all the appearance of an ancient Arabian city. The streets are so extremely narrow that a man on a donkey—one of the native ways of traveling—completely fills one. In the coffee-shops the native men sit for hours listening to tales related to them by professional story-tellers.

"The Habanera," of Oriental character and established rhythm, is a dance of great antiquity, which takes its name from Havana, the capital city of Cuba. It is said to have been introduced into Cuba many generations ago from Africa, and from Cuba taken to Spain. It is generally danced to the accompaniment of song, in a slow and stately manner, a choral refrain being a feature of the form.

Le Cid it was who displayed so much shrewd prowess in warfare that his skill is still recounted in Spain after over nine hundred years. After his death, which was, at his own order, kept secret, his body was tied to the back of his own war-horse in sitting position—this was also a plan of the Cid's—and the horse then led at the head of the troops in the battle, which resulted in victory.

Massenet, who wrote the opera and ballet, tells in his book, "My Recollections," of first hearing the Spanish air which he made the important feature of the ballet. "I remember I heard the *motif* which begins the ballet, in Spain," he writes. "I was in the very country of Le Cid at the time, living in a modest inn. It chanced that they were celebrating a wedding and they danced all night in the lower room of the hotel. Several guitars and two flutes repeated a dance tune until they wore it out. I noted it down. It became the *motif* I am writing about, a bit of local color which I seized. I did not let it get away."

Castile, in the north central part of Spain, is, in the main, a broad, treeless plateau. The capital of Old Castile was the city of Burgos. It is highly appropriate that the "Castillane" should be a part of the "Cid" ballet, for here in the old Castilian city of Burgos there is still a castle near which stand three stone monuments which mark the site of the birthplace of the Cid. He and his wife were buried for many years in San Pedro, about twelve miles from Burgos, but their bones now repose in the Town Hall of Burgos.

Andalusia, a southern province of Spain, owes its quaint name to the reply given by a Spanish peasant to a question asked him, in very early times, by a band of Moorish soldier-explorers. They asked him the name of the land through which they were traveling. He, not understanding their language, ordered his donkey—whose name was Lucia—to move on, with the Spanish "Anda Lucia" (On! Lucia). The soldiers, taking his remark for the name of the province, wrote it on the map, where it has remained until this day.

HISTORICAL NOTES

The MacDowell "Indian Suite" was written in the music-room of the MacDowell home, "Hillcrest," in Peterborough, before the Log Cabin, in his famous woodland studies, had been built. The Indian themes used by MacDowell were some that had been collected by Dr. Theodore Baker, long before anyone else had done such collecting scientifically. The *Suite* had its first performances in Boston and New York City in 1896, within a few weeks of each other, with Emil Pauer as the conductor of the Boston Symphony and Anton Seidel, of the New York Philharmonic. The Boston concert was a remarkable one for MacDowell, for not only was the *Suite* played, but he played his Second Concerto, as well, and received a tremendous ovation. In the music-room at "Hillcrest" there still hangs a huge wreath presented to him on that day.

The title *Cid* comes from the Arabian *sidi,* meaning lord or master. The Cid of Spanish fame was married to a sister of King Alphonso the Sixth. His name is always associated with the city of Valencia, which stronghold he captured from the Moors in 1094 after a twenty-year siege. He was then made Governor of Valencia. The public gate of Valencia, used at the present day, has, ever since, been known as Puerta del Cid (Gate of the Cid).

QUESTIONS AND TOPICS FOR DISCUSSION

1. How do modern and old classic suites differ?

2. What is meant by "nationality"? What musical traits help to determine musical nationality? Discuss.

3. Name nationality features individual to music of Arabia, Spain, Norway, the Orient, and the American Indian. How can you often recognize the nationality which the composer wished to suggest in a piece of music, even when you know neither title nor composer of the music?

4. Why are two types of national music presented in the "Peer Gynt Suite"? How have musical instruments aided Grieg in doing this?

5. Discuss the folk-songs of Russia. In what ways do they resemble the music of the Orient? Contrast the "Danse Russe," by Tschaikowsky, and the "Arabian Dance," by Grieg. How does each make its musical appeal to you?

6. What is meant by an "idealization" of a folk-air?

7. Why has MacDowell chosen the wind instruments to carry the air or melody of his "Love Song"?

8. The melody or main theme of the "Marche Militaire Française" is conventional rather than Oriental in type. Explain how Saint-Saëns has contrived to suggest Oriental or Moorish influence in the music. In what sections of the "Marche" are these traits most evident?

9. Discuss the importance of rhythmic "pattern" as a musical force in suggestion of nationality. Contrast the underlying rhythms of the two Spanish dances suggested. Which, in your opinion, is more typical of Oriental dance music? Why? Which is the more important in these two Spanish numbers, the melody or the rhythm? Give reasons for your answer.

10. What is a *rondo*? How many times is the main theme heard in *Castillane*? What other Spanish dance is similar in rhythm to this *Andalouse*? What noted composer has used this rhythm in a famous operatic *aria*? Name it and the opera of which it is a part.

11. Discuss the three features which seem to you to be most characteristically Russian in the *Trépak*.

12. Why has MacDowell not considered the tribal music of the American Indian a basis for a national school of composition? What is meant by such a "school"? What nation employs in many of its

oldest songs the same five-toned scale as that upon which was built
the Iowa tribal melody which MacDowell has used?

13. Discuss characteristics of Indian tribal music. Name two
favorite instruments of the American Indian. How has MacDowell
imparted a truly "Indian" atmosphere to the "Love Song"? Tell
what you know of MacDowell's life, home, and writings.

14. What is meant by "parallel" minor? How does it differ
from "relative" minor? Contrast the moods of the two themes in
"Solvejg's Song." How does the mood of the first theme in any way
reflect the home conditions of many people who live in Norway?
Explain.

Library Reading. "Edvard Grieg," by Henry T. Finck; "Rambles
in Spain," by J. D. Fitzgerald; "The Nutcracker," "Fairy Tales,"
by Hoffman; "The Indian in Song and Story," by Alice Fletcher.

PART TWO—CHAPTER THIRTEEN

FAMOUS CONCERTED MUSIC FROM OPERA *

In spite of the great favor with which the opera-going public
always has regarded, and always will regard, the beautiful *arias* for
which all opera is noted, it is undoubtedly true that many of the
extraordinarily realistic effects, the stirring climaxes, and the poetic
appeals of opera are created by its ensemble music.

The smallest form of vocal ensemble is the duet. Between the
forms of duet and operatic chorus there are ranged such effective
vocal combinations as trio, quartet, and sextet, all interesting to hear
and learn about, whether known as independent concert numbers or
in connection with their legitimate stories and backgrounds as parts
of a complete opera.

"May Angels Guard Thee," from "Force of Destiny," by Verdi,
is one of the most beautiful duets of operatic literature. The duet
occurs during the *Finale* of the second act of this highly dramatic
work, an opera (four acts) in which all the principal characters meet
a violent death. It is sung by soprano and bass, accompanied by
chorus and orchestra. The scene is within a church. Leonora is departing for her solitary abode and is receiving a prayerful blessing
from the Abbot. The duet proper (*adagio*) is preceded by an introductory measure of staccato, harp-like chords from the orchestra,
pianissimo. Contrary to the usual custom, the chorus is heard before

* See also "Toreador Song" from "Carmen"; "Misérere," "Anvil Chorus," and "Home
to Our Mountains" from "Il Trovatore"; "Farewell, O Earth" from "Aïda"; and "Barcarolle" from "Tales of Hoffmann."

the soloists, their song at once establishing the devotional atmosphere in which are sung the Abbot's prayer—"Let Angels of God Watch Over You"—and Leonora's devout responses.

"Solenne in quest'ora (Swear in this hour), from "Force of Destiny," by Verdi, is a duet between Alvaro (tenor) and Don Carlo (baritone), in which the latter, unconscious that he is thus serving his old-time but unrecognized friend, swears to carry out the dying wishes of Alvaro, a new-found friend, by burning, unopened, a casket of precious letters. The duet is beautifully melodious and intensely emotional, and serves to contrast most forcibly the characteristics of these two types of male voice.

"O Somme Carlos" (O Noble Carlos), from "Ernani," by Verdi, is a great operatic ensemble which expresses the martial triumph of Carlos, who has been accepted as King by the Electors, at their final meeting. The young king has concealed himself in the gloomy royal sepulcher to which he has come to overhear the plotting of his enemies, who draw lots for the privilege of killing him. Carlos, in the following dramatic scene, in a darkness lighted only by torches held by his soldiers, pardons them all. There is then heard the stirring Finale, "O Somme Carlos," a trio and chorus at first declamatory in effect, then made brilliant by its vigorous dynamic shadings—from *pianissimo* to *fortissimo*—and by its superb climax.

"Bella figlia dell' amore" (the Quartet), from "Rigoletto," by Verdi, is, without doubt, one of the most masterly vocal ensembles ever written. It is heard in the third act of the opera. The four parts are sung by Gilda (a soprano rôle long a favorite with prima donnas); Maddalena (contralto); The Duke (tenor), and Rigoletto (bass). Rigoletto is the hunchback court clown who

QUARTET FROM "RIGOLETTO"

must always jest, though his heart may be breaking. Gilda, his daughter, loves the Duke.

In the quartet each character sings a different emotion, and it is in the blending of these that Verdi has shown his great art. The

Duke, who is inside the inn, begins the quartet, closely followed by Maddalena, the young gypsy woman who is there talking with him. Gilda is watching them from outside, accompanied by her father, who is threatening vengeance upon the Duke, for his treachery. Each of the four parts is characterized by brilliant vocal accomplishments, and the dramatic climax—capped with a high *A* for the soprano— is calculated to win attention and admiration from all hearers.

"Chi mi frena" (the Sextet), from "Lucia di Lammermoor." Donizetti, another Italian master of operatic melody, has composed

SEXTET FROM "LUCIA DI LAMMERMOOR"

a marvelous masterpiece of concerted singing in this famous sextet. The gorgeous ensemble is heard at the moment when Edgar (tenor) who loves and is loved by Lucia (soprano), appears at her wedding feast after she has been deceived and persuaded to marry Arthur (second tenor), having been told that Edgar is false to her and that Arthur can save her family from ruin. Lucia's brother Henry (baritone), who has plotted against her, the Priest (bass), and Alice, her companion (alto), complete the sextet.

The number opens with a two-measure introduction from the strings, *pizzicato,* the rhythm being that upon which the entire sextet is built. Then there is heard the chief air, considered by many to be

one of the greatest melodies in the history of Italian opera. One by one the six characters take up their parts until in the magnificent climax, all are singing. Each is, for a short time, the most prominent voice.

This *Sextet* may well be heard as a brilliant piece of vocalism without any reference to the opera story. It is popular because it is well-written, melodious, singable, and easy to remember.

Operatic Choruses. While the operatic ensemble numbers written to be sung by carefully selected solo voices attract by their resplendent beauties, there are, among the gems of operatic literature, no greater nor more effective masterpieces than some of those works written for the regular chorus. Among them are these skillfully constructed and vivacious choruses, "They're Here!" (Son Qua!), the

"PAGLIACCI"—ARRIVAL OF THE PLAYERS

opening chorus of the opera "Pagliacci,"* by Leoncavallo, and the same opera's pleasing "Bell Chorus."

"They're Here!" (Son Qua!), the opening chorus of the opera, shows a scene at the entrance to the Calabrian village. Here a theatre tent has been set up by a troupe of strolling players (the pagliacci), who prepare for the evening performance. The music is thoroughly Italian in its melodiousness, and in its stirring motion.

Sounds of trumpets are heard, slightly out of tune, and a drum is beating behind the scenes as the curtain goes up. The clowns have been parading and some of the villagers have been waiting near the tent to see them return. After several calls, confused shouting, all in keeping with the scene, the chorus begins, with clever passing of the theme from one voice to another. The sopranos have a four-note arpeggio-figure which passes, without loss of rhythm, no overlapping and no rest, to the tenors. From there it moves to the

* See also the story of the "Pagliacci" "Prologue" in Chapter One, Part Two—"Famous Preludes."

basses. Here the theme develops, on the tones of a simple triad. Presently it is sung in thirds by the sopranos. All the while the orchestra is adding a masterly and colorful accompaniment which is built upon so simple a little figure as a running passage of five notes. All of the music expresses the good-natured anticipation and excitement of the villagers.

The "Bell Chorus" shows the same scene in the little Italian village. Canio, the master of the troupe, has been inviting all the villagers to the evening performance. Suddenly the church bells begin to ring the Angelus, and the peasants troop away to the vesper service singing their delightful "Bell Chorus" as they go—"Ding dong! The shadows fall!"

The scene is a fascinating one. The showman's oboe is heard within the tent, contrasting with the ever-ringing bells in the orchestral accompaniment, and the purposely monotonous "bell" chords of the singers as they repeat their plaintive "ding-dong!" Toward the end an exquisite echo is heard as the music diminishes to a tender *pianissimo finale* as the crowds disappear in the distance.

"Pilgrims' Chorus," from "Tannhäuser," by Richard Wagner, is a chorus equally melodic, but entirely different in its appeal. The scene is laid in a valley near the famous Wartburg Castle, noted through the centuries for its tournaments of song. The peaceful atmosphere of the scene is emphasized.

Elizabeth's "Prayer" and Wolfram's "Evening Star" have been sung, when, from a distance, comes the faint sound of singing Pilgrims as they move along on their return from their religious pilgrimage to Rome. As they approach, the chant of the chorus grows louder and louder. Presently it is interrupted by a snatch of the melody from the shepherd's flute. Becoming more eloquent, the music of the Pilgrims passes directly by, then diminishes as the sound of the voices recedes in the distance.

The melody is classic in its chant-like form and makes a dramatically religious appeal. It is also a unique study in tone shading on the part of a chorus.

"Ma perchè tu ei abbandoni?" (Wilt Thou Leave Us all Unprotected?), from "Boris Godounow," by Moussorgsky, is thought by many to be the most brilliant of all the choral numbers in the sumptuously gorgeous Russian opera. The opening chorus is sung by a gathering of the people who have been clamoring at the gateway of the royal retreat and demanding that the Tzar shall again assume the scepter of Russia. This he has refused to do, again and again. Now comes the beseeching prayer to his loyalty, in which the Tzar is addressed by his subjects as "little father." *

Opening *fortissimo,* with a short prelude for full orchestra in which the constant roll of the drums and rhythmic effects "set the scene" for the superbly brilliant military pageant. The simple theme of the music is made doubly effective by being sung, for some time, by all of the chorus in unison.

This theme is notable for its odd rhythms, and its frequent alternations of three- and five-beat measure.

MUSICAL ILLUSTRATIONS

8097 *May Angels Guard Thee from "Force of Destiny"—Duet (Verdi)*
       Ponselle, Pinza and Metropolitan Opera Chorus

8069 *Solenne in quest' ora from "Force of Destiny"—Duet (Verdi)*
            Gigli and de Luca

8174 *O sommo Carlo from "Ernani"—Trio (Verdi)*
   De Luca, Tedesco Antony and Metropolitan Opera Chorus and Orch.

10012 *Bella figlia dell' amore from "Rigoletto"—Quartet (Verdi)*
        Galli-Curci, Homer, Gigli and de Luca

10012 *Chi mi frena from "Lucia di Lammermoor"—Sextet (Donizetti)*
        Galli-Curci, Homer, Gigli and de Luca

4028 {*Son Qua! (They're Here!)* } *from "Pagliacci"—Choruses (Leoncavallo)*
    {*Bell Chorus* }
           Metropolitan Opera Chorus

20127 *Pilgrims' Chorus from "Tannhäuser"—Chorus (Wagner)*
            Victor Male Chorus

9399 *Ma perchè tu ci abbandoni? from "Boris Godounow"—Chorus*
  (Moussorgsky) Royal Opera Chorus and Royal Covent Garden Orch.

INFORMATIONAL NOTES

"The Force of Destiny" had its first performance in the Imperial Theatre in St. Petersburg (now Leningrad) on November 10, 1862.

The *pagliacci* is the Italian name for the strolling players who wander from town to town in Italy. They usually carry with them, in a cart drawn by a donkey, a small tent, and this they set up in whatever convenient place they can find near the market square of the village. This rural custom is made the background of Leoncavallo's very melodic opera.

Richard Wagner drew much of his inspiration and many of his subjects from the legends and myths known to all cultured Germanic peoples. The Wartburg Castle, which is the scene of many of the

---

* This was a customary title in the days of the old Russian Empire.

incidents which occur in "Tannhäuser," is located on the heights above the town of Eisenach, famous as the birthplace of Johann Sebastian Bach.   This castle first became famous at the opening of the thirteenth century, on account of the "War of Wartburg," a poetic title given to the contest of song held there in 1206.   The castle was then the home of Hermann of Thuringia, who made the place the refuge of all musicians, scholars, and artists who needed protection or patronage.   The castle is said to have been built in 1060, and remains today one of the most picturesque palaces in existence.

"Boris Godounow" is a four-act opera, the libretto of which is founded upon scenes from a historic tale of the same title, written by Pushkin.   Boris is a counsellor of the Tzar, and has caused the brother and heir of the ruler to be assassinated.   A young Russian impostor attempts to impersonate the murdered prince.   The entire story is filled with gloom and tragedy.   The music is characterized by remarkable beauty and color, and suggests deep national feeling. The opera had its first performance in St. Petersburg (now Leningrad) in 1874.

The real Boris Godounow was a usurper, a man who had served Ivan the Terrible, and who was held responsible for the disappearance of the heir to the throne at the death of the Tzar.   Boris then ruled for many years.

QUESTIONS AND TOPICS FOR DISCUSSION

1. What is meant by vocal ensemble?   Name at least five types of vocal ensemble.

2. Discuss the voice types heard in the concerted works mentioned in this chapter.

3. Contrast the moods of the duet and the trio here suggested. By what musical means have the composers achieved these effects? Mention at least three ways.   What is the mood of the "Pilgrims' Chorus"?

4. What picturesque custom of provincial Italy has Leoncavallo perpetuated in his opera "I Pagliacci"?   What unusual musical feature of this opera has been suggested in a previous chapter?   Mention and discuss at least five ways in which Leoncavallo has, through the music alone, suggested the simple happy life of a small Italian village.

5. Discuss any other music from these same operas which you may have heard in connection with your study of music, in opera performances, or in concert form.

Library Reading.   "The Bride of Lammermoor," by Sir Walter Scott.

PART TWO—CHAPTER FOURTEEN

CONCERT OVERTURES

In spite of the romantic glamour which will always surround the classic instrumental compositions of Haydn, Mozart, and Beethoven —including the numerous charming chamber music works, and symphonic works for the orchestra as it had been developed in their day, it has been possible for the orchestra itself, through its own continued development (both in size and in variety of instruments included in it), to offer composers of the later nineteenth century still more alluring inducements for writing poetically expressive, elaborate, or spectacular works for it.

Some independent concert overtures * which have won for themselves an enduring popularity were written originally for a definite occasion (and are so-called "occasional" music) and contain within themselves unique personal or historic elements.

"Overture 1812," by Tschaikowsky. This overture is an expression of the deepest and most sincere patriotism on the part of its composer. The event which it commemorates is the historic repulse of Napoleon's invasion of Russia in 1812. The defeat at Moscow and the retreat of the French army are spectacular events in world history.

THE KREMLIN AT MOSCOW

When invited, in 1881, to prepare an orchestral work to be played in Moscow for the celebration of an important cathedral's dedication, Tschaikowsky decided to include in his new work a pictorial description of the older event.

The music was played out-of-doors in the Public Square, and in the shadow of the great Kremlin. A huge orchestra was assembled, with an auxiliary brass band, and cannons that were to be fired at certain dramatic moments in the music. A part in the music was also arranged for the church bells.

The music of "Overture 1812"—now a perennial favorite, although the "parts" for the cannon are usually omitted—taxes the utmost resources of the modern symphony orchestra. It opens with a slow Introduction in which two themes—an old Russian chant or hymn, and the air of an old Russian war song—are heard.

* See Chapter One, Part Two. page 1.

Presently the "Marseillaise" of France is heard, and throughout the composition this air is repeated whenever the French troops are to be suggested. As they were, at first, victorious, the "Marseillaise" seems to come nearer and nearer, with ever-increasing power. They are, at the end, overcome, and the Overture ends in a wildly triumphant orgy of brilliant music, the air of the Russian war song, the surge and apparent confusion of cheering, the thunderous roar of the Russian hymn, and the noisy pealing of the bells, uniting in a thrilling wave of sound which vividly suggests the tremendous wave of patriotism which swept the city in 1812.

The "William Tell" Overture, by Rossini, equally patriotic, but in quite a different manner, was written originally as a part of the opera of the same name.

The "William Tell" Overture * is usually thought of in four parts. It is a faithful description of Alpine life. Part One is a prelude,

PUBLIC SQUARE OF THE KREMLIN, WHERE THE 1812 OVERTURE WAS FIRST PLAYED

"Dawn," a suggestion of sunrise in the mountains. Part Two, "The Storm," is a vivid description of a mountain storm in the Alps. Part Three, "The Calm," is a *pastorale,* depicting the quiet life of the mountain shepherd. In this part of the Overture is heard the "Ranz des Vaches" (Swiss shepherd song) played by English horn and flute in much the same way that it sounds and echoes when played by a Swiss shepherd on his Alpine horn. Part Four, the "Galop" or "Finale," brings the Overture to a brilliant close.

The Overture begins with a short 'cello figure which soon is lost in the unfolding of beautiful harmonies depicting the coming of dawn.

* For detailed analysis see "Music Appreciation for Children," pages 240-241, and "What We Hear in Music," page 534.

A dreamy melody by 'cello then continues throughout the movement. The mutterings of a storm are suggested, by tympani, in the distance and suddenly the tempest breaks in fury in one of the most forceful

AN ALPHORN BLOWER, SWITZERLAND

musical descriptions ever written. The third section, opening with the "Ranz des Vasches," is a *pastorale*—a scene on the mountain top —in which the woodwind instruments convey the serene calm after the storm. The finale begins with a fanfare of trumpets which usher in a stirring march melody, the principal theme.

The Overture closes with a brilliant *coda*.

The "Flying Dutchman" Overture, by Richard Wagner, is founded upon an old legend of the sea. The hero was a Dutch sea captain named Van Straaten, who was condemned to sail the high seas in a spectral ship, the sight of which was regarded as a bad omen by sailors. Similar legends are current in Germany and England. Originally it was related that the captain was delayed by head winds while trying to turn the Cape of Good Hope and swore blasphemously that he would beat around it if it took him until the Judgment Day. The "phantom vessel" with blood-red sails—the superstition—and its captain, who is doomed to sail forever except for a landing of a few hours once in each seven years, was brought to Wagner's attention on a stormy voyage which he took from the continent to London.

The Overture breathes the out-of-doors, and the composer has also cleverly suggested throughout the sweep of the wind and the

SCENE FROM "THE FLYING DUTCHMAN"

scurrying of water and foam in an angry sea. Other features of the Overture are the song of a chorus of sailors and Senta's melody (it is Senta whose love, in the operatic version of the old sea tale, finally rescues the Dutchman from the awful curse). The ending is triumphant, as the curse is finally lifted.

The Overture opens with a long-held tremulous chord from the woodwind instruments and violins, giving a feeling of mystery. Almost immediately the Call of the Dutchman (sometimes also known as the Curse), horns and bassoons, is also heard, as he nears the shore upon which he hopes to land for the one short visit allowed him each seven years. This is followed by a rushing ascending and descending scale passage (each note of which is sounded twice), after which the Dutchman's Call is heard again from trombone and tuba—this time an "echo" call as though from far out at sea. *Motifs* from the Call are sounded loudly from all instruments, and once more soft echoes resound (viola and 'cello). The music which follows is one of the grandest of all musical pictures of the sea.

The theme which is known as Senta's melody (or the Redemption theme), is interwoven with the music of the Overture and is easily recognized at its first appearance as it comes as so strong a contrast to the wild tempestuous music of the sea. The Senta theme is filled with tenderness and quiet sentiment, and at last grows to heroic proportions, a symbol of Senta's final heroism in giving her life for the Dutchman.

The entire Overture moves in the general *tempo* of an *Allegro*.

This popular Overture contains several characteristic themes from the opera which follows it. It is descriptive music of a very definite type, in which are heard a number of themes, each suggestive of one or more characters, or of a phenomenon of nature: as the theme which Wagner identified as the curse of the Dutchman, the personal *motif* (or musical symbol) which represents the Dutchman; the Sailor's song; and a wonderful theme suggesting the motion of the sea.

First is heard the theme which identifies the Dutchman, and, since his condemnation is really a part of himself, also his Curse. This theme is heard again and again throughout the Overture.

The second important theme in the Overture is Senta's melody, which appears following the first rush of the storm, and which, as the Redemption theme, closes the Overture.

Another *motif* which is plainly heard is used as a symbol of unrest, although it is also identified with the Norwegian sailors, who sing it, in the opera.

Concert Overtures

Another sailors' song, which is clearly identified because of the contrast of its light melody with the surging of the storm, is this:

All of these themes are heard and developed to considerable extent in the opera, of which this Overture is such a magnificent introduction.

"Midsummer Night's Dream" * Overture, by Felix Mendelssohn. Especially happy is this fanciful Overture written by Mendelssohn when only seventeen, after reading the Shakespeare story of Titania, and Oberon, the Fairy King. Many episodes in the play are suggested in the exquisitely beautiful music. It opens with four lovely chords played by the wind instruments—mysterious charms which admit the hearer to Fairyland. The music of the fairies follows—gay swirls of sound suggestive of dancing feet. Then is heard the more stately theme suggestive of the Duke and his retinue, the clownish caperings of the rural entertainers, and the braying of Bottom, who, by fairy magic, is turned into an ass. At the close appear again the four chords of magic which dispel the dream, just as did the magic juices which mischievous Puck placed on the eyes of Shakespeare's sleepers. Dainty and bewitching though it is, this is truly dramatic music.

MUSICAL ILLUSTRATIONS

9025, 9026 *Overture 1812* (*Tschaikowsky*)   *Royal Opera Orchestra*
20606, 20607 *William Tell Overture* (*Rossini*)   *Victor Symphony Orchestra*
6547   *Flying Dutchman Overture* (*Wagner*)   *N. Y. Philharmonic-Sym. Orch.*
6675, 6676 *Midsummer Night's Dream—Overture* (*Mendelssohn*)
                                     San Francisco Symphony Orchestra

INFORMATIONAL NOTES

One of the sights of Russia is the Kremlin, the royal castle, in Moscow, before which the "Overture 1812" was first played. Rising above a graceful bend in the Moscow River is a steep hill and on it stands the Kremlin. Its many cathedrals, with their pink, blue, mauve, and golden domes, and its great palace look down over the whole of Moscow over a triangular wall more than a mile long and forty to fifty feet high. Over the gates the double-headed golden eagles of the former Czar gleam in the sunlight. Within the palace are marvelous exhibits of ancient armor, textiles, gowns worn by empresses

---

* For detailed analyses see M. A. C., pp. 227-228.

of long ago, and many valuable pieces of gold and silver plate and enamel work.

The "Ranz des Vaches," an Alpine song, is so dear to the Swiss that when the Swiss troops have, at various times, been away from their native land on duty, officers have had to forbid the playing of the melody because of the extreme homesickness it caused.

"William Tell." The historic incident upon which the opera is based is the story of the Swiss patriot, who was required, by the

PUBLIC SQUARE AT ALTDORF, THE SCENE OF THE STORY OF WILLIAM TELL

tyrant Gessler, to shoot an apple from the head of his little son. The incident happened hundreds of years ago, but the Swiss nation still so honors the brave patriot that stories of his act are told in every school; a statue of Tell and his son has been erected in the village square of Altdorf (where the event took place) ; and a beautiful "William Tell Chapel" is erected and maintained in his memory on the shore of Lake Lucerne at the spot where he is said to have escaped from his captors.

High in the Alps in the heart of Switzerland are three Forest Cantons, and in one of these lived William Tell. The reigning Hapsburg Dukes claimed these Swiss highlands, and Gessler was sent to represent the Emperor. Naturally cruel, Gessler was so tyrannical that patriotic Swiss leaders met one night in a lonely meadow and vowed to work together for their freedom.

Soon after this, Gessler, wishing to assert his authority still further, set up a pole in the market-place of Altdorf, placed his cap upon it and gave the order that everyone who passed by it should bow to it in submission to his rule. This, William Tell (who, with his little son, had just come down to the village from his home on the nearby mountain-side) refused to do. The punishment followed and it was a dramatic moment when Tell sent the arrow through the heart of the apple which rested on his son's head.

Just as he accomplished that a second

CLOSE VIEW OF WILLIAM TELL MONUMENT AT ALTDORF

arrow fell from his belt to the ground. Asked by Gessler what it was for, William Tell bravely answered: "For you, sir, had I killed my son."

This angered Gessler still further, so that he ordered William Tell imprisoned. As he was being rowed across the lake by his captors, a storm arose, during which Tell managed to escape.

"Midsummer Night's Dream,"by William Shakespeare, was written during the later years of the sixteenth century. By some, it is thought to have been written for and first performed at a celebration held in honor of the marriage of the Earl of

WILLIAM TELL CHAPEL, LAKE LUCERNE

Essex in 1590. Oberon, the King of the Fairies, is first mentioned in the French romance of Huon of Bordeaux. The name Titania, given to his Queen, is thought to have been Shakespeare's own invention. Puck, the elf who causes so much of the mischief, is a sprite mentioned in fairy lore as old as the sagas of Iceland. Bottom, the village rustic who is, through magic, given an ass's head, is a clever satire on an old form of punishment in England. Old English court orders of the sixteenth and seventeenth centuries disclose the fact that persons convicted of brutality in their dealing with others were often placed in stocks on public squares, attired with an ass's head upon their shoulders, hay set before them, and a placard announcing their beastly actions prominently displayed, from "six in the morning until six of the clocke at night."

QUESTIONS AND TOPICS FOR DISCUSSION

1. How has Tschaikowsky used national airs in music to represent the people of a nation? Can you name other composed music in which this has been done? Discuss the emotional appeal of such a use of melody.

2. What is meant by "occasional" music? Name and discuss

several examples of it which have been mentioned in this and previous lessons.

3. The first two overtures suggested in this lesson are based upon historic events, the last two upon legendary tales. Discuss the appeal of the two types of background. Contrast the "Flying Dutchman" and the "Midsummer Night's Dream" Overtures.

4. Which of these Overtures are examples of *realistic* and which of *impressionistic* music?

5. One of the most popular themes included in any overture mentioned in the chapter is that given from the "William Tell" music. Learn this so well that you will recognize it whenever you hear it. Is it its rhythm or its melody which gives this theme its greatest charm?

6. Identify the Dutchman's Call and Senta's theme, in the "Flying Dutchman" Overture. What are the musical devices used by Wagner to so definitely impersonate these characters? How does he suggest the sea? What instruments of the orchestra does Wagner use in each case? What is the mood of this Overture? Contrast its mood with that of the "William Tell" music, and also with that of the "Midsummer Night's Dream" Overture. What one word will, in each case, best describe the outstanding appeal of each Overture?

7. Is the Mendelssohn Overture to be classed as "descriptive" or "suggestive" music? Give reasons for your answer. How has Mendelssohn at once suggested the alluring fantasy and atmosphere of the Shakespeare play? Discuss the various incidents of the play which are portrayed in the music.

8. Is nationality suggested in any of these four overtures? If so, how?

Library Reading. "William Tell," by Schiller; "Midsummer Night's Dream," by Shakespeare.

LATER ITALIAN OPERA, "AÏDA," BY VERDI

What Is Meant by "Later Italian Opera." During the fifty years between 1843 and 1893, Verdi, the renowned composer of Italian opera, kept pace with the musical development of his time.

In early Italian opera it had become quite the fashion that the work should contain, not only many lovely singable melodies, but that it should also provide elaborate opportunities, throughout, for the display of the unusual vocal abilities of those who sang it. The music contained, therefore, many showy cadenzas, or long-extended passages upon very high notes, which had little or nothing to do with the telling of the opera's story. Such an opera is "Il Trovatore."

But presently, through the influence and the reforms of Gluck, and later Wagner, both composers and public came to feel that the music of an opera—while still beautifully melodic—should play a definite part in the unfolding of the dramatic plot, or story, of the opera.

So it was that, during the last twenty years in which Verdi wrote, he devoted himself to creating such truly dramatic music, and first of all among his works of this type stands the inspired opera "Aïda," a perennial favorite since 1871, when it was given its initial performance at Cairo, Egypt.

How "Aïda" Came to Be Written. It was during the year 1869 that the building of the Suez Canal—one of the greatest engineering feats of the world—was accomplished and the Canal formally dedicated. To commemorate this event, and, at the same time, celebrate the completion of his magnificent new Opera House in the city of Cairo, the Khedive of Egypt, Ismail Pasha, decided to commission someone to write a new opera.

LOUISE HOMER AS
AMNERIS

The choice of a composer was not difficult, and within a short time, Verdi, the most popular Italian composer of his day, received the invitation to undertake the work. It was only after some time and much persuasion that he consented, but once the opera was promised and he began to plan for it, his imagination was greatly stirred by a suggestion that in it he endeavor to create a truly national opera founded on Egyptian life and history.

The Characters Who Take Part in "Aïda." Although, in performances of "Aïda," vast numbers of people are needed for the presentation of the mass scenes—in which all the court, soldiers, slaves and temple attendants are in evidence—there are, in reality, but six principal characters. These are:

Aïda, a captive slave in attendance upon the Princess of the realm, in reality the daughter of
Amonasro, the King of Ethiopia
The King of Egypt, one of the Pharaohs
Amneris, his daughter
Rhadames, Captain of Egyptian troops
Ramfis, High Priest of the Temple

The Time of the Opera. The historic days of the Pharaohs, who ruled Egypt in Biblical times.

The Scenes in Which the Opera Is Set. Two very old Egyptian cities, Memphis and Thebes.

The Story of "Aïda." The Scene of the first part of Act One is in the King's Palace at Memphis. Rhadames is being informed by the High Priest that he has been chosen to lead the Egyptian troops in an expedition against the Ethiopians. Left alone, Rhadames sings the renowned aria, "Celeste Aïda," in which he discloses his love for the captive maiden, whose real identity is unknown to any of her cap-

© *Mishkin*

CARUSO AS RHADAMES

tors. Amneris, the King's daughter, who loves Rhadames dearly, enters the room and questions him about the coming war. Following their conversation Rhadames is called before the King and the Court who invest him with due authority and bid him and the army farewell. Aïda sings her famous aria, "Return Victorious," although his victory will mean ruin for her own family. Thus she discloses the depth of her love for the young Captain.

In the opening Scene of Act Two, Amneris is being made ready for the festival of welcome which is to be extended to Rhadames and the troops who are returning victorious. Suspecting that Aïda is her rival in love, she tricks the girl into a confession of her love for Rhadames by telling her, untruthfully, that he has been killed in the battle. It is during this scene, also, that a group of Moorish slaves do an Oriental dance in Amneris's apartment to entertain her.

In Scene Two of this act, the King and all his Court go out to the city gate to welcome the victorious troops and their captain, Rhadames. The scene is one of great excitement and exaltation, as, in the manner of the olden days, all the troops, the prisoners of war, and finally the Captain—borne aloft by a group of slaves—pass in homage before the King. The procession is escorted, in a colorful and finally the Captain—borne aloft by a group of slaves—pass in trumpets and trombones. Among the prisoners of war, Aïda suddenly recognizes her own father, the King of Ethiopia, who quickly signals to her not to disclose his identity. According to old custom, the death of all the prisoners is called for by the King of Egypt, but Rhadames saves all their lives by asking for them as his reward.

The King is so pleased with Rhadames's successes that he not only grants this request, but offers him Amneris for his wife, and makes him heir to the throne.

© *Mishkin*
PONSELLE AS AÏDA

Scene One of Act Three is one of artistic perfection. The charm and mystery of a moonlight night on the banks of the Nile are suggested by the short orchestral prelude before the rise of the curtain. The pagan Temple is half seen in the distant background. As the curtain rises an unseen chorus within the Temple is heard chanting a hymn of praise.

Aïda, protected by a disguising veil, appears, hoping to meet Rhadames, and while she waits, sings the exquisite aria, "My Native Land." Her father appears and suggests that she use her influence with Rhadames and secure from him military information which will be helpful to her native land. Reluctantly Aïda obeys, but, unfortunately, not only the hidden Amonasro but also the jealous Amneris overhear his confidence. She calls loudly to the guards. Amonasro and Aïda escape, but Rhadames is captured and cast into prison.

Galloway
THE NILE RIVER NEAR THEBES, WHERE VERDI LISTENED TO FOLK AIRS OF EGYPT

Scene One of Act Four discloses a room in the Palace. A door at one side leads to Rhadames's cell, and here Amneris comes, begging that he shall save his life by giving up Aïda and marrying her, instead. But when Rhadames refuses, she calls for the guards to come and conduct him to the judgment room, and cries loudly for vengeance.

In Scene Two—the closing scene of the opera—Rhadames is being punished for treason, according to the custom of the times, by being given a living burial in a tomb built underneath the pavement of the Temple. Just after the stone which buries him forever has been lowered into place above him, Rhadames discovers Aïda, who has hidden in the tomb so that she may perish with him. This scene is made doubly effective by a stage setting devised by Verdi, in which the stage is arranged in two parts—the Temple, full of chanting priests above, and the lonely tomb below. Here Aïda and Rhadames sing their plaintive duet, "Farewell, O Earth," while above, Amneris, repentant too late, falls weeping upon the fatal stone.

The Music of "Aïda." In the music of this opera, Verdi glorified pure melody. Although the type of the opera is essentially Italian, it has also a strongly Egyptian national note and, in a wonderfully colorful and impressive manner, suggests the tropical splendor of the Orient.

In Act One, two Egyptian folk-melodies are used in their original form—in the first Finale (the chant of the Priestesses, with harp accompaniment) and in the ballet.

Mention should be made of the rarely beautiful effects which Verdi achieved in the orchestral accompaniment, and of the Oriental atmosphere suggested by the frequent and timely use of numbers of harps and flutes.

"Celeste Aïda." Verdi's main interest was in the human voice and its possibilities, with appropriate orchestral accompaniment as his secondary interest. "Celeste Aïda"—*recitative* and *aria*—is music characterized by declamatory style, short vocal phrases, and an alternating of the vocal part with military trumpet calls very suitable to the scene. It is very interesting to contrast the elaborate style of an Aïda *aria* with the infinitely more simple early style of Verdi, as displayed, for example, in "Stride la Vampa," in "Il Trovatore."

"Celeste Aïda" comes directly at the opening of the opera, following the brief dialogue between Rhadames and Ramphis concerning the choice of a new commander for the Egyptian armies; and a short recitative in which Rhadames communes with himself:

> "What if 'tis I who am chosen? . . . .
> I, the chosen leader . . . .
> To thee returned, Aïda,
> My brow entwined with laurel."

The two-measure theme of the expressive *aria* is constructed from an almost complete scale passage.

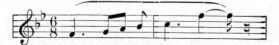

This is immediately repeated in the same key (starting on *F*), then in sequential manner from *G*, from *A*, and again from *F*.

Later Italian Opera

The second theme, in parallel minor key, is more passionate in mood. Following it the first theme is heard again, and a *Coda*—partly spoken on one tone (*parlante*) and containing a brilliant although *ppp* closing figure built upon ascending notes of the simple arpeggio. It closes dramatically with a high *pianissimo* B-flat.

The *aria* is in three-part song form with *Coda*.

"Return Victorious," sung by Aïda, again makes use of a simple scale passage as thematic material. The main theme is in minor mode. It is, in part, *recitative* in style, and expresses, throughout, agitation and fervid emotion.

"Dance of the Moorish Slaves," in Act II—preceded by a chorus of women, and a harp-like introduction—makes much use of minor mode; of *staccato* thirds; of frequent *basso ostinato;* and, at times, the very old Oriental scale (especially in the bass accompaniment to the melodic figures in the soprano).

The dance music is simple in construction and produces a primitive effect as old as the monotonously charming and colorful Oriental dance after which it is patterned.

"Triumphal March," in Scene I, Act II, is a "favorite" melody among opera-lovers.

Played, in the opera, amid a scene of splendor and pomp, the march is tremendously vigorous and dramatic. The main theme is repeated three times in the original key; then, following an abrupt modulation, in a higher key. This procedure is repeated, each abrupt rise in pitch suggesting an immediate rise in emotional intensity. It is then heard once more in the first key of *A*-flat.

In the opera this gorgeous air is followed by a *ballabile* (like the word *ballet,* from the Italian *ballare,* and meaning a piece of music to be used for dancing) to the rhythm of which a group of slave girls bring in and display the spoils of the conquered. The theme, embellished by many musical ornaments of an Oriental type, is played *staccato* and almost entirely in double sixths.

"O Patria Mia" (My Native Land) makes an instant appeal

because of its tenderly emotional quality. It is accompanied, in the main, by a delicate murmuring in the basses.

"The Fatal Stone," sung by Rhadames and Aïda, is one of the finest duets ever written for or sung in a stage production. Opened by Rhadames in a *recitative* sung on one tone, it becomes more agitated, although remaining *pianissimo,* as he thinks he sees a phantom which resembles Aïda, not realizing that it is indeed the real Aïda who awaits him in the tomb.

In "Farewell, O Earth," the latter part of this final duet, Verdi has made constant use of a short theme complete within itself, rather than the usual type of "question and answer" theme. The theme is repeated, by either Rhadames or Aïda, or by both in unison, nine times.

Notice should be made of the stress given each time to the seventh tone of the scale.

The duet (and at the same time, the opera) closes *pppp,* as the curtain slowly descends.

MUSICAL ILLUSTRATIONS

Act One:

6595   *Celeste Aïda (Heavenly Aïda) (Sung by Rhadames)*   Martinelli
9411   *Return Victorious (Sung by Aïda)*   *Giannini and La Scala Orchestra*

Act Two:

35780   {*Introduction and Moorish Ballet*
        {*Grand Triumphal March*   *Creatore's Band*

Act Three:

7106   *O Patria Mia (My Native Land) (Sung by Aïda)*   Rethberg

Act Four:

3040   *La fatal pietra (The Fatal Stone)*   *Ponselle and Martinelli*
3041   *O terra addio (Farewell, O Earth) (Sung by Aïda and Rhadames)*
        Ponselle and Martinelli

INFORMATIONAL NOTES

Literary Sources of "Aïda." The tiny "germ" from which the tragic story of "Aïda" developed was discovered by Mariette Bey, a renowned French Egyptologist, who had spent many years in Egypt hunting amid old manuscripts, and deciphering hieroglyphics, in search of historical data of other days. Among his "finds" was an old history tale, an incident which occurred in the days of the Pharaohs.

When it became known that Verdi was seeking a "theme" or

story for the proposed opera to be written for the Egyptian ruler, Bey suggested this old historic incident. Verdi welcomed the suggestion eagerly. Although incidents which might possibly occur in modern times were necessarily included in the libretto (or story of the opera) the plot is chiefly of ancient origin.

Verdi at once engaged Camille du Locle, a French librettist, who worked out the story into French prose under the composer's watchful eye. As soon as this was done, Verdi engaged still another writer —an Italian named Antonio Ghislanzoni—who translated the French prose into Italian verse. Verdi, the composer, contrary to usual custom, aided in the writing of the "Aïda" libretto to such an extent that he should be mentioned as one of the four men who really created it.

Origins of the Historic and Nationalist Atmosphere of the "Aïda" Music. Before the libretto of "Aïda" had been entirely completed, Verdi set himself to work to absorb as much Egyptian musical atmosphere as possible. For this, he went to Egypt and spent much time sailing up and down the River Nile in a *dahabiyah* (a picturesque native river boat) listening to the songs of the natives, some suggestions from which he used in his opera themes. Here he heard old boatmen's songs; the songs of the Egyptian *fellah* (peasant) plowing in the fields; and those sung by the native laborers—often working in pairs— who, either with or without the assistance of camels and oxen, still turn the awkward primitive *sâkiyehs,* or water wheels, and so carry water, in woven reed baskets, from the surface level of the Nile, up terrace after terrace, until it reaches the thirsty fields. These Egyptian working songs have been unchanged for thousands of years, and unconsciously still create the same quaint atmosphere that they did at the dawn of history.

In addition to the atmosphere and thematic material which Verdi received, first hand, because of his Nile journeyings, the great composer set himself the task of a minute study of early Egyptian art. The earliest Egyptian paintings and carvings—some of them more than six thousand years old—found in the Pyramids, and in the Tombs of the Kings in the Thebes district, show clearly that the early Egyptians studied the art of music with great detail. Quaint handmade harps of exquisite workmanship and great antiquity have been taken from these royal tombs, and similar harps, and long trumpets of truly Oriental design * were utilized by Verdi in the music of the opera.

---

* The long slender trumpets always carried by soldiers in the "Triumphal March" in Act Two were made to order for the first performance of "Aïda," according to specifications laid down by Verdi. Similar trumpets or long horns are used, as they have been for centuries, by the Devil Dancers in Tibet.

The opera was originally ordered for 1870, but on account of the political disturbances of the Franco-Prussian War, it was not completed nor performed until December 24, 1871.

"Aïda" also lends itself readily to out-door pageantry, and in 1912 it was given a spectacular presentation in the open air in Egypt, on the sands before the Pyramids. Since then, the opera has been sung out-of-doors many times in America—at the New York City Polo Grounds; at Ravinia Park, Chicago; and in Ohio, California, and other places.

Historical Setting. Egypt is a "land of long memories" and also of massive monuments, its civilization going back thousands of years B. C.

Memphis and Thebes—the two cities mentioned as scenes of the opera "Aïda"—are very old.

Memphis has, for nearly fifty centuries, commanded admiration, wonder, and respect. Now little remains but interesting ruins. The city was the first capital of the united kingdom of upper and lower Egypt, a seat of learning, and the site of the pagan temples mentioned in the music and libretto of "Aïda." It also played an important political rôle in Egypt's history, and presently the city became a battle-ground for conflicting armies, was plundered repeatedly, and finally destroyed.

Near Memphis stand the Colossal Statues of Rameses II. It was at Memphis that Mariette Bey (who first suggested the "Aïda" story to Verdi) unearthed, in his archæological diggings, an entire avenue of sphinxes.

At, and near the historic city of Thebes—just across the Nile River from

RUINS OF TEMPLE AT LUXOR.

the more modern city of Luxor—archæologists have, for many years, sought the hiding places of the Pharaohs, and it was just a short distance away that the English scientists found the tomb of Tutankhamen, with its fabulously rare and valuable treasures.

Ancient Thebes was built on both sides of the Nile, and the word Luxor (the name of the city on the east bank) is an old Arabian name meaning "The Palaces."

Egypt is now an independent kingdom.

Later Italian Opera

QUESTIONS AND TOPICS FOR DISCUSSION

1. Contrast earlier and later periods of Italian opera. What great Italian composer developed his art at the same time Italian opera was developing, and wrote operas of all types?

2. How have nationally characteristic folk-airs and traditions colored the plot, atmosphere, and music of "Aïda"?

3. How do musical themes and musical instruments used in "Aïda" suggest the music of the Orient? Give your reasons as to why and how Egyptian and Oriental music may be said to resemble each other.

4. The "Triumphal March" suggests a very vivid scene. Describe it in your own words.

5. Listen to the voices of the Brass Choir in the "Triumphal March." Give reasons why these orchestral instruments are most appropriate for use in this music.

6. Locate the River Nile, and the historic cities of Memphis and Thebes on a map. Find Nubia (Ethiopia) also.

7. What incidents in the opera prove Rhadames's true nobility?

8. Discuss the art of Verdi in closing the opera as he did.

Theme Topics. Character sketches of each of the principal characters in the opera.

Library Reading. You will find ancient Thebes referred to in the *Iliad IX*, where mention is made of its "hundred gates" and of its "twenty thousand war chariots." You may learn about Egypt's romantic past by reading "Reconstructing Egypt's History" and "The Resurrection of Ancient Egypt"—both articles in the "National Geographic Magazine" for September, 1913; and "A Dramatic Moment in History," in "The Mentor," January, 1924.

PART TWO—CHAPTER SIXTEEN

OUTSIDE STUDENT PROJECT

A program may be made up of musical numbers heard and studied during the semester, the selection and arrangement of which have been made by members of the class. See Part One, Chapter Sixteen, for further suggestions.

FOLK-MUSIC FROM OLD RUSSIA AND POLAND

Russian Folk-Music a Reflection of Russian Life. The peoples of every country of the globe have their own songs, each country's airs being influenced by climatic and geographical conditions and by differing degrees of political, social, and industrial advancement, and therefore expressing a communal feeling and sentiment.

RUSSIAN ITINERANT MUSICIAN

There is an old Russian saying, "Song is truth; and the expression of our life;" and so in Russia every activity of daily life has a song which may appropriately accompany it.

Life in Russia differs widely because of the great size of the country, and the varied industries of the people. There are really three Russias: the great territory to the North, known as Great Russia; a district to the West, known as White Russia; and the more fertile land to the South, known as Little Russia. The music of the Russian folk reflects these differences in the wild and barbarous airs of the Cossacks* of the eastern steppes (in what is known as Little Russia), the working songs from the Volga, the Oriental melodies from the South, and the lively airs of Ukrainia.

There are, among Russian folk-tunes, ceremonial songs, cradle songs, love songs, working songs, and dance songs—in fact, a song for every activity of life. Many of these airs are comparable to old church modes, and a large percentage of them reflect Tartaric influence. National characteristics are the uncertain tonalities and the use of irregular rhythms.

Characteristic Musical Instruments of Ancient Russia include the gousli,† with its five or seven strings; the reed-flute, in which is recognized a descendant of the short pipes used by Russian shepherds; and the balalaika, a guitar-like instrument, played by peasant and soldier alike.

General Characteristics of Russian Folk-Melodies. Many Russian airs resemble or suggest the fiery, impetuous, and picturesque melodies and fascinating syncopated rhythms of the Orient. At least three

---

* The Cossacks are sometimes spoken of as the "Rough Riders of Russia."
† Used by Rimsky-Korsakow in his opera "Sadko."

causes are suggested for this: one, the geographical location and close physical relation of Russia to the Orient; second, the historic invasions of the Tartars in the twelfth century;* and third, the absorption of many alluring musical traits from the gypsies who wandered through Russia and the Orient during the centuries.

Numbers of Russian folk-songs † had their origin in pagan rites or orgies, or in very early religious ceremonies; many reflect the austere modes of the Greek Church.

The atmosphere of a Russian folk-tune is always one of color and vitality, whether it be in the prevailing minor, or in wildly exuberant major, mode. It is noticeable that even the gayest folk-dances are often played and sung in minor mode, and many songs which begin in the major end in the minor.

A Russian air is frequently very short and simple, and within the compass of a very few notes, the singers seeming never to weary of repetition of the same phrases. One reason for this may lie in the fact that in primitive times in Russia, each singer had his own tunes —usually only two or three of them—and that to these he sang all his songs. As the singer was untutored, his song was always very simple, and in this lies much of its charm.

Two Russian folk-melodies which illustrate the infusion of Oriental gypsy characteristics are "Two Guitars" and "Shining Moon."

"Two Guitars," which had its beginnings in a gypsy air of great antiquity, is in three-part song form. The melody opens in slow *tempo* and minor mode, moves into an impetuous second section, and lapses into the first mood. Intervals and rhythms are picturesquely Oriental.

"Shining Moon" is a folk-song which moves with the marked rhythm and brisk *tempo* of a typical dance. The first theme is immediately answered and imitated, but at an interval of a third lower, the shifting of the tonality being very marked. The second melody is carried by the bass instruments, which again shift the melody a third lower. As the music continues it gathers momentum, marked by great *crescendos* and rapidly executed scale passages. The number ends at a very fast *tempo*.

Irregular and Decisive Rhythms. Decisive and intense rhythm is an underlying feature of Russian song. Many airs are characterized by extreme rhythmic irregularity, one measure being sung, for example, in 4/4 measure, the next in 5/4, and so on. In other airs, phrases may be of unequal length.

The Songs of Toil seem, even without the words, to have been

---

* Retold in Hero Songs devoted to the memory of Prince Igor of Novgorod, and idealized in the "Polovetzian Dances."
† See "One Hundred Russian Folk-Songs," by Rimsky-Korsakow.

"made up" to be sung as an accompaniment for some regular kind of labor. Here the sense of rhythm is very strong. When loading or unloading a barge, when a building is being erected, or other work done, it is usually done rhythmically under the influence of song. This is true even in the play-songs of the Russian children.

"Volga Boat Song" is the most familiar illustration of this type of Russian folk-song. Only by the aid of rhythmic song are the barge-haulers of the Volga River able to withstand their terrible labor. It not only assists them in their work, but gives them equal moments of relaxation. By repeating the words of the native text "Ei Ukhnam" ("Oh, heave ho!"), the steady impulse of the music is felt.

A BALALAIKA ORCHESTRA, SHOWING BOTH BALALAIKA AND DOMRA

This song is in the favorite minor, with a repeated drop from the fourth tone of the minor scale to the first tone, which is sung nine times within the course of its thirty-two measures. Of severe and majestic character, it has been suggested by some as an appropriate song to replace the old-time Russian National Hymn ("God Preserve the People"), which may not be played since the revolution.

The Social Folk-Songs and Dances of Russia are filled with natural eloquence, with flowing and expressive melody, and, usually, a lively rhythm. The same song may be heard in many different localities, and in slightly varied versions, on account of the differing circumstances of life and surroundings in each village.

Folk Music From Russia and Poland

"The Red Sarafan."* A national folk-song which expresses an age-old folk-tradition of Russia is the "Red Sarafan." It is the song of a daughter who asks her mother, "Why toil, O Mother dear, at the sarafan, by day and night?" to which the fond mother replies, "For memory's sake I weave the red sarafan."

The text of the song will be more greatly appreciated when it is known that the word "red" means to the Russian peasant the same as "beautiful" in the English language. There is always, in a well-ordered Russian home, the "red corner" in the parlor, in which honored guests may sit, and the red shrine, for worship. The red sarafan is a handsome dress worn by all women of the Russian peasantry on holiday occasions.

The melody† to which this tender conversation is sung is one of simple beauty and form.

This song is one of the best-loved airs of central Russia.

"Song of the Shepherd Lehl" is an old Russian folk-song which the composer Rimsky-Korsakow incorporated in his ballet opera "The Snow Maiden." The opera is based on the fairy-story play of Ostrovsky and tells of Snow Maiden, the daughter of King Frost and Fairy Spring, who longs to be mortal so that she may win the love of the Shepherd Lehl. In the opera the song is sung by Lehl during a festival celebrating the first day of summer. As a reward for his song, the Czar permits the shepherd to choose a wife, but he passes by Snow Maiden to pick a peasant girl. Snow Maiden, in despair, ventures into the forbidden sunlight and is melted away.

The introduction and the interludes present a fascinating archaic melody which suggests, in the instrumentation as well as in the melody itself, the playing of the rustic shepherd pipes. The voice then sings, to an old folk melody, the ancient legend of how the clouds and the thunder plotted together to bring the summer. The song and story furnish an excellent example of the use of authentic folk material in the larger types of composition, yet with the folk characteristics kept unchanged.

The Hopak, another national Cossack folk-dance—both form and style of which have been idealized in a composition for piano solo, by

---

* Composed many years ago by Varlamov, now accepted as a folk-song.
† It was, some years ago, made the central musical figure of an elaborately embellished composition by a Russian composer, Henri Wieniawski, in his brilliant piece for violin, "Souvenir de Moscow."

Moussorgsky, an eminent Russian composer—is of wild and furious rhythm and tempo. It is danced by men who wear heavy boots, to

POLISH GIRL IN NATIVE COSTUME

the heels of which little bells or clappers are often attached for the dance. The dancers jump into the air and crack their heels together, shouting in a rather boisterous and barbarous manner, and also use a step in which the feet are thrust forward rhythmically in rapid alternation, from a crouching position.

Polish Folk-Dance. As the last ray from the setting sun falls across the fields about any village in Poland, the peasant farmers may be seen returning wearily to their homes in the village. For a time, no sounds may be heard but those which have to do with the preparation and eating of the evening meal. Then the music of a violin, and possibly a flute, is heard from some spot in the center of the cluster of houses. Men and women, and boys and girls come from their homes, stand for a moment listening to the musicians, and then, by pairs and by groups, the villagers enter the open space and dance the ancient Polish dances.

These dances play the part in the lives of the Polish peasants that athletic games and all forms of social events do in the lives of the American people. The steps are gymnastic in their vigor, more so than the steps of many social dances, and offer a relaxation, in the quick skipping of the circle figures, and in the rhythm and swing of the instrumental music and the songs which accompany the dances. The children grow up watching the graceful steps and patterns of the dance, and in a short time know every minute movement. The Mazurka, Polonaise, and Polka are all popular dance forms.

Galloway

THE ROYAL PALACE AT KRAKOW, POLAND

Krakowiak. One of the most popular of the old folk-dances in the Polish district of Krakow—in which is Krakow, the first capital of Poland—is the Krakowiak. This is a wild and lively dance participated in by many couples in a circle.

When danced at festivals it is made extremely picturesque by the brightly colored and interesting costumes worn by the peasants.

The Mazurka, a national dance in 3/4 measure, known since the seventeenth century, somewhat slower than a waltz and more irregular and spontaneous in its *tempos,* is also a native of Poland, although it has been, for many years, danced in all parts of Russia. It originated in a singing-dance, and this is the manner in which it is still retained, as contrasted with dances accompanied by musical instruments. Many composers have used the *mazurka* as a basis for idealized composition. A peculiar characteristic of many composed mazurkas is the use, by composers, of a *basso ostinato,* suggesting a primitive instrument—as a bagpipe—which has a drone bass. In the district of Massovia, in which the *mazurka* originated, it was the feature of the men's dancing to click their spurs together on the second pulse of the measure.

MUSICAL ILLUSTRATIONS

20037	*Two Guitars (Russian-Gypsy Folk-Air)*	*Victor Salon Orchestra*
19960	*Shining Moon (Russian Folk)*	*Kirilloff's Balalaika Orchestra*
20309	*Volga Boat Song (Russian Folk)*	*Kibalchich's Symphony Choir*
78619	*Red Sarafan (Russian Ukrainian Air)*	*Kirilloff's Balalaika Orchestra*
4066	*Song of the Shepherd Lehl—Snow Maiden*	*(Rimsky-Korsakow)*
		Zelinskaya
1161	*Hopak (as idealized) (Moussorgsky-Rachmaninoff)*	*Rachmaninoff*
80393	*Krakowiak (Polish Folk-Dance)*	*Europa Orchestra*
1327	*Mazurka (as idealized) (Chopin)*	*Horowitz*

INFORMATIONAL NOTES

Krakow, the early capital of Poland, is filled with buildings of the Middle Ages, some of which were already old when the Crusaders from the North passed through it on their way to Palestine. Old customs carefully adhered to, may be seen at its picturesque festivals. The city was founded in the eleventh century, was sacked and burned by the Mongolians, afterward rebuilt by the Germans, and was the residence of the Polish kings until about 1610. Its decline began when the court was moved to the gayer city of Warsaw, three hundred miles distant.

Gypsy music contains many Eastern elements and resorts to strange old modes upon which to form its melodies, rather than standard major or minor scales. It is essentially vocal, using the instrument for decorative purposes, for accompaniment, and between the verses. It often does not conform to regular set forms, or patterns, but each melodic phrase is extended to fit the sentiment or emotion

of the words, or to allow florid ornamentation. An unusual characteristic feature of gypsy music is the insistent repetition of one note,
accompanied by a grace note.

QUESTIONS AND TOPICS FOR DISCUSSION

1. Name and describe the folk musical instruments of Old Russia.
How may the folk-music of Russia be divided or classified?

2. Discuss the "Songs of Toil." How do they compare in rhythm
with working songs of the American Negro or the American Indian?
How do they compare in mood? Name at least four features which
all have in common.

3. Discuss at least five outstanding characteristics of Russian folk-
music. How does it resemble Oriental music? Name three or more
ways in which the influence of Oriental music has been brought into
contact with Russian airs.

4. What are some general characteristics of all gypsy music?
Mention folk-music of other lands to which these same musical characteristics have been carried. Contrast the Russian and the Spanish
folk-song; Russian and Bohemian; which is the most brilliant in general style? Which is most exhilarating? Which, most poetic? Give
reasons for your answers.

5. How is nationality expressed in Russian folk-song? How does
such folk-music as that of Russia lay a solid foundation for a "national school" of musical composition?

6. What musical elements contribute most largely to the enduring charm and vitality of the folk-music of any land?

Library Reading. "Three Days on the Volga," by Mott, in
"Scribner's Magazine," March, 1905.

PART THREE—CHAPTER TWO

NATIONALITY IN ART MUSIC—RUSSIA AND POLAND

Characteristics of Russian Music. Upon the solid foundation of
one of the most remarkable and most virile bodies of folk-music known
to the world, Russian composers have built an equally marvelous national "school" of musical composition.

Russian composed music is noted for its extreme emotional appeal, for its extended use of national folk-melodies and rhythms, and
for its frequent use of folk or history tales for its "story" or "program" subjects. The truly Russian art music also shows in its blend-

ing of major and minor scales (sometimes of the Oriental whole-tone scales)

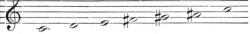

the strong influence which the primitive music of neighboring Oriental countries has had upon it.

Glinka, the "Father of Russian Music." To Michael Ivanovich Glinka has been given this proud title because, before him, most of so-called Russian art-music was inspired by foreign sources—such as French or Italian tales. His national opera, "A Life for the Czar," which had its first performance in November, 1836, is the first really Russian opera. He drew both story and many musical themes used in it from folk-history and the folk-life of Russia.

SERGEI RACHMANINOFF

It relates, in dramatic manner, a tale of the seventeenth century, when the Polish soldiers were yet in possession of the city of Moscow. The military fortunes of their enemies—the Russians—were at a low ebb, and when a Romanoff * was elected Tzar of Russia, the Poles planned to capture him.

A band of the Polish soldiers, disguised as Russians, start overland to seize him. Arriving at a rural dwelling they ask information concerning the new ruler's whereabouts, as, they say, they wish to visit him and pay him homage.

Soussanine, a loyal peasant subject of the Tzar, suspects treachery, and, at the certain cost of his life, offers to guide them personally, and thus leads them astray until his son has had time to ride ahead and warn his sovereign.

The Polish soldiers, finding themselves apparently lost in a swamp, at last suspect Soussanine of deception. This he proudly admits in his thrilling *aria*.

"Aria of Soussanine" *Adagio non tanto,* in *D* minor, opens—following a brief orchestral prelude—with a dramatic *recitative,* "The Truth Is Suspected." Certain that his loyalty to the Tzar, and his subsequently false guidance of the Polish soldiers, have been discovered, Soussanine sings of his hopeless situation. In the main

---

* The dynasty of Russia was founded by Michael Romanoff at the time of his election as Tzar (1613). This Tzar was the grandfather of Peter the Great, a ruler who did so much to bring to Russia modern ideas, habits, customs and industries of other European countries.

aria, which is separated from the *recitative* by a short interlude, he predicts that

> "When the day shall break again
> 'Twill be the last time
> I shall see the sun on high."

The melody to which these words are sung still further suggests the tragedy of his almost certain fate:

Presently Soussanine prays for mercy and strength to bear the coming torture, and ends his aria with a short but brilliant cadenza-like passage, typical of his undying courage.

Glinka was not only a composer of marvelous music, but was also the teacher of the gifted composer Balakireff, who was, in turn, the teacher of many others of those remarkable composers who have made Russia famous, including Borodin, Cæsar Cui, and Rimsky-Korsakow.

A RUSSIAN PIPER

"Polovetzian Dances," by Borodin. Another truly Russian opera in that it is built upon a real history tale, is "Prince Igor," by Borodin. Chief among its many attractive features is the somewhat barbarous ballet, the "Polovetzian Dances," which occur in the second act.

The dances take place in the encampment of the Khan Kontchak, to whom, as prisoners of war after an encounter with the Slavs, have fallen Prince Igor and his son, Vladimir.

While the daughter of the Khan and Prince Vladimir are in conversation, the Khan comes and suggests to Vladimir that he purchase his liberty by promising to never again take up arms against the Polovetzi. This the Prince refuses to do, and in hope of changing his decision the Khan decides to tender him his most princely hospitality. So he summons the tribe and orders the dance to begin.

In the opera this dance is accompanied by a chorus from the voices of those who mass themselves around the spot cleared for the dancers. The music—furnished entirely by orchestra when done as a concert number—is fiercely martial, almost primitive in its vigor.

The dance music (as recorded) opens with a violently rhythmic, though Orientally monotonous beating, upon which a characteristically Russian air—which shows distinct influence of their Mongolian neighbors—enters in the woodwind.

One of the beautiful and characteristic melodies, played first by the oboe, and later by other instruments of the orchestra, is the alluring air:

dolce

Instruments of percussion—triangle, tambourine and tympani—and the harps add to the fascinatingly Oriental background. Near the close is the "dance of the savage men," characterized by a lively tune for the clarinet.

"Le Coq d'Or" (The Golden Cockerel), by Rimsky-Korsakow, is a fantastic and poetic fairy-tale opera based upon an old Russian Skazka (or fairy tale), by Pushkin, in which the old King Dodon is presented by one of his subjects, The Astrologer, with a wonderful golden Cockerel, which, he tells the King, will always give warning when danger is near. The Cockerel soon proves its magic power by telling of a coming invasion. Later, while in a rage, the King kills the Astrologer who had given him the Cockerel, which revenges its former master by killing the King.

"The Golden Cockerel" was, at first, a conventional opera, but is now given as an opera-pantomime. For this, a ballet on the stage silently enacts the rôles of the four principal characters (the King, the Queen,

NICOLAI RIMSKY-KORSAKOW

the Voice of the Cockerel and the Astrologer), and the chorus; while those who sing the enchanting music which Rimsky-Korsakow has written are seen at one side of the stage. Thus there are two people engaged in impersonating each character in the opera, every movement of singer and actor being perfectly synchronized.

The music of the opera reflects the piquant spirit of Russian folk-lore. Folk-melodies are sung by the chorus in the first and last acts; there is a rousing phrase played by muted trumpets for the Cockerel;

and Oriental characteristics are heard in the humorous music for the old King's clumsy dance, to which he is urged by the Queen, and in the gorgeous "Hymn to the Sun," sung by the Queen in the second act. Here the Queen, attired in a red silk robe, richly embroidered with gold, a white turban on her head, comes out to view the rising sun, followed by four slaves who carry native goussli* and violins. They accompany her as she sings.

"Hymn to the Sun" has a melody of strongly nationalistic flavor. The *aria* is introduced by a brilliant Orientally colored melody played by the clarinet, a chromatic downward-moving air which sets the atmosphere for the song.

The air of the song is of a mystic Oriental type, with strange chromatic arabesques and cadences and contains many small cadenza-like passages. It very strongly suggests the "Song of India," by the same composer, both songs being perfect examples of the Oriental characteristics heard in much Russian music.

"Caucasian Sketches," by Ippolitov-Ivanov, is a modern Russian suite for symphony orchestra, in which are heard melodies of a genuinely Oriental character and origin. The music suggests in a gorgeously descriptive manner, the wild, lawless life of the nomadic tribes of herdsmen who inhabit the district round about the fabled Colchis Strand. The composer, Ippolitov-Ivanov, gained the musical material from which the Sketches are evolved, during his visit and residence in the Caucasus Mountains. He taught in Tiflis in Caucasia, and took his themes from the life he actually saw. He disappeared during the World War and has not been heard of since.

"In the Village," the first of the "Sketches," opens with a remarkable introduction, which at once establishes the Oriental setting —a village in Southeastern Europe—for the village dance. The beginning of the Introduction is a *cadenza,* in most Oriental type, from

---

* The Russian goussli (sometimes spelled goosli) is a small stringed instrument which resembles the harp.

English horn. It is soon divided into a cadenza-like duet between a muted viola and the English horn. Then enters the announcement of the theme melody, strongly accented, from the English horn, followed at its sixteenth measure by another *cadenza,* this time from muted viola.

Now begins the graceful dance. The movement (3/8 measure and *allegretto*) is characterized by much typically Oriental rhythm; much use of *staccato* and *pizzicato* by the strings; and a rhythmic accompaniment of Oriental drum, tambourine and the harp. The first theme, which makes a syncopated use of an Oriental scale,* is played just by oboe and then repeated in octaves by unison oboes and clarinets. A striking feature of this music is the unvarying beat of the Oriental drum and the constant rhythmic figure ♩♫♫ ♩♫♫ in the accompaniment.

At the close of the piece *cadenzas* are again heard from the English horn and from muted viola, after which a three-measure *Larghetto* (*pianissimo* chords from *pizzicato* strings and English horn) brings the quaintly Oriental sketch to a close. The composition is built almost entirely upon one theme and a rhythmic "figure," and offers a great opportunity to become familiar with the Oriental scale and with the voices of the viola, English horn, and oboe.

"March of the Caucasian Chief" (or March of Sardar), from the suite, is conspicuous as a composition which stresses rhythm, insistently. It opens with a light but relentlessly rhythmic figure played by kettle-drums (tympani), drums, triangle, and cymbals. The rhythm of the march definitely established, there begins a shrill, piercingly sweet melody played by piccolo and bassoons. Other instruments join in the wild air—woodwind, more percussion, the brass, and finally the strings. There now enters a descending melody, weirdly Oriental, played, by clarinets, several times in succession. At the same time a unique octave passage, which moves a step upward each time heard, is played repeatedly—more than a dozen times—by the violins.

After a lively development and a tremendously brilliant *fortissimo* climax, there is a gathering of all the orchestral forces, in a slower, broader *tempo* for a return to the gorgeous first theme. All the wind instruments and the trumpets join in a thrilling performance of this stirring melody while the remainder of the orchestra beats an insistent rhythmic accent until the $\frac{4}{4}$ end of the composition.

"Lord Have Mercy," by Lvovsky, is a characteristic piece of

---

* An Oriental minor scale (*a b c d-sharp e f g-sharp a*) is notable for the augmented second which gives it its weird effect.

Russian liturgical* music. A characteristic feature of Russian church music is the customary doubling of the bass part one octave lower than written, by the second basses, whenever this is harmonically possible. The Russian male singers are noted for their deep voices.

This chant-like prayer creates a profound musical impression by the abrupt modulations, and by the skilfully planned monotony of both melody and rhythm. Following the first phrase, in 4/4 time measure,

there is added a new phrase in 3/4 measure, each measure of this music (to which is chanted the same complete word-phrase, "Lord Our God Have Mercy"), being repeated three times. This is continued through twenty-three measures, after which the first rhythm is resumed. The music creates a very emotional atmosphere and appeal.

"Souvenir de Moscow," by Wieniawski. This brilliant and difficult concert solo for violin was written by Wieniawski—himself a brilliant virtuoso—to display his own ability to play violin harmonics. The story is told that, not satisfied with his ability to play these weird embellishments, he retired one summer to his little estate in Russia and there spent several months working hours each day on technical exercises. At the end of the long period of special practice, he had more than mastered the technique of harmonics, and so wrote this elaborate "Souvenir of Moscow," in which harmonics are prominently used, and played it in his Fall concert to prove his accomplishment.

The composition is built in the form of a set of variations upon a folk-air of Russia, "The Red Sarafan" (see previous chapter). It opens with a two-measure chordal introduction from the piano, which is followed by a long and elaborately ornamented *cadenza* for violin, made up of florid scale runs and arpeggiated chords, double notes, trills, mordents, and harmonics.

It then moves directly into the simple strains of the "Red Sarafan."

The piano now takes up the simple air while the violin plays above it an extremely brilliant accompaniment of scale and arpeggio figures.

This is followed by a variation of brilliant harmonics and arpeggios, also in the key of *G* Major.

The next variation—in *E* Minor—is in the manner of a simple

---

* A liturgy is music related to a form of public worship.

counter-melody in the piano part, followed by brilliant passages, elaborate rhythmic figures, harmonics and *pizzicato*-chords.

The closing variation—also in *E Minor*—is entirely in harmonics, and the solo closes with a short and lively *Coda*.

"Military Polonaise," in *A* Major, by Chopin. This stirring composition for piano, originally a popular dance, owes this form to an ancient custom in Poland of opening a formal ball with a Polonaise. It therefore became rather a march or processional than a dance, although the Polonaise is usually spoken of as a dance form. In the days of the six-teenth century, when Poland was a kingdom, it was the custom for return-ing heroes to pass in a very stately re-view before the king.* The officer highest in com-mand, or the oldest of a group of such men of similar rank, was accorded

Galloway

MARKET SCENE IN NOVOGRODEK, POLAND

the honor of leading the march, which was, appropriately, called the *polonaise* and therefore in such case a *military polonaise*.

The great Polish composer, Frederic Chopin, idealized this form in his series of art-polonaises, of which this one in *A* is most familiar. It is related that while he was working upon the composition of the piece, his imagination took such violent possession of him that he one day fancied that the walls of the room opened before him, allowing the entry of prancing war-horses and their brave riders, as they surged forward in a victorious procession. The illusion was so strong that Chopin is said to have fled from the room, to which he could not be persuaded to return for several days.

This "Polonaise" is written in three "big parts" (the form may be diagramed *A B A*). It opens with a rousing martial theme, two measures in length, and built upon a vari-ation of the prevailing polonaise rhythm

* The first "court" polonaise was held in Krakow by Henry III, of Anjou, in 1573.

A contrasting theme of like figure and rhythm and a repetition of the opening melody complete this part, after which the *trio* or middle section is heard with, first, a soaring trumpet-like melody in the right hand accompanied by the persistent polonaise rhythm in the bass; and a second division which clearly suggests the stirring roll of drums.

The repetition of the polonaise proper brings the work to a close.

MUSICAL ILLUSTRATIONS

*6534	*Aria of Soussanine from "A Life for the Czar" (Glinka)*	*Chaliapin*
6514	*Polovetzian Dances from "Prince Igor" (Borodin)*	
		Stokowski and Philadelphia Sym. Orchestra
——*	*Hymn to the Sun from "Le Coq D'Or" (Rimsky-Korsakow)*	
1335	*March of the Caucasian Chief* ⎰ *from "Caucasian Sketches"*	
6514	*In the Village* ⎱ *(Ippolitov-Ivanov)*	
		Stokowski and Phila. Sym. Orch.
78890	*Lord Have Mercy (Lvovsky)*	*Russian Symphony Choir*
——*	*Souvenir de Moscow (Wieniawski)*	
*6234	*Military Polonaise in A Major (Chopin)*	*Paderewski*

INFORMATIONAL NOTES

The opera "Prince Igor" was given its first performance at the Imperial Opera House at St. Petersburg, Russia, October 23, 1890. It echoes the spirit of the most heroic days of the former Empire of Russia. Borodin began to plan for the opera as early as 1866, and made many sketches of the various scenes. He first made a conscientious study of the old chronicle, "The Story of Igor's Band," which tells of a twelfth-century expedition of the Russian princes against a nomadic tribe, called Polovetzians, related to the Turks of ancient days, who had already invaded Russian territory.

Borodin wrote the libretto himself, working at it spasmodically for over seventeen years, but died with it still unfinished. The overture was written out from memory by his friend Glazounow. Rimsky-Korsakow and other friends completed the work and its orchestration, which, from its first performance, won many ardent admirers. The most popular act of the opera is the second, in which are heard and seen the picturesque, animated, and energetic dances. Many of the melodies of the dances were given to Borodin by Hunplvi, a traveler, who had heard them sung by tribes of Central Asia.

The American premiere of "Prince Igor" was held at the Metropolitan Opera House, in January, 1916.

The opera "Coq d'Or" (The Golden Cockerel), by Rimsky-Korsakow, is built upon a legend of Moorish origin. Brought to Spain by way of Africa, it has, for centuries, been a popular favorite there. It was brought into Russia, during the eighteenth century, where it was jotted down by Pushkin and elaborated by him into the fanciful tale used by Rimsky-Korsakow in his opera. Washington Irving, an American novelist, also rewrote the old tale during his years of residence in Spain, to which he had been sent as United States Ambassador. His version of the tale is found in the two stories, "House of the Weathercock" and "Legend of the Arabian Astrologer."

The Caucasian villages, such as are described musically in the "Caucasian Sketches," are said to be situated upon the site of the Colchis Strand first made famous by the mythical tales of Jason and the Golden Fleece. The inhabitants of these villages are a mixed people, in nationality, in religion, and in traditions. (For further information concerning these villages see pages 187-192 in "Music Appreciation Readers," Kinscella, Book Five.)

QUESTIONS AND TOPICS FOR DISCUSSION

1. Name the principal characteristics of the art music of Russia. What is the effect of the use of the whole-tone scale upon composed music? Who was the first Russian composer to use folk-material in composed music? What are the essential features of the music of the Polovetzian Dances?

2. What instrument of the orchestra impersonates the Golden Cockerel in the opera of the same name? What musical characteristics of the "Hymn of the Sun" suggest Oriental folk-music?

3. Tell what you know of Ippolitov-Ivanov and his music. Is rhythm or melody the predominating feature of the "Caucasian Sketches"? Give reasons for your answer. How does the "Oriental" minor scale differ from the "whole tone" scale? Why are the oboe and English horn appropriate instruments to be used in "In the Village"?

4. Name five definite characteristics of Russian church music which are illustrated in the liturgical music heard in this lesson.

5. What is a violin harmonic? What is the effect given by elaborate use of harmonics in a violin composition?

6. What is the characteristic rhythm of the polonaise?

Library Reading. "House of the Weathercock," "The Legend of the Arabian Astrologer," in "The Alhambra," by Washington Irving; "My Musical Life," by Rimsky-Korsakow; "In the Cosmopolitan Caucasus," in "Travel," December, 1916.

PART THREE—CHAPTER THREE
"PETROUCHKA," A RUSSIAN BALLET BY STRAWINSKY

(It is suggested that the student review at least the opening sections of Chapter Ten, Part One—"Ballet—Telling a Story in Music and Dance"—before taking up the study of this Chapter.)

The Russian Ballet. Although men of many countries have written, produced, or danced ballets, the most perfect known to the world is thought by many people to be the Russian Ballet. There are two great reasons for this. One is that the great Russian musicians have given much of their time to the composition of beautiful ballets, many of which owe their charm to the richness of Russian folk-music and folk-lore. The other is that—until the World War—Russia had special schools supported by the Government in which ballet dancers were trained in their difficult art.

"Petrouchka" is a real Russian ballet, for it tells a story of Russian life a hundred years or more ago, and has, in all its music, a flavor of the wildly beautiful Russian folk-music.

The plot of the ballet is not that of any Russian historical tale, or of an old folk-tale, but is a bit of fantasy. The ballet has four scenes, all of which are laid in the market-place of old St. Petersburg (now Leningrad) during the Carnival, or Street Fair.

The time is about 1830.

The four principal characters are The Showman, Petrouchka, The Dancing Doll, and The Moor. There are many less important characters in the ballet, including coachmen, nurses, grooms, merchants, and people attending the Fair. There are also a dancing bear and a merry-go-round to help furnish amusement.

The Story of "Petrouchka." "Petrouchka" is sometimes called the "ballet of the Jealous Puppets." Petrouchka, a wooden puppet-doll owned by a Showman who has a tent at the Fair, is in love with another puppet, The Dancing Doll. As Petrouchka is only a clown, and a very homely one, too, The Dancing Doll prefers The Moor, the third of The Showman's puppets. While the carnival is in full swing, and the hurdy-gurdy is grinding out tunes to amuse the crowds, The Showman comes out of his tent and begins to attract attention by playing on his flute. While the fun is at its height, it is interrupted by Petrouchka's sudden flight into the street from the little theatre tent, pursued by the angry Moor, who kills the clown with his sword.

The crowds are horrified, thinking that something terrible has happened. But The Showman reassures them by telling that Petrouchka is, after all, a wooden doll which he (The Showman) has, by the aid of magic, made to seem alive; and by holding up the lifeless wooden body for them to see.

This satisfies the crowd, which starts dancing again as The Showman begins to drag Petrouchka into the tent to put him back in his box. Something seems to warn The Showman, who turns about just in time to see the ghost of the clown doll leering at him above the little booth. Petrouchka seems to have been quite alive, after all. The Showman runs away in fright. Snow begins to fall, and the crowd finally disperses and goes home.

The Music of "Petrouchka." Not only is Strawinsky's brilliant music written for the accompaniment of ballet, but it is now arranged by the composer (who has written a special concert ending) so that it may also be played and heard as an independent suite for symphonic orchestra.

IGOR FEDOROVITCH
STRAWINSKY

The music is, for the greater part, full of fantasy, action, intense vigor, and grace. Although Strawinsky is said to have stated that the ballet contains no authentic folk-airs, it has an unmistakable folk-atmosphere.

In it the composer has used many strikingly unusual instrumental combinations, such as a solo trumpet which vies with a flute, while a bassoon plays the accompaniment; the use of saxophones and other wind instruments to play certain short passages; a xylophone to suggest the stiff-legged doll-dancer; and the dainty flute with piano for the little Ballerina's dance music.

The score suggests not only the action of the puppets, but that of the entire carnival crowd. It contains merry dance tunes, hilarious carnival music in which the street-fair confusion is cleverly imitated, music of a hand-organ, heavy basses playing for the clumsy dancing bear, and the quaint tune played by the visiting peasant on his simple shepherd pipe.

"Danse Russe" opens abruptly, full orchestra with piano, *forte.* The entire dance is built upon a theme, simple in itself, but a part of the general complexity of the music brought about by the composer's use of large, consecutive, full chords and spectacular accompaniment features. The two-measure theme in piano

is repeated immediately, four times, being combined with a similar melody in flute and clarinet; with a *pizzicato* chordal accompaniment in the strings; and a rhythmic accompaniment on the "figure" or pattern from the rest of the orchestra.

Following this four-fold statement of the main dance theme, the solo is passed, measure by measure, from muted trombone to clarinet, then to oboe, while at the same time harps and piano furnish a rhythmic accompaniment. Sweeping *glissandos* are heard from piano and xylophone.

The complexity of the music increases with the greater agitation of the dance and the development of the theme (this development being more a rhythmic than a melodic one). Here violins and flutes carry the wild air, and an atmosphere of dashing, vigorous motion is lent by much further display of *glissando* from piano and xylophone. This section of the dance comes to a close in an explosive climax, full orchestra, after which it quite abruptly diminishes to a milder mood in which an oboe carries the solo, a counter melody is played by the solo violins, and a constant rhythmic accompaniment is heard from English horn, bassoons, and *pizzicato* strings.

In Petrouchka's Room. This episode in the Suite is theatrical in its musical allusions. It opens with a tiny one-measure fanfare in the woodwind, and the beating of drums behind the scenes. This short *Introduction* is followed by much use of scattered rhythmic groups each of which is made up of irregular note patterns.

Here the piano offers a tiny arpeggiated *cadenza*, the notes evenly divided and alternated between the two hands.

STAGE SETTING FOR PETROUCHKA AT LA SCALA OPERA HOUSE

Now the music which, in the ballet proper, attends the "Malediction" (or Curse) of Petrouchka is heard. It moves along furiously, a confusion throughout, which is carefully constructed by the composer by means of arpeggio calls *fff* from trumpets and trombones; long-held chords from the horns; tremolo and arpeggio figures from the woodwind; and trill passages from the strings.

"*Petrouchka*"

A more thoughtful strain (*Adagietto*) enters the music. Solo flute and piccolo make much use of embellishments. The theme passes from them to English horn, then back to flute and bassoon, leading to the *Coda* or *Finale,* a climax built upon *motifs* drawn from the several themes.

"Grand Carnival." The brilliant music of the Carnival Scene is precisely what its composer wished it to be, the height of jolly confusion, created by the assembling of many thematic *motifs*—as there are many people in the gay company—full orchestra.

"Dance of the Bear and the Peasant." The happy incident of the appearance of the Dancing Bear at the Russian Fair is told in a jolly manner. This movement of the Suite moves more slowly than many of the others, with a stolidity about it which suggests the clumsiness of the bear. As the bear enters slow *sostenuto* chords from the bassoons—just two chords which alternate with each other, back and forth, over a period of several measures, are heard. Similar treatment is given to a simple figure in 'cellos and basses, while the clarinet provides a song of the Carnival unrest by its restless quaverings.

Soon the very typical "bear" melody or theme is heard, given out, most appropriately, by the tuba.

"Dance of the Coachmen and the Grooms." Clumsy rhythm and an apparent lack of melodic thematic material characterize this number, which is begun with a *basso ostinato* in tuba and trumpet, heavy chords from the strings, and a swirling rhythmic figure played by clarinet and horns. An interesting incident in the music is the entrance of a series of calls (built upon the simple triad) from solo horns.

"The Masqueraders," in agitated *tempo,* opens with dance rhythm in woodwind, celesta, and harps. Here the composer has made much use of chromatics.

MUSICAL ILLUSTRATIONS FROM "PETROUCHKA" SUITE

Informational Note

The ballet music was written in May, 1911, by Igor Strawinsky, a young Russian composer who had at first been educated to become a lawyer. However, he had, as a boy, been allowed to cultivate his talent for music, and although he has now spent many years in other parts of Europe, and in America, he is said to have never lost touch with the old-time atmosphere of life in his native land. It is said that he wrote all of the enchanting music for "Petrouchka" in thirteen days, while on a visit to Rome, Italy.

Questions and Topics for Discussion

1. While first listening to the Petrouchka music, which is decidedly descriptive, try to follow the "story" of the ballet, and identify the various incidents mentioned in it. Notice the great art shown by the composer in opening and ending the ballet in the same scenes and with the same care-free carnival spirit.

2. Contrast the Petrouchka ballet music with other Russian ballet music you have heard, such as the "Valse" from Tschaikowsky's "Sleeping Beauty," or the "Russian Dance" (Trépak) from the same composer's "Nutcracker" ballet (and suite). What characteristics, if any, are common to all?

3. How does Strawinsky make use of folk-atmosphere, or the "folk-idea" in "Petrouchka"? Where and how does the music suggest the mechanical dancing of the puppets? Where and how is the dancing bear suggested? Compare the music for the "Coachmen's Dance" at the end of the last scene with the ballet music for the opening carnival scene.

4. Does the "Petrouchka" music belong to the "classical" type, or to the "modern" type? Give reasons for your answer.

5. What characteristics are common to both composed ballet music and the simplest folk-dance air?

Library Reading. "The Russian Ballet," by A. E. Johnson; "Interpretations," by Anna Pavlowa, in "Ladies' Home Journal," September, 1924; "Music of the Russian Ballet," in "New Republic," January 22, 1916.

Part Three—Chapter Four

SONATA FORM—THE SONATINA, SONATA, AND SYMPHONY

What a Sonata Is. The most perfect of all forms is that known as the sonata form. The word *sonata* comes from the Latin *sonare*, meaning to sound, and thus, at first, the sonata was simply a "sounding piece.'' Gradually it developed—learning from its forerunners, the *suite* and the *Theme With Variations*—into a definitely planned composition.

The name sonata at first meant a piece of music that was to be played (or sounded) upon a musical instrument, in direct contrast to a cantata, or composition intended for singing. The word sonata is now come to refer more directly to the *sonata form,* although the title is still given, in a general way, to an entire work of several movements. Great care should be taken to differentiate between a *sonata* as a piece of music and the *sonata form* which is common to all formally constructed works of this nature.

Sonata Form. The sonata pattern or form (the first movement) is divided into three general parts: the Exposition, the statement or announcement of the themes, of which there must be at least two; the Development, in which the themes are elaborated; and the Recapitulation, in which the themes are repeated, in the key of the composition. The rule for the appearance of the main themes is that the first shall appear in the key of the composition, and the second—and additional themes—in contrasting keys. This form or plan affects only the first movement of the complete sonata. Other movements of the complete work may include a slow movement (as an *Andante*); and one or more lively movements frequently copied in style from old suite dance forms.

BEETHOVEN IN HIS THIRTY-EIGHTH YEAR

A piece in sonata-form (or with first movement in this form), written for one solo instrument with accompaniment, is called a *concerto;* for a string quartet or other small group of instruments, it is called by the name of the instrumental combination, as, *trio, quartet* or *quintet;* and for full orchestra it is called a *symphony.*

A miniature sonata which is, however, perfect in its simple form, is the *sonatina.* A study of a sonatina, a sonata, and a symphony will make clear in the student's mind such use of themes.

''Sonatina, in *C,*'' by Clementi (in three sections, divisions or movements), is held by many musicians to be the most perfect example of very simple sonata form in existence.

The First Movement—*Allegro,* written in four-four time and in the key of C Major, has three divisions. The first division (from beginning to first double-bar, if music lies before one) includes the presentation of both themes. The second division begins at double-bar and continues to the end of the development section. The third division begins with the return of the first or principal subject in tonic and continues to the end of the movement.

The first theme is built on the intervals of the broken chord of *C* (like a bugle call) :

The bass offers the simplest possible accompaniment, with a scale passage leading to repetition of the first *motif.* After this repetition and modulation, by means of sequence-like series of pairs of broken thirds, to the dominant (key of *G*), the simple second subject is heard. It ascends (in dominant, key of *G*) with extra (octave) repetitions of principal notes.

The bass is built from a broken chord.

This is repeated in the score, but not on the record.

In the short development section, there is a transpositional development of the first theme, in the dominant (key of *C* Minor), with a counter-melody in the bass. This is followed by a return of the first theme, now transposed to the tonic (key of *C*), and the second theme, also in the tonic (key of *C*).

This section is also repeated in the score, but not on the record.

Andante Cantabile (The Second Movement) is song-like in style, with a simple flowing melody in the key of *F* Major. The principal theme is an augmentation or elongation of the type of the First Movement, with broken chord accompaniment. In fact the general design of all three movements is similar.

Vivace (The Third Movement), written in the key of *C*, sounds like a jolly dance in major key. The simple accompaniment in the bass is made up, for the most part, of simple broken chords.

"Sonata in *A*" for violin and piano, by Mozart. A sonata may be participated in by two equally important instruments. Such is the case in this Mozart work for violin and piano, in which the responsibility of announcing and developing the various themes is shared equally by the players. Among the long lists of his chamber music compositions there are forty-two sonatas for violin and piano alone. None of these is more perfect in form, more tuneful or of greater musical value than this dainty Sonata in *A*.

BEETHOVEN IN HIS STUDY

An analysis of the thematic structure follows: The first theme, *a,* pronounced by the piano and violin in unison, is built upon a descending triad or arpeggio in the key of *A* Major, and, with its question and answer, occupies eight measures. This is immediately repeated.

Then the violin announces *b,* the second theme, also in the key of *A* Major, which is followed by a modulatory episode carrying the music into the key of *E* Major.

The third subject, *c,* in the key of *E* Major, also built upon a simple triad, is introduced by the violin while the piano plays a delicate tremolo accompaniment. After eight measures the melody of *c* is taken up by the piano which now carries the air while the violin plays the tremolo accompaniment.

A comparatively long *Coda* completes this exposition of the three themes.

Now follows a short development section in which *a* appears first in the key of *E* Minor, in ascending motion; then in *F* Minor, ascending; immediately followed by a sequential modulatory passage which carries the players to a recapitulation of *a* in the original key of *A* Major.

Figures from *b* now appear, first in the piano, then in the violin, then again in the piano, the theme descending in thirds in a sequential manner.

After an episode, *c* (which was first given out in *E* Major) appears in the key of *A* Major, the melody being first presented by the violin and then, in octaves, by the piano. A brilliant Coda, reminiscent of preceding thematic material, brings the sonata movement to a close.

"The Eighth Symphony," by Beethoven. This cheerful symphony, which the composer, in a letter to a friend called "a *little* symphony in F,'' was written at Lintz, Germany, during the summer of 1812.

There is so much that is beautiful about this work, and also so much that is jolly and bright, that Sir George Grove said it

PHILADELPHIA SYMPHONY ORCHESTRA

might be called the ''Humorous Symphony.'' The size of the composition is also less than that of the symphonies written directly before and afterward.

The first movement is written in strict sonata form. There is no real slow movement, or *andante,* as is customary with the classic symphonies, but instead a droll *scherzando* and a lilting minuet; then the closing *Finale.*

The first, or sonata movement (*Allegro vivace e con brio*) is in the key of *F* Major. It has no *Introduction,* but the orchestra plunges at once into the delightful four-measure first theme which is played by the first and second violins,

to a full orchestra accompaniment. The mood is one of serenity, and it is interesting to note that the symphony is scored for the old type of orchestra, smaller in size and lighter in volume than many modern orchestras. There are no trombones.

The reply (or answer) to this first theme comes from the clarinets, and is the same, both in spirit and in the type of its thematic material.

During the next four measures the strings play a variation of the same theme, followed by a longer intermediate phrase in which the graceful air is prolonged in various keys.

The second theme, first played by the first violins and the seconds in the octave

is made easily familiar by being repeated, immediately, by the wind instruments (flutes, oboes, and bassoons).

After modulations, the third melody (flutes and oboes in octaves) is heard,

followed by a series of *staccato* "figures" like those which preceded it. This poetic melody is also repeated and developed to a climax.

The development section of the movement follows, built up by many skipping octave figures, enhanced in beauty by dainty little note "patterns,"

which are heard repeatedly from the voices of the various woodwind instruments, then the violins in canon form.

Snatches of the second theme are also heard alternating with tiny "patterns" of five notes which skip about among the stringed instruments as though taking part in a merry game. This combination of the themes leads at last to a brilliant climax which completes the formal part of this sonata movement, *sforzando,* in a long-held chord. The *Coda* now begins softly, in direct contrast, in a gentle downward-moving figure.

During the *Coda* the bassoon plays a solo on a figure

which is repeated eight times. With supreme art Beethoven closes the movement *pianissimo,* upon the identical six notes with which he started it, played now, as then, by the stringed instruments.

The second movement—*Allegretto Scherzando.* The great charm of this happy music is two-fold, first its playfully jolly as well as elegant tune and second, its equally delightful "tick-tock" accompaniment. The *Allegretto* is founded on a simple three-voiced canon or round, "Ta, ta, ta, lieber (dear) Mälzel," which, it is said, was written by Beethoven, who was fond of fun and joking, some time before, as a playful tribute to his friend Mälzel * at a farewell dinner given on the eve of his departure for a long trip.

"I, too, am in the second movement of the Eighth Symphony," Beethoven wrote a friend, "Ta, ta, ta—the canon on Mälzel. It was a right jolly evening when we sang this canon. Mälzel was the bass. At that time I sang the soprano."

So, throughout almost the entire movement, the persistent "ticking" of the wind instruments in sixteenth notes is heard in imitation of the metronome.

The "ticking" begins with the first note (all woodwind), and at the end of the first measure the lovely, delicately *staccatissimo* air (the first theme, first violins) begins.

After a little echo down in the basses, the second theme is heard.

The bass keeps on, as if unable to stop.

---

* Mälzel was the inventor of the metronome and many mechanical devices.

Sonata Form

The same tiny pattern skips about briskly through all the strings, one after another, the movement ending, at last, in a tumultuous climax.

The third movement, *Minuet,* in three-beat stately dance rhythm is perfect in its form, and genial in its melody. Here, after a two-measure *Introduction,* Beethoven has taken four notes as a theme, and seemingly amused himself with them, for they appear over and over, in various keys and positions, and in all voices of the orchestra.

The first theme has its announcement in the strings and basses. The second theme is announced by the solo bassoon.

The *Trio* (third "large part") opens with a pastoral melody of the folk-song type, played by the solo horns, and answered by the solo clarinet.

The minuet is then repeated.

The fourth and final movement, *Finale, Allegro Vivace.* Like all other movements of this Eighth Symphony, this *Finale* is without elaborate *Introduction.* The carnival spirit is continued from the earlier movements by the immediate entrance of the strings in a restless triplet figure. The second theme possesses a quiet and lovely beauty, and is "sung" by the violins and oboes. The movement is written in rondo style, with five large sections and a *Coda.*

MUSICAL ILLUSTRATIONS

20160	*Sonatina in C (Muzio Clementi)*	*Kinscella*
22018	*Sonata in A (piano and violin) (Mozart)*	*Kinscella and Schmidt*
9342		
9640 }	*Symphony, No. 8 (Beethoven)*	*Vienna Philharmonic Orchestra*
9641		

INFORMATIONAL NOTE

The autographed manuscript of the Eighth Symphony now lies in the Royal Library at Berlin, with this inscription in Beethoven's own hand: "Symphony, Lintz, in month October, 1812." The first performance was in Vienna, February 27, 1814.

QUESTIONS AND TOPICS FOR DISCUSSION

1. What is a sonata? How does the modern sonata differ from the understanding of the term in early days? Which movement of

the complete sonata is written in sonata form? What are three essential divisions of the real sonata movement?

2. What is meant by Exposition? By Recapitulation? What is a sonatina? What is a symphony?

3. What were two forerunners of the sonata form?

4. Discuss the mood of the Beethoven Symphony. By what musical devices has the composer accomplished this atmosphere? Try to become entirely familiar with the important themes of each movement of the symphony before listening to the whole work. What has Beethoven done in his completion of the *Finale* to increase the unity of the entire symphony?

5. What is the character of the first theme of the Clementi Sonatina? Upon what is it built? How has Clementi preserved unity in the three movements of the Sonatina?

6. Identify the theme of the Mozart Sonata in its first presentations by both piano and violin. How many times is the theme played by each instrument?

Part Three—Chapter Five

THE "PASTORAL" SYMPHONY—PROGRAM MUSIC BY A CLASSIC WRITER

Absolute and Program Music. There is no hard and fast line between Absolute and Program music, although each has a separate

and distinct field of expression. There is, however, a shadowy middle ground where expression may be both formal and descriptive. Some music really belongs to both classes, being written with due regard for form, and at the same time suggesting a definite "program."

Up to about the year 1800 much stress was laid upon formal beauty in composition. Beethoven, the great master of form, in his Sixth or "Pastoral" Symphony, completed in 1808, did something quite new, for in it he combined formal beauty and the more dramatic side of art. With this symphony he opened the door of music to program music.

BEETHOVEN IN THE COUNTRY

In "Pastoral Symphony" Beethoven presents a poetic picture of country life and, in charming melodies, recalls the sounds of Nature he loved so well. He not only describes country scenes and incidents, but—greatest test of a composer's ability—he expresses the inner feelings or mood which the story or picture suggests. Some of the tone-pictures are purely imitative, as the songs of the birds, the thunder and the wind; others are merely suggested.

Beethoven also displays rare humor in his musical description of a village band and its bassoonist, who has only three notes left on his battered instrument. These he plays full force whenever he should, and sometimes when he should not.

The entire symphony * is written in a major key with the exception of a short passage in the fourth movement, "The Storm," in which Beethoven made use of the key of *F* Minor to suggest the darkening of the skies and the coming of the rain.

Local color is added by the use of two Croatian folk-songs, one in the first, and one in the fifth movement of the Symphony.

I. Awakening of Joyful Feelings on Arrival in the Country. This movement begins without any introduction, and with the first theme given out by the first violins of the orchestra. This is one of the themes which Beethoven is said to have taken from an old folk-song.

Upon these four measures almost the entire first movement is constructed, for throughout it Beethoven made constant use of bits of the melody or rhythm from the theme. Certain of the tiny phrases which he took from it are repeated over and over, sometimes as many as twenty times in succession, to suggest the constant sounds of Nature.

This is played ten times in succession at one point by the violins.

Sometimes the theme is heard in another octave as in this little example, which the oboe plays.

It is not for some time that the full orchestra sounds, the first

---

* See preceding chapter for discussion of sonata form and symphony.

part of the movement being played by small combinations of instruments. Throughout the movement a happy mood is felt, as the persistent monotony of running brooks and songs of birds, all suggested or imitated by the tiny arabesques from the flutes, the tremolo in the 'cellos, and the little rhythmic "patterns" or figures heard.

The second theme or subject—a more thoughtful melody than the first—begins almost immediately following the first climax from full orchestra. It can easily be recognized, as it is repeated by each part of the String Choir in turn—the first violins, the second violins, the violas, the 'cellos, then the double-basses.

It is then repeated by the wind instruments. Accompanying it are many delicate passages of *staccato* notes, dainty flourishes from the flutes, and the delightful sameness (not to be confused with monotony, as Nature is seldom monotonous) brought about by repetition of little passages.

Following this is a development section in which both themes—more especially the first—are repeated, inverted, and otherwise altered, culminating at last in a tremendous full orchestra climax. After much further repetition of the first theme by all instruments and by full orchestra, the music moves at once into the rather long and very brilliant *Coda*.

There are really four distinct divisions in the music of this first movement of the "Pastoral." They are:

1. The statement of the first theme, in the key of *F* Major, and the statement of the second theme in the key of *C* Major.

2. Development of the themes.

3. A repetition of the first theme in almost its original version.

4. The *Coda*.

II. By the Brook. Here Beethoven has immediately suggested the rippling of a running brook through "shimmering" music played on the violins. In a sketch book already five years old when the "Pastoral" was completed, Beethoven has set down a passage in this same rhythm and labelled it "murmuring of brooks," adding the words "the more water, the deeper the tone." So he places

BY THE BROOK

this ceaseless "brook murmur" at the very begining of the movement, in the music which the lower strings continue for fully two-thirds of the entire composition. The suggestion is that of water going somewhere.

The first theme is introduced by little *motifs* taken from it and played by the first violins over an accompaniment of the other "murmuring" strings.

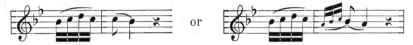

These *motifs* bring on, at last, this lovely melody for violins, played, later, by clarinets, then flutes, while the strings add charmingly delicate string embellishments.

The second theme (also introduced by strings) is more singing in style and appears very soon—just at the close of the first twelve measures.

After a rather long and elaborate development, in which is much embroidery of both themes, is the short twenty-measure *Coda,* that famous passage in which Beethoven imitated the singing of the birds, and was so anxious that it be recognized that he wrote an explanation on the margin of his score. For nightingale, he used the high-pitched voice of the flute; for quail, the oboe; and for cuckoo, the clarinets.

III. Village Festival. This picture of a merry gathering of the country folk is a real *scherzo,* jolly and carefree. The movement begins with a soft and lightly tripping downward-moving tune, the first theme, which is played by the stringed instruments.

Flutes, bassoons and oboes then take up the melody, one after the other, and the rustic music is brought to a climax, with many instruments playing in octaves, *fortissimo.*

The real dance now begins, time-beating chords being played

in thirds or fifths by various groups of instruments. The *one*-two-three, *one*-two-three, old-fashioned waltz rhythm is vigorously suggested by four measures of tiny chords which are played by the first and second violins and which introduce the second theme, a gay waltz tune played by the oboes.

This is accompanied by a continuation of the little chords from the violins, and by the humorous bassoon solo. The solo is made up of just three notes

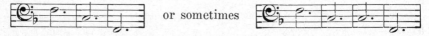

or sometimes

and is said to imitate a rural bassoonist whom Beethoven had heard playing in a village band. He could play just these three notes and kept playing them continuously and industriously whether they were in harmony with the rest of the band's music or not.

All this leads directly into the *Trio* (in two-beat measure), another rustic dance air played by first and second violins against a simple harmonic accompaniment.

This music is developed *fortissimo,* full orchestra, and leads without any pause back into a repetition of the first theme, then on to

IV. The Storm. Suddenly, just as storms are apt to come when a village festival is in progress, comes the distant thunder (suggested by the basses and kettle-drums in the orchestra), the wind and the lightning—all of them suggested by easily recognized musical symbols. Beethoven stops the dancing abruptly. Trumpets, trombone, and piccolo, not heard before during the symphony, are here introduced. A very brief introduction by strings ushers in a clarinet call which is at once echoed by a horn. A repetition of this horn "reply" is followed by the first theme, which is given out by strings, and played three times in succession. Hurried, agitated passages by basses and 'cellos, and firm blasts from trumpets and trombones, portray the surge and swish of the storm.

Just before this reaches its climax there is a sudden lull—a descending chromatic scale played softly creating this impression.

The final clearing off of the storm is now suggested by an oboe solo.

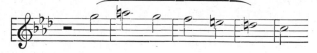

The end of this fourth movement is indicated by the gentle upward-going scales, played by flute

moving directly, without pause, into

V. The Shepherd's Song. This is in the nature of a thanksgiving after the storm. It begins with a shepherd's call from the clarinet, similar to the sound of an Alpine horn on a Swiss hillside, playing the *Ranz des Vaches.**

The call is echoed, and then follows the Shepherd's Hymn—the principal theme—played by first violin and repeated by the second violins, against a *pizzicato* accompaniment and repeated chords in the wind section and the horns.

VI. Gladsome and Thankful Feelings, the last section of the symphony, is a rich development of the shepherd's melody, building from the parts of this beautiful theme a great force of emotional thanksgiving at the passing of the storm. During this development bits of the melody are tossed from one instrument and from one section of the orchestra to another. The violins play the entire tune as the orchestra accompanies with arpeggio-like chords; the flutes play a suggestion of it, or it is plucked by the strings while other instruments have arabesque scale passages; and again the 'cellos repeat the entire theme as the horns echo the *Ranz des Vaches* figure in the distance. The climax is reached in full orchestra after which the violins descend, in an unusual passage, from high *G*, an octave above the staff, to first

---

* See Part Two, Chapter Fourteen, for information concerning *Ranz des Vaches.*

line *E*, and at the same time decrease in volume from *sforzando* to *pianissimo*.

A short peaceful *coda*, in which the shepherd's melody takes on a hymn-like character, brings to a close a work which gave Beethoven, as well as many, many thousands of people who have lived since then, much pleasure.

MUSICAL ILLUSTRATIONS

	Pastoral Symphony (Beethoven)	*Koussevitzky and Boston Sym. Orch.*
6939	*I. Arrival in the Country.*	
6940, 6941	*II. By the Brook.*	
6941, 6942	*III. Village Festival.*	
6942	*IV. The Storm.*	
6942	*V. The Shepherd's Song.*	
6943	*VI. Gladsome and Thankful Feelings.*	

QUESTIONS AND TOPICS FOR DISCUSSION

1. By what means has Beethoven most effectively suggested his picture of rural life—through local folk-melody, country dance rhythms, instrumentation, or his own thematic material? Give reasons for your answer.

Galloway
ENTRANCE TO BEETHOVEN'S BIRTHPLACE AT BONN

2. How may a composition combine within it the characteristics of both Absolute and Program music?

3. Suggest way in which Beethoven, in small musical episodes in the "Pastoral Symphony," displayed his rare artistry.

4. What instrument of the orchestra is often chosen by composers to suggest humor? How has Beethoven made use of major and minor to suggest mood?

5. What two uses has Beethoven made of folk-song in this symphony? Name specific instances.

6. Name several ways in which Beethoven has suggested the sounds of Nature. What instruments are best fitted for this use on ordinary occasions? In time of storm? What is a *motif*?

7. How may the first (or sonata) movement of the "Pastoral" be divided into sections? Discuss each of these sections and the themes and instruments which play them. What is the most famous episode in the second movement? What use of instruments makes it attractive? What is a *scherzo*? Name at least three distinct ways in which Beethoven suggested rural atmosphere in the third movement.

8. What is the *Ranz des Vaches*?

9. Contrast the "Storm" movement of the Beethoven "Pastoral" with the "Storm" section of the "William Tell" Overture, by Rossini, which you have already studied. (Chapter Fourteen, Part Two.) Contrast also, Beethoven's "Shepherd's Song" (Part V of the "Pastoral") with "The Calm" in the "William Tell" Overture. How differently have the two composers depicted the same scenes and moods?

PART THREE—CHAPTER SIX

BEAUTIFUL MELODIES PLAYED UPON SOLO INSTRUMENTS

Melody the Basis of All Musical Art.   Melody has been said to be "the very soul of music." That this is true has been proven by the survival of certain melodies from prehistoric times. Naturally these old airs were songs handed down from one person to another in a hereditary fashion.

Use of Musical Instruments as an Aid to Melody.   With the advent and development of solo instruments, upon which every shade of poetic fancy might be expressed, melody took on new and added beauty. The combination of a beautiful melody with the personality of various instruments is an interesting study.

Some Important Solo Instruments.   Not all musical instruments are possessed of enough charm, variety, and individuality of tone to make them useful as solo instruments, with the ability to interest the hearer when played singly over a long period of time. Such instruments, however, add variety of color in instrumental harmonies and accompaniment.

The Violin, a great favorite among solo instruments, has ability not only to display to the utmost the technical facility of the performer, but has also great power of emotional expression. Its *G* string is often used when tone of great purity and sonority is desired; its tremolo may express great agitation; mystery may be suggested by the use of delicate harmonics; use of the *mute* muffles the tone and creates a mysterious atmospheric effect; correct use of *pizzicato, glissando,* and *vibrato* produces special effects which may be desired by the composer; and its unusual range—from low *G* to *C* in the sixth space above the staff—offers great variety in pitch and resulting tone color.

The Viola, tuned a fifth lower than the violin and of a deeper compass, is sometimes heard as a solo instrument. In the few works written for the viola, its peculiarly individual effect is less emotional in appeal than that of the violin.

The 'Cello, one of the most expressive of all solo instruments, possesses a mellow singing tone of rich quality, and is frequently used to suggest romantic fervor, tenderness, and other forms of deep emotion.

The Flute, the soprano of the Woodwind Choir, is capable of producing a varied tone, either brilliant and far-carrying, or of remarkable sweetness. It has a wide range and is capable of great delicacy and tenderness.

The Harp, one of the oldest of all musical instruments, was used for centuries as an accompaniment to melody. It may, however, in the hands of an artist, become a very effective solo instrument. It was a forerunner of the *Piano,* as the *Flute* was of the modern *Pipe-Organ.*

Types of Melody. Melody may vary in its appeal because of the type of rhythm—also harmony and form—upon which it is built. Each century and each composer have had an individual style of musical expression to suggest moods. A study and comparison of these varied types of melody, as played upon solo instruments, is of great interest, and is also helpful to an appreciation and understanding of larger works.

"Prize Song," from "The Mastersinger of Nüremberg," by Richard Wagner. The opera of which this *aria* is the climax owes its existence to the system of apprenticeship which existed in the Old World for centuries.

The city of Nüremberg was, in the Middle Ages, governed by a council. One member of this council, at the time this opera opens (the sixteenth century), is Burgomaster Pogner (a master goldsmith) who, in his eagerness to encourage art, offers a very precious prize—his own daughter Eva—to the one who shall sing best at the coming Contest of Song.

This Contest is held each year by the Mastersingers, who are also members of the various trade guilds. Walter, a descendant of Walter von der Vogelweide—the greatest of the historical minnesingers—leaves his medieval castle and comes to democratic Nüremberg to hear the Mastersingers sing. Here he learns of the strict formal rules which must rigidly govern the composition of the songs entered and sung by the contestants. Walter feels that too close an observance of rule without inspiration may lead to a mechanical art. He dreams the "Prize Song" which he sings the next day at the Contest held in the meadows outside the town and across the River Pegnitz, and by its performance wins the approval of the Mastersingers and the people, and the prize.

The famous "Prize Song" has been transcribed for many musical instruments, but for none so effectively as for the

WALTER'S TRIAL

'cello, which so ably duplicates the mellow tenor voice of Walter. The lyric melody begins after a short harp-like introduction. The accompaniment is an important feature of this *aria,* throughout the progress of which it frequently repeats *motifs* taken from the main theme.

"Après un rêve" (After a Dream), by Fauré. This French composer is best known to the general musical public through his piano compositions and works written in the smaller forms. His writing is notable for its delicacy of style and grace. This transcription for 'cello by Casals, of an air by Fauré, is spiritual in its simplicity and beauty, and displays the expressive possibilities of this "favorite" instrument. The mood of the composition is one of meditation.

The theme, in minor mode, is announced in sonorous manner, and is then repeated an octave higher. The effect is that of a two-verse ballad. The repetition is slightly more passionate than the first announcement, and after a brief development of the theme, the "dream" comes to a quiet close.

"Souvenir," by Franz Drdla. This short work composed, not arranged, for violin, is a sincere tribute of one artist and composer to the memory of other composers. Drdla is said to have received inspiration for the composition of this number while passing the entrance of the old Central Cemetery in Vienna on a street-car. As he rode his glance rested upon the stone monuments to Beethoven,

Gluck, Mozart, and Schubert, and without conscious thought, a simple, but beautiful, original melody came into his mind. Having no other paper at hand, Drdla jotted the notes of this air down upon his paper street-car transfer, that he might not forget it. Later, the spontaneous little melody was developed and the completed composition appropriately entitled "Souvenir."

It is built upon a curious rhythmic figure, with an important accompaniment for piano which often uses the same figure in contrary motion. The first theme offers an opportunity for display, by the soloist, of a piercing sweetness of tone. The second theme, more vivid in character, and in double-notes, closes with a delicate *cadenza*. After a repetition of the first theme, a *Codetta*, based upon thematic material, closes the composition. The form is *A B A* and *Codetta*.

"Ave Maria," by Bach-Gounod. This famous melody adapted by Gounod to the first Prelude from the "Well Tempered Clavichord," by Johann Sebastian Bach, follows closely the main tones of the accompaniment. In Chapter One, Part One, there is given an outline of the "air" of the Bach Prelude, by which is meant the prominent notes of the broken chords or arpeggios of which the entire composition is formed. A comparison of this outline (which is here repeated) with the Gounod melody (which uses the Bach number as its accompaniment), measure by measure, will disclose the close relationship between the two.

The Bach "air."

The Gounod melody.

The Gounod melody is introduced by four measures of broken chord. As transcribed for the pipe-organ, the devotional mood of the original composition is enhanced.

"Ave Maria," by Schubert-Wilhelmj. This beautiful arrangement for violin of the Schubert art-song (of the same name as the previous selection) is a most grateful solo number. As in the song, so in the violin transcription, the accompaniment (arpeggio figures made up of simple chords) not only provides a suitable atmosphere for the lovely melody, but is a charming example of Schubert's constant use of rhythm, although here of a subtler type than that of march or country dance. In the song, there are three separate stanzas with their musical settings. In the violin arrangement, only two are given, the first in simple flowing style, the melody entering after a short harp-like introduction by the accompaniment. After a brief interlude the second section enters, the repetition of the first melody being here varied by use of octaves, sixths, and double-stopping. An expressive *Coda* of similar style closes the piece.

"Blue Danube" Waltz, by Strauss-Schultz-Elver, is a much-transcribed set of melodies, here arranged as a brilliant concert solo for piano. The composition is, in fact, a series of waltzes, after the old-time Viennese custom of combining many short contrasting movements of similar type and rhythm. The theme of the first of the waltzes, in its original form, is said to have come to Johann Strauss, its composer, while he was preparing to conduct an orchestral concert, and after hearing someone quote the first lines of a poem of the same name:

> "River so blue
> So blue and bright."

Attracted by the rhythm of the words, he jotted down the little theme on his stiff white cuff. By the time the concert was over, the entire incident had been forgotten and had it not been for the observation of his wife, the alluring waltz theme would have been lost. Written first for male chorus, then as a composition for orchestra, the set of waltzes achieved a popularity which has lasted until the present time. The concert arrangement for piano opens with an introductory series of delicate arabesques which suggest, in musical fantasy, the murmuring of the two tiny brooklets which are the source of the mighty Danube. The waltzes which follow are a highly idealized version of one of the most perfect examples ever written of the combination of swinging rhythm and delectable melody.

"Old Folks at Home" (Swanee River), by Stephen Collins Foster, a composed folk-air which claims, with "Home, Sweet Home,"

the distinction of being the most widely known song in the world, was written for the performance of the Christie Minstrels. The song, originally written so as to call up a vision of life upon a Southern plantation, has become general in its tender appeal as a "home" song.

STEPHEN FOSTER MEMORIAL HOMESTEAD,
PITTSBURGH

Played as an instrumental solo upon the harp—an instrument which is capable, in the hands of an artist, of producing at the same time both the solo and the accompaniment parts—the exquisitely simple melody takes on an added charm. The form is binary, or two-part song form, with four phrases (*a a b a*), the first two of which are repeated.

"Sanctissima," by Corelli-Kreisler. A beautiful melody in which the "voices" of two favorite solo instruments are blended and contrasted, is this quaint Old World air of the seventeenth century by Corelli—the renowned Italian violinist and composer—which has been garbed in modern dress and put into duet form by Fritz Kreisler, Viennese virtuoso. The melody is first introduced by the 'cello, which is, at the conclusion of the first phrase, joined by the dulcet tones of the violin. Refined in style, of rare symmetry and grace, the quiet air proceeds, the instruments being, throughout, in perfect balance.

ARCHANGELO CORELLI

The work, though in old-time style, is almost entirely free from embellishments. As it moves along, the melodies presently mount, both in pitch and emotional intensity, the violin, for a brief moment, offering *pianissimo* but vivid contrast to the generally thoughtful mood of the composition. The duet, which has been in minor mode, closes softly with a chord in parallel major key.

MUSICAL ILLUSTRATIONS

6620	*Prize Song from "Die Meistersinger" (Richard Wagner)*	*Casals*
1354	*Souvenir (Franz Drdla)*	*Elman*
21216	*Ave Maria (Bach-Gounod)*	*O'Connell*
7103	*Ave Maria (Schubert-Wilhelmj)*	*Elman*
6840	*Blue Danube (Strauss-Schultz-Elver)*	*Lhevinne*
4001	*Old Folks at Home (Stephen Collins Foster)*	*Salvi*
8090	*Sanctissima (Corelli-Kreisler)*	*Hugo and Fritz Kreisler*

(It is suggested that the student hear also the flute solos in L'Arlésienne "Minuet," in Loeillet "Sonata" No. 7, and in "Danse des Mirlitons," from the Nutcracker Suite; the viola in "Reverie du Soir," by Saint-Saëns; English horn in the Händel "Pastoral Symphony"; the violin or 'cello in "Serenade," by Schubert; "Meditation," by Massenet; "Romance in F," by Beethoven; "E-flat Nocturne," by Chopin, and many other beautiful melodies discussed in other chapters.)

INFORMATIONAL NOTES

The Mastersinger of Nüremberg. It has been said that in this

opera Wagner wrote his own biography; that Walter was an impersonation of Wagner's own intention to bring to the world (as Walter
brought to Nüremberg) something new in music.

The *minnesingers* were the German counterpart of the Troubadours of Southern France, but lived and sang at a somewhat later
date. They were always of noble or gentle birth and the most famous
ones known through literature are Walter von der Vogelweide (who
learned to sing from the birds), Wolfram von Eschenbach and Tannhäuser.

The harp is an instrument of great antiquity. The modern instrument is a descendant of the shepherd's lyre, and of the more skilfully made instruments of the Greeks, the Romans, and the Egyptians.
Carvings of harps are seen in nearly all the tombs at Thebes. The
Assyrians improved upon the Egyptian harp by adding sound holes
to it. Earliest history of the Celts gives the harp a prominent place.
A harp may be seen carved upon a church near Kilkenny, the date of
which cannot be later than 830. The earliest and oldest example of
the Irish harp, as it is now known, is the famous harp in Trinity College, Dublin, which was made in the fourteenth century. The modern
harp owes much of its facility to the art of Sebastian Erard, a French
harp-maker of the eighteenth century.

Questions and Topics for Discussion

1. What melody suggested in this chapter is the most dramatic
in its appeal? Which is the most lyric? Which the most poetic?
Which is the most devotional in type? Give reasons for your choice.

2. Contrast the extremely simple melody of "Old Folks at Home"
with the more complex and formal melody of the "Prize Song."
What are the musical elements in each which make the strongest emotional appeal?

3. How many distinct waltz melodies are heard in the "Blue
Danube"?

4. How may the use of an expressive solo instrument greatly enhance the beauty of even a very simple melody? Discuss the characteristics of the various solo instruments. Tell what you know of
the origin and development of each instrument discussed. What can
you say concerning the "personality" of these various instruments?

5. How much do such elements as simplicity, tunefulness, frequent repetition of *motifs* from a theme, decisive rhythm, and use
of a simple form, affect the "appeal" of a melody?

6. Are the melodies suggested in this chapter examples of Pure
(Absolute) or of Program music?

7. How are national tendencies strongly expressed in some of these melodies?

8. Reread Chapter One, Part One. Discuss the essentials to the composition of a beautiful melody.

Part Three—Chapter Seven

THE MUSIC OF EDWARD MacDOWELL, AMERICAN COMPOSER

Edward MacDowell, the Man. As the years go by, it becomes more and more apparent that MacDowell's is quite the rarest musical genius that has ever been fostered on New England's soil.

The MacDowell Music.* From first to last, MacDowell worked

EDWARD MAC DOWELL

stedfastly in a single direction, and from the life about him gathered impressions to be woven into the magic web of his dreams. This is especially true of the later years of his musical life, when the happy summers were spent at Peterborough, for much of the music he wrote during these years—especially the "Woodland Sketches"—is colored by his Peterborough environment.

Great composers are, and often wished to be, judged by the success of their larger works, but the fact remains that many of these larger works—and their composers as well—would often remain unknown to the general public were it not for the interest awakened by some of the same writer's less complicated and more universally appealing work. Then, too, only a very great artist can dare to venture into the realm of miniature writing or painting. A great painter once advised his pupils to begin by painting life-size portraits, and only when they had completely mastered the technique of their art, to begin working on the jewel-like scale of the miniature. In the work of all great composers this principle is clearly shown. The

---

* See also "Love Song," from "Indian Suite," by MacDowell, Chapter Twelve, Part Two.

The Music of Edward MacDowell

great miniature writers are never merely "little" masters, but have been able to show, within a small compass, as notable and permanent results as they and others have produced on a larger scale. *The size of a composition has nothing to do with its real quality.*

Edward MacDowell had a remarkable gift for extremely compact expression. When, in the summer of 1896, there came a little time for writing at the Log Cabin at Peterborough, MacDowell wrote the "Woodland Sketches," many of which have such a charm that they have made his name and writings

HILLCREST, THE MAC DOWELL HOME AT PETERBOROUGH

known to even the most unmusical concert-goer. Colored as they are by the scenes about the Log Cabin in which they were written, they appeal to nearly everyone. They run the whole gamut of fancy, from whimsical and humorous, to stately and somber. MacDowell himself wished each of the "Sketches" to express but a single musical thought. Each of them reflects a single image—as a simple wild flower—and is, in fact, a poetical story with its own individual charm.

"To a Wild Rose," a two-page tone-poem, is a miracle of concentrated grace and beauty, and is notable for its simplicity. To accurately sense the phrase limits of the themes of this little gem one should know MacDowell's own "trick" of counting it and having his students count it—to say the counts on one breath from the beginning to the end of the phrase (here, eight counts in four measures) instead of counting for each separate measure. Two such phrases combined (the question and answer) create a "large part." The form of the "Wild Rose" is extremely simple:

a (a "large part"—eight measures) key of *A* Major
a (an echo)
b (hear the three-note *motif* from the first theme in this twelve-measure phrase)
a (as at first)
b (with a prominent counter-melody)
Coda—reminiscent of both themes

Music and Romance for Youth

"From an Indian Lodge" MacDowell has here preserved the chief characteristics and atmosphere of native Indian music, and in this brief composition has written a tone-poem of great effectiveness

THE LOG CABIN

and dignity. Both its themes are original and genuinely Indian in style, and here MacDowell has made suggestion, rather than imitation, the basis of his setting. The mood of the dirge, with its insistently monotonous muffled drum beats, is more than suggestive, it is convincing: and while the first impression is that of a stately procession, as it winds up through the pines following the body of a young chieftain, there is a still more subtle symbolism about the music, as in it the Indians lament not only the death of the dead brave but mournfully foresee the tragedy of the passing of their race.

The first section of the piece, built of octaves and chords, is in the type of declamation of a stately and dignified type. (When played as a piano solo it suggests orchestra, the long tremolos in the bass suggesting the roll of tympani, or of the Indian drum.)

The second part of the composition is a mournful dirge, its most unique touch being the single dull-toned chord which comes monotonously on the second beat of each measure, having no *crescendo* or *diminuendo,* no matter what changes there may have been in force, or mood of the melody. This clearly suggests the beating of the Indian drum, in dirge rhythm. The four-measure *Coda* is a phrase similar to the opening section of the composition.

THE GRAVE OF EDWARD MAC DOWELL ON HIS FARM

In the Peterborough woods where the "Indian Lodge" was written, there was much to remind MacDowell of the Indians, and in his strolls about the Log Cabin he frequently found and picked up stone arrow-heads. Some of these are still on the shelves in the Log Cabin where he placed them.

"To a Water Lily" is an idyl which, for poetic beauty and sincerity of feeling, is unrivaled in modern musical literature. A real composer does not always try to imitate a thing—he may suggest it. He often has, however, a definite picture or fancy in mind while writing, and this may color his music to a very great extent. The beautiful water lilies, as they look upward to the light and sway with the water, while their long stems reach down through the water to the earth below, are clearly suggested by the gently swaying rhythm of the music. The composer's direction—"In dreamy, swaying rhythm"—taken in conjunction with the title, gives the clue to the mental picture he had in mind.

The form of the "Water Lily" is:

a (first theme)

a (repetition)

b (an eight-measure questioning theme)

A transitional passage made up of three sequential phrases of two measures, each.

a

a (in altered form)

Coda.

"A Deserted Farm." In this number MacDowell has revealed much of the Celtic romance which was so much a part of him. He has written as one who comprehends that the very precious things of life are often the very simple things, and with the simplicity of real art.

Scattered among the New Hampshire hills, and even in his own Peterborough forest, MacDowell often came, in his strolls, upon the ruins of a deserted home. The abandonment of the stony farms, which, beginning in the 1850-1860 period with the gold fever, became really serious after the close of the Civil War, has left the country-side, in many places, desolate, and crumbling ruins of walls, and fire-places are all that is left, in many instances, to tell the pathetic story of fruitless struggle. In "A Deserted Farm," MacDowell has given a definite poetic suggestion of an intimate scene of life—the leaving of the old home—the old schooner, the man, with his wife and children and their bundles starting out for new scenes, but looking back with wistful eyes to the old home.

The form of the "Deserted Farm" is as follows:

a (in the key of *f*-sharp minor)

a (in altered form)

Trio a (in parallel major-*F*-sharp)

　　b (with extension of phrase)

a (as at first)

a (very slightly altered)

Other examples of pictorial classics among the MacDowell works are his "Fireside Tales," "New England Idyls," "Sea Pieces" and the "Orientales." The "Indian Suite" for orchestra, four piano sonatas, and his delightful songs, are also worthy contributions to American art music. Of particular interest is his Concerto in *A* for piano and orchestra, a mature work, though written when MacDowell was only seventeen years old.

"Of a Tailor and a Bear"—founded upon a tale by Hans Christian Andersen—is a clever bit of musical story-telling. It is one of the "Marionettes" which MacDowell wrote under the name of Edgar Thorne, at a time when he wished to raise some money for the relief of a needy friend.

This gayly expressive little description begins with a happy dance melody in which short *staccato* chords take a prominent part. After four measures, a deep bass melody is heard which tells that the Dancing Bear has arrived. Then the gay dance tune is resumed—to be interrupted by a pompous little passage and the bear's growl in the bass. Another episode—the tuning of his fiddle by the tailor—is now introduced. These various musical incidents combine and carry the "forgotten fairy tale" on to completion. The little dance tune, heard three times, each time more softly, and a repetition of the bear's growl, far in the distance, bring the music to a close.

"A Maid Sings Light," is a romantic song of delightful lyric quality. The thematic content of the first two-measure phrase is simply a downward-moving scale, and in the brief song a whole scale of emotions is run as well. Much whimsical advice is given, to a melody in which—in the second part—are many large skips, including four measures of octave skips. An exact repetition of the first theme concludes the song. The accompaniment is of light and dainty character.

"The Swan Bent Low," an art-song—composed throughout—is notable, not only for its exquisite melody, but for its pianistic accompaniment, harp-like in its first part, and sturdy in the more passionate middle section. The melody has a swinging rhythm—much assisted by the rolled chords of the accompaniment—and is to be sung in the very flowing *legato* manner which to MacDowell was suggestive of a "liquid" quality to tone.

"The Sea" is a dramatic tragedy in miniature. It tells of a sailor who sails away, and of his sweetheart, who stands on the shore and cries. The sailor meets with shipwreck and never returns, but sleeps beneath the ocean in a coral bed. One of the most superb "sea" songs in existence, the music has, at first, all the gay sweep of an old sea chanty.* Simple chords in the accompaniment lie low in the bass, symbolizing the depths of the sea. The rarely poetic first theme,

---

* A chanty is a rhythmic song sung by sailors to help them in their work.

in major key, gives way to an air of simple pathos, in minor, on the words "many and many a year," and to *pianissimo* and peaceful phrases on the last "asleep," which is repeated gently, twice. There is an absolute reflection of the verse in the music. Rich, colorful harmonics enhance the tragic atmosphere of this American art-song.

MUSICAL ILLUSTRATIONS

	From *"Woodland Sketches"*	
1152	To a Wild Rose	Stock and Chicago Symphony Orchestra
1152	To a Water Lily	Stock and Chicago Symphony Orchestra
20342	From an Indian Lodge	Victor Concert Orchestra
22161	A Deserted Farm	Eaver
	From *"The Marionettes"*	
20153	Of a Tailor and a Bear	Victor Orchestra
	Songs	
4017	A Maid Sings Light	Murphy
4017	{ The Swan Bent Low } The Sea	Dadmun

INFORMATIONAL NOTES

Madame Teresa Carreño, the noted Brazilian pianist who was MacDowell's boyhood teacher, was the first person to play MacDowell music in America. It happened that while MacDowell was studying in Europe, he sent Madame Carreño, who was then in America, a roll of manuscript along with a letter in which he said: "Dear Teresa: You know how I have always valued your advice. Look these over. If they are no good, put them in the paper basket and tell me, and I'll never write another note." Madame Carreño opened the bundle and there she found MacDowell's First Suite, the "Witches' Dance," "Erzahlung," "Barcarolle," and several others of the numbers which later helped to make him famous. "I played them over," she once related. "They were splendid. I was to give a recital in Chicago in two weeks, so I learned some of them, played them there—and that was the first MacDowell ever played in concert in the New World."

The Log Cabin, in which MacDowell wrote so many of his loveliest compositions, is situated deep in the woods, several hundred yards north of his New Hampshire home, "Hillcrest." The home was one of the deserted farms, an old New England homestead, well over a hundred and fifty years old. The first summer that the MacDowells lived there, they added the music room to the north end of the house. But as MacDowell still craved more seclusion and a complete separation from the noises of house and farm, the Log Cabin was built, at what was then the extreme edge of the MacDowell property. Since that time more acres have been bought and added beyond the Cabin, but it is still "In Deep Woods"—the name of a short composition which the composer wrote in description of it.

During Mr. MacDowell's last illness, realizing the opportunity for more and better work which had been afforded him because of the peaceful seclusion of his beloved Log Cabin, he pledged Mrs. MacDowell to bring to realization a dream which he had had for many years. This was that he might provide similar opportunities to other creative artists. This Mrs. MacDowell has done, in the formation and maintenance of the wonderful MacDowell Colony, in which, each summer, several score of creative workers in the allied arts—painting, sculpture, literature, and music—work in separate studios which have been built in isolated spots in the many wooded acres of the MacDowell homestead at Peterborough, New Hampshire.

"To a Wild Rose" is sometimes made into a song, by using, with it, words which were a part of the "Pageant of Peterborough," given a number of times in the MacDowell woodland above the Log Cabin:

> "Come, oh, songs! come, oh, dreams!
> Soft the gates of day close—
> Sleep, my birds! sleep, streams!
> Sleep, my wild rose!"

"A Deserted Farm" was also used as a song in the "Pageant of Peterborough." These words were sung by the "Farmer's Wife" to the "folk" type melody of the composition's middle section, in the scene which enacted the historic departure to the gold fields:

> "Here our babes were born, and here
> Glad through all our toil were we.
> Never, never half so dear
> New homes shall be!
> Weed and wind!
> Storm be kind!
> Here our hearts still dwell.
> Farewell! Farewell!"

At the close of this song, in the Pageant, the rest of the short number (which is almost a repetition of the first part) was played softly by musicians concealed amongst the trees, as the wagon and the departing family moved slowly away and were lost to sight.

QUESTIONS AND TOPICS FOR DISCUSSION

1. Has MacDowell used suggestion or realism in the majority of these compositions? Name selections from his works which are examples of each kind of writing.

2. Why is it often more difficult to create a miniature—whether it be in music or painting—than a larger work?

3. Tell what you know of the Log Cabin, and discuss its real influence upon MacDowell's writings.

4. Discuss the numbers which you know from the "Woodland Sketches," from the angles of poetic thought, mood, descriptive content, and story-telling music.

Library Reading. "The Boyhood of Edward MacDowell," by Abbie Farwell Brown; "Edward MacDowell," by Gilman; "The Peterborough Pageant," by Herman Hagedorn; MacDowell's own small book of poems.

PART THREE—CHAPTER EIGHT

MUSIC OF THE AMERICAN NEGRO

The Underlying Feature of Negro Music. The story of the Negro is inseparable from a story of song, for, from cradle to the grave, his life is attuned to melody. The songs of which the Negro is now so justly proud, are a heritage to him from his ancestors who, in the midst of toil, and often sorrow as well, found time to sing.

TUSKEGEE QUARTET, TUSKEGEE INSTITUTE

The underlying feature of all Negro song is its rhythm, peculiarities of which have been imitated by less clever artisans than the Negroes themselves, in rag-time, jazz, and "blues."

The music of the Negro may be divided into two distinct groups —the working songs and his social songs and dances; and his religious spirituals.

The Working Songs. The Negro has always used singing to help him with his work and to ease his toil. In Africa all the work done by the Negro—as the pounding of wheat and turning of waterwheels

—has always been done to the rhythm of music. In Abyssinia, where teff, a kind of millet, is the principal cereal crop, the threshing is all done by hand flail, by relays of about six men at a time. The lusty singing of these Negro workers while they thresh is said to be easily heard for at least two miles, the men flailing energetically as they sing the threshing song. There are frequent musical climaxes in the song, and as these are being reached, the flails descend faster and faster, beating the heads off the straw, harder and harder, with the men often actually bending to the ground as they slam the wooden flails to the rhythm of the primitive song.

This rhythmic use of singing in connection with work was, and is, also true in the South, where a working song is often improvised to fit the occasion.

One singer will begin an improvised air—the words also improvised to suit the work at hand. Other workers will follow him in unison, and by the time the refrain is reached, all the workers are singing in exquisite and spontaneous harmony. These songs emphasize the art of cheerfulness and of co-operation, and the kind of rhythm used in an individual song is usually determined by the number of men at work and the nature of the work itself.

Social Songs are very frequently composed in the same spontaneous manner, and are often narrative in style.

The Spirituals. There is probably no one race whose religious songs are so unusual or so beautiful as those of the American Negro. His religious songs are called "spirituals," a name given to them long years ago, and are the expression of the Negro faith. They cannot be separated, in thought, from rhythm and melody.

The words of an old Negro spiritual may often seem quite strange, but a reason for this is easily understood. Most of the early Negroes who created the spirituals were unable to either read or write, and so their knowledge of Bible stories came only through hearing them read or told. They frequently had an imperfect understanding of the meaning of the stories heard in the camp meetings, and so heaven was always thought of as a happy place where they would never have to work again. People of the Bible and of heaven were very real and were made to seem so in the spirituals. Some of the songs which have been sung in America for decades are thought to have been greatly influenced by incidents which happened in Africa, before the first Negro was brought to these shores.

"Go Down, Moses" is a Negro spiritual which contains, within itself, a miniature drama. Although its certain origin is lost in mystery, it is known that the melody is very old, and is said to have been sung in Africa for many centuries. Learned scholars have professed to see and hear in it likenesses to a Jewish chant of great antiquity. Many Negro songs are like the earliest *rondeaus,* the chorus beginning and ending the song. Of this type is "Go Down, Moses." The melody is simple. The song is in minor mode, many of its phrases ending dramatically in the major mode.

"Swing Low, Sweet Chariot." The Old Testament story of Elijah and Elisha is the foundation for one of the most exquisite of all the spirituals. The verse reads: "There appeared a chariot of fire, and horses of fire, and Elijah went up by a whirlwind into heaven."

In the old spiritual, the Negro sings of his longing to go to heaven in the same way. So he sings:

> "Swing low, sweet chariot,
>   Comin' for to carry me home,
> Swing low, sweet chariot,
>   Comin' for to carry me home."

This spiritual also begins with the chorus, the words of which have just been given. Then a soloist sings a line, the chorus or congregation joining in with harmony on the responses. This custom prevails throughout all the verses of the song.

Characteristics of Negro Music. One of the principal characteristics of Negro song is that it is always sung in harmony, in direct contrast to the Indian custom of singing in unison. Many Negro songs are in the quaint pentatonic, or five-tone scale, the use of which seems to antedate all written history,* and some use the Oriental minor scale employed by his African forefathers.

The rhythm of the songs is nearly always syncopated, and, combined with luscious melody; rich, musical, and often bizarre harmonies; lack of conventionality in form; sudden changes of key; frequent plaintive imagery; and a genuine creative ability, seems to aid the singer in his emotional utterance.

Use of These Characteristics in Composed Music. No greater tribute can be paid the folk-music of any race or peoples than its inclusion in the art music of a great composer, or the direct influence of its rhythms or melodies upon his writings. The melodies of some Negro songs—especially the spirituals—have been taken in their entirety and either harmonized or idealized into concert form.

"Deep River," an example of such use of a Negro melody, is an old spiritual arranged and harmonized by H. T. Burleigh. It sings,

---

* The Chinese are known to have used it in 2800 B. C.

in tender devotional mood, of the "home across the Jordan," "the Promised Land" and "the heavenly campground."

It opens with a two-measure introduction which suggests the playing of a harp (never used with a spiritual in its primitive setting). The main theme, with its falling inflections, as developed, makes much use of the characteristic interval of a falling minor third.

Deep . . . . riv - er

"Juba Dance," by Nathaniel Dett, is one of five numbers which make up a characteristic suite "In the Bottoms" (originally for piano, but transcribed for orchestra), giving scenes from Negro life. Dett, the Negro composer, has given this rhythmic *motif* to the entire suite.

"Pattin' juba" is a Negro term for beating of hands and feet at an impromptu Negro dance on an old Southern plantation, in substitution for the rhythmic beating of a drum. In primitive times, the accompaniment to all dances was made by clapping of hands, and the Negroes of the South follow this method to this day.

NATHANIEL DETT

In "pattin' juba" those who watch the dance, stamp on the ground and follow this with two quick pats on their hands, in 2/4 measure. About a third of the crowd keeps time in this way, while the other two-thirds dance. Sometimes this is done in a solo dance, all but the soloist keeping time. Music is usually furnished by the local "fiddler" or banjoist.

Dett's "Juba Dance" has a steady quick motion, and is characterized by many double-note passages. The first theme—a downward-moving figure in 2/4 measure —is heard four times in succession. The second theme (chords, with heavy octave response) then enters. It is followed by a return of the first theme and the introduction of a succeeding melodic third theme—a combination of a melody and a stirring rhythm. The first theme returns once again, slightly altered at intervals, in melody, but not in rhythm. There is a lively chordal *Coda*. The form is that of a rondo.

"From the Canebrake," Opus 5, No. 1, by Samuel Gardner, reflects the atmosphere of Negro music, especially in its rhythms. The main theme (introduced by the strings) begins, following a two-measure introduction. Peculiarly effective are the percussion effects, and the insistent bass accents from the tuba. There is a slight rhythmic variation in the accompaniment of the immediate repetition of the first theme. The second theme is mellow and *legato* in style, with much slur-

THE DVOŘÁK HOME IN SPILLVILLE, IOWA, 1893

ring of short phrases. It is a decided contrast to that of the first section. At its close, the first section is again played and repeated, *fortissimo*, thus placing the short composition as a three-part song form.

Symphony, No. 5, in *E* Minor, "From the New World," by Antonin Dvořák, is one of the largest works to have been directly inspired by the melodies and rhythms of the American Negro. The Symphony was written during Dvořák's sojourn of three years in this country (1892-1895) and was, as he is said to have remarked, "a legacy which makes free use of the native idioms of the Negro's musical language." The music was written partly in New York City, and partly in the little village of Spillville, Iowa, where Dvořák spent some months with Bohemian friends. This was Dvořák's last composition in symphonic form, and is a rarely beautiful and appealing work.

I. Adagio: Allegro molto. This first movement in *E* Minor has a slow introduction, after which the main theme (*Allegro molto*, in 2/4 measure) is announced by the horns. It is arpeggio in effect and produces a gay atmosphere.

The main theme is followed by such episodical passages as these, which suggest not only the syncopated rhythms of the Negro, but also the lilt and gayety of a peasant folk-dance in Dvořák's own land.

The famous second theme, appearing in the flute (accompanied by a drone *D* from violins and horns) has more than a chance kinship to the exquisite Negro spiritual "Swing Low, Sweet Chariot." This will be seen by comparing the two themes.

(Theme of "Swing Low")

(Theme of "New World")

II. Largo. (See Chapter One, Part One, for analysis of this popular movement.)

III. Scherzo (*Molto vivace, E* Minor, 3/4 measure) is built upon two main themes, each introduced by flute and oboe; and a lively *Trio* in *C* Major. The movement is repeated after the *Trio* has been played.

The *Scherzo* opens with a brilliant octave passage, after which the first theme (flute and oboe in unison) is heard with its unusual two-measure phrases, each beginning and ending upon the second beat of a measure.

Although in minor key, the air is a gay one, and passes in turn from flute and oboe to first violin, to 'cello, double bass and horns. A curious undertone of primitive rhythm is kept in motion by the instruments not busy with the melody.

The second theme (flute and oboe with string accompaniment)

harks back to the *Largo* and the artful simplicity of its opening theme. This melody is repeated once by clarinets in octaves, with a dainty triangle accompaniment feature; and then by 'cello and bassoon.

The first jolly dance tune of the *Trio* maintains the unity of the whole movement by its arpeggio character.

The second theme of the *Trio* is another reminder of Dvořák's nationality, for in it he has written a gay Old World waltz. It, too, moves by leaps and bounds, and is arranged in two-measure phrases.

After the *da capo* (the repetition of the *Scherzo* proper) a short *Coda* is heard in which, as in the first movement of the symphony, the composer has subtly suggested both rhythm and melody of "Swing Low, Sweet Chariot."

IV. Allegro con fuoco (*E* minor, 4/4 measure). Throughout the entire symphony, Dvořák has proven conclusively that the use of a minor key does not make necessary the expression of a sad or doleful sentiment. The fourth movement is no exception. The first theme, with its intense rhythms, is literally shouted by horns and trumpets, after a short introduction.

The second and less important theme is sung by clarinet over a delicate tremolo accompaniment; after which a development section brings in reminiscences of the first three movements by presenting in turn the principal theme of the first movement, the lovely English horn melody of the *Largo,* and the brilliant opening theme of the *Scherzo.*

Music and Romance for Youth

20518	Go Down, Moses (Negro Spiritual)	Tuskegee Quartet
20068	Swing Low, Sweet Chariot (Negro Spiritual)	Robeson
1276	Deep River (Negro Spiritual) (H. T. Burleigh)	Flonzaley Quartet
21750	{Juba Dance (Nathaniel Dett) {From the Canebrake, Opus 5, No. 1 (Samuel Gardner) }	Victor Orchestra
6565 to 6569	Symphony No. 5, in E Minor, "From the New World" (Antonin Dvořák)	Stokowski and Phila. Sym. Orch.

QUESTIONS AND TOPICS FOR DISCUSSION

1. Name and discuss the types of Negro song.

2. What other races are known to make use of rhythmic working song?

3. Name several musical characteristics which are repeatedly featured in all Negro song.

4. How has Dvořák made conspicuous use of thematic and atmospheric material chosen from the music of the Negro race? Which has he used the more—themes, rhythms or mood and atmosphere of the Negro music? Name three ways in which he has created the unity which exists between the various movements of this Symphony.

Library Reading. "The Negro and His Song," by Howard Odum.

OUTSIDE STUDENT PROJECT

Class members should hear and study at least one concert program each semester, in addition to those presented in class. See Part One, Chapter Eight, for instructions to be followed in listening to these programs.

PART THREE—CHAPTER NINE

FAMOUS TRANSCRIPTIONS

What a Transcription Is. A *transcription,* in its original meaning, is an arrangement of any piece of music for some instrument, or group of instruments, other than that for which the composition was originally written.

For many years the use made of the art of transcription was not especially gratifying, being, like the music of the earliest operas, often little more than a showy and often distorted version of some popular air arranged for the purpose of displaying the technical abilities of the performer.

Presently, however, the greatest of composers gave attention to this branch of their art, and by careful study of the principal features, or expressive meaning of a composition, have often been able to either enhance these beauties, or, by arrangement of the music for an instrument, or combination of instruments, frequently played and heard, have given the composition a wider performance and hearing than it otherwise would have had.

MORRIS DANCE OF OLD ENGLAND

New beauties are also often added to familiar melodies by the careful choice and use, by the transcriber, of one or more instruments whose natural tone quality is most appropriate to the style or mood of the composition.

It is always of especial interest, when studying a transcription of any piece, to also hear, when possible, the original composition, to contrast the two versions of the music, and thus learn, if possible, by what artistic means the transcriber has enhanced the beauty of the themes.

"On Wings of Song," by Mendelssohn, transcribed for violin by J. Achron, will be better appreciated and understood if the form and style of the original composition—a well-loved art song—is well understood. The inspired poem by Goethe, the words of which begin,

"On wings of music roaming,
With thee, sister dear, I glide,"

are set by Mendelssohn in a musical form of art song known as the "Minnelied form" (after the songs of the *minnesingers* of the Middle Ages), a form in which two verses use the same melody and the third an altered or varied form of the melody, or an altogether new one.

The main melody, with its many appropriate and graceful upward flights,

is introduced by two measures of a fluttering harp-like figure from the accompaniment, a figure which, continued in the accompaniment of the verses, serves well as a foundation for the melody of the song and also as an expression of the words.

A secondary melody also floats along within the accompaniment figures. A short interlude separates each verse from that which precedes it. The climax comes during the third verse, the air of which is a somewhat varied version of the earlier melody. After another brief interlude, instrument and accompaniment join in a thoughtful five-measure *Coda,* a prolonging of the graceful sentiments expressed in the song. The subdued close is played *pianissimo.*

"Country Gardens" (also known as "Handkerchief Dance")* by Percy Grainger is often heard and is very popular in its arrange-

PERCY GRAINGER

ment for piano solo,† a transcription of the original form of the composition which was written as "room music" in 1908.

The attractive composition is in itself a transcription of an old Morris dance tune from the valuable collection of Cecil Sharp, an English musician. However, contrary to usual custom, Grainger has not left the melody of the old folk-dance in its original form. The folk-dance has four distinct parts, phrases, or "strains," and it is the fourth of these with which "Country Gardens" opens. This "fourth strain" is at once repeated.

Then the second phrase of the old folk-dance is brought into the composition; then the third, and finally the first (with a few slight alterations of the rhythmic figures).

The first is then repeated; then, in their original order, the second, third, and fourth—the fourth being now heard in a broadened chordal phrase.

The remainder of "Country Gardens" is a refreshingly original and harmonious development of these four simple melodic phrases. Rhythm, melody, and harmony—the three essentials of music—are here skilfully combined to produce an effective concert number.

"O Thou Sublime Sweet Evening Star," from "Tannhäuser,"

---

* The subtitle, "Handkerchief Dance," is given this work because of the old custom of Morris Dancers to carry fluttering handkerchiefs during the dance.
† Upon the score of the piano transcription, the composer wrote, "Birthday gift to mother, July 3, 1918."

by Richard Wagner, is sung by Wolfram in the third act of this opera. Elizabeth, the heroine, has been watching for the return of Tannhäuser, as bands of Pilgrims pass on their return from their pilgrimage to Rome.* Still Tannhäuser does not come. Wolfram, who loves Elizabeth and suffers at seeing her sad and in tears, has been watching her as she departs for the castle. He now seats himself and begins to play on his minstrel harp, sings this exquisite ode to the evening star, which has appeared upon the horizon, and invokes it to guide Elizabeth to her home.

In the effective transcription for 'cello, the mellow tone of the instrument is well chosen as a substitute for the baritone voice for which the melody was originally written. The piano accompaniment of both the recitative, with which the number opens, and the *aria* itself, also suggests the harp with which the original *aria* is, in effect, accompanied. The form is three-part song form with *Coda*.

"Air for *G* String," by Bach-Wilhelmj, was originally written as a movement of the Bach orchestral suite No. 3, in *D* Major, where the lovely "Air" is sung by the violin section of the orchestra. As transcribed for violin solo by August Wilhelmj, the celebrated violin virtuoso, it has had an even wider hearing, and is known as one of the most popular bits of absolute or pure music, in the world.

The transcription, transposed to the key of *C* so that the melody might have the added eloquence of the *G* string's mellow sonority, is given in *Lento* tempo and 4/4 measure. The accompaniment, here an important feature, is partly in flowing melodic style, and partly in sequential "patterns" and octave skips. The short composition is in simple two-part song form, with each part repeated.

"The Swan" (Le Cygne), by Saint-Saëns, written originally by this composer as a number in his orchestral suite, "The Carnival of Animals," † has become one of the composer's most widely known small compositions. It was also a favorite with Saint-Saëns, as he is said to have made a transcription of the air for every solo instrument of the symphony orchestra. It is essentially a bit of impressionistic program music, its delicate wavering accompaniment figures suggesting the motion of the water, while the elegantly simple melody portrays the graceful motion of the swan.

The form of the composition is *A B A*, with a short *Coda*.

"March Hongroise-Rákóczy," by Berlioz, is a transcription for orchestra of a spirited national folk-air of Hungary, said to have been composed in its present familiar form by a gypsy court musician in the service of Prince Rákóczy. The melody is one of the most widely known of all Hungarian tunes and became especially dear to Hungarian hearts because of their adoration of the patriotic Prince who, at the beginning of the nineteenth century, unsuccessfully opposed the power of Austria in an attempt to gain for them political freedom. The martial song became a sign of insurrection and its performance on public occasions was forbidden by the Austrian Government.

HECTOR BERLIOZ

Berlioz, the French composer, while on a visit to Budapest, found the cherished melody in an old volume of songs, and, inspired by its stirring rhythms, wrote a brilliant concert march which used the air as its main theme. Later, when preparing the score of his opera, "Damnation of Faust," * Berlioz made a place in it for the thrilling march, so arranging a scene that a regiment of unseen Hungarian troops march past the fortress, in time to its music. This spectacular bit of stage-craft, combined with the patriotic fervor aroused by the magnificent march, won a wild enthusiasm for the Berlioz opera.

Without reference to its patriotic background, the March is notable for its fine simplicity of theme; its sudden stirring climaxes; its frequent use of unison passages; effective use of kettle-drums; abrupt modulations; and gradual and skilful crescendos from *piano* to the *fortissimo* climax.

Scored for full orchestra, the March opens (*allegro*) in marked rhythm, and with military fanfare from horns, trombones, and trumpets. After a momentary pause, the theme of the old folk-air is announced softly, but with brisk rhythm and a double-quick tempo, in flute, piccolo, and clarinet, accompanied by simple harmonies in oboes, horns, and *pizzicato* strings.

* Based upon scenes from Goethe's "Faust."

The main theme develops a quick crescendo and climax, and the whole short section is then repeated.

With the second section there enters a bold and stirring arpeggio figure given out by woodwind and accompanied in typical "gypsy" manner by sharp sweeping chords from plucked strings. Not a note is sounded which does not enhance the bold martial mood of the music. Drums and triangle are used sparingly. The tiny figure of three notes is repeated in contrapuntal  manner between groups of instruments, and in sequence, each first note of the group receiving, at each repetition, a defiant accent.

The first notes of each group of one such descending passage, with their accented prominence, bring vividly to the hearer, that Oriental or gypsy minor scale upon which the entire composition is based.

Presently the theme is heard for a brief moment in parallel major key, the shrill piccolos at all times lending brilliance of a military style to the already stirring melody. Minor mode (pure and unaltered) reappears shortly in the unison fanfare, but gives way again to major. Thematic and accompaniment features become, all the time, more complex. Rolling of drums, brilliant *fortissimo* rhythms sounded from tambourine and triangles, unison passages in the melody with its new rhythmic developments, and massive chords from accompanying instruments, bring to a gorgeous culmination this superb military march.

MUSICAL ILLUSTRATIONS

6848 *On Wings of Song (Mendelssohn-Achron) (composed for voice,
        transcribed for violin)*   *Heifetz*

20802 *Country Gardens (Handkerchief Dance) (Percy Grainger) (Old
        English folk-tune transcribed for piano solo) (double
        transcription for orchestra)*   *Victor Concert Orchestra*

6620 *O, Thou Sublime Sweet Evening Star (Richard Wagner) (com-
        posed as baritone aria, transcribed for 'cello)*   *Casals*

7103 *Air for G String (Bach-Wilhelmj) (composed for orchestra,
        transcribed for violin)*   *Elman*

1430 *The Swan (Camille Saint-Saëns) (composed for orchestra,
        transcribed for organ)*   *Dupré*

6823 *March Hongroise-Rákóczy (Gypsy Folk-Air—National Air)
        (Berlioz) (transcription of folk-tune, for orchestra)*
                                    Stokowski and Phila. Sym. Orch.

The wild folk-melody which formed the thematic basis for the Berlioz "March" was played at all public concerts in cities of Hungary for many years. It was equally popular among gypsy musicians and members of the nobility. It has been included in art work many times, one of the most notable of these being the fifteenth "Hungarian Rhapsody," by Franz Liszt, a work given its first public performance in America by Rafael Joseffy, the brilliant Hungarian pianist.

QUESTIONS AND TOPICS FOR DISCUSSION

1. What is a transcription? How do the transcriptions of later years differ in value from those made long ago? What are the main reasons for this? How may a transcription of a composition sometimes enhance its beauty and emotional effect? Give at least two ways.

2. Compare the emotional appeal of the Bach-Wilhelmj "Air for *G* String" with the Berlioz "Rákóczy March." What are the causes—whether thematic, rhythmic, or instrumental—which create the different effects?

3. What is meant by "Minnelied form"? Who were the minnesingers?

4. What is meant by instrumental "tone-color"? How is the use of such tone-color a feature in the successful creation of fine transcriptions? Discuss the art of Percy Grainger and also of Hector Berlioz in using orchestral tone-color to increase the rhythmic and melodic appeal of simple folk-airs.

5. Why is the transposition of the "Celebrated Air" to another than the original key an advantage to the effectiveness of the Bach melody?

6. Give several reasons why you think that "The Swan" is so eminently fitted for transcription. Is it its melodic style, its type of theme, its type of accompaniment, or its programmatic features, which are its greatest charm?

7. Which compositions suggested for study in this chapter would you list under the heading of absolute music? Under program?

Library Reading. "Musical Memories," by Camille Saint-Saëns; Berlioz' Autobiography.

PART THREE—CHAPTER TEN

MUSIC FOR THE PIANO AND ITS ANCESTORS

Popularity of Keyboard Music. It is probably true that no type of instrumental music is more popular, more generally heard, or more frequently participated in than that written for the piano.

This was also true of keyboard music in early days before the invention and development of the modern piano, when its ancestors —the clavecin, harpsichord, and clavichord—were probably used in homes, palaces, and concert-halls. Much of the music written for these older instruments is now played upon the modern piano, where it retains much of its quaint old-time charm.

Characteristics of the Early Keyboard Instruments. The early instruments were very small and light, so that they might easily be

A HARPSICHORD, 1658

carried from room to room in a home. Their tone was correspondingly delicate. As they were not equipped with pedals with which to prolong the tone—as in the case of the modern piano—composers were forced to add many extended trills and other embellishments to keep the tones sounding.

The Harpsichord, which was so popular and in such constant use in the sixteenth, seventeenth, and early eighteenth centuries, had two keyboards and mechanical provision was made for certain variation of the tone. The fact that the single strings * (the large instruments sometimes had two or four strings) were plucked by quills rather than being struck by hammers, also tended to produce a quaintly delicate atmosphere in the music played upon them. Many of these early instruments were beautifully decorated with painted pictures, with carvings, and sometimes with gold and precious stones.

The Clavichord and **Clavecin** took their names from the Latin *clavis,* meaning key, and *chorda,* meaning string. Thus a clavichord

CLAVICHORD

was a sweet-toned stringed instrument having keys. The earliest clavichords had only a few keys, twenty being thought sufficient to use in playing the simple songs of the day. It was, in fact, much similar to a harp to which a keyboard had been attached. Unlike the harpsichord, however, the clavichord strings were set in vibration by means of a metal bar, called tangent, which struck the string at points designed to give different pitches to the tone. Often a single string served for two tones of the scale.

The Invention of the Piano. The first piano came from Italy. There, in the city of Padua, lived a man named Bartolomeo Christofori, who was known to be the best harpsichord maker in Europe. The Prince di Medici, hearing of him, invited him to come to Florence, and there it was, while he was in the employ of the Prince, that he made the first piano.

As it was so constructed that it might produce either soft or loud music, its maker combined the two words which, in his language, meant *soft* and *loud,* and called his new invention *pianoforte.* The tone of this instrument was distinctly individual as compared to that of other keyboard instruments. Ever since that time (about 1720) the finest artists and the most skilled workmen have taken pride in developing the appearance, the mechanical construction, and the tone of the piano.

---

* A modern piano has three strings for each key throughout the entire middle and upper register.

Main Divisions of Piano Literature. It will be interesting to hear and contrast the music of composers who wrote for those earliest instruments with that written at the present time. Because of the enlargement and development of the instrument, and also because of the development of form in music, many differences in type and general style will be noted. Each has its own beauties.

For the sake of clearness it is customary to divide the literature of the piano into five general divisions, as follows:

1. Very Early Classics: Those written in the simple forms—often imitations of folk-dances—and for the clavecin, clavichord, or harpsichord. Composers of this period of piano music include Scarlatti, Couperin, Daquin, and Rameau.

2. The Later Classics: Some of these works were written for harpsichord, as this was the transitional period between the use of harpsichord or clavichord and the piano. However, musical form—such as sonata and fugue—had been greatly developed. Composers of this period include Bach, Händel, Beethoven, Mozart, and Haydn.

3. The Romantic Period: At this time composers, wishing variety from the strictly formal music of those who had preceded them, began to use form only as it suited their needs, and preferred rather *to express mood* through music than to follow formal rules. Prominent composers of this period are Chopin and Schumann.

4. Early Moderns: Composers of this period—who include Liszt, Grieg, and MacDowell—used form, but in a free and an individually expressive manner. Many of the early modern composers were so individual in their writings that their works may easily be recognized when heard, even when title or composer is unannounced. This kind of writing is often spoken of as "individual idiom."

5. The Ultra-Moderns: This term does not apply to all recent writers, for some still living write their music in an extremely formal manner. It refers to modern writers who have developed some new and striking style or manner in music. Such a composer is Debussy, who, in France, developed what is sometimes called *impressionism* in music, through very free use of both form and tonality. Other ultra-moderns have made great use of complex harmonies and rhythms, and often, of less familiar scales.

"Le Coucou," by Louis Claude Daquin, is one of the most charming of the early classics. Daquin lived in the age of courtly manners, and his music—written for the clavecin—reflects the intimacy of the court concerts of his day. He played at the court of Louis XIV at the age of six.

"The Cuckoo," one of his cleverest bits of imitative music, needs no title to suggest its "program." The theme of the music is the short two-note call of the cuckoo. The form of the dainty composition is that of the rondo, the first theme reappearing at regular intervals.

"Tambourin," by Rameau. This charming dance for early harpsichord is one of the formal dances in the tragedy "Castor and Pollux," for which Rameau wrote the music in 1737. The dance movements in the music written for the tragedy are examples of early classic music of the highest level. The soft melodic lines, the elegant grace, and the charming rhythm are reflections of the elegance of the music heard at the French courts of the day, and suggest, more than words, the limitations and possibilities of the harpsichord.

JEAN PHILIPPE RAMEAU

The Rameau "Tambourin" is a lively dance in 2/4 measure, with much octave skipping in the melody, which is also decorated with many mordents.

The *tambourin,* as known in its folk-form, is a sprightly dance which came from Provence —the land of the Troubadours—in southern France. It received its name from the quaint historic drum—shaped like a small barrel—which was held and beaten by one hand of the folk-musician, while with the other he held and played his primitive flute.

The Preludes and Fugues by Bach. The piano-playing world probably owes more to Johann Sebastian Bach than it does to any other one composer of the classic period of composition. There are many excellent reasons for this.

Previous to Bach's time, owing to a system of tuning then in vogue, in which there was little elimination of the overtones, it was possible to play in only a limited number of keys. This is suggested in the famous series of fifteen "Two-Part Inventions" by Bach, which are so familiar to students of the piano.

An examination of these will show that each one of the fifteen is written in a different key (as *C* Major, *c* minor, *D* Major, *d* minor, *E*-flat Major, etc.). Thus fifteen keys in all were employed. (Fifteen major keys and fifteen relative minor keys, are now used, thirty in all.) The reason for the omission of the other keys, in the Inventions, was, that at the time of their writing, the old system of tuning was still in use.

Presently Bach (who had always tuned his own instruments) completed his private experiments and began to sponsor what he called "tempered tuning," a system which made it possible for him to play with equal ease and pleasure in all major and minor keys.

Then, to prove to the musical world that the new system of tuning was entirely practical, he wrote his "Well-Tempered Clavichord," which is a set of preludes and fugues, a pair of

MORNING PRAYERS IN THE HOUSE OF BACH

which is written in each major and each minor key.

In these *Preludes and Fugues,* Bach wrote much *contrapuntal* music, by which is meant the use of one (or more) theme which appears over and over in the various voices (as soprano, alto, tenor, or bass) of the music. He also began a systematic use of the thumb in playing, a custom not general in earlier times. The use of the thumb, as well as the development of the piano itself, did much to bring the use of chords into piano music.

The "Prelude and Fugue" in *C* Major with which the "Well-Tempered Clavichord" opens, illustrates many phases of Bach's music.

The "Prelude"* is very simple in its construction, being little more than a charming series of broken chords, and a study in tone shading.

The "Fugue" is built upon a very simple theme

which appears first in one voice, then another. The fugue has three separate divisions: the statement of the theme in each voice, the de-

* This Prelude was used by Gounod, many years later, as an accompanying base over which to lay the exquisite melody of his song, "Ave Maria." See Chapter One, Part Two, "Famous Preludes"; Chapter Six, Part Three, "Beautiful Melodies."

335

velopment section in which *motifs* from the theme are heard in various forms and the final restatement of the theme and *Coda*.

"Gavotte in *F*," by Beethoven. This quaint piano composition, originally for four hands, is in old-time dance form, and, true to form, begins on the last half of the measure. The first theme is notable for a delicate lilting melody, slightly embellished by grace notes.

The form of the composition is *A B A C A Coda*.

"Berceuse," Opus 57, by Frederic Chopin, is one of the loveliest of all compositions written by this most prominent composer of the Romantic period of piano composition. The characteristic rhythmic feature of the music is the unchanged bass "figure" which persists throughout the entire lullaby, including the two-measure Introduction, but excepting the final two cadences of the music. The main theme

is continued throughout the composition in a set of exquisite variations—although not so labeled. A special feature of the second variation is the unusual fact that the grace notes carry the melody. Other variations feature running passages, double-note figures and a free use of tremolo, and the most delicate arabesques. The "Berceuse" comes to gentle close in a simple restatement of the opening theme.

"To Spring," by Edvard Grieg, a charming portrait of a well-known phase of Norwegian life, is one of the many "Lyrical Pieces" for piano which have won for Grieg the undying admiration of thousands of music lovers. It tells a story of life among the mountains of Norway. Here, each Spring, the cattle, with the sheep and goat herds, are taken up onto the mountains to graze throughout the Summer. Girls from the family go, too, to attend them and to care for the milk and cheese products.

To assist the herd-girl to follow the progress of the herds, many of the animals are equipped with a tiny bell tied about the neck. Thus, as the herds graze along the mountain-side, the delicate tinkling of the bells is constantly heard.

"To Spring" is "program" music, and its first two measures will take on added significance if, in imagination, the listener hears in each of the two groups of five *pianissimo* and *staccato* chords a suggestion of the tinkling of the little bells on a distant mountainside. Similar chord groups are soon intermingled with the song of the shepherd. Later the melody is elaborated with a set of variations, but throughout the piece, it suggests the simplicity of out-of-doors, as it might be on a Spring day on a Norwegian mountain-side.

"Little Shepherd," by Debussy, is a dainty musical picture of a shepherd boy watching his flock on a lonely mountain-side, and entertaining himself by playing on his simple home-made shepherd's pipe. The first little tune he plays is strongly reminiscent of the old whole tone scale which may have been used, and taught him, by his shepherd ancestors. This little tune alternates with a quicker and sprightly rhythm, suggestive of a satyr's whimsical dancing.

"The Golliwogg's Cake-Walk" is a picturesque composition in which Debussy glorifies, for the moment, the caperings of a golliwogg —a French rag doll. It employs, in part, old scales and modes, and, throughout, the contagious rhythm of the American Negro's cake-walk, a dance-rhythm which was, in 1908 (the time of Debussy's writing), a popular novelty to European ears. The composition is full of mood, from the first challenging rhythms of the dance, through the more seductive middle portion, and back to the recurring cake-walk.

In form, the "Golliwogg's Cake-Walk" is very simple. The first section in the key of *E*-flat—following a nine-measure introduction made up of a rhythmic unison passage and a series of rhythmic chords —contains two well-defined themes. The middle section in the key of *G*-flat is of contrasting mood. At its close, following a modulatory passage, the first themes are repeated as given at first. This is three-part song form.

MUSICAL ILLUSTRATIONS

1199 {*Le Coucou (Daquin)* / *Tambourin (Rameau)*}		*Landowska*
9124	*Prelude and Fugue, in C Major (Johann Sebastian Bach)*	*Samuel*
6592	*Gavotte in F (Beethoven-Bauer)*	*Bauer*
6752	*Berceuse (Chopin)*	*Cortot*
22153	*To Spring (Grieg)*	*Eaver*
21945 {*The Little Shepherd* / *Golliwogg's Cake-Walk*} *(Debussy)*		*Kinscella*

Informational Notes

The Dulcimer (or Zither) was the name given to an early ancestor of the pianoforte much played by early Assyrians and Greeks. It was an instrument shaped like a shallow box, over which metal strings were stretched. The instrument was held horizontally and was played by means of little hammers. Such instruments are pictured on many ancient monuments of the Orient, and often in settings which suggest their use in connection with singing and dancing. In medieval days the instrument was very popular and is sometimes mentioned in connection with the music of the *minnesingers.**

The Harpsichord was created by the addition of a keyboard to the Dulcimer. For each key there was one corresponding string, the length of the strings varying according to the pitch desired. The harpsichord was an important instrument in the early orchestra and was frequently presided over by the conductor himself. This was especially true during the century which began about 1730, when it was the custom for the conductor to sit at the harpsichord upon which he accompanied, at the same time he directed, the ensemble. For opera, two harpsichords were often used, one at the side of the stage for use in accompaniment, and the other placed in the center of the orchestra for the use of the conductor. The harpsichord was also a favorite solo instrument.

Beethoven and Mozart, both of whom contributed largely to the literature of the piano, were both also acquainted with the older keyboard instruments which preceded it. Mozart frequently played the harpsichord in public concert; and Beethoven, during his earlier years, used the clavichord largely as the instrument upon which he taught.

"Gavotte in *F*." This composition was unpublished until a few years ago. Found in manuscript after Beethoven's death, it was, for a time, thought to be a copy of a work by Mozart. It was presently proven, however, that the composition had been written by Beethoven about the year 1786. The first performance of the composition in America was under the auspices of the Beethoven Association of New York City, on January 13, 1890.

"The Little Shepherd" and the "Golliwogg's Cake-Walk" are both parts of a suite of highly descriptive compositions written by Debussy in 1908 as a birthday present for his own daughter.

QUESTIONS AND TOPICS FOR DISCUSSION

1. Contrast the characteristics of early clavier music with those of the music written at the present time. Name and discuss the types of five general divisions of piano literature. Name a composer of each type.

2. How do the Early Classic and the Later Classic composers differ in their writings?

3. Name five general characteristics peculiar to the "Cuckoo"

---

* The Cembalom, an instrument used by the Hungarian gypsies, is the modern form of the Dulcimer.

and the "Tambourin." Is this "program" or "pure" music? Why? What was the early "tambourin"?

4. For what four important developments in piano music is Bach noted? How have they affected modern piano music?

5. What is a *fugue*?

6. What is meant by the "Romantic" period in piano music?

7. How do the Ultra-modern writers differ in manner of composition from early composers in their methods of writing?

8. Name two important features of the "Berceuse." Memorize the melody, if possible, so that you can recognize it in all its varied forms.

9. What is meant by "impressionistic" music?

10. Classify the piano selections heard and studied in this lesson, as to type (Program or Pure); as to form; mood; and special musical characteristics. Is nationality expressed in any of these numbers? If so, which? Is it the rhythm, melody or general style which suggests it?

Library Reading. Pages 138-148 in "Music of the Past," by Landowska.

PART THREE—CHAPTER ELEVEN
SACRED CANTATAS AND ORATORIOS

Early Cantatas. Both the cantata and the oratorio are direct outgrowths of opera.

In the sixteenth century the term *cantata* was applied to any large composition meant to be sung—whether to sacred or secular words—the word itself coming from the Italian *canto,* meaning song. For over a century it was used in the south of Europe in this way, coming, more and more, to mean music which could be used as a part of a church service.

Presently the word *cantata* was used entirely with those combinations of solos and choruses in which religious devotion was expressed. The music of many of these was written to Biblical texts.

The Development of Oratorio. The cantata was gradually developed into a real art form, and the term *oratorio* came to be applied to this type of religious dramatic music because of the way in which it was used in Florence, Italy, about 1565. Here singing was used by a Florentine named Neri, to enhance the beauty and effectiveness of the addresses being given in the oratory (from the Latin *oratio*—speech). For a time oratorio was, in reality, a sacred music drama, but was established by Händel, in the eighteenth century, as a form of religious concert music which includes solos, concerted passages, and sometimes orchestral accompaniment whether sung in the church or elsewhere.

In *oratorio,* Biblical texts are used, or poetic texts that are Biblical in character and sentiment.

The Bach Cantatas. No classic composer was more successful than Bach in the creation of religious cantatas. He wrote more than three hundred sacred cantatas, and as he was, for many years, in charge of the music in the court chapel, most of these works were sung as soon as they were completed. In them Bach combined great devoutness of thought and feeling, a detailed development of the sentiment of the words in the music, and a strikingly original type of accompaniment.

"My Heart Ever Faithful," from the sixty-eighth cantata, "God So Loved the World," is one of the most famous of all sacred *arias.**

In the cantata this *aria* is preceded by a chorus number and is immediately followed by a short concerted number for instruments. The *aria* opens with a five-measure *Introduction* or prelude in which the tenor part, clearly marked through the first two measures, is a forerunner of the main melody. For the remaining three measures the upper notes of the Introduction carry the air.

The unity with which Bach has created the song as a whole is marvelous. In many cases a single phrase is divided between the voice and the accompanying instrument. This is illustrated at the very beginning when the voice sings the first half-phrase

after which the instrumental interlude at once takes up and completes the phrase.

As the voice again takes up the air the instrument keeps up a running counterpoint in the accompaniment. There is in the *aria* much repetition of the first theme and its melodic characteristics, with frequent wide skips and brilliant passages.

The Oratorio "The Messiah," by Händel. It is upon his magnificent oratorios that the permanent fame of Händel rests. The greatest of these is the "Messiah," which, written to a masterly libretto, is wholly devotional in character and of an enduring musical value.

---

* The word *aria* is used in connection with vocal solos in oratorio as well as in opera.

Händel was, first of all, a dramatic musician, and in the oratorio he wrote on a grand scale, employing the chorus and smaller vocal combinations in a manner calculated to command instant attention and interest.

"Why Do the Nations So Furiously Rage Together?" A florid *aria* for bass which occurs in the "Messiah" suggests not only the devotional atmosphere of the entire work, but also the brilliancy which had characterized Händel's early opera writing. In the first performances (and many times since) the singer of this solo number was accompanied by an orchestra made up of the strings, the woodwind instruments, trumpet, and tympani, all of which participated in the brilliant Introduction.

HÄNDEL

The clever theme of the distinguished aria is built upon the simple chord of *C* and the *C* scale.

Why   do   the   na - tions so   fu - rious-ly rage   to - geth - er?

The Introduction gives out the main song-theme, as is often the case with "Messiah" *arias.* In spite of the simplicity of the theme, Händel has developed a magnificently gorgeous *aria* which includes many "coloratura" passages (such as one with triplets to be sung upon every note of the descending scale) which require the utmost facility and breath control. The *aria* is in the established three-part song form; moves presently into minor mode; then returns to the theme and key of the opening section.

"He Shall Feed His Flock," sung by contralto, another *aria* from the "Messiah," is of peaceful and comforting atmosphere. It is preceded by a short *recitative.* When accompanied by orchestra, a mystical effect is produced by the use of muted strings. The gently moving air, *legato,* is announced by the instrumental introduction. The same devotional theme continues, with slight changes of harmony which alter the key. The accompaniment—especially in the short interludes—is written so as to suggest canon form, following the voice part in direct imitation. With no loss of rhythm or tempo a final two-measure interlude leads the same melodic theme into a higher key, where it is taken up by the soprano.

"Come Unto Me," for soprano, identical in type and mood with the contralto *aria* which immediately precedes it, closes with a four-measure instrumental *Coda*. Throughout, it retains its spirit and atmosphere of simplicity and devotion.

THOMAS CHURCH, LEIPSIC, WHERE BACH
WAS CANTOR

"I Know That My Redeemer Liveth," for soprano, is one of the most gracious *arias* in existence. When accompanied by orchestra, the instruments used include string quartet, flute, clarinet, and bassoon. Characterized by a mood of worshipful triumph, the music may be said to be "composed throughout" in the manner of an art song. The theme, first given out in the accompaniment, is taken up by the voice. The accompaniment then echoes it, the vocal and instrumental part completing each other, formally.

"Hallelujah Chorus." This famous chorus from the "Messiah" displays to the uttermost Händel's skill in simple and effective choral writing, his use of vigorous counterpoint, of brilliant contrasts and climaxes, and a broad majestic style. Features of the chorus in addition to its supreme worth as a piece of worshipful music are the responsive shouting back and forth of the "Hallelujah" theme between chorus and accompaniment; unison of both choral forces and accompaniment on the words "For the Lord Omnipotent Reigneth"; its grandeur and piling up of noble masses of sound; the impressive vocal figure on the words "And He shall reign forever," in which voice after voice enters with the stirring refrain; and the exciting culmination of the music on the theme "King of Kings."

"Stabat Mater," by Rossini, is a departure from the style of writing usually associated with this composer's works. The "Stabat Mater" is Rossini's greatest religious work, and is both fervent and sincere in mood. It is also intensely dramatic, reflecting, subtly, characteristics common to Rossini's highly popular operatic works.

"Cujus Animam" ("Saviour, breathe forgiveness o'er me"),

aria for tenor, is a prayer set to music. The Introduction opens with a dramatic octave passage, followed by a presentation of the main melody. The tenor voice then takes up the extremely lyric air in unison with the accompaniment. Operatic in type, the rhythm of the accompaniment remains unchanged and

$$\left(\frac{4}{4} \middle| \, \flat \, \flat \, \middle| \right)$$

is repeated over and over. The melody is characterized by fluency and spontaneity, by its great range, wide skips in its latter half and by its perfect reflection of the sentiment of the words. The aria is in three-part song form.

"Gloria," from the Twelfth Mass, by Mozart, is a striking display of the magnificent use, by a great composer, of

GIOACCHINO ANTONIO ROSSINI

very simple means. The theme, which rises in an exulting phrase, is this.

Glo - - - - ri - ous

This number is musically and also historically important, for here Mozart not only used his own skill, but in addition imitated the Italian style of writing, much in vogue at the close of the eighteenth century. The highest art is exhibited in Mozart's unity between the sentiment of the words and music. The "Gloria" is divided into four movements, and here magnificent effects are produced by the bringing together of the voices in a great *fortissimo* climax. The *Coda* is unconnected with what has gone before, and is added solely for the sake of a brilliant conclusion. The unison of voices and instruments in three-octave range in syncopated melodic passages suggests the *finale* of an Italian opera.

MUSICAL ILLUSTRATIONS

——* *My Heart Ever Faithful, from Cantata No. 68, "God So Loved the World" (Johann Sebastian Bach)*

Music and Romance for Youth

9654	*Why Do the Nations So Furiously Rage? from ''The Messiah''* (*George Frederich Händel*)	*Radford*
4026	*He Shall Feed His Flock from ''The Messiah'' (George Frederich Händel)*	*Baker*
4026	*Come Unto Me from ''The Messiah'' (George Frederich Händel)*	*Marsh*
9104	*I Know That My Redeemer Liveth from ''The Messiah'' (George Frederich Händel)*	*Marsh*
35768	*Hallelujah Chorus from ''The Messiah'' (George Frederich Händel)*	*Trinity Choir*
19967	*Cujus Animam (Saviour, Breathe a Blessing) from ''Stabat Mater'' (Rossini)*	*Andrews*
35768	*Gloria from ''Twelfth Mass'' (Mozart)*	*Trinity Choir*

INFORMATIONAL NOTES

Extremely rapid in composition, Händel is said to have written the ''Messiah'' in twenty-four days. He used, for his writing, a sharp quill, and, when he had completed a page, blotted it, as was then the custom, by sprinkling sand over it. The sand would be shaken off when dry, and so rapid was Händel in his work and so stirred by his own inspiration, that many of the manuscript pages— which may now be seen in the British Museum—are smeared across their surface, so hasty was the composer in dashing the sand from them that he might continue his writing.

The Händel ''Messiah,'' written during August and September, 1741, had its first performance in Dublin, Ireland. When the ''Hallelujah Chorus'' was sung, the King rose to his feet in a simple gesture of devotion and, with the audience, which followed his example, remained standing throughout the entire number. The custom, so impulsively inaugurated, has continued until this day. The first American performance of music from the ''Messiah'' was in New York City on January 9, 1770, when sixteen numbers were given, with harpsichord accompaniment. The entire oratorio was first given in America by the Händel and Haydn Society of Boston, in 1818.

Rossini's great ''Stabat Mater'' was completed in 1832, although the composer added three extra numbers in 1841. The first performance was in 1842.

QUESTIONS AND TOPICS FOR DISCUSSION

1. From what type of music did the cantata and oratorio spring? Give historical facts of their beginnings. Under what composer did the oratorio become established as concert music? To what nation are we indebted for the beginnings of this type of music? Name one essential feature of the libretto of an oratorio.

2. Name a feature of musical construction common both to ''My

Modern Chamber Music

Heart Ever Faithful" and "I Know That My Redeemer Liveth."
How does this suggest the construction of an "art" song?

3. Compare the thematic structure of the opening airs of "Why
Do the Nations?" and the Mozart "Gloria." How has the composer
of each made use of simple means?

4. How do any of the works studied in this lesson suggest operatic
characteristics?

5. Name and discuss at least five distinctive characteristics of the
"Hallelujah Chorus." Contrast this with the less complex "Gloria."
How has each composer achieved his musical effect of triumph and
praise?

Part Three—Chapter Twelve

MODERN CHAMBER MUSIC

(The student should review the opening paragraphs of Chapter
Seven, Part One—"Chamber Music—Instrumental Combinations"—
before continuing with this chapter.)

Modern Developments in Chamber Music. During the latter half
of the nineteenth century, a spirit of "romanticism"—a striving for
fanciful, romantic, or "program" effects—began to influence chamber music. At first the intrusion of the "pro-
gram" affected only the spirit or atmosphere
of the composition, but later it affected its
form also, and brought in a new element of
emotional appeal.

ANTONIN DVOŘÁK, TAKEN IN
1893

Especially is this true of the Slavic
composers of chamber music of whom may
be mentioned Tschaikowsky, Borodin, and
Dvořák—the first two, natives of Russia, the
latter, of Bohemia—who in their writing of
chamber music included not only emotional
appeal but strongly nationalistic colorings.

"Andante Cantabile," from "String
Quartet, Opus 11," by Tschaikowsky. This
entire movement is played with muted strings,
producing a veiled and mystic tone. The
mood of the "Andante" is tenderly wistful. One of the striking features
of the piece is the *basso ostinato*—played *pizzicato* by the 'cello in the
middle section. There are also many plucked chords in the accompaniment and in one section of the solo melody a display of the warm tone
produced by use of the *G* string. Tschaikowsky also made a striking

use here of the Slavic manner of repeating a single phrase over and over again.

The origin of the main theme of the "Andante Cantabile" is unknown. It is an exact repetition, with only an altering of time, signature, and the placing of measure bars, of an old Russian folk-air * which Tschaikowsky heard a servant singing one day. Rimsky-Korsakow, in his "One Hundred Russian Folk-Songs" gives the old air, with its odd combination of 4/4 and 5/4 measures, its wistful four-measure theme twice repeated, ending each time in a questioning, unfinished way. He adds, in a footnote, "the melody is certainly very old." It is interesting to compare the old folk-melody with the first eight measures of the "Andante Cantabile" and see the use to which Tschaikowsky has put it.

Just at the beginning of the second theme comes the entrance of the *pizzicato* figure in the 'cello, which continues *pianissimo* for twenty-six measures.

The second theme equals, if it does not surpass, the first, in beauty and emotional appeal.

* The title of the Russian folk-song is "Johnny on the Sofa."

The first theme then returns.

The "Andante Cantabile" is written in three-part song form.

"Nocturne," a quick movement from another Russian string quartet—the "Second String Quartet" in *D* Major, by Borodin—pre-

FLONZALEY QUARTET

sents a different type of Slavic melody and accompaniment. The Quartet is dedicated by Borodin to his wife, and the lovely "Nocturne" is unsurpassed in rare poetic beauty. It is the most popular single number of all of Borodin's compositions. The music is extremely Oriental, in melody, in the copious use of ornamentation, and in the syncopated rhythms of the delicate chordal accompaniment.

The first theme begins in the first measure in the 'cello, an exquisitely lovely air embellished in an Oriental manner, its beauty enhanced by a simple, artfully monotonous syncopated accompaniment in viola and second violin.

Cantabile espressive

After a time the violin takes up the air. Then the new theme appears, a vigorous two octave scale passage and a tiny "figure" of notes.

The same scale figure is repeated in the second violin, and the small group of notes appears alternately in the parts of all the instruments, and unison in first violin and 'cello. The first theme then returns in a lovely *canon* between first violin and 'cello, while the inner voices add an odd undulating accompaniment. The piece ends quietly.

"Quintette in *E*-Flat Major," by Robert Schumann. In this masterly work for piano and four-stringed instruments (two violins, viola, and 'cello), Schumann was said to have invented a new form, although piano trios and quartets had been familiar for many years. Schumann's new work (first published and performed in 1843) came at a time when the modern piano was already a well-developed instrument, and its possibilities are reflected in the modern manner in which the Quintette is composed. The combination of instruments has been a favorite one with many later day composers, none of whom, however, have surpassed, in their writings, the sonorous, dramatic dignity of this great masterpiece. The work has four movements.

The first of these *(Allegro brilliante, E*-flat major, ₵) opens abruptly with a massive succession of chords from the piano, the melody which they carry being doubled in the strings. After this brilliant introduction, a lovely lyric theme, which permeates all the movement, is heard, being first announced by the piano, then taken up, in turn, by each of the other instruments.

This movement is, throughout, notable for beauty of form and melody, and for its unity.

In modo d'una Marcia, the second movement of the Quintette is, as the subtitle suggests, a slow march. The sorrowful first theme, in *C* minor, given out by the first violin,

to a soft chordal accompaniment from piano, 'cello, and second violin.

A change of mood is later effected by a change in both rhythm and *tempo,* as a *staccato* triplet figure *(agitato)* is given out by the piano.

A brief return to the first theme is followed by a second *agitato* section in which varied rhythms are combined. Presently the mellow voice of the viola is heard in the first theme, *marcato,* over a fluttering accompaniment in piano and other strings. The second theme, altered and transposed, and a final pianissimo reappearance of the first slow march melody, bring the movement to a close. The form is that of a simple rondo, *a b a c a b a.*

Scherzo (*molto vivace, E*-flat Major, 6/8). This dazzlingly brilliant movement relies for its thematic material upon series of scales and note patterns. The swift galloping rhythm is maintained throughout. The opening theme is an ascending scale run which terminates in a syncopated chord.

Throughout the lyric second movement *Trio* I the speed is unabated. Here the melody is one of whimsical charm, and is developed briefly in canon form. The theme of the second trio is given out in unison by first violin and 'cello. The *coda* is built upon reminiscences of the opening theme.

Finale (*Allegro, ma non troppo, C* Minor, ₵ opens in a sturdy, melodious manner, with prominence given to the piano. There is, in this movement, frequent use of *pizzicato* in the strings, much unison melody (strings and piano), and clever contrapuntal development. During the canonical development of the first theme, the subject is announced, in turn, by piano, second violin, first violin, 'cello, and viola. A gorgeously brilliant, and technically difficult *coda* closes this poetic composition.

The simple, but original, theme which opens the *Finale*

is reflected in the entire movement, both in structure and in mood.

"Concerto Grosso," by Ernest Bloch. This remarkable composition for string orchestra, with piano *obbligato,* is a modern version of an eighteenth-century form. Written by a contemporary composer, it reflects the spirit of modern music without having suffered, in the least, the loss of old-time melodiousness and formal beauty. It follows the early understanding of the word concerto, in that it is not a work for a solo instrument, but a concerted work for a combination of musical instruments.

The composition is divided into four distinct movements:

Music and Romance for Youth

1. "Prelude" (*allegro energico o pesante*). Individual characteristics of this movement are a decisive rhythm—founded upon alternating duple and triple time—and much energy. The "Prelude" opens with an Introduction created by a half dozen measures of heavily accented chords in measures of differing time values. These are followed by a direct and vigorous statement of the principal theme.

2. "Dirge" (*Andante moderato*—3/4 time-measure). This begins with a simple statement of the dignified first theme by the strings alone. This statement is followed by "lament" sections in which the strings, doubled and reinforced by the piano, perform a series of strikingly effective descending chromatic passages. The time-signature now changes to 4/4, and the solo violin, accompanied by the piano (in arpeggio patterns) and the strings, presents an exquisitely tender melody.

During this middle section of the "Dirge" (which is suggestive of a Chant), a complex and mysterious effect is added by the simultaneous use, by the composer, of many tonalities. Here the 'cellos and double-basses play and repeat a single figure, in *B*-flat; the violins are in *F* Sharp; and the viola and other instruments in still other keys.

ERNEST BLOCH

The descending passages are again heard—now in thirds—under a poignantly effective high and sustained tone from the solo violin.

The climax of the movement is effected through a dramatic return to the first subject; which closes on a *pianissimo* chord, unexpectedly in the major mode.

3. "Pastorale and Rustic Dance" (*assai lento*, 3/4 time-measure). Melodies are here employed which immediately suggest those of Bloch's native Switzerland, and France. An eight-measure prelude introduces short solos by both viola and violin which are accompanied by soft chords from muted 'cellos. The gentle atmosphere of a *pastorale* is thus established. Both *tempo* and time-signature are altered very soon, and a gayly contrasting mood is introduced by the solo violin (*allegro*, 6/8). The return of the opening theme of the viola, in the original *tempo,* echoed, in turn, by 'cello, piano, and strings, is followed by acceleration of the *tempo* and enrichment of the harmonies. The 'cellos suggest the drone bass of the bag-

pipe frequently played by old-time shepherds. The pastorale division of this movement is in simple three-part song-form.

The music passes, without pause, into the "Rustic Dance" (*allegro giocoso,* 6/8). All strings and the piano unite in a *forte,* and brilliant announcement of the colorful tune of the dance, which is here clearly reminiscent—in both melody and rhythm—of the ancient French folk-air "Marching Through Lorraine." * This is now heard, with heavy rhythmic accenting, suggesting the steady tramping of the peasant dancers.

The thoughtful mood and theme of the "Pastorale" now returns. Subtly combined with a suggestion of the melodic figure from the preceding "Dirge", the rustic dance is again heard; after which the entire movement comes to a close, *molto allargando.*

4. "Finale" (Fugue) (*allegro,* 4/4). This bit of Pure or Absolute music is typical of the Händelian music so cleverly suggested by Bloch in the complete composition. The main theme is announced, *marcato,* and in the key of *D* minor, by the violas. Each group of instruments enters, in turn, with repetitions, inversions, and developments of the original melody. The violins are the first to answer the violas, and they are followed by an announcement of the theme in bass, then in treble. The complexity of the development grows until about midway through the "fugue," the theme is played by the inner voices (or inner instruments in the multiple string quartet formation) in its familiar form and *tempo,* while the violins take up the theme and play it at twice as slow a *tempo.* This unique harmonic effect is followed by presentations of the theme, in both original and inverted or altered forms. First in the bass, then in treble; by a growth in dynamics and velocity; and by an abrupt but impressive ending.

MUSICAL ILLUSTRATIONS

6634 *Andante Cantabile (Tschaikowsky)*	*Elman String Quartet*
——* *Nocturne (Borodin)*	*Budapest String Quartet*
8092-8095 *Quintette in E-Flat Major (Schumann)*	
	Gabrilowitsch-Flonzaley Quartet
9596-9598 *Concerto Grosso (Bloch)*	*Phila. Chamber Str. Simfonietta*

QUESTIONS AND TOPICS FOR DISCUSSION

1. How do classic and modern writings in chamber music forms differ? What is meant by "romanticism" in music? Give an example of it.

2. Name characteristics of Slavic or Oriental music heard in any chamber music selections studied in this lesson.

---

* For history of this air, see Chapter Two, Part One.

3. Upon what type of a melody is the "Andante Cantabile," by Tschaikowsky, written? Mention a Slavic use of a theme employed by Tschaikowsky in this music. What is meant by *basso ostinato*?

4. Contrast the moods of the "Andante Cantabile" and the Borodin "Nocturne." Which is the more Oriental in manner of writing? Why?

5. Compare Tschaikowsky's use of folk-song with Grainger's. Which is more true to the primitive characteristics of the folk-music? Which is more poetic?

6. Contrast the early and the modern meanings of the term *concerto*. Contrast the meaning and mood of the words "dirge" and "elegie." How have the composers indicated these differing moods? What is a *pastorale*?

7. What can you tell of the history of "Marching Through Lorraine"? Name three outstanding peculiarities of its music. How has Bloch used its characteristics in his "Rustic Dance"? What has he meant to suggest by such a use?

PART THREE—CHAPTER THIRTEEN

INFLUENCE OF MODERN LIFE UPON MUSIC—COMPARISONS OF FOLK AND CLASSIC MUSIC

Characteristics of Modern Music. It is not possible nor desirable to ignore certain changes that have come into standard musical composition through the influences which many features of modern life have brought to bear upon it. The fashion of doing everything as quickly as possible; the use of mechanical inventions; the crowding together of many people in comparatively small spaces in large cities, and the restlessness which accordingly frequently prevails; these have all led to new experiments in music. As there was a Classical age in music, and a Romantic age, there is now an age of Realism, and a seeking for expression in a new or novel manner.

In modern composition can be found certain such common ideals and methods as realism (direct imitation); a prevailing tendency to write music to some kind of a text rather than a seeking for formal beauty; an unusual care for detail, expressed in the music of some moderns in a very sensitive and refined way; expression of a great deal of clever humor; activity; a tendency to use unconventional melodic and harmonic "patterns"; a lack of tonality, by which is meant a failure to remain within certain keys for a given period of time.

"By the Waters of Minnetonka," by Thurlow Lieurance. An

opportunity to contrast a folk-air, the same melody in an art idealization, and then in a jazzed version, may be offered in the Sioux Indian tribal melody, best known through Thurlow Lieurance's wonderfully artistic art version of it, in which the unique accompaniment ably portrays the swishing and circling of water.

THURLOW LIEURANCE

The Indian legend concerning the tribal song is the story of two Indian lovers. One belonged to the Sun Deer clan, the other to the rival Moon Deer clan. When their families tried to separate them, the lovers fled together, and, rather than be captured, flung themselves into the waters of Lake Minnetonka (in Minnesota). Here, the old legend says, the rippling waters still mourn for them and sing their names each day above their heads.

"By the Waters of Minnetonka" is built upon this old Sioux melody. It is characterized by quite disconnected *motifs* in its theme. Its form is simple—a two-measure *Introduction*; the first theme (eight measures long) and its repetition; the more agitated second theme, also repeated; and the return of the twice-repeated first theme. (*Introduction, a a b b a a*). A harp-like accompaniment is one of the notable features of the song.

"The Fountains of Rome," by Ottovino Respighi, a suite of tone-poems, is an exquisite example of modern realism, also suggesting water, as does the Lieurance "Minnetonka," but in a totally different manner.

I. *"La fontana di Valle Guilia all' alba"* (The Fountain of Valle Guilia at Dawn), *Andante Mosso,* suggests a pastoral landscape. The early morning droves pass, as is common in all Italian cities, and disappear into the gray mists of a Roman dawn.

Here Respighi has recorded an exquisitely lovely tone-picture of an Italian fountain at dawn. The composition opens with a fluttering "figure" of notes played by muted second violins, while at the same time the first violins play weird harmonies, the combination establishing at once a delicate sense and atmosphere of mystery. Soon a tender melody is "sung" by the oboe, which is—beginning with its third measure—accompanied by flutes and English horns.

Presently the body of the music becomes very slightly more firm —although retaining, all the while, its impressionistic character—

through the addition of clarinets, bassoons and the lower strings, all *piunissimo*. A triangle gently taps, eight times. Muted instruments, tremolo in the strings, and delicate running passages from the sweet-voiced celesta are all artfully used to create and maintain an atmosphere as vague and mysterious as the quiet hours of dawn. Suddenly a loud insistent blast of horns is heard above the delicately dainty trills and twitterings of all the birds (this is played by the whole orchestra), which introduces the second poem.

II. "The Triton Fountain at Morn," *Vivo,* is a subtle, fanciful bit of music. A joyous call summons a troop of naiads and tritons who come running up and step a frenzied dance between the shimmering jets of water. The difference in mood and atmosphere between this bit of impressionistic music and that which has just been played is felt with the first measure, which brings a *fortissimo* call from the horns. The remainder of the four-measure phrase is a marvelously elegant arabesque from the entire orchestra (woodwind, horns, harps, carillon, piano and strings, with triangle and cymbal). The same effect is repeated three times and leads to the *fff* climax with which the *Introduction* ends.

A light and playful rhythmic figure in flutes, clarinets, and harps, serves as the first theme, the harps also furnishing airy embellishments which suggest the play of the waters in the fountain. The same melodic figure is next taken up by the first violins, and is then passed to and fro among all the instruments. Many trills are heard, as well as much *pizzicato* from violins and other strings, and *glissando* from celesta, harp, and piano, the varied combination suggesting the singing and twittering of birds, and the dance of the naiads and tritons, as morning approaches. The music is brought to its poetic *Finale* through a beautifully shaded *diminuendo* and the muting of instruments of first one, then another choir of the orchestra.

III. The "Fountain of Trevi at Midday" is built upon a solemn theme which is shifted from the wind instruments to the brass, and which, in a triumphal peal, announces the approach of Neptune's chariot across the water. As the procession vanishes, a faint trumpet call is heard, as in the far distance. This tone-poem is characterized by a solemn theme first announced by woodwind, then passed to the brass instruments. The piano adds arpeg-

FOUNTAIN TREVI AT ROME

giated chord accompaniment, and additional atmosphere is inspired by the *glissando* passages which are heard from the harps throughout the first large division of the composition. At the *Trio*, or second large division, the tempo increases and the atmosphere becomes one of buoyant triumph, full orchestra, pealing trumpets contributing to the brilliant effect. Then the mood of the beginning returns, the music becoming again slower, more calm, and finally diminishing to a *pianissimo* above which faint trumpet calls are heard softly, as though from a distance.

IV. The "Villa di Medici Fountain at Sunset" is sad in theme, suggesting the dying day. Above the subdued warbling of the sleepy birds is heard the echoing and re-echoing of tolling bells. The music becomes more gentle and quiet. Day sinks to rest, and the silence of night follows. This romantic atmosphere of early evening is here suggested by the introduction of a subdued hymn-like melody, *pppp* (in divided first and second violins), the expressive theme singing above it (in flute and English horn) to a constant accompaniment of delicate arabesques in celesta and harp.

The predominating feature of this fourth section of the "Fountains of Rome," as a whole, is not so much melody as atmosphere, sounds as of rustling leaves and bird noises being produced by the downward-moving *glissando* of the harps, and delicate "patterns" of notes on the silvery-toned celesta and muted strings. Toward the close the string basses are silent; the violas (muted) are divided into a four-part chorus; the second violins are muted; and the first violins are divided into three parts, one of which carries the final tender melody. All sound sinks gradually away to silence.

"The Hurdy-Gurdy Man," number three in the "Kaleidoscope," a book of twelve small pieces for piano by Eugene Goossens, is a brief but telling example of the modern ability to inject humor into music, through the pictorial use of unconventionally discordant harmonies. The main theme of this little waltz is an old, old folk-tune from Germany which is here modernized by means of surprisingly humorous ultra-modern harmonies which ably suggest the old-style "grind-organ." The little piece is of simple construction—three "big parts" and a *Coda*. So alluringly entertaining and so correct is this miniature picture and clever imitation of the very jolly and noisy street musician, with his frequently out-of-tune barrel-organ, that a title is really unnecessary.

"In Springtime" Overture, by Carl Goldmark, though performed for the first time in 1889, is modern in many of its characteristics, being a gorgeous illustration of program music, and a composition which utilizes the facilities of a modern symphonic orchestra to their fullest extent. It is scored for three flutes, two oboes, two clarinets, two bassoons, four horns, three trumpets, three trombones, one bass tuba, kettle-drums, and the strings.

The long first theme (*Allegro*, *A* Major, 3/4 measure), played by violins, is fiery and impetuous, and is, in its immediate development, notable for its remarkable and dazzlingly brilliant series of modulations.

The second, and contrasting, theme—played by strings, with embellishments and arabesques from instruments of the woodwind—suggests, gracefully, the awakening of all nature and the singing of birds. After a development and stormy episode section, the third theme is introduced (violins), then developed canonically. A return is next made—by means of graceful cadenza-like passages—to the first or main theme, which is again heard in its original key.

The development and recapitulation of all three themes follows and fulfills the requirements of the sonata form in which the work is written. A sparklingly animated *Finale* brings the famous overture to a close.

"Afternoon of a Faun," by Claude Debussy, is a modern composition in which the composer has illustrated, most exquisitely, his ability to use the instruments of an orchestra as a medium for the creation of vague, mysterious, and elusive mood and atmosphere. This music tells the story of a faun—an imaginary creature—who awakens at dawn in a forest, and tries to recall his experiences of the previous afternoon. He thinks that he was visited by nymphs, but is not certain—the "shadow of the vision," which is all that has remained with him, is not more substantial than the shower of tones which come from his precious flute.

The chief theme of the composition is introduced by the flute (9/8 measure) and is then immediately developed in turn by oboe and clarinet.

At the end of each phrase a delicate *glissando* from harp is heard.

The second theme, very similar in style, is slightly contrasted in mood. There is an almost immediate return to the first theme and its languorous atmosphere of veiled loveliness. It is now played over and over, flute alternating with 'cello, and the whole momentarily interrupted by the distant call of horns and by the limpid flood of harp tones.

Influence of Modern Life Upon Music

Accompanying the theme, toward the close of the composition, is the soft rhythmic beating of the very small cymbals which Debussy introduced into the orchestra for the purpose of reproducing effects heard in connection with ancient dances of Pompeii. The composi-

RICHARD STRAUSS

tion closes with a recurrence of the first theme, now accompanied by muted strings, harmonics, and soft *pizzicato*.

"Till Eulenspiegel's Merry Pranks," by Richard Strauss, is a decidedly modern symphonic tone-poem which tells of the romantic, picturesque, and roguish pranks of Till, the best known of all German medieval heroes, whose name is also sometimes given as Till Owlglass because he once held up a mirror for the owls (the wise folk) to look at themselves in.

So familiarly known are Till's name and personality in Germany even today—several centuries after his death—that all tricks or practical jokes, the authorship of which cannot be traced, are commonly laid at the door of "Till Eulenspiegel." Till was a strolling vagabond, the victims of whose pranks and roguish tricks included not only his democratic neighbors and acquaintances, but also even noblemen, princes, and parsons.

The Strauss music is written to describe the various activities of Till and his numerous victims. The composition is written somewhat in the form of a rondo. In it Till is represented, throughout, by a highly descriptive prankish theme, introduced by the French horn, in the key of *F* Major.

This theme is repeated constantly, as Till meets his numerous victims, and is announced, in turn, by bassoon, 'cello, and by various groups of instruments, among which the shriller woodwinds predominate. The announcement of the theme by the bassoon is supposed to suggest Till's encounter with a parson; the 'cello, his romantic love affair.

The *tempo*, usually fast and filled with rollicking rhythm, varies slightly as the moods of the composition change. The music changes in character, in turn, from a lively and sprightly mood, to moods of a grotesque, violent, tender, jolly, or farcical nature. Clownish burlesque and humor is the predominating characteristic.

The theme is freely developed. Presently shrill dissonances introduce a jolly and melodious folk-dance in four-beat measure. This is soon rudely interrupted (as were the dancers) by Till, who then continues to create bedlam and confusion until the end of the musical story. Extremely abrupt changes of *tempo*, rhythm, harmony and instrumentation, sharp phrase endings, liberal use of chromatic scale runs, clownish screams from the flutes, and tremolo in the strings, are some of the musical devices by which Strauss has composed this work and created what he is said to have called his "musical joke."

MUSICAL ILLUSTRATIONS

21972	*Sioux Indian Flute Melody (Tribal Air)*	*Lieurance*
21972	*By the Waters of Minnetonka (Thurlow Lieurance)*	
		Lieurance and Barone
9126- 9127 }	*The Fountains of Rome (Respighi)*	*Coates and London Sym. Orch.*
21945	*The Hurdy-Gurdy Man (Goossens)*	*Kinscella*
6576	*In Springtime Overture (Goldmark)*	*Chicago Symphony Orchestra*
6696	*Afternoon of a Faun (Debussy)*	*Philadelphia Symphony Orchestra*
9271- 9272 }	*Till Eulenspiegel's Merry Pranks (Strauss)*	*London Symphony Orchestra*

INFORMATIONAL NOTES

The public fountains of Rome are among the most interesting of the many public places visited annually by tourists. One of the most magnificent of them is the Fountain di Trevi, which was built in 1762, although the site of the fountain is nearly two thousand years older, its waters having been brought to Rome by King Agrippa in 19 B. C. The original fountain was a simple basin, but the background is now formed by the south side of the noble Palazzo Poli. The bas-reliefs at the top represent the maiden pointing out the spring to the Roman soldiers and Agrippa approving the plans. The four statues represent the four Seasons. The constant running of the waters fills the whole piazza with a rippling noise. There is a tradition that whoever throws a coin into this fountain will surely return to Rome. The Fountain del Tritone was built in 1640.

"The Fountains of Rome." These four tone poems were given their first performance at a war benefit in Rome, under direction of the famous Toscanini, February 10, 1918. The first American performance was in New York, exactly a year later.

The "small Cymbals" used by Debussy in his "Afternoon of a

Faun'' are similar to the antique cymbals found in the ruins of ancient Pompeii. These were made of bronze, and were found to vary greatly in size. Some were as small as a silver dollar, but the majority were about the size of the palm of a man's hand. These small cymbals were used in the hands of dancers of the seventeenth century to mark the rhythms of the dance, and are thought to be forerunners of the modern castanet. They are played by being struck on their edges, and produce a soft but high-pitched metallic sound.

Till Eulenspiegel, the son of a German peasant, is said to have been born at Kneitlingen in Brunswick, Germany, during the latter part of the thirteenth or the beginning of the fourteenth century. He died in 1350, and his grave is still shown at Lübeck, surmounted by a stone upon which is carved a characteristic pun, and a picture of an owl and a glass. Till was said to have used a picture of an owl as his signature, and was fond of drawing this emblem upon windows and doors, or walls of public buildings. A unique memorial fountain, semi-circular in form, stands in a public square of the city of Brunswick, the water pouring forth from the mouths of little monkeys and owls.

QUESTIONS AND TOPICS FOR DISCUSSION

1. Name several causes for new elements which appear in much of the modern composed music.

2. Name and discuss some of the ways in which modern composers have created a new type of music.

3. Contrast modern descriptive music—such as the ''Fountains of Rome''—with classic descriptive music which you have already heard and studied, as the ''Pastoral'' Symphony, by Beethoven. Discuss.

4. Is the composition ''Fountains of Rome'' to be considered as realistic or as impressionistic music? Give reasons for your answer. By what instrumental means has Respighi achieved his atmospheric effect—as the suggestions of bird noises, of splashing water, of the clear light of midday as contrasted with the downcoming dusk? Contrast the moods of the four poems. What is the predominating feature of both?

5. What musical means has Strauss employed to suggest the various episodes in the life of Till Eulenspiegel? What is the most characteristic mood of the tone-poem? How is it expressed? How are different instruments used to suggest the personalities of Till's various victims? How has Strauss suggested a village festivity?

Library Reading. ''Romantic Germany,'' by Robert Schauffler; ''Master Tyll Owlglass,'' by Mackenzie.

A SYMPHONIC POEM—"THE MOLDAU," BY SMETANA

What a Symphonic Poem Is. The *Symphonic Poem* is a comparatively new classic form. It was not until Franz Liszt, the brilliant Hungarian pianist and composer, wrote his remarkable series of "Preludes" that the form was invented, or developed.

The name of the new form, in which he had written these "Preludes," was also the invention of Liszt, as a general title of an orchestral work of large design which was not intended to be so strict as the sonata in form, but which endeavored to express a definite "program," or poetic thought. A general title is generally given each symphonic poem by the composer, to assist him in conveying his story to the imagination of the hearer.

FRIEDRICH SMETANA

No two symphonic poems are ever exactly alike in form, just as no two stories are exactly alike. Each case is governed by its own needs, and contains the special incidents or elements which give it its own individual style and charm.

The Symphonic Poem, "The Moldau." Of all the later composers who used the Symphonic Poem form in their writings, none was more successful than Smetana, the musical pioneer of Bohemia, who was once a pupil of Liszt and had learned from him a fondness and preference for the symphonic poem form.

Smetana had a great love for his home-land, and in all his composition it was his supreme desire that his music might, in such a degree as was possible, express the beauties and charms of that home-land, to the world.

So, in 1874, Smetana set himself the huge task of glorifying his native land by composing a whole cycle of six Symphonic Poems, under the general title of "My Fatherland." All of these are distinctly program music of the most descriptive sort. The whole cycle is dedicated to the city of Prague. The second piece of the cycle is the "Moldau," a picture, in sound, of Bohemia's principal river, and of the scenes through which the beloved river flows, the beauties of nature, and of the historic buildings which stand upon its banks.

A Symphonic Poem

That music is able to tell such a story, or follow so elaborate a "program," is proven by a hearing of even the first section of the Symphonic Poem—"The Source of the Moldau."

The "Program" of "The Moldau." The symphonic poem, "The Moldau," contains several distinct parts which, taken together, describe the river from its humble source in the forest to its impressive and triumphal passage through the capital city, Prague. These parts, in their order, are:

1. Source of the Moldau River.
2. Hunt in the Forest.
3. Peasant Wedding.
4. {Moonlight.
   {Dance of the Nymphs.
5. St. John's Rapids.
6. Grandeur, Widest Part.
7. Castle Vyšehrad.

The Composer's Story for "The Moldau." When "The Moldau" was completed—it was written in the very short time between November 20 and December 8—Smetana added, in his own handwriting, the following Preface:

Galloway

TYPICAL COUNTRY SCENE NEAR THE MOLDAU

"Two springs start their courses in a shady Bohemian forest: one is warm and sparkling, the other cool and tranquil. Their clear waters, that run so gayly over stone and pebble, unite and sparkle in the morning sun. The rapid forest brook, rushing on, becomes the River Moldau, which, as it takes its course through the fields and valleys of Bohemia, grows into a mighty river, flowing through thick forests wherein the joyous clanging sound of the hunter's horn seems to approach the listener. It pursues its way through meadows and farms. A rustic wedding is being joyfully celebrated with music and song and dance. The water nymphs disport themselves by moonlight in the river's glittering waters, in which are reflected towers and castles as reminders of the departed glory of chivalry and martial fame. At St. John's Rapids the stream winds its way through the foamy rapids of the cataract and through a deep and narrow rocky cleft into the broad river-bed, along which it rolls majestically on to Prague, welcomed on its way by the venerable Vyšehrad, and disappears in the distance from the composer's vision."

The music begins with a gently undulating theme—not really a melody. There is, at first, just one tiny air, played softly in unison by the sweet-voiced instruments. Then another rippling theme is added by the restlessly "waving" strings—just as one small brooklet joins another—bits of harp and string music, the number growing as the waters come together. Smetana is said to have told a friend that this musical story of a gradually growing river is a symbol of his nation's career.

THE MOLDAU AS IT PASSES UNDER THE BRIDGE AT PRAGUE

Galloway

I. In "The Sources" Smetana suggests the tiny beginning—a single brook—by means of a single flute part which plays, softly, a weaving, waving figure. Soon the clarinets enter with a similar melodic figure (portraying a second brook which joins the first), and then the violas (another brook), all these accompanied by delicate bits of music from *pizzicato* strings and harp, suggestive of sprays of water. The number of instruments playing the weaving figure grows constantly, bassoons, then strings, joining. Presently the main melody or theme is heard—a symbol of the river whenever it appears— brought in by oboes and first violins.

This theme is repeated four times, immediately, in the same key; twice more in transposed version, each time a third lower—as the water in the brook grows deeper; is then joined by flutes and bassoons; and repeats itself over and over, gradually building up the body and volume of the music and its chordal accompaniment.

II. Hunt in the Forest. Now the Hunter's Call is heard (built upon a common chord, as is a bugle call) in oboes, horns, and bassoons; while the ceaseless flowing of the waters, still suggested by the strings, ends very softly as in the distance.

This call is echoed from individual instruments in all the choirs of the orchestra. The entire short movement is built upon this one theme.

III. Peasant Wedding. The "Hunt in the Forest" comes to a close with a prolonged note of the horn. Immediately afterward all the instruments of the orchestra, except the horn, join in the rustic wedding procession music, which moves lightly along. The first four-measure phrase repeats itself four times in succession (like a folk-air) and then, as the procession moves away into the distance, the tinkling of the church bells (triangle) is heard as they alternate with the kettle-drum in softly accenting the rhythm. The music becomes gradually softer, but not slower. To produce the effect of distance, Smetana has muted all the strings, the clarinets and the kettle-drum.

IV. Moonlight and Dance of the Nymphs. Above a quiet chord played by muted strings, delicate "patterns" played by flute set the scene for the fairy revels. Harp arabesques are tossed into the ensemble to suggest the splashing of water. The principal theme enters, a sweet and sustained song-like melody, on the muted violin,

which is repeated again exactly, except that *D* natural replaces *D* flat.

This is the main content of the music, played as softly as possible by the main body of the orchestra, while above it, flutes, piccolos, and clarinets play frolicsome passages.

Presently the trumpet begins to assert itself, though at first very softly, and in martial rhythm.

Trombones and tubas join and help lead the music back into live-lier strains. Suddenly, from the flutes, piccolos, oboes, bassoons, and violins is heard a bit of the "river" theme, which carries the hearer directly (as the water flows in the river) to

V. St. John's Rapids. The string section now furnishes the "surge of waters." Snatches of the "river" melody are heard con-stantly at the same time from first one instrument, then another, until a vast confusion (like the waters in the rapids) is accomplished. A huge climax, from the midst of which are heard the brass instruments constantly asserting themselves in *motifs* from the "river" theme, is built up, only to sink suddenly into a quiet hush, just as do the waters after the rapids are passed. A delicate upward-moving scale passage (violins and violas) leads to

VI. Grandeur, Widest Part. Here the Moldau flows in grandeur over a smooth bed through broad open meadows. The swelling chorus of the "river" theme is heard from the woodwind section, to an ac-companiment of full chords from the double-basses, drums, triangle, harps, and strings. This is a short movement preparing for entry into the stately music of the

VII. Vyšehrad. All the instruments of the orchestra (except the strings) in *fortissimo* octaves, work, in broad majestic rhythm, into a hymn-like strain—an old chant melody from the cathedral that stood in early days within the Vyšehrad castle walls. Unity of the entire composition is preserved by the final reappearance of the "river" theme, which now soars out, in a slightly altered version, from the entire string section. The chant dies away, followed by a gradual leave-taking of the "river" theme as the Moldau "disap-pears in the distance from the composer's vision." Two chords—silence.

MUSICAL ILLUSTRATIONS

21748⎫ *The Moldau (Bedrich Smetana)*   *Victor Symphony Orchestra*
21749⎭

GEOGRAPHICAL NOTE

The source of the river Moldau is on the Bohemian-Bavarian border in south Bohemia. The river is navigable for river boats up to the St. John Rapids, situated about ten miles south of Prague. The river is used for passenger shipping, and for trade shipping for the needs of the city of Prague (with a population of 675,000) and its quite large industry. But the main trade on the Moldau is the floating of rafts or wood from the Sumava forests on the Bohemian-Bavarian border. The river's whole course is about 270 miles.

A Symphonic Poem

Much of the history of the Bohemian nation may be traced by following the Moldau. As Bohemia is situated in the heart of Europe, so Prague—the "city of the hundred spires"—is in the heart of Bohemia, and it is very fitting that the climax of the river's history—as the climax in Smetana's symphonic poem—should be reached at Prague.

The city is built in the valley of the Moldau and lies on both banks of the river. Here five bridges span it, some of them elaborately handsome and also very old. (A wooden bridge that once stood on the present site of the magnificent Charles Bridge was, history tells us, swept away before Columbus's time.)

The Castle Vyšehrad, mentioned in the eighth episode of Smetana's music, is situated in the city of Prague. It is an unused fortress of remote origin and in early times formed the point round which settlements were made on the right bank of the river Moldau. In the fortress there is situated the old church which was built in 1070, and on the same height is the Roman rotunda of a chapel. Some years ago archæological excavations were carried out on the site of the old citadel. Here traces of prehistoric times dating back to 1600 B. C. have been found, as well as two burial places dating from the eleventh century. Remnants of a church dating from the eleventh century and the tremendous wall of the former royal palace have also been brought to light.

Wars and battles have waged about the walls of this famous old fortress, and its ruins form a desolate reminder of past glories.

Prague is now the seat of government of the Republic of Czecho-Slovakia.

QUESTIONS AND TOPICS FOR DISCUSSION

1. What is a Symphonic Poem? How does it differ from a sonata or symphony?

2. Who wrote the first symphonic poem and also invented the form-title?

3. How does the music of "The Moldau" suggest the "program" which Smetana has set out for it. Discuss in detail your impressions of the various sections of the music. How has the use of various musical instruments helped to secure the effects desired?

4. Why is Smetana often spoken of as a great "nationalist" in music?

5. Trace the course of the Moldau upon a map.

6. Become familiar with the "river" theme, so that you can

recognize it whenever it enters the music. Notice the folk-character of the theme melody. How has the composer suggested the Hunt in the Forest? Upon what is a hunter's call built? What is meant by "muting" an instrument? How are the various instruments muted? What is meant by *pizzicato?* How has Smetana secured unity in the writing of the Moldau?

Library Reading. If possible read the chapter on "The Vltava" (the Bohemian spelling of *Moldau*) in "Czechoslovakia," by J. Mothersole.

Part Three—Chapter Fifteen

MUSIC-DRAMA—"THE RING OF THE NIBELUNGEN"

What a Music-Drama Is. For many years operas—especially those by the earliest Italian writers—were composed primarily for

THE WAGNERIAN OPERA AT BAYREUTH

the purpose of exploiting the vocal abilities of operatic singers. Later operatic history tells of composers who sought to unite real plots with beautiful music.

Richard Wagner was a composer who felt that a still closer union should exist between the "story" of the opera and the music which was intended to express it. In this ideal combination of music and drama which Wagner had in mind certain features were stressed:

Arias by soloists should not overshadow other parts of the opera.

The music of the opera should not be written to "catch the ear."

The dialogue of the opera must exhibit the inner motives of the characters.

No note should be sounded by soloist, chorus, or orchestra which had not a definite part in the expression of the "story" or plot.

There must be a decisive event to mark the close of each act.

Each bit of the stage scenery should also have an interpretative meaning.

Such a combination of ideals Wagner was able to bring to pass in operatic works for which he wrote both libretto and music, and to which he gave the general title of *Music-Drama.*

Music Drama

The Subjects of the Wagnerian Music-Dramas. After many years of experiments in the field of dramatic music, Wagner developed at last his own original type of writing, and began to study deeply and to dramatize the sagas of the early Norsemen, and the legends and myths of the Germanic peoples. Many of his librettos were based upon combinations of incidents taken from these very old epic tales.

"WAHNFRIED," WAGNER'S HOME AT
BAYREUTH

Wagner's Use of Leitmotif. That each character, or the *influence of that character* (even though he might not be seen upon the stage) should stand out clearly, Wagner originated a type of musical symbol, which he called *leitmotif*. These motifs (or bits of music) were each characteristic of some definite person or object, and were played by the orchestra whenever that character or important object was to be suggested.

There is, for example, in Wagner's "Rheingold," a certain phrase

which is a symbol of the River Rhine, and which suggests the surge of its waters whenever heard.

To truly appreciate a Wagnerian music-drama, the hearer should seek to know the more important of the *leitmotifs* which are heard during its performance.

"The Ring of the Nibelungen," Wagner's most important work, is a series of music-dramas four in number, each of which is an independent work, although each is a part of the others and related to them.

The mythology from which Wagner drew the material for his libretto for these four dramas is very old, some of it from Icelandic tales of the fifth century, and much of it from the Germanic Nibelungenlied, which was the first great epic poem of Germanic literature.

It is a story of treasure coveted and unlawfully used by its possessors, and the curse which follows such use.

Wagner localized the incidents by placing the scene along the River Rhine in Germany, somewhere near the city of Worms. This is thought by many people to be quite appropriate, for the coat of arms of the city of Worms has, for many years, been a two-winged dragon, a key in one of its claws. This is in reference to the Siegfried legends.

Some people say that the exact spot at which the treasure is seen in the music-drama, in the opening act, is near the fabled Lorelei Rock. And it is certain that many of the characters which play an important part, are characters either in old historical tales or in the mythological tales of the Rhine country. Siegfried, for example, is a popular hero in the myths of the old Nibelungen, the most popular tale recited by the minstrels of the Middle Ages, and is supposed to have been born at Xanten, on the Rhine.

THE LORELEI ROCK, NEAR WHICH THE RHEINGOLD WAS HIDDEN

Wagner was twenty-eight years in his completion of the four music-dramas, the first performance of which was in 1876. He had thought, at first, to tell the whole tale in one drama. His reasons for not doing so are related in a letter which he wrote to a friend:

"When I tried to dramatize the most important of the myths of the Nibelungen in 'Siegfried's Death' (the fourth of the music-dramas, now known as 'The Twilight of the Gods') I found it necessary to indicate a vast number of antecedent facts so as to put these main incidents in the proper light. . . . So I came to write 'Siegfried' (the third of the music-dramas). But here again the same difficulty troubled me. Finally I wrote 'The Valkyrie' (the second of the music-dramas), and then 'Rheingold' (the first of the series with which 'The Ring' formally begins), and thus contrived at last to incorporate all that was needful to make the action tell its own tale."

Historical Background of "The Ring." Old history tales tell of a nation of dwarfs—at least people smaller than the average European ancestors of the present race—who lived for many years on the main continent of Europe, until they were finally driven into England, Wales, and Scandinavia. These dwarfs, the old tales relate, were highly civilized and skilled in the arts of making beautiful objects from ivory, bones, and precious metal. So they were thought to be possessors of magical power, and many folk- and fairy-tales came into being which told of the clever smiths who lived beneath the ground, or flew through the air in magical ways. These dwarfs were called "Nibelungen" and were said to live in "a land of mist" (England) for the people of the British Isles knew, in earliest times, of the uses of valuable metals.

It is this fanciful history of the skillful dwarfs which Wagner has taken for the background of all the miraculous happenings of which he relates in "The Ring of the Nibelungen."

The operatic story of "The Ring," in each of its four dramas, is as follows:

I. The Rheingold opens with an earthly scene, and in a prehistoric time, when everything is perfection and beauty. Even the treasure of the world—which is here symbolized by a magic golden ring which lies shining below the surface of the waters of the Rhine—exists only as a bit of beauty. There it is carelessly guarded by three beautiful Rhine-maidens, who swim about in the water above it.

It is only when Wotan, the ruler of the gods, becomes envious of any power possessed by others, and wishes, in his greed, to have all power—including that of the magical golden ring—in his own hands, that the presence of the treasure on earth becomes a curse to humanity.

As the Rhine-maidens are singing, they are interrupted by the appearance of the ugly Alberich, chief of the Nibelungs, who calls down this curse upon himself by stealing the gold and disappearing with it into the depths of the earth.

Wotan, wishing to have a magnificent palace of unparalleled beauty, bargains with two giants—Fafner and Fasolt—for its construction, promising to give his sister Freia to Fafner when the palace is finished, forgetting the fact that Freia is the Goddess of Youth, and that were she to leave them, all the gods would grow old and die. The palace is soon completed and Fafner asks for his reward. Loki, the cunning God of Fire, now suggests that Wotan secure the palace —which is to be called Walhalla—but that he do so without paying the agreed upon price. He suggests that Wotan try to take the ring of magic power away from the Nibelungen and give it to Fafner in exchange for Freia. As they take the ring from Alberich he repeats to them the curse that will bring its owner only sorrow and death.

Having secured the ring, Wotan wishes to keep it, and also a magic cap which, he is told, will make its wearer invisible. Fafner finally secures both the treasures, and as he receives his reward, a radiantly beautiful Rainbow Bridge appears, over which the gods, led by Wotan, pass in procession to Walhalla.

II. The Valkyrie. Here the gods are enjoying the pleasures of Walhalla Among the company are the nine War Maidens—known as the Valkyrie—the daughters of Wotan, whose fabled duty it is to ride above the battlefields of earth and from there bring to Walhalla (another name for Heaven) the souls of the bravest of the fallen heroes.

Meanwhile Wotan comes to realize that whosoever is in possession of the Ring and the Magic Cap is in possession of mighty power.

Still greedy for power, Wotan begins to plan for the theft of the treasure from Fafner. This is not an easy task, for by means of the Magic Cap, Fafner has changed his form into that of a terrible dragon, and, lying across the mouth of an open cave in

THE RIDE OF THE VALKYRIES

which he has placed the Ring, he guards it by night and day. Wotan knows that he would not be able to struggle against the dragon, and begins his search for a youth of blameless life and fearless presence who may be able to conquer the dragon and restore the Ring to him.

Because of a direct disobedience of her father's orders, Brunnhilde, one of the Valkyrie, and Wotan's best-loved daughter, loses her immortality as a goddess, and is doomed to sleep through the years upon a rock upon the mountain-side until some man courageous enough to fight his way through the wall of magic fire which surrounds her, shall awaken her to life again.*

III. Siegfried. During the long years that have elapsed since Brunnhilde began her sleep upon the mountain-side, Fafner, in his shape as a dragon, has continued to guard his treasure.

Meanwhile Mime, another of the Nibelungs, has wished to secure possession of the Ring. He, too, is searching for a fearless youth who shall help him win it, for Mime knows that only someone who is strong enough to weld and wield a certain magic sword,† shall be able to conquer the dragon.

---

* This is another version of the old "Sleeping Beauty" tale. See Chapter Eight, Part Two.
† This suggests the magic sword of the King Arthur tales.

Siegfried, an unknown youth for whom Mime has cared as a foster-father, proves his ability to do this, and so, accompanied by the deceitful Mime, sets out to find the dragon's cave. On his way, Siegfried listens to the birds, whose songs he is able to interpret as speech, and answers them by playing a sweet melody on his horn.

Arriving at the cave, Siegfried confronts the hideous dragon, and, in spite of its huge size and fearful strength, succeeds in killing it and securing the treasure. Upon his return from the cave, Siegfried passes by the lonely mountain upon which Brunnhilde is sleeping behind her magic wall of fire. Penetrating the fire, which has no ter-

SIEGFRIED'S RHINE JOURNEY

rors for him, Siegfried discovers Brunnhilde and wakens her to life again.

IV. The Twilight of the Gods. Siegfried has given the Ring to Brunnhilde, but although neither of them has coveted power, the curse still remains. Although told of the doom which awaits all the gods—including the destruction of Walhalla—unless she returns the Ring to the River Rhine, where the Rhine-maidens still mourn its loss, Brunnhilde refuses to part with it, and trouble follows her decision rapidly.

Brunnhilde, robbed of the Ring, is carried to the castle of an enemy, Gunther, and presently finds that Siegfried is already there, that he is again wearing the Ring, and that, because of a magic potion that he has drunk, he has forgotten his vows to her. Angered, Brunnhilde plans revenge. She relates to Hagen (Siegfried's arch enemy) the secret of Siegfried's one weakness. After slaying the dragon, Siegfried had bathed in its blood *—a pagan ceremony thought to make the bather immune from all harm. In doing so one spot on his back had not been touched, and in that spot he might still be wounded.

Being told of this Hagen lures Siegfried to a wood on a pretext of hunting, and while his guest kneels at a brook to drink, stabs him with a sword.

Brunnhilde, now filled with remorse, realizes that the curse is still active. Ordering the flames of Siegfried's funeral pyre lighted upon the banks of the Rhine, she mounts her horse—which she formerly rode as one of the Valkyrie—and rides upon the blazing pile.

SIEGFRIED AND THE DRAGON

As she disappears, the waters of the Rhine rise and overwhelm the flames, and the coveted Ring, purged of its curse by its passage through the fire, is returned to the Rhine-maidens, its rightful owners.

The Music of "The Ring of the Nibelungen." Wagner left little to be desired in his orchestral accompaniment, and sought many new and unusual orchestral effects. For the opening of the "Rheingold," with its scene of waving water and the Rhine-maidens swimming about, he has used eight horns, with an unique effect. At the close of this first music-drama, while the gods pass to Walhalla over the glistening Rainbow Bridge which spans the valley of the Rhine, an

* Suggests Hercules and the River Styx.

exquisite effect of mystery is achieved by the use of eight harps, each
of which plays a separate part.

The "Rhine *leitmotif*" has already been given. Here follow
four other important *motifs* which are heard in the musical illustrations from "The Ring," which are suggested at the close of the chapter:

The Valkyries' War Call.

The Valkyrie (notice the galloping rhythm).

The Magic Fire.

The Siegfried motif (The Youth).

"Forest Murmurs" from "Siegfried," by Richard Wagner. This
highly descriptive composition—a bit from Act II of the opera—was
arranged by the composer himself for separate concert use. During
the scene in the opera, Siegfried, the hero, is found journeying to the
cave which shelters Fafner, the terrible dragon. As he passes through
the forest, Siegfried listens to the forest voices—the murmur of the
insects, the singing of the birds, and the rustle of the leaves and
branches. Presently he stretches himself under the trees and tries to
understand what the birds are saying. He tries to imitate them on a
simple reed which he cuts with his sword, but, disappointed with the
result, plays a woodland call to them on his own silver horn:

His music awakens the sleeping dragon, who now advances toward him. During the fight which follows, in which the dragon is killed, Siegfried's hand is splashed with some drops of its blood. Hastily raising his hand to his lips, he, by chance, tastes the blood, and at once finds himself able to understand all that the bird above him is saying. It tells him of the hidden treasures within the dragon's cave, and also of Brunnhilde, the beautiful woman who lies sleeping on a rock nearby within the ring of magic fire.

The music follows this program very closely, opening with a mysterious, fluttering movement. Presently the rustle of the forest grows louder, and the Bird Song *motif* is plainly heard (in oboe, flute, clarinet, then other wind instruments). The horn call is clearly heard, and as the fight between Siegfried and the dragon progresses, magnificent and dramatic music is heard. In the closing phrases (*vivace*) the Siegfried *motif*, Fire *motif*, and the exquisite slumber *motif*, are heard.

Slumber *motif*.

MUSICAL ILLUSTRATIONS

From *"Ring of the Nibelungen"* (*Wagner*)

9163	*Prelude of Rheingold*	*Coates Symphony Orchestra*
9163	*Ride of the Valkyries from "The Valkyrie"*	*Coates Symphony Orch.*
35936	*Magic Fire Music from "The Valkyrie"*	*Schendel*
7192	*Forest Murmurs from "Siegfried"*	
	Mengelberg-N. Y. Philharmonic Symphony Orchestra	
9007	*Siegfried's Rhine Journey from "Twilight of the Gods"*	
	Coates-Chorus-Symphony Orchestra	
9049	*Siegfried's Funeral March from "Twilight of the Gods"*	

Informational Notes

Much of the actual composition of these four music-dramas was done by Wagner under the direct sponsorship of King Ludwig II of Bavaria, who not only gave him his patronage, but also financial support. Wagner now began to long for a "perfect theatre" in which he might dictate all the stage-settings and surroundings of the performances of "The Ring." This object he finally achieved in his "Festival House" at Bayreuth, a Wagnerian theatre which has, since 1876, been devoted entirely to performance of Wagnerian opera. The season is a short one, during the summer, and is considered a gala occasion. Here the orchestra is seated entirely out of sight of the audience, so as not to distract the attention of the listeners. Instead of a bell to recall the audience to their seats after an intermission between acts, they are recalled by a group of musicians, who go to the entrance of the theatre and play *motifs* from the act about to be given.

Wagner's skill in the creation of stage-settings capable of picturing the events of "The Ring" was very great. In the opening scene he was able, by clever use of gauze curtains, painted canvas and, for that day, strikingly unusual lighting effects, to create the illusion of a stage filled with water.

Wagner's home, a marble palace named "Wahnfried," stands not far distant, and he himself lies buried on the grounds of his estate.

QUESTIONS AND TOPICS FOR DISCUSSION

1. What is meant by music-drama? How does it differ essentially from opera?

2. What is a libretto? A *leitmotif*? How has Wagner used the leitmotif?

3. Upon what is the libretto of "The Ring" based? How has Wagner localized the scene? Does this add plausibility to the story, or not? Give reasons for your answer.

4. Who were the Nibelungs? Where are they said to have dwelt? In what way are they said to have been skilled? How does this contribute to the strength of the Wagner libretto?

5. Name several ways in which Wagner has created unity, from the opening of the "Rheingold" to the close of "Twilight of the Gods."

6. Contrast one of the Wagner selections here suggested with a prelude or overture from some early Italian opera. In what essential points do the two numbers differ? Compare the Prelude to "Rheingold" with Wagner's own Overture from "Flying Dutchman" (see Chapter One, Part Two), which was written in an earlier stage of the composer's development. How has his work changed? What outstanding characteristics still remain?

7. Discuss the appropriateness of the *motifs,* as, the "Rhine" and the "Magic Fire" *motifs.* How has Wagner so definitely suggested the object he has in mind?

8. What are the greatest appeals to the imagination and the emotions in the "Ring" music to which you have listened? Is the Wagner orchestral music of the absolute type, or is it program music?

9. Notice the similarity in general outline of many old legends, and their manner of differing when told in different locations. How

does this suggest the influence of geographical location upon types of folk-music?

10. Notice the art of Wagner in keeping the same scene—the River Rhine—before you at the beginning and again at the very close of the complete "Ring."

11. What have you learned about Wagner the man, by listening to his music?

PART THREE—CHAPTER SIXTEEN

OUTSIDE STUDENT PROJECT

A program may be made up of musical numbers heard and studied during the semester. See Part One, Chapter Sixteen, for further suggestions.

Biographical Notes

(For extended notices for all these composers see "What We Hear in Music," also consult bibliography.)

DON ISAAC ALBENIZ (1861-1909) was a court pianist in Spain, where his influence has been greatly felt in the renewed interest in Spanish music. As a boy he toured, giving concerts. He wrote much for his instrument, and because of his study of the folk-music of his native land, his compositions show a very strong folk character.

JOHANN SEBASTIAN BACH (1685-1750) was born in the storied village of Eisenach, Germany. He came of a musical family, having among his ancestors more than forty professional or semi-professional musicians. Orphaned at ten, he went to live with an older brother, also a musician. From him he learned much of music, and also learned much musical literature by copying music. At eighteen he was a violinist in the band of a Prince, and many years of his later life were spent in writing and directing music for royal households. He wrote in almost every musical form, was the first contrapuntal composer, and introduced the use of the thumb in playing a keyboard instrument.

ANTONIO BAZZINI (1818-1897), an Italian composer and violinist, was known as a concert artist, as a teacher at the Conservatory of Milan, and as a composer of distinction. His important works include an opera, sacred cantatas, symphonic works, and much splendid chamber music. However, his lasting monument is the delightfully spontaneous "Ronde des Lutins" for violin solo.

LUDWIG VAN BEETHOVEN, whose works were the beginning of a new epoch in the history of music, was born in Bonn, Germany, in 1770. He took a long course of lessons with Haydn, in Vienna, and among his own famous pupils was the great technician, Carl Czerny. Four strings were attached to each key of his piano, in his later life, because of his increasing deafness. Beethoven died in 1827.

HECTOR BERLIOZ (1803-1869), the son of a French country doctor, was at first educated for the practice of medicine. Going to Paris at the age of eighteen to continue this study, he changed his course, and was presently enrolled as a pupil at the Paris Conservatory, where he studied for seven years. His composition is noted for brilliancy of orchestration and instrumentation, and has been the guide of almost every composer since his day.

SIR HENRY BISHOP (1786-1855) the composer of "Lo, Here the Gentle Lark," is best known as having given to the world the well-loved song "Home, Sweet Home," an old Sicilian tune, which was, originally, a part of the opera, "Clari, the Maid of Milan." (Words by our own John Howard Payne.)

GEORGES BIZET, the composer of "Carmen," was born in Paris on October 25, 1838, and died at Bougival, near Paris, on June 3, 1875, being only thirty-seven years old at the time of his death. He became one of the most distinguished of all French composers. His first attempt at composition was the writing of a one-act operetta. Three years later his work won the coveted Prix de Rome, which prize entitled him to residence and study in that Italian city. In addition to his ability as a composer, he was a brilliant pianist.

ERNEST BLOCH (July 24, 1880-   ) was born in Geneva, Switzerland. As a youth, he became a student first with Jacques Dalerozi, then with Ysaye in Brussels. Later he studied in Germany and France. Bloch's residence in the United States dates from 1916. Since coming to this country Bloch has won distinction by his winning of the *Musical America* $3,000 prize for an orchestral composition with his rhapsody, ''America.'' Other works of large proportions include the ''Concerto Grosso'' for String Orchestra and Piano, which, written in 1924-1925 in Sante Fe, New Mexico, and Cleveland, Ohio, had its world premiere at a Hollywood Bowl concert in August, 1925.

LUIGI BOCCHERINI (1743-1805) is most noted as a brilliant 'cellist and as a composer. Given much encouragement from members of royal families of both Italy and Spain, Boccherini later spent some years as private musician to the King of Prussia. Very industrious as a composer, he left more than one hundred and twenty-five string quintets and ninety-one string quartets. He may be said to have created a new style in chamber music.

ALEXANDER BORODIN (1834-1887) was born at St. Petersburg, in Russia. Early in life he chose medicine as his profession, and at the close of his studies was appointed Professor of Chemistry at the Academy of Medicine, at St. Petersburg. From the time of this appointment until his death, Borodin's active interests were about equally divided between chemistry and music. Among his intimate friends were included such Russian masters as Rimsky-Korsakow and Balakireff.

JOHANNES BRAHMS (1833-1897) is sometimes called ''the last of the old German masters.'' His father was a professional musician, and the boy grew up in the atmosphere of music. His great interest in folk music—more than 120 of his works are said to have been either directly or indirectly inspired by folk airs—was inspired through his association with the gypsy violinist, Eduard Remenyi. Some of the folk songs were idealized, others were used as thematic material in larger compositions. He made contributions to all branches of music except opera. It is interesting to know that at his first public appearance as a concert pianist, at the age of fourteen, one of his program numbers was his own set of original variations on a folk-air.

HENRY T. BURLEIGH (1866-   ), well-known for many years as a church and concert singer in New York City, has written many strikingly beautiful songs, and has arranged a number of Negro spirituals for concert use.

CHARLES WAKEFIELD CADMAN was born in Johnstown, Pa., in 1881. His first study of music was with private teachers of Pittsburgh, including Emil Pauer. After a short career as an organist and music critic, he became greatly interested in Indian melody, and visited several tribes and Indian reservations. He has idealized many Indian melodies, and included twenty or more in his Indian opera, ''Shanewis,'' which had a successful premiere at the Metropolitan Opera House, in New York City, in March, 1918.

ALEXIS EMMANUEL CHABRIER (1841-1894) took up music first as a hobby while studying law in Paris. Soon he decided to devote himself entirely to music. His ''España Rapsodie''—the results of observations made while traveling in Spain—was first played at the concerts of the Château d'Eau, in Paris, in November, 1883. Chabrier wrote operetta, opera, for piano, and for orchestra. His works are noted for extreme brilliancy.

FREDERIC CHOPIN (1809 or 1810-1849) was born near Warsaw, in Poland. His father was a French professor in the University of Warsaw, and his mother was a Pole. He himself, grew up an ardent Polish citizen. Like the Mendelssohn family, the Chopin children were all musical and talented, and were constantly getting up festivals, plays, and concerts. Frederic was an accomplished pianist at the age of eight. Zywny was his teacher. He soon played before Emperor Alexander. In 1828 Chopin visited Berlin and saw Mendelssohn, who greatly inspired him; and in 1831 he visited Paris, where he later played in concert, taught, and wrote. He died in Paris in October, 1849.

MUZIO CLEMENTI (1752-1832) a native of the city of Rome, was an organist,

Biographical

composer, and pianist of great attainments. He toured England, France, Austria, Russia, and Germany as a concert pianist. He was a fine performer and once played a friendly contest with Mozart. His style of composition was strictly classical, and his writings did much to display the possibilities of the instruments for solo playing. In his writings he was very exact and his correct forms were held in esteem by even Beethoven.

SAMUEL COLERIDGE-TAYLOR (1875-1912), the son of a West-African Negro who came to England to study medicine and married an English woman, began playing the violin at the age of five, and was later admitted to the Royal College of Music on a scholarship. One of his greatest friends was Sir Edward Elgar, who got him a hearing (with his orchestral ''Ballad in *A* Minor'') at the Gloucester Festival. Soon after this, his choral work, ''Hiawatha's Wedding,'' was given its first performance at a concert held under the auspices of the Royal College.

ARCHANGELO CORÉLLI (1653-1713), was a contemporary of Antonio Stradivari, the violin maker of Cremona who set a standard in violin making which has never been surpassed. Corelli, in his turn, developed the technic of the violinist to a high degree. He wrote many dozen sonatas for violin, and a number of *concertos* (ensemble pieces) for the ''string band'' of his day. He is known as a great violinist and as a composer who determined much of the technical status of the violin by his writings. He became a favorite in social circles of Rome and owed much of his opportunity to establish chamber music upon a permanent foundation to the assistance given him by royal patrons. He was a friend of both Scarlatti and Handel.

FRANÇOIS COUPERIN (1668-1733), the son of Charles Couperin, a musician, was born in Paris and spent the greater part of his life in that city. A pupil of his father, he became, presently, organist in a Paris church in which both his uncle and his grandfather had played before him. At the age of twenty-five he entered a musical competition, held at Versailles, and was honored by being chosen by Louis XIV, of France, to become royal organist. The rest of his life was spent in the service of the royal household.

CÉSAR CUI (1835-1918) was the son of a French officer who had been unable to accompany Napoleon's troops on their historic retreat from Moscow in 1812— the incident celebrated in Tschaikowsky's ''Overture 1812''—and so remained in Russia. Cui combines in his writings the lyric refinement of the French, with the mystic orientalism of the Russian school. His work is notable for elegance, melodic grace, and great originality.

LOUIS CLAUDE DAQUIN (1694-1772) was born in Paris. At the age of twelve he was already a professional organist, and from 1727, until the time of his death, he was organist at the Church of St. Paul. His first book of pieces for the harpsichord (of which ''Le Coucou'' is a favorite) was published in 1735.

CLAUDE ACHILLE DEBUSSY (1862-1918), one of France's most modern composers, both in point of time and in originality of musical thought, left behind him much beautiful music notable for its refinement and its impressionistic, expressive qualities. As a student, he won the Prix de Rome. During one summer, at about this time, he spent several months in Russia as pianist in the home of a wealthy family. There he heard much oriental music, much use of the whole-tone scale—for which many of his own later works are notable—and met several of Russia's leading musicians, including Rimsky-Korsakow and Borodin. The influence of his Russian visit is felt in many of his compositions.

MANUEL DE FALLA, born in the Spanish city of Cadiz on November 23, 1877, is one of the outstanding musicians of modern Spain. Driven by his interest in Spanish paintings to search out old folk lore and song of his native land, he has become an inspired painter in sound, bringing to his compositions the very breath of the atmosphere of Andalusian tales and rhythms. De Falla was only fourteen when the Madrid Academy of Music awarded him first prize for his piano playing.

LEO DELIBES (1836-1891) is one of the world's greatest writers of ballet music. Though born at St. Germain-du-val, he was brought to Paris at the age of ten, and there he at once began his connection with the musical interests of the city. As choir boy, then as an honor-winning student at the Conservatoire, and as accompanist and chorus-master at the Opera, he learned the art which he was later to so greatly adorn. His first commission of importance for a complete work was given him by the director of the Opera, who asked him to compose ballet music on the old tale of Coppélia, the mechanical doll. In this music he displayed those gifts for delicate beauty and rare charm in composition which were displayed in many succeeding works. The ballet ''Sylvia'' was produced on the same stage nearly ten years later. Delibes is said to have been the first composer to write music perfectly adapted to ballet, which is at the same time entirely worthy of use as independent concert material. He is known as the ''Father of Ballet.'' In 1877 he was made Chevalier of the Legion of Honor of France, and in 1889 promoted to officer.

LUIGI DENZA is a native of Italy, having been born there in 1846. He entered the Conservatory of Naples at the age of sixteen. Although he won some fame as a composer of opera, his chief composition was in the form of song, of which he wrote several hundred. His song ''Funiculi Funicula'' has also been so frequently sung as to be thought a folk song.

NATHANIEL DETT (1882-   ), Negro musician, has for many years been director of music at Hampton Institute, Virginia, and conductor of the Hampton Singers. Dett's compositions featuring the characteristics of Negro music have won him prizes, medals, and commendation of prominent critics.

GRETANO DONIZETTI (1797-1848), who lived and wrote during the first half of the nineteenth century, was born in Bergamo, Italy, the village made famous by the Bergomask dancers. (These dancers were imitated by Shakespeare in his ''Midsummer Night's Dream,'' Act V, Scene I.) His father was a weaver, who gave his son every opportunity to receive a splendid education. Donizetti wrote much chamber music, and many sacred works, but his fame rests mainly upon his brilliantly inspired operas, of which he wrote sixty-five. He was, for ten years, an official and instructor in the Naples Conservatory.

FRANZ DRDLA (1867-   ), a contemporary composer of Moravian birth, was a classmate of the famed violin virtuoso, Sevcik, and has, for many years, conducted at the Volksopera at Vienna.

PAUL DUKAS (1865-   ), one of the most renowned and distinguished of the modern French composers, was born in Paris. He chose music as his favorite study and became a pupil at the Paris Conservatory. His writing of a highly individual cantata won for him the Prix de Rome. As a composer he excels in dramatic music, whether it be written for vocal or instrumental ensemble. One of his outstanding works is the ''Sorcerer and Apprentice.''

ANTONIN DVOŘÁK (1841-1904) lived, during his youth, in a tiny Bohemian village, in which his father was inn-keeper. Dvořák absorbed the musical atmosphere of a simple Bohemian village as a boy, learning many of the sprightly tunes he played on his violin or piano from the village bandmaster or from the strolling gypsies. By the time he was fourteen years old, the boy had learned to play on violin, viola, and piano, and often played folk tunes at the country

Biographical

dances. When he was sixteen, he made his first important visit to Prague, where he studied, though he was so poor that he had to earn all he had by playing in a restaurant on week days and in a church on Sunday. At first he burned all the music that he wrote, his ideal was so high. He at one time lived for three years in New York City, where he taught at the National Conservatory, and it was during this short residence in this country that he became interested in the quaint melodies of the American Indian and the Negro, which he immortalized in his famous "New World Symphony."

SIR EDWARD ELGAR (1857-   ) comes of a musical family. His father was an organist, and also kept a music shop in which the young lad had his first glimpses of orchestral music. He first became deeply interested in such music through study of "Beethoven's First Symphony." That he might be able to enjoy such music better, and later that he might become entirely familiar with the needs of the various instruments, he learned to play the piano, the organ, violin, 'cello, double-bass, and bassoon.

GABRIEL URBAIN FAURÉ (1845-1925) was an eminent French organist and composer, who has long been known as a teacher in the Paris conservatoire. His first prominence as a composer came through a group of songs, of which the beautiful "Après un rêve" is one. In 1905 he succeeded to the directorship of the conservatoire.

STEPHEN COLLINS FOSTER (1826-1864) was born in Pittsburgh, Pa., where much of his youth was spent idling along the river banks listening to the Negro stevedores whose singing had so great an influence upon his later writings. He was never a profound musician, but possessed the ability to create melodies that touched the heart. The citizens of Pittsburgh have dedicated the old Foster homestead in that city as a Memorial, and Foster's piano, upon which he played most of his songs as soon as they were completed, is carefully treasured in the Carnegie Institute.

ALEXANDER GLAZOUNOW (1865-   ), born in St. Petersburg, began to compose at the age of thirteen. His general studies, as well as the study of music, were thorough, and he was enrolled at the University of St. Petersburg. He later became a student with Rimsky-Korsakow, and with him, reconstructed the Borodin "Prince Igor" music at the death of its composer. He himself wrote out the entire overture from his memory of having heard the composer play it at the piano. His own music is notable for its Oriental melodies and general polished style.

CHRISTOPH WILLIBALD GLUCK (1714-1787) had every opportunity, as a boy, for study of music, learning to sing and to play harpsichord, organ, and violin, as his father was in the service of the Prince. Beginning composition at an early age, his main and constant desire was to create dramatic music. When twenty-two years old, he went to England to visit Händel, and to observe the public music of the day. Gluck's first important and successful opera was founded upon the old myth of *Orpheus* and *Euridice*. Gluck also taught in Paris, where one of his distinguished students was Marie Antoinette. He was, for a time, Court Musician to Queen Maria Theresa. Gluck first introduced the cymbals and the bass drum into the orchestra, and is known as the "father of classic opera."

CARL GOLDMARK (1830-1915) was born and spent his boyhood in Hungary. Taught at first by the village schoolmaster, Goldmark evinced, at an early age, a talent of such proportions that he was soon sent (at the age of fourteen) to the Conservatory at Vienna, for further study. The next ten years were spent in the gaining of a mastery of the technique of both composition and orchestration. Many of Goldmark's compositions are extremely Oriental in character, and he is widely known as the composer of the opera "Queen of Sheba." "In

Music and Romance for Youth

Springtime'' was first played in Vienna in December of 1889, and had its first American performance in New York City during the same year.

EUGENE GOOSSENS (1893-   ) is a young English musician, a member of a musical family. He has, for several years, been musical director of the Rochester (N. Y.) Symphony Orchestra. His ''Kaleidoscope''—a series of short pieces of pictorial type—from which the ''Hurdy-Gurdy Man'' is taken, is a clever bit of modern writing.

CHARLES FRANÇOIS GOUNOD (1818-1893) was born in Paris, in which city he spent much of his musical life. He devoted his first years of composition to sacred music but was afterward known for a wide variety of composition, including works for piano, the church, orchestra, and opera. His most successful operas were ''Faust'' and the romantic ''Romeo and Juliet;'' Gounod was unsurpassed in the composition of exquisite melodies, and in his use of the orchestra as accompaniment and background.

PERCY GRAINGER (1882-   ), born in Brighton, Melbourne, was the son of a well-known Australian architect and a musically talented mother. His mother was his first teacher, later he studied in Germany. He became an intimate friend of Edvard Grieg, and was, during the summer of 1907, a guest at the Grieg home, Troldhaugen. It was Grieg's love of the folk song that led Grainger to his enthusiastic study of the folk airs and dances of Great Britain. Of these he has written many idealized settings or arrangements for piano solo, for two pianos, string choir, and orchestra. In his orchestral writings Grainger makes much unique use of percussion instruments. ''Molly On the Shore'' is dedicated to the memory of Edvard Grieg. Percy Grainger is now an American citizen, and served in the World War as an American soldier.

ENRIQUE GRANADOS (1869-1916), the son of a Spanish army officer, was the greatest master of the modern Spanish School. His opera ''Goyescas'' met with instant approval both in Europe and America. Granados, who had come to this country to conduct the first performance, and his wife, lost their lives on their return voyage to Spain, when the ill-fated Lusitania, upon which they were passengers, was torpedoed in the war zone.

EDVARD GRIEG was born in Bergen, Norway, June 15, 1843, and died there September 4, 1907. His mother was his first teacher. At the age of sixteen he heard Ole Bull— the renowned Norwegian violinist—who was his first direct musical inspiration. Later he studied in Germany at the Conservatory founded by Felix Mendelssohn. After his graduation, he returned to Norway where he devoted himself and his talents to the cause of a national Norwegian music. When he was about thirty years old the Norwegian government pensioned him for life so that he might, in leisure, devote his entire time to composition. Many of his most popular compositions were written at his country home at Troldhaugen where, down the hill from his home and toward the fjord, stood his tiny ''music house.'' At his death fifty-seven governments sent official representatives to attend his funeral—an honor seldom accorded anyone save rulers.

GEORGE FREDERICH HÄNDEL was born in 1685, the same birth year as that of Bach. These two men, whose composition so greatly influenced the development of the art of music, wrote in somewhat similar manner and style and lived for many years within thirty miles of each other, but never met. Händel's father was a surgeon who at first intended that his son should follow the profession of law. Much of Händel's studies were in Germany, after which he spent some years in Italy, where both his music and his performance were very popular. The latter part of his life was spent in England where he wrote and conducted his own works under royal patronage. He is buried in Westminister Abbey.

Biographical

JOSEPH HAYDN (1732-1809) was born in the little Austrian village of Rohrau, where his father was a wheelwright. His first introduction to concerted music was in the informal evening and Sunday singing-hours in which his father and mother used to lead from their front porch, the mother playing a harp and the father singing. The most important part of Haydn's life, in many ways, was the period of about thirty years spent as director of music in the household of Prince Esterhazy. The Esterhazy family had been music lovers and patrons since 1635.

VICTOR HERBERT, the composer of "Natoma," is often spoken of as an American, because of his long years of public service as a musician before the American public. He was, however, an Irishman. Born in Dublin, in 1859, he was sent to Germany for education at the age of seven. There he specialized in cello. Coming to America in 1886, he became solo cellist at the Metropolitan Opera House. He held many other important posts, and for many years served as conductor of the Pittsburgh Orchestra. He was the grandson of the famed Samuel Lover, Irish composer of songs, including "Believe Me If All Those Endearing Young Charms" and "The Low-Backed Car." As a naturalized American citizen, Herbert became famous as a composer of exceedingly charming and tuneful operettas and light operas.

ENGELBERT HUMPERDINK (1854-1921) was born in the Rhine country in Germany, and during his early childhood absorbed many of the fanciful tales and quaint folk airs which he later used in his art writings. He was a great friend of Wagner, and assisted that artist in his preparations for the first performance of "Parsifal" at Bayreuth. The "Hansel and Gretel" opera was given its first public hearing in 1893. A second famous opera dealing with the life of the folk is the "Konigskinder," the first American performance of which brought the composer to America as guest conductor.

MICHAEL IPPOLITOV-IVANOV was born at Gatchina, Russia, in November, 1859. His father was an employe at the Imperial Palace. He studied at Petrograd, part of his work, for six years, being under the direction of Rimsky-Korsakow. In 1882 he went to Tiflis as Director of the Music School. He was also conductor of the symphonic concerts of the Imperial Musical Society. He became very interested in the folk music of the Caucasus regions, and finally published a volume of these folk songs, which he had collected. Later he taught in Moscow, and as conductor of the opera there gave several works the *librettos* of which were based on folk life. The "Caucasian Sketches" were written in 1895. He disappeared during the World War and has not been heard of since.

ARNAS JÄRNEFELT (1869-   ) is a modern Finnish composer best known by his short compositions. A musician of great ability, he has been director of the National Conservatory of Helsingfors, opera director in Stockholm, and court music director.

FRITZ KREISLER (1875-   ) is a native of the city of Vienna, and displays in his compositions much of that charming musical grace and style for which that city has long been noted. He was admitted to the Vienna Conservatory at an unusually early age, and while there was a student in violin of Leopold Auer, and in theory of Delibes. Kreisler is known throughout the world as a man of wide general education and culture, and as a concert artist of first rank.

RUGGIERO LEONCAVALLO (1858-1919) was the son of an Italian magistrate. He went, at an early age, to the Neapolitan Conservatory, where he was a student of piano, harmony, and composition. At the age of eighteen he wrote his first opera. However, it was many years before he became known as a successful composer, and his first opera to win acclaim was "I Pagliacci." Leoncavallo combined rare literary ability with his musical talent, and not only wrote many of his own *librettos,* but helped with those used by other composers.

THURLOW LIEURANCE (1878-   ), American composer, has been one of the pioneers in recording and bringing to public attention and interest the music of the American Indian. Through his more than thirty visits to Indian villages and reservations, he has written down hundreds of Indian tribal airs and ritualistic music and customs which might otherwise be lost to history.

JEAN BAPTISTE LOEILLET (-1728) began the study of the flute at a very early age, and attained a virtuosity remarkable for his time. In 1702 he went to Paris where he wrote a number of works for flute. Three years later he removed to London where he established himself as an orchestral and chamber music player, composer, teacher, and concert soloist. His complete works include lessons for the clavecin (upon which he was a skilled performer); sonatas for various instruments; and many brilliant compositons for flute and piano.

JEAN BAPTISTE LULLY (1633-1687) was born near Florence, Italy, but spent much of his life at the court of King Louis XIV of France, where for fifteen years before his death he was director of the Opera. He was very successful in his composition of ballets for the court and also of sacred music.

EDWARD ALEXANDER MacDOWELL (1861-1908) was born on Clinton Street, in New York City, his ancestors being of Quaker faith, and of Scotch-Irish descent. His first study of music in New York (where Carreño, the most renowned woman pianist of her century was his teacher) was followed by study in France and Germany. Some further years were spent in Europe after his study was over, and there his music was received by such artists as Raff and Liszt, and by the general public, with intense interest.

Later he returned to America, where he was known as a composer, teacher (he established the department of music at Columbia University, New York City), and as a brilliant concert pianist. At his death he was buried in a little private cemetery on his own grounds at Peterborough, New Hampshire; his tombstone, a huge boulder in the shadow of which he had loved to lie and rest while alive; and his marker a bronze tablet placed upon the boulder by the MacDowell Society of Boston.

PIETRO MASCAGNI (1863-   ) was born at Leghorn, Italy, the son of a baker. He was trained at the Milan Conservatory and took up the conductorship of a town orchestra in Cerignola. His ''Cavalleria Rusticana'' won him a prize and fame in 1890, and has kept his name before the public ever since. In 1890 he received the Order of the Crown.

JULES MASSENET (1842-1912), eminent French composer, is noted for the composition of many successful operas, suites, and ballets, in which melodic tunefulness and clever rhythms play an important part. He received his early musical education at the Paris Conservatoire where, one after the other, he won three first prizes, then the coveted Prix de Rome which entitled him to a period of study in that Italian city. Upon his return to Paris from Rome, he entered seriously upon the work of composition and was, during his lifetime, honored by election to the Legion of Honor of France, and to the Academy of Fine Arts.

FELIX MENDELSSOHN was born in Hamburg, Germany, in 1809, the son of a wealthy banker, and the grandson of a scholar. He grew up in an atmosphere of refinement and culture. It was the custom of the Mendelssohn family to give weekly musicales, when Felix and his sister Fanny would take part, and most of Mendelssohn's early works were written for these social occasions. He wrote his ''Midsummer Night's Dream Overture'' for a party in the garden house of his father's estate, in the year 1826. For three years he toured Europe and the

British Isles as a part of his education. In August, 1835, he became director of the famous Gewandhaus Orchestra, at Leipsic. He died in Leipsic in November, 1847, and a contemporary wrote at the time: "An awful stillness prevails. We feel as though the king were dead."

GIACOMO MEYERBEER (1791-1864) was born in Berlin, the son of wealthy and cultivated parents. His education was varied and thorough, and his later operas— of which "Dinorah" is a type—are notable for their intensely romantic subjects. He was gifted with a fertile and artistic imagination and displayed in his composition a genius of the highest order.

MODESTE MOUSSORGSKY (1839-1881), born at Karevo in Russia, was the son of musical parents. At the age of ten he was sent to the city to school, and there the study of music was added to the curriculum. He prepared for a military career, and became a member of a famous company of royal guards. He later became intensely interested in the national music of Russia and the development of a national "school" of composition, and was the first to suggest the informal organization known as "The Five." This group of Russian composers included Moussorgsky, Borodin, Balakireff, Cui, and Rimsky-Korsakow. He is noted for his dramatic music dealing with historic incidents in Russian national life. His most famous work is the national music-drama "Boris Godounow."

JESÚS DE MONASTERIO (1836-1903), the composer of the "Serenata Andaluza," was a child prodigy, came under royal patronage at the early age of seven, and later studied music in both Madrid and Brussels. He was, for many years, one of the leading violin instructors at the Conservatory of Madrid.

FELIX MOTTL (1856-1911), who arranged the Gluck "Ballet Suite," was a celebrated and highly gifted European conductor of symphony and opera. He is also known as an editor and as a composer of opera, chamber music, and song cycles.

WOLFGANG AMADEUS MOZART (1756-1791), the son of a violinist and composer, is noted for the symmetry and charmingly clear style of his writings, in which melodic and formal beauty are agreeably blended. The enchanting city of Salzburg, in eastern Austria, was Mozart's native city. Here his father was Chapel Master to the Duke of Salzburg, Court Musician, and Court Composer. As a child, he and his sister toured Europe as "wonder children," playing often before royalty. Many of Mozart's earliest compositions were written for these public appearances. The city still treasures the memory of its illustrious citizen. In the older part of the city, where the Mozarts lived, are narrow winding streets, on one of which may still be seen Mozart's birthplace, designated by a bronze tablet. Not far away is the quaint garden house in which he wrote most of the music of his "Magic Flute" opera. In a certain tower of Salzburg is a *glockenspiel*, or chime of bells, which each hour remind those who dwell or visit there of Mozart by playing some of the sweet melodies which he and his father composed so long ago.

JACQUES OFFENBACH (1819-1880) was born Jacques Levy, but adopted the name of the town of his birth, Offenbach-on-Main. He studied in Paris and also played there in the orchestra of the Opéra-Comique, where he absorbed much knowledge which became very valuable to him in his later writings. He presently became a conductor of orchestra and theatre manager, and was known as a composer of attractive and popular operettas. He visited America in 1875, and died in Paris in 1880.

AMILCARE PONCHIELLI (1834-1886) ranked, in Italy, very close to Verdi as a writer of tuneful operatic music. His most famous work, "La Gioconda," of which the "Dance of the Hours" is so important a feature, was given its first performance at the La Scala Opera House in Milan, April 8, 1876.

JEAN PHILIPPE RAMEAU (1683-1764), one of the most noted of the early French composers and concert performers, was intended, by his family, for the profession of magistrate. He became noted as a performer on harpsichord, organ, and violin. For lack of a teacher, he was required to work out for himself his knowledge of harmony and composition, and became, some time later, one of the first rank authorities on theory of music. One of his most important works was his "Pieces for Clavecin." He was master of opera (as it was developed during his lifetime), of ballet music, and chamber music. He was finally accorded every honor that the French nation was capable of paying him.

OTTOVINO RESPIGHI, born in Bologna, Italy in 1879, is a modern writer on Italian subjects, and well-known as a composer of opera and symphonic music. His father was his first teacher, and later he studied with the Russian master, Rimsky-Korsakow. As a youth he traveled much, according to the European custom among families of means. The "Fountains of Rome" is really a suite, although often called (by the composer as well), a symphonic poem.

NICOLAI RIMSKY-KORSAKOW (1844-1908) was born in the Russian province of Novgorod. During his youth he took many trips into the interior of Russia and learned, first hand, many of the primitive customs and songs. He often jotted down old airs heard at festivals and rural homes, and made a collection of "100 Russian Songs," in which he made note not only of the melodies, but also of the characteristic rhythms and scales used. His first musical impressions were gained by listening to the primitive orchestra (made up of violins, cymbals and tambourine) organized among the servitors on the family estate. Of aristocratic birth, he was educated at the governmental Naval College, music being studied as a cultural subject. After leaving the college, Rimsky-Korsakow spent several years of his life on the sea, as a naval officer, before he took up the profession of music. But even there he worked upon musical composition.

Soon he gave his entire time to music. His intense interest in all Oriental music and legend led him to become much interested in the gorgeous Spanish folk music so closely related to it. This, in turn, led to his composition of the "Caprice Espagnole," in 1887.

GIOACCHINO ANTONIO ROSSINI (1792-1868), whose operatic compositions exerted a more potent influence upon the whole operatic world than had been exerted by the writings of any other Italian composer since Scarlatti, won for himself an immediate and lasting fame by the wonderfully melodic and dramatic qualities of his works. Rossini was, for a time, director of the Italian Theatre in Paris, and was appointed Royal Composer. His many public duties, kept him in prominence. At his death his property was divided between the giving of a prize to the Institute for dramatic composition, and the establishment of a conservatory in his birthplace, Pesaro.

CAMILLE SAINT-SAËNS (1835-1921), born in France, was a child prodigy, playing a piano recital in Paris when only ten years old, the program of which included compositions by Händel, Bach, Beethoven, and Mozart. He also played them entirely without notes (a custom, not then—in 1846—so common as it now is). He composed music in almost every known form.

He was born in the same quarter of Paris as was Gounod, who was later his friend and teacher. Exceedingly well read in all subjects, Saint-Saëns wrote his first suite for orchestra at the age of sixteen, and from that time on, for over seventy years, he was constantly before the public as either organist, concert pianist, or composer. During the World War he lent the support of his name

Biographical

and his art to many charitable and patriotic movements. He conducted an orchestra in the United States (as guest conductor), and traveled much in South America, Africa, and Asia. The French government honored him by many official distinctions, including election to the Legion of Honor. For many years he made his winter home in Algeria, and died there, after a brief illness, in 1921.

PABLO SARASATE (1844-1908) was of Spanish birth, but Parisian education. He was known both as a brilliant concert violinist and as a worthy composer, and won the favor of royalty in his native land. The "Zapateado" permits a display, on the part of the violinist, of much brilliant technic, including double-stopping, violin harmonics, *pizzicato*, and a lovely flowing melody.

DOMINICO SCARLATTI (1685-1757) was one of the outstanding geniuses of his time, a noted composer and artist. He once met Händel in a friendly contest on both the organ and the harpsichord. His compositions include many pieces for the harpsichord as well as several operas.

ERNEST SCHELLING, the composer of "The Victory Ball," was born in 1876, in New Jersey. At the early age of four he appeared in public as a pianist, and later, studied with Paderewski. He was a soldier in the American Expeditionary Forces during the World War. In recent years he has won fame, not only as a composer and a concert pianist, but also as a conductor of children's orchestral concerts in New York City.

FRANZ PETER SCHUBERT, was born in Vienna, January 31, 1797, and passed nearly all his life there. He was descended from a family of Moravian peasants, and his father was a schoolmaster. He was the thirteenth child, and, as many of the children were gifted, musically, it early became the custom for them to play together, on Sunday afternoons, to an audience of relatives and neighbors. Franz began to play the piano as soon as he was tall enough to reach the keys, and began to write tunes as soon as he knew how to form notes. When a little older he became a student at the Imperial School, but returned home each Sunday to play in the family Sunday concerts. A piano sonata for four hands, which he wrote when eight years old is still played. At one time he taught primary grades in his father's school while studying composition. He died in 1828. Schubert is possibly best known as a writer of beautiful songs, and is said to have written the "Erl King" in one hour.

ROBERT SCHUMANN (1816-1856), the son of a book-seller, was, through his father's influence, brought into early contact with literature and languages. He displayed an interest in, and talent for music at an early age, but was sent to the University of Leipzig to prepare himself for the profession of law. He also studied at Heidelberg, but finally decided that music was of supreme importance to him, and gave up the study of law. His music is notable for decidedly individual characteristics. He wrote much for piano, many beautiful songs, and a famous piano quintet.

JEAN SIBELIUS (1865-   ) is considered the greatest of Finland's composers. He is thoroughly Finnish in his patriotism, as may be proven by his choice of musical subjects. His father, a surgeon with the rank of Major in the Finnish army, died when his son was very young, and he was educated by his grandmother. Sibelius gave particular study to Greek and Latin, and attended the University of Helsingfors. He studied music and made attempts at composition from childhood on, and was later honored by his government with a pension, because of his musical attainments. Of his short numbers the "Romance," originally a piano solo, is a good example of lyric music, a Finnish "song without words." But it is in his larger works that he displays his true greatness.

CHARLES SANFORD SKILTON was born in Northampton, Mass., August 16, 1868,

Music and Romance for Youth

Mr. Skilton had a broad education, and studied music both in this country and in Germany. He is known as a composer of great idealism, and also as one who takes a profound interest in the tribal music of the American Indian. Among his best known works are the cantata "The Witch's Daughter" (a folk tale of North Carolina as its text); "Two Indian Dances"; and the suites "Primeval" and "East and West." Mr. Skilton is also widely known as an organist. He is a descendant of veterans of both Revolutionary and the French and Indian Wars; is a member of MacDowell Colony; and of many musical Societies of England and France.

BEDRICH SMETANA was born on March 2, 1824, in Leitomischl, one of the most picturesque of Bohemian towns, often called a "fairy tale in stone." Its stone churches of the fourteenth and sixteenth centuries, and the fine Public Square, have all been mentioned in literature. Smetana's first public appearance was at the age of six and a half, when he was presented as a child pianist at a patriotic celebration. At eight he wrote dance music. He was well educated in all branches, but even when at school was so interested in composing that he often neglected his other studies. He became a virtuoso, also taught, and studied composition. His entire aim was to write music entirely Bohemian in spirit, and in manner of writing. When he died, in 1884, Smetana was honored by being buried in the cemetery on the historic Vyšehrad, celebrated in his "Moldau." In 1924 the entire world celebrated the centennial of Smetana's birth.

AUGUST JOHANN SÖDERMANN (1832-1876) was the son of a professional musician, his father being the director of a small orchestra. The boy thus grew up with a splendid knowledge of musical instruments, and at the age of eighteen directed an orchestra of his own on tour through the provinces of Finland. He is well known as a composer of operetta, his music being notable for having in it the vigor and energy so typical of the Scandinavian folk music.

JOHANN STRAUSS (1825-1899), known as the "Waltz King," was born in the city of Vienna, the son of another Johann Strauss, also an orchestral conductor and composer of famous waltzes. The "Blue Danube" was first heard on February 13, 1867, at a concert by the Vienna Men's Singing Society. Strauss was also known as a composer of tuneful operettas.

RICHARD STRAUSS (1864-   ) was born at Munich, where his father was first horn-player in the Court orchestra. The boy began the study of music at the early age of four, and wrote music when only six years old. Later a student at the University, he combined musical and collegiate studies. His works are notable for great complexity.

IGOR STRAWINSKY (1882-   ), the son of a Russian opera singer, was given thorough musical training when a young boy, as a part of his general education. Later he specialized in music, studying composition with the Russian master, Rimsky-Korsakow, after which he decided to devote himself entirely to music. He is known for his great individuality and for his daring unconventionalities in methods of composition.

JOSEF SUK (1874-   ), pupil and son-in-law of Dvořák, has shown an interest in all the Slavic legendary world, having written much chamber music based, for poetic thought, on Bohemian folk lore.

CHARLES AMBROISE THOMAS (1811-1896), who lived and wrote during the end of the nineteenth century, did much to advance the progress of French opera. He wrote more than twenty operas, of which the most enduring and popular are "Mignon," "Hamlet," and "Le Caïd." Thomas was a student of the Paris Conservatory, where he won, consecutively, the first prize in piano (1829), the first prize in harmony (1829), and the grand prize (1832). The winning of

Biographical

the coveted Prix de Rome allowed him study in that Italian city. He was later a director of his own Conservatory. His first permanent success was with "Le Caid," his light opera first performed in 1849, and in which he wrote a witty satire upon what he considered the absurdities of the old Italian opera. He was presented, in turn, by the honors, Knight of the Legion of Honor (1845), Officer of the Legion of Honor (1858), and Grand Cross of the Legion of Honor (1894), this last honor coming on the occasion of the 1000th performance of "Mignon." The first American performance of "Le Caid" was in New York City, November 8, 1866.

CARLOS TROYER (1837-1920) was a pioneer in the work of recording and making known the songs of the American Indian. Born in Mainz, Germany, he was educated in the Old World, and became a concert violinist. He was a friend of Franz Liszt. Coming to America he became, presently, intensely interested in Indian lore, and his records of it are among the treasurers of prominent museums. He worked also among the Indians of South America.

PETER TSCHAIKOWSKY (1840-1893) was born not many miles from the historic Russian city of Nizhny-Novgorod. His father was the Superintendent of a copper mine in the Ural Mountains. His mother was his first teacher. Later the lad studied in St. Petersburg at the Conservatory. He was also a student in instrumentation with the renowned Anton Rubinstein. He studied for the profession of law, but finally came to adopt music as his greatest interest. As his unique talent for composition became evident, his works were received with acclaim, and he even received special commissions to write definite compositions, from the royal house. He was noted throughout his later life as a conductor and composer, and wrote for voice, piano, violin, chamber music, opera, ballet, and for the opera stage.

GIUSEPPE VERDI (1813-1901) was born in the little Italian village of Roncole, where his father owned a tiny inn and shop. During visits which he made to the neighboring village of Busseto, he became greatly interested in music through airs he heard played by an old organ-grinder. Later he was able to study music, learning to play first upon the spinet, then upon the organ. When he grew older, his greatest work in music was the composition of opera. His operatic airs are so singable, tuneful, and spontaneous, that they possess a lasting charm and win the hearts of all hearers.

Verdi was showered with honors by his own and other governments, but until his death he remained a modest, simple-hearted gentleman. When he was quite old he purchased a country estate near Busseto. There, when he went out for his daily walks, the music-loving peasants would honor him, as he passed them on the road, by singing to him popular choruses from his own operas.

HENRI VIEUXTEMPS, celebrated violinist, was born in Belgium, February 20, 1820. His father was a retired military officer, an instrument-maker, and a musician. As a child he was so brilliant that at the age of six he played a Rode "Concerto" in public with orchestral accompaniment. At the age of seven, he made his first concert tour, followed in later years by many others. During the course of these travels—in which he was accompanied by his father, the boy made the acquaintance of such notable musicians as Paganini, Robert Schumann, Richard Wagner, Carl Czerny, Henselt, Spohr, and De Beriot. The first of three American tours was in 1844.

Vieuxtemps was well known as a teacher (as Professor of the Royal Conservatory in St. Petersburg, and at the Brussells Conservatory), and as a composer for violin whose works have been played constantly by concert artists during a period of nearly a hundred years. He died in Algiers in 1881.

Music and Romance for Youth

RICHARD WAGNER (1813-1883) was born in Leipzig, the youngest of nine children. He was left an orphan at an early age, but, brought up by a devoted step-father who was attached to a theatre, Wagner absorbed, as a child, much information which he later found to be of great value to him. At the age of nineteen he wrote his first dramatic libretto. His great ambition, in composition of his later music dramas, was to write music which might more nearly reflect the spirit of the libretto and really help to tell the ''story'' of the opera—as does the accompaniment of an art song—rather than to write merely tuneful music destined to display the vocal abilities of the opera singers.

CARL MARIA VON WEBER, composer of ''Oberon'' was born in 1786. He was a cousin of Mozart's wife. His father was the local choirmaster in the village, and the boy's first teacher. Weber was the first composer to use dance rhythm as a medium for standard composition of single works to be played in concert. His ''Invitation to the Dance'' was the first piece of dance music to be used thus on the concert platform. Weber died in 1826.

Glossary

ADAGIETTO—Slightly faster than *adagio*.

ADAGIO—Very slow, usually dignified or sad.

ALLEGRETTO—A little slower than allegro.

ALLEGRO—Moderately fast.

ALTO—The lowest female voice.

ANDANTE—Leisurely, moderate tempo, after fashion of walking.

ANIMATO—With spirit.

ARABESQUE—A light fantastic composition. A lacy, ornate pattern. "Arab" like. Oriental.

ARIA—A vocal air or melody; a term usually applied to the formal songs in opera and oratorio.

ARPEGGIO—The playing of the tones of a chord in succession, rather than simultaneously, as on a harp.

BADINERIE—A light bantering composition, same as badinage.

BALLET—A story told in dance and music.

BARCAROLLE—A boat song; may be instrumental.

BARITONE—A male voice placed between tenor and bass.

BASS—The lowest male voice.

BASSO OSTINATO—Ground bass; the constant repetition of a tone or group of tones, in the bass, of a part or a whole composition.

BERCEUSE—A cradle song; may be instrumental.

BOLERO—A lively Spanish dance; in 3/4 time; often used for theatrical or exhibition purposes.

BOURRÉE—A French dance; quick 2/4 or 4/4, rhythm beginning on up beat.

CADENCE—The end of a part or a phrase of a composition; a close.

CADENZA—An extended ornamental solo passage or flourish inserted between regular rhythmical beats of either vocal or instrumental music.

CANON—A composition in which two or more imitations of a melody or part follow each other at definite intervals. A real *round* may be said to be a perfect *canon*. (From Greek meaning "a rule.")

CANTABILE—In singing style.

CANTATA—A vocal composition in dramatic style for solo voices and chorus.

CANZONETTA—A short song or instrumental composition, having a singing lyric melody.

CAPRICCIO—A composition in free, vivacious style.

CAPRICE—A whimsical, playful composition.

CARILLON—A set of bells; a chime.

CASTANETS—Small, spoon-shaped snappers made of ivory or hard wood. They are held in the palm of the hand and used by dancers in Spain and other Southern countries to mark the accent of music.

CELESTA—A keyboard instrument in which bars of metal are struck by hammers, as in a piano, producing a dainty, bell sound.

CEMBALOM—A wire-stringed folk-instrument of the Hungarian gypsy.

CHANSON—A song, usually for single voice, but sometimes arranged for part singing.

CHROMATIC—Tones not belonging to the scale; a modified or altered interval.

CODA—An ending; Italian for "tail"—therefore the tail piece of the music.

CODETTA—A diminutive *coda*.

COLORATURA—A term for decorative effects in vocal music, also applied to a type of voice which can sing ornate and embellished melodies.

CON BRIO—With life and fire.

CONCERTO—A Sonata written for solo instrument (or instruments) with orchestral accompaniment, designed to display the skill of the performer or the scope of the instrument.

CON MOTO—With motion.

CONTRALTO—Same as alto. The solo alto.

COUNTERPOINT—The combination of two or more melodies or voices which move in the same general direction.

CRESCENDO—A steady increase in loudness.

DA CAPO—From the beginning.

DIMINUENDO—A steady decrease in loudness.

DOLCE—Sweetly.

DOUBLE—Very old name for variation of melody by embellishment, also implied a doubling of tempo. A fugue having two subjects.

DOUBLE STOPPING—The bowing of two strings, producing two tones at one time.

DUET—A composition for two voices or instruments.

ENSEMBLE—Together; a group; the opposite of solo.

ENTR'ACTE—An intermezzo; a piece suitable for playing between the acts of a play.

ETUDE—From the French, meaning "study," hence a musical composition designed to assist a student. Also a selection for artist's performance.

FANDANGO—Spanish dance for two dancers; in 3/4 measure; much resembling bolero.

FINALE—The concluding portion of a composition.

FORTE—Loud, usually abbreviated to *f*.

FORTISSIMO—Very loud, usually abbreviated to *ff*.

FUGUE—A composition in which two or more independent voices or parts combine at regular intervals to state, contrast, and develop the characteristic features of a single theme.

FURIANT—A Bohemian dance, with sharp alternating rhythms.

GAVOTTE—An old dance of French origin, in quadruple measure, commonly found in the Classical suites. It was named for the people called "Gavots," inhabitants of Gap in the province of Dauphiny, France.

GIGUE—Old English dance, for single dancer, rapid 6/8 rhythm.

GLISSANDO—Produced by rapidly sliding over the keys or strings of an instrument instead of playing them in the usual manner.

HABAÑERA—A Spanish dance in triple measure, which originated in Havana, Cuba.

HARMONIC—A light, delicate tone produced by so touching the string to be sounded that it is forced to vibrate in segments and so give out an artificial or over tone.

HAUTBOY—Oboe.

HEY OR HAY Name of a figure of a dance; from French for "hedge," the dancers standing in two rows like a hedge.

HUMORESQUE—A fanciful, capricious composition.

IDYLL—An instrumental or choral work of pastoral or romantic character.

IMPROVISATION—An impromptu or unplanned performance.

INTERLUDE—Same as intermezzo; also an instrumental passage between themes or sections of a composition.

INTERMEZZO—A musical selection, usually light, performed between the acts of a drama or opera, or in an interval of a serious musical work.

Glossary

JOTA—Spanish dance, rapid triple rhythm, much resembling a free waltz.

LARGO—A slow, broad, dignified movement.

LEGATO—Connected; the sound of one tone being held until the next is heard.

LEGGIERO—A rapid passage for piano in which the keys are struck with only force enough to produce sound.

LEITMOTIF—A theme or figure used in dramatic music to indicate a character, a mood or a situation.

LENTO—Quiet, slow *tempo*.

LIBRETTO—The words or text of an extended vocal composition, such as an opera or oratorio.

LYRIC—A short, song-like poem or instrumental piece.

MADRIGAL—A song of a pastoral character, usually rather elaborate.

MAZURKA—A national Polish dance; in 3/4 time, much slower than waltz, with accented second beat.

METER—The rhythmic element of music measured by beats and bars.

MEZZO—Half or medium; middle voice.

MINUETTO OR MENUETTO—A little minuet.

MODERATO—In moderate time.

MODULATION—A changing from one key to another, within a composition.

MORDENT—An embellishment which makes a quick alternation with the next tone above or below.

MOTIF—A group of notes which produce a complete musical impression. A figure or musical subject.

NOCTURNE—A night piece, usually instrumental, peaceful and meditative in character.

OBBLIGATO—An auxiliary melody, usually instrumental, but one of independent value, which accompanies harmonized music.

OBOE—An instrument sounded by means of a double reed.

OPERA COMIQUE—A French opera in which the ending is happy and the dialogue is spoken.

OPUS—Latin for work. Used by composers to designate and index their works.

ORATORIO—A serious composition for chorus, soloists, and orchestra, with a text usually based on a religious subject. Given without scenery, costumes, and dramatic action.

OVERTURE—Generally an instrumental prelude to an opera or oratorio, but may be an independent composition or concert overture.

PASTORALE—A composition of rustic character, suggesting shepherds and grazing flocks.

PENTATONIC—Five-toned scale. An example of the pentatonic scale may be heard by playing in succession the five black keys of the piano—*C*-sharp, *D*-sharp, *F*-sharp, *G*-sharp, *A*-sharp.

PHRASE—A short musical thought ending in complete or incomplete cadence.

PIANISSIMO—Very softly; usually abbreviated to *pp*.

PIANO—Softly; usually abbreviated to *p*.

PICCOLO—The octave or small flute.

PIZZICATO—A term applied to music for stringed instruments, indicating that the strings are plucked instead of bowed.

POCO—A little; rather.

PORTANDO—Sliding the voice from one tone to another. Same as Portamento.

PREAMBLE—See Prelude.

PRELUDE—An introductory instrumental section, a preliminary section.

PRESTO—The very fastest *tempo*.

PROLOGUE—A prelude to be sung.

QUARTET—Commonly understood as a selection for four performers; technically a sonata for four instruments.

QUINTET—A selection for five performers; a sonata for five instruments.

RECITATIVE—A vocal declamation, but without fixed rhythm and with little accompaniment.

RHYTHM—Systematic grouping of notes with reference to their duration; the pattern of beats upon which a composition is built.

ROULADE—A rapid vocal run sung to a single syllable.

SARABANDE—An old dance form in triple measure, commonly found in the classical suite.

SCHERZANDO—Jokingly, in the manner of a *Scherzo.*

SCHERZO—From the Italian, meaning ''jest,'' literally a ''musical joke,'' hence a fanciful, happy composition.

SEQUENCE—The repetition of a definite group of notes from different starting places in the scale.

SEQUENTIAL—In the manner of a sequence.

SERENADE—An evening song; may be instrumental.

SERENATA—A dramatic or imaginative composition for voices, or an instrumental form intermediate between suite and symphony.

SEXTET—A selection for six performers.

SFORZANDO—Forced, to be especially emphasized, usually abbreviated to *sf* or *sfz.*

SOLO—A selection for one performer.

SONATA—A serious instrumental composition of three or four movements (usually four), one of which (usually the first) is written in sonata-form. The other movements may or may not be in sonata-form. The common arrangement of the movement is a quick movement, followed by a slow movement, then a minuet or scherzo, then another fast movement.

SONATA FORM—The distinctive first movement structure of a Sonata, based upon two themes presented in contrasting keys, often with transitional material, and conforming to the following plan:

(1) Exposition, giving out the two subjects with episodes.

(2) Development, a thematic working out of both subjects.

(3) Recapitulation, repeating both subjects in original key and sometimes closing with a coda.

There may or may not be a short introduction before the Exposition.

SONATINA—A small sonata.

SOPRANO—The highest female voice.

SOSTENUTO—Sustained.

STACCATO—Detached; each note short and separated from every other.

SUITE—A set of instrumental dance forms in the same or nearly related keys, with contrasts in tempo.

SYMPHONY—A sonata written for full orchestra.

TEMPO—The rapidity with which a piece is to be performed; from Latin *tempus.*

TENOR—The highest male voice.

THEME—A fragment of melody or a complete tune.

TIMPANI—Kettle-drums; the form of drum most suitable for orchestra because it may be tuned.

TRANSCRIPTION—An arrangement of a composition for some instrument (or instruments) other than that for which it was originally written.

TRANSPOSITION—The changing of a piece from one key to another by moving its key note.

Glossary

TREMOLO—A wavy tone produced by rapidly alternating two tones which lie close together in the scale.

TRIAD—A chord made up of three tones.

TRIO—Commonly understood as a selection for three performers; technically a Sonata for three instruments. Also applied to the middle part of certain compositions originating from the old usage of writing that portion for three instruments.

VIBRATO—A tremulous effect on a single tone, used in vocal or stringed instrument performance to produce emotional quality.

VIVACE—Vivacious, with spirit.

VIVO—Same as *vivace*.

Pronunciation Table

Acuzena (*Ahz-you-chay-nah*)
adagietto (*ah-dagh-ĭ-ĕt-'toh*)
adagio (*ah-dagh'-yo*)
Æolian (*Ay-oh'leahn*)
Aïda (*Ah-ee'-dah*)
Air du Tambour (*Ayr doo Tahm-boor*)
Air Gai (*Air Gay*)
Alberich (*Ahl'-ber-ich*)
Alborado (*Ahl-boh-rah'-doh*)
Algerienne (*Al-jee'-ree-en*)
Alhambra (*Ahl-ham'-bra*)
Aljaferia (*Ahl-ha-fer-ee'-ah*)
Allegro (*Al-leh'-groh*)
Allemande (*Al-leh-mahnd'*)
Almaviva (*Al-mah-vee'vah*)
Amaryllis (*Ah-mahr-yl'-lees*)
Amneris (*Am-nay'-ris*)
Amonasro (*Ahm-oh-nahz-'roh*)
Andalouse (*An-dah-loos'*)
Andalucia (*An-dah-loo-chee'-ah*)
Andaluza (*An-dah-loo'-thah*)
Andante (*An-dan'-tay*)
Anitra (*A-nee'-trah*)
Antonio (*An-toh'-nee-oh*)
Arabe (*A-rahb'*)
Arabesque (*Ar-a-besk'*)
Aragon (*Ar-a-gohn*)
Archangelo (*Ark-an'jel-loh*)
aria (*ah'-ree-ah*)
Arlaten (*Ahr-lah'-ten*)
Arles (*Ahrl*)
Arlesienne (L') (*L'Ahr-lay'-see-enn*)
Armas (*Ahr'mah*)
Armide (*Ahr-meed'*)
arpeggio (*ahr-pay'-jee-oh*)
Ase (*Oh-seh*)
automaton (*o-tom'-a-ton*)
Auvergne (*Oh-vayrn'*)
Ave Maria (*Ah-vay Mah-ree'ah*)
Avignon (*Ah-veen-yon*)

Bacchus (*Bok'us*)
Bacchanale (*Bahk-an-nahl'*)
Bach (*Bahk*)
Badinerie (*Bah-de-nay-'ree*)
Balakireff (*Ba-lahk'-i-ref*)
balalaika (*bal-ah-lī'-kah*)
ballet (*bahl-lay*)
Balthazar (*Bal-thaz'ahr*)

Baptiste (*Bap-teest*)
Barbarossa (*Bar-bah-roh'-sah*)
barcarolle (*bahr'-kah-rohl*)
Basle (*Bah'-zel*)
basso ostinato (*bah-so os-tee-nah'-tah*)
Bazzini (*Bah-zee'ny*)
Beethoven (*Bay'-tow-ven*)
Bella figlia dell 'amore
        (*Bel'lah fee'ly-ah del-ah-mohr'*)
Berceuse (*Bair'-suhs*)
Beriot (de) (*Day Bair'-y-oh*)
Berlioz (*Bair'-lee-oh*)
binary (*bī'-nah-ree*)
Bizet (*Bee-zay'*)
Blidah (*Blee'dah*)
Boccherini (*Bohk-ayr-een'-y*)
Boemus (*Bay'-muss*)
bolero (*boh-lay'-roh*)
Borodin (*Boh'-roh-deen*)
Bordeaux (*Bohr'doh*)
Bougival (*Boo-gee-vahl*)
Bourée (*Boo-ray'*)
Brahms (*Brahmz*)
bravura (*bra-voo'rah*)
Brindisi (*Brin-dee'sy*)

cadenza (*ka-dent'-zah*)
Cadiz (*Ka-dith'*)
Caid (le) (*Le Kah'-eed*)
Cairo (*Ky'roh*)
Camille (*Ka-meel'*)
canon (*kan'on*)
cantabile (*kan-tah'-bee-lay*)
cantata (*kan-tah'-ta*)
canzonetta (*kan-zoh-net'-ta*)
capriccio (*ka-pree'-chee-oh*)
caprice (*ka-prees'*)
carillon (*kar-il'-yon*)
Carreño (*Ka-rayn'-yoh*)
castanet (*kas-ta-net'*)
Castile (*Kas-teel'*)
Castillane (*Kas-til-layn'*)
Catalonia (*Kat-ah-lohn'-ya*)
Cavalleria Rusticana
        (*Kah-vahl-er-ree'-ah Roos-teh-kah'-nah*)
Celesta Aïda (*Chel-es'-tah Ah-ee'-da*)
cembalom (*sem'-ba-lum*)
César (*Kay'zar*)
Chabrier (*Sha-bree-ayr'*)

Pronunciations

chanson (*shan-sohn'*)
Chapelou (*Shop'-ay-loo*)
Charlemagne (*Shar-la-mayn'*)
Château d'Eau (*Sha-toh' Doh'*)
Chibiabos (*Chee-bee-ah'-bōs*)
Chi mi frena (*Chee mee fray'na*)
Chinois (*Shee-naw'*)
Chopin (*Shōh'-pan*)
Christofori (*Krees-toh-foh'-ree*)
chromatic (*kroh-mat'-ik*)
Cid (Le) (*Le Theed*)
clavichord (*klav'-i-kord*)
Clementi (*Klem-en'-ti*)
coda (*koh'-dah*)
coloratura (*kol-ohr-ah-too'rah*)
con brio (*kon bree'oh*)
concerto (*kon-chair'-toh*)
con moto (*kon-moh-'toh*)
contre (*kon'-tra*)
Coppélia (*Ko-peel'-yah*)
Coq D'Or (*Cok Dohr'*)
Corelli (*Koh-rel'-li*)
Corentino (*Koh-ren-tee'-noh*)
Cöthen (*Kay-ten*)
Couperin (*Koo-pair-an'*)
courante (*koo-rhant'*)
crescendo (*kres-shen'-doh*)
Cremona (*Kre-moh'na*)
Croatian (*Kroh-ay'-shi-an*)
Cui (*Kwee*)
Cujus Animam (*Ku'-jus Ah'-nee-mam*)
cymbals (*sim'-bals*)
Czecho-Slovakia (*Chĕk'-o-slo-vah'-ki-a*)

da capo (*dah-kah'poh*)
dâhabiyah (*dah-hah-bee'-yah*)
Dapertutto (*Dap-air-too'-toh*)
Daquin (*Dah-kan'*)
Daudet (*Doh-day'*)
de la Hale (*Duh lah Hahl'*)
Delila (*Duh-lee'la*)
Dies Irae (*Dee'es Ee'ray*)
diminuendo (*dim-in-u-en'doh*)
Dinorah (*Dee-noh'ra*)
di quella pira (*dee quel'la peer'ah*)
dolce (*dohl'-chay*)
Don Juan (*Don Hwahn'*)
Donna è Mobile (La)
       (*Luh Doh'-na ay Moh-beehl'*)
Drdla (*Derd'la*)
Dukas (*Doo'-kah*)
Dumka (*Dum'-kah*)

du Soir (*Doo Swar'*)
Dvořák (*Duh-vohr'-zhak*)

Échoes (*Ay'-kōz*)
Enrique (*Ahn-reek'*)
ensemble (*on-som'-bl*)
entr'acte (*on'-trahkt*)
Erl King (*Airl King*)
Escamillo (*Es-ka-meel'yoh*)
Espagnole (*Es-pahn-yohl'*)
España (*Es-pahn'-yah*)
Esterhazy (*Es'-ter-hay-zy*)
Euridice (*U-rid'-i-chee*)
Euryanthe (*U-ree-ahn'-thy*)

Fafner (*Faf'-ner*)
fandango (*fan-dang'oh*)
Farandole (*Far'-ahn-dohl*)
Fasolt (*Fas-ohlt*)
Faust (*Fowst*)
Fernando (*Fur-nahn'-doh*)
Figaro (*Fig'-ah-roh*)
finale (*fee-nahl-lay*)
flageolet (*flaj-oh-let'*)
forte (*for-teh*)
fortissimo (*for-tiss'ee-moh*)
Française (*Fran-say'*)
Francesco (*Fran-ses'-koh*)
François (*Fran'-swah*)
Freia (*Fry'-ah*)
fugue (*fūg'*)
fuguée (*fū-gay'*)
Furiant (*Foo'ree-ahnt*)

Gabrielle (*Gay-bree-el'*)
Galicia (*Ga-lis'-y-ah*)
Garzia (*Gar'-tzee-ah*)
gavotte (*ga-vŏt'*)
Giacomo (*Jah-koh-mo*)
gigue (*geeg*)
Gioconda (La) (*Luh Joh-kon'-dah*)
Giuletta (*Jee-uh-let'-tah*)
Giuseppe (*Joo-sep'-pah*)
Glazounow (*Glah-zoo-nof*)
Glinka (*Glink'-ah*)
glissando (*gliss-ahn'-doh*)
glockenspiel (*glok'-en-speel*)
Gloria (*Gloh'-ree-ah*)
Gluck (*Glook*)
Goethe (*Gay'-tah*)
Goossens (*Gōō'-sens*)
Gounod (*Gc̄ō'noh*)

397

gousli (*gōōs'-ly*)
Goya (*Goy'ah*)
Goyescas (*Goy-es'kas*)
Granada (*Gran-ah'-dah*)
Granados (*Gran-ah'-dohs*)
Grau (*Grou*)
Grenadier (*Gren-a-deer'*)

Habañera (*Ah-bah-nay'-rah*)
Hagen (*Hah'-gen*)
Händel (*Hen-del*)
harpsichord (*harp-si-kord*)
hautboy (*oh'-boy*)
Haydn (*Hy'-dn*)
Hebrides (*Heb'-ri-dees*)
Heidelberg (*Hy'-del-berg*)
Hoël (*Hoh-ayl*)
Hopak (*Hoh'-pak*)
Hopi (*Hoh'-py*)
Huon (*Hwon*)

Iagoo (*Ee-ah'-goo*)
Iberian (*Y-behr-ian*)
Ibsen (*Ib'-sen*)
idyll (*y'dl*)
Ignaz (*Ig'natz*)
Igor (*Ee'-gohr*)
Il Trovatore (*éel Troh'-vah-tohr*)
intermezzo (*in-ter-met'-zo*)
Ionian (*I-ohn'-ian*)
Iphigénie en Aulide
　　　　(*Ee-fee-zhay'-nee-ah in Au'leed*)
Ippolitow-Ivanow
　　　　(*Ee-pohl'-ee-toff Ee'-vah-noff*)

Jacques (*Zhahk*)
Järnefelt (*Yair'-ne-felt*)
Joseffy (*Zhoh-sef'-fy*)
jota (*hoh'tah*)
Jules (*Zhul*)

kantéle (*kan-tel'*)
Khedive (*Kee'dīv*)
koto (*koh'-toh*)
Krakowiak (*Krah-koh'-vi-ak*)
Kreisler (*Krys'-ler*)

Largo (*Lahr'-goh*)
legatissimo (*leg-ah-tiss'-ee-moh*)
leitmotif (*līt-moh'-teef*)
lento (*lahn'-toh*)
Leoncavallo (*Lay-ohn-kah-vahl'-low*)
Lieurance (*Leu-rahnc'*)

Loeillet (*Loy-yay'*)
Loki (*Loh'-ky*)
Longjumeau (*Long-jum-moh'*)
Lucia di Lammermoor
　　　　(*Lōō-chee'-ah di Lam'-mer-mohr*)
Lucretia Borgia (*Lōō-kree'sha Bohr'-zha*)
Luigi (*Lōō-ee'-gee*)
Luxor (*Luk'-sor*)
Lvovsky (*Lvoff'-sky*)
lyre (*lȳr*)
lyric (*lȳr'ik*)

Macabre (*Ma-kah'br*)
madrigal (*mad'-ri-gal*)
Maffeo Orsini (*Mah'-fay-o Or-see'ni*)
Mahulena (*Mah-n-lay'nah*)
Malaga (*Mah-lag'-ah*)
Malagueña (*Mah-lah-gu-ay'-nah*)
Manrico (*Man-ree'-koh*)
Marche Hongroise (*Marche Ahn'-grwa*)
Marseillaise (*Mar-say-yayz'*)
Marseilles (*Mar-sy'-yah*)
Mascagni (*Mas-kahn'-yee*)
Massenet (*Mass'n-nay'*)
mazurka (*mah-zoor'kah*)
Medici (*Med'-ah-chee*)
Mendelssohn (*Men'd'lsohn*)
Mère Renaud (*Māir Rahnoh*)
Meyerbeer (*My'-er-baer*)
mezzo (*met'-zoh*)
Mignon (*Meen'-yon*)
Militaire (*Mil-y-tayr'*)
Mime (*Meem*)
Mirlitons (*Meer-eel-tohn*)
Misérere (*Mee-sair-aeray*)
Mistral (*Mis'trahl*)
moderato (*mod-er-ah'-toh*)
Moldau (*Mol'dau*)
Monasterio (*Mon-as-tair-ee'oh*)
Moussorgsky (*Moo-sorg'skee*)
Mozart (*Moh'-tsart*)
musica di camera
　　　　(*mōō'-see-kah dee kam'-air-ah*)
Muzio (*Moo'-tzee-oh*)

Neri (*Nair'ee*)
Neruda (*Nair-ōō'-dah*)
Nibelungen (*Nib'-el-ung-en*)
Nizhny-Novgorod
　　　　(*Nyizh'-nye Nov'-go-rot*)
nocturne (*nok'-toorn*)
Nüremberg (*Noo'-rem-burg*)

Pronunciations

obbligato (*ob-li-gah'-toh*)
Oberon (*Oh'-ber-on*)
oboe (*oh'-boh*)
Ombra leggiero (*Om'brah-lay-jee-roh*)
Omphale (*Om-fahl*)
opéra-comique (*oh-pay'rah koh-meek'*)
opus (*oh'-pus*)
oratorio (*oh-rah-toh'-ree-oh*)
orientale (*oh-ree-en'tahl*)
O terra addio (*Oh tair'-rah ah'-dee-oh*)
overture (*oh'-vair-tur*)

Pablo (*Pab'-loh*)
Padua (*Pad'-wah*)
Pagliacci (*Pahl-yat'-chee*)
Paquiro (*Pah-keer'-oh*)
pasodoble (*Pas-oh-doh'-bla*)
pastorale (*pas'-toh-rahl*)
Patria mia (*pah'-tree-ah mee'-ah*)
Pavlowa (*Pav-loh'-vah*)
Peer Gynt (*Pair Gynt'*)
Pepa (*Pep'pah*)
Petrouchka (*Pah-trōōsh'-kah*)
Pharaoh (*Fair'-roh*)
piano (*pee-ah'-noh*)
piccolo (*pik'-oh-low*)
pifferari (*pif-er-air'y*)
pizzicato (*pit-zi-kah'-toh*)
poco (*poh'-koh*)
Poitou (*Pwah-toh'*)
polonaise (*poh-loh-nayz'*)
Polovetzian (*Poh-loh-vet-zian*)
Ponchielli (*Pohn-chee-ell'-ee*)
Portillo (*Pohr-teel'-yo*)
Praeludium (*Pray-loo'-dee-um*)
Prague (*Prahg*)
preambule (*pray'-am-bool*)
presto (*pres'-toh*)
primeval (*prim-ee'vahl*)
Prix de Rome (*Pree duh Rohm'*)
prologue (*proh'-log*)
Provençal (*Proh-vahn'-chahl*)
Provence (*Proh-vahns'*)
pueblo (*poo-eb'loh*)

Rachmaninoff (*Rakh-mah-neeh-noff*)
Radúz (*Rah-duth'*)
Rameau (*Ra-moh'*)
Ramfis (*Rahm'-fis*)
Ranz des Vaches (*Rahn'day Vash*)
recitative (*re-ci-tah-tiff*)
religioso (*re-ligi-oh'-so*)

Respighi (*Res-pee'gee*)
Rhadames (*Rahd'-ah-maze*)
Rheingold (*Rīn'gold*)
Rigoletto (*Rig-oh-let'-toh*)
Rimsky-Korsakow
    (*Rim-sky-Kohr'-sah-koff*)
ritornello (*rit-ohr-nel'-loh*)
Rohrau (*Roh'-raw*)
Roncole (*Ron-cohl*)
rondeau (*ron'-dow*)
Ronde des Lutins (*Rond day Loo-tan'*)
rondino (*ron-dee'-noh*)
Rosario (*Roh-sahr'ee-oh*)
Rosina (*Roh-zee'-nah*)
Rossignol (Le) (*Luh Roz'-in-yol*)
roulade (*rōō-lahd'*)
Royaux (*Roy-oh'*)

saeter (*set'er*)
saga (*sah'-ga*)
Saint-Saëns (*Sahn-Sanss*)
Salzburg (*Sahltz'-boorg*)
Santa Lucia (*Sahn-tah Loo-chee'-ah*)
sarabande (*sar'-ah-bahnd*)
Saragossa (*Sar-ah-goh'-sah*)
Sarasate (*Sar-ah-sah'-tay*)
sardaña (*sahr-dahn'-yah*)
Satie (*Sah'-tee*)
Scala (La) (*La Scah'-lah*)
Scarlatti (*Skar-lah'-tee*)
Schahriar (*Shah-ri-yar*)
Scheherazade (*Sha-hair-a-zah'-dee*)
scherzando (*skairt-zahn'-doh*)
scherzo (*skairt-zo*)
Schubert (*Shoo'-bairt*)
Schumann (*Shōō'man*)
Seguidilla (*Seg-wa-dil'-lah*)
sequential (*se-kwen'-shial*)
serenade (*sair-a-nahd'*)
serenata (*sair-a-nah'-tah*)
sforzando (*sfohrt-zahn'-doh*)
Sibelius (*Si-beel'-i-us*)
Siciliana (*Si-cil-ee-ah'-nah*)
Siebel (*Sēē'bl*)
Siegfried (*Sēēg'-freed*)
Sierra Morena (*See-air'-ra Moh-ray'-nah*)
Sigurd Jorsalfar (*See'-gurd Jor'sal-far*)
Slezak (*Slay'-zahk*)
Smetana (*Smět'ă-na*)
Södermann (*Say'-der-man*)
Solvejg (*Sohl'-vehg*)
sonata (*soh-nah'-tah*)

sonatina (*son-a-tee'-nah*)
Son Qua (*Sohn Kwuh*)
Sor (*Sohr*)
Stabat Mater (*Stah-bat Mah-ter*)
staccato (*stak-kah'-toh*)
Steyr (*Stair*)
Strauss (*Strowss*)
Strawinsky (*Strah-vin'-sky*)
Stride la vampa (*Streed la vahm-pah*)
strophic (*stroh-fik*)
Suk (*Sook*)
Symphony (*Sym'-fohn-y*)

tambourine (*tam-boo-reehn'*)
Taos (*Tows*)
Tartini (*Tar-tee'-ni*)
Tausig (*Tow'-sig*)
tempo (*tem'poh*)
Thaïs (*Tah-ees'*)
Thibaut (*Tee'bow*)
Thomas (*Tohm-ah'*)
timpani (*tim'-pan-y*)
Toreador (*Toh-ray-ah-dohr'*)
Traumerei (*Troy'-mair-y*)
Trepak (*Trĕp-ak*)
Trevi (*Trev'y*)
Triste (*Treest*)
Triton (*Tree'ton*)
Trio (*Tree'oh*)
trobar (*Troh'-bahr*)
troubadour (*troo'-bah-dohr*)
Tschaikowsky (*Chī-koff'-ski*)

Turridu (*Tur-ree-dōō*)
Tutankhamen (*Too-tahnk'-ah-men*)

Valencia (*Val-en-'chee-ah*)
Valkyrie (*Val-kee'ry*)
Valle Guilia (*Vahl Jul-'ee-ah*)
Valse Lente (*Valse Lahnt'*)
Varlamov (*Vahr-lah'-mof*)
Verdi (*Vair'-dee*)
Vermeland (*Vair'-mah-land*)
Versailles (*Vair-sä'-y*)
Vieuxtemps (*Vyuh-tohmp*)
viola (*vee-oh'-lah*)
virtuoso (*vir-tu-oh'soh*)
Visigoth (*Viz'-i-goth*)
vivace (*vee-vah-chi*)
vous dirais-je (*vōō deeray-zha*)
Vysehrad (*Vee che rahd*)

Wagner (*Vahg'-nair*)
Walhalla (*Val-hahl'-lah*)
Wartburg (*Vahrt'-boorg*)
Weber (*Vay'-ber*)
Wotan (*Voh'-tan*)

Xanten (*Zahn'-ten*)

Zapateado (*Zah-pah-tay-ah'-doh*)
Zaragossa (*Zar-agoh'-sah*)
Zeyer (*Zay'-er*)
Zoellner (*Zĕl'ner*)

List of Illustrations

Music and Romance for Youth

List of Illustrations

Music and Romance for Youth

Numerical List of Records Used, Grouped According to Parts

PART I

1099	6567	7006	9030	20245	22018
1127	6586	7058	9113	20248	22053
1128	6589	7059	9245	20309	22081
1166	6592	7060	9296	20440	22082
1178	6593	7120	9398	20445	22144
1199	6595	7124	9598	20614	22162
1204	6606	7125	9646	20620	22174
1242	6615	7126	9647	20636	35781
1319	6616	7177	19723	20641	35788
1386	6617	8097	19783	20665	35793
1414	6634	8105	19854	20737	35800
1422	6649	8109	19961	20744	35833
3043	6663	8124	20011	20842	35878
3046	6664	8130	20043	21616	35879
4023	6665	8131	20080	21621	35958
*6159	6691	8132	20127	21945	68823
H6447	6703	8133	20158	21947	*72165
6513	6844	9013	20164	21948	79182
6563	6869	9016	20227	21950	80701
6566					

PART II

1140	4114	6710	7059	9278	20983
1143	P5865	6738	7106	9296	21972
1153	H6364	6739	7110	9327	35763
1174	6505	6740	7152	9399	35780
1180	6547	6741	7179	9411	35885
1193	6579	6742	7200	10012	35977
1196	6587	6766	7201	19923	35978
1335	6591	6823	7202	20043	42480
1337	6592	6841	8069	20127	45531
1354	6595	6844	8091	20151	50170
1367	6603	6847	8097	20169	50279
1406	6614	6868	8109	20342	50314
1445	6615	6872	8174	20374	73466
3040	6635	6914	9015	20432	77555
3041	6639	6915	9025	20450	78280
3047	6648	7021	9026	20606	D1053
3048	6675	7047	9075	20607	
4014	6676	7048	9122	20614	
4028	6695	7049	9124	20805	

Numerical List of Records

1083	6514	6840	8121	9598	21216
1152	*6534	6848	8122	9640	21748
1161	6565	6939	8123	9641	21749
1199	6566	6940	9007	9654	21750
1276	6567	6941	9104	19960	21945
1327	6568	6942	9124	19967	21972
1335	6569	6943	9126	20037	22018
1354	6576	6998	9127	20068	22153
1430	6592	6999	9163	20153	22161
4001	6620	7000	9271	20160	35768
4017	6634	7103	9272	20309	35936
4026	6696	7192	9342	20342	78619
4066	6752	8090	9596	20518	78890
*6234	6823	8120	9597	20802	80393

Numerical List of Records Used

1083	*6234	6740	8097	19723	21749
1099	H6364	6741	8105	19783	21750
1127	H6447	6742	8109	19854	21945
1128	6505	6752	8120	19923	21947
1140	6513	6766	8121	19960	21948
1143	6514	6823	8122	19961	21950
1152	*6534	6840	8123	19967	21972
1153	6547	6841	8124	20011	22018
1161	6563	6844	8130	20037	22053
1166	6565	6847	8131	20043	22081
1174	6566	6848	8132	20068	22082
1178	6567	6868	8133	20080	22144
1180	6568	6869	8174	20127	22153
1193	6569	6872	9007	20151	22161
1196	6576	6914	9013	20153	22162
1199	6579	6915	9015	20158	22174
1204	6586	6939	9016	20160	35763
1242	6587	6940	9025	20164	35768
1276	6589	6941	9026	20169	35780
1319	6591	6942	9030	20227	35781
1327	6592	6943	9075	20245	35788
1335	6593	6998	9104	20248	35793
1337	6595	6999	9113	20309	35800
1354	6603	7000	9122	20342	35833
1367	6606	7006	9124	20374	35878
1386	6614	7021	9126	20432	35879
1406	6615	7058	9127	20440	35885
1414	6616	7059	9163	20445	35936
1422	6617	7060	9245	20450	35958
1430	6620	7103	9271	20518	35977
1445	6634	7106	9272	20606	35978
3040	6635	7110	9278	20607	42480
3041	6639	7120	9296	20614	45531
3043	6648	7124	9327	20620	50170
3046	6649	7125	9342	20636	50279
3047	6663	7126	9398	20641	50314
3048	6664	7152	9399	20665	68823
4001	6665	7177	9411	20737	*72165
4014	6675	7179	9596	20744	73466
4017	6676	7192	9597	20802	77555
4023	6691	7200	9598	20805	78280
4026	6695	7201	9640	20842	78619
4028	6696	7202	9641	20983	78890
4066	6703	7253	9646	21216	79182
4114	6710	8069	9647	21616	80393
P5865	6738	8090	9654	21621	80701
*6159	6739	8091	10012	21748	Gramaphone
					D1053

H—Acoustic records which appear only in Historical Catalogue No. 2.
*—Indicates Acoustical Method of Recording.

Alphabetical Index of Records

——* Record in Preparation.
* Denotes Acoustical Recording.

Alphabetical Index of Records

Music and Romance for Youth

Alphabetical Index of Records

Music and Romance for Youth

Alphabetical Index of Records

Music and Romance for Youth

Alphabetical Index of Records

Music and Romance for Youth

Alphabetical Index of Records

Music and Romance for Youth

Alphabetical Index of Records

Music and Romance for Youth

Alphabetical Index of Records

Music and Romance for Youth

VICTOR DIVISION, R C A Victor Company, Inc., Camden, N. J.—Form No. 2206—ITA—Printed in U. S. A